Jun 16

EVERYTHING EXPLAINED THAT IS EXPLAINABLE

Hugh Chisholm, editor in chief, the Eleventh Edition.
Portrait by William Strang, 1907

EVERYTHING

Explained

THAT IS

Explainable

On the Creation of the
Encyclopædia Britannica's Celebrated
Eleventh Edition, 1910–1911

Denis Boyles

Alfred A. Knopf
New York · 2016

THIS IS A BORZOI BOOK
PUBLISHED BY ALFRED A. KNOPF

Copyright © 2016 by Denis Boyles

www.aaknopf.com

Library of Congress Cataloging-in-Publication Data
Names: Boyles, Denis.
Title: Everything explained that is explainable : on the creation of the
Encyclopedia Britannica's celebrated eleventh edition, 1910–1911 /
Denis Boyles.
Description: First edition. | New York : Knopf, 2016.
Identifiers: LCCN 2015029960 | ISBN 9780307269171 (hardback) |
ISBN 9781101947777 (ebook)
Subjects: LCSH: Encyclopedia Britannica–History. | Encyclopedias
and dictionaries–History and criticism. | BISAC: HISTORY / World. |
REFERENCE / Encyclopedias. | HISTORY / Study & Teaching.
Classification: LCC AE5.E3633 B69 2016 | DDC 031–dc23 LC record
available at http://lccn.loc.gov/2015029960

Jacket design by Stephanie Ross

Manufactured in the United States of America
First Edition

To my FAMILY

and to

RORY CHISHOLM MBE,

whose help and

encouragement

is gratefully acknowledged

Contents

Prologue ... ix

The Savoy's Banqueting Room, New Year's Eve, 1907,
as seen by the artist from the Illustrated London News

Prologue

HOGARTH, JANET ELIZABETH (1865–1954), Oxford-educated British editor and writer, first female employee of the Bank of England, former librarian of the Times Book Club, member of the executive board of the Women's National Anti-Suffrage League, and the only female senior editor of the *Encyclopædia Britannica*, stepped under the huge canopy covering the magnificent Savoy Hotel's Embankment entrance, went up to the foyer and into the formal banqueting hall, and quickly greeted a small collection of colleagues. You couldn't have known by looking at her—she was a tall, big-boned, middle-aged, apparently confident Victorian professional woman in a serious gown, except for that sweetheart neckline and the lace insert—but she was very anxious. In fact, she admitted later, "I was never so frightened in my life."

It was the night of December 13, 1910. The occasion was a banquet to celebrate the work of the "women contributors" to the soon-to-be-published Eleventh Edition of the *Encyclopædia Britannica*, an enterprise so heavily and persistently publicized that the appearance of a new edition alone seemed to be the appropriate climax to a climactic decade, the first of the twentieth century. Of all the great reference works in the English language, the Eleventh Edition of the *Encyclopædia Britannica* is among the most famous. It's now more than a century old, but whether you know it or not, your view of the world has been shaped by the Eleventh's insightful and deep comprehension of what has mattered most in the modern world. It was—and for many still is (the forty thousand entries from the Eleventh, now in the public domain, provide an important content

The Cecil and the Savoy, two of the great Edwardian London hotels

backbone to Wikipedia)—*the* encyclopedia that counted, the ultimate authority, the unimpeachable source of highly credible information in a world, then as now, dizzy with change. Janet Hogarth was there to represent and salute those women who helped create it, to give a rousing speech in their honor, and to call attention to the way the new *Britannica* heralded the birth of a truly modern era for truly modern women—which, as a freethinking, employed, unmarried, Oxford-educated woman, she certainly was.

Barely ten years after the death of the old empress, and after decades of obsession about social order and transition, "modern" was becoming less a destination and more a settled state. By 1910, most educated people felt certain that the massive upheaval and change driven by the growth of literacy, democracy, science, and secularism at last had delivered them all to a world that had achieved the dependable stability of a great pyramid, especially to an English-speaking man or woman. For Hogarth and her colleagues, blocks of knowledge had been piled atop one another through all of history— each layer lifting mankind higher and higher, setting Romans on Greeks, materialism on faith, whites on blacks. Modern life seemed finally to conform to a rational structure, one nourished by commerce, enlightened by charity and good works, governed by order, and devoted to Progress. A Union Jack, representing the global supremacy of the English language, flew confidently from the apex of that pyramid. All the old explanations from all those earlier, dimmer ages—about God, women, science, art, literature, technology, anthropology, and politics—no longer seemed to apply. Now the entire world—all of existence, really—could be explained, if only one knew where to look.

And as of December 1910, thanks to Janet Hogarth and her coworkers, it had that, too. They had made the Eleventh Edition the book of the age, the obituary of the Victorian epoch and an essential snapshot, not a preview, of a very modern era, the arrival of which came as a bit of a surprise, less than a century after Waterloo. "A completely new *Encyclopædia Britannica* was called for by the remarkable changes which have profoundly affected all departments of human life," said a source no less authoritative than the *Encyclopædia Britannica* itself.

Of course, in the decades leading up to 1910, there had been dozens of encyclopedias published—many of them versions of pirated earlier editions of the *Britannica*. But the Eleventh Edition was not just another encyclopedia in an age of encyclopedias. This was the latest, and greatest, *Britannica*!—the exclamation point made essential after the decade-long marketing blitz that had preceded publication. In phrases lifted from the blizzard of *Britannica* sales pieces and circulars, the Eleventh Edition was all this: The Sum of Human Knowledge! All that is new and new views of all that is old! The most costly literary venture ever brought to completion! Everything Explained That Is Explainable! In less than 150 years, what had begun in 1768 with the appearance of weekly numbers, sold at sixpence each, that would eventually be compiled into a three-volume "dictionary of arts and sciences" under the editorship of a writer named William Smellie and a self-styled "Society of Gentlemen in Scotland" (the First Edition, comprising all three volumes, was finally published in 1771), had become the greatest general reference work in the English language, "an inventory of the universe" in which "every article . . . is founded on the *fullest knowledge* and gives the results of the *most recent progress*," a "library of universal information" containing more than 44 million words. A century later, the Eleventh is still judged

Janet Hogarth addresses "a dinner held in celebration of the part played by women in producing the Eleventh Edition." Hugh Chisholm is seated four places to Hogarth's right, with Millicent Fawcett on one side and Lady Strachey on the other. Illustrated London News, *24 December 1910*

one of history's great encyclopedias, an unparalleled editing feat and a favorite of scholars and writers since T. H. Huxley and T. S. Eliot.

Its various proprietors had struggled—sometimes heroically, usually futilely—to keep the *Britannica* relevant through edition after edition. Hogarth had seen the Eleventh barely escape collapse, working feverishly even as the plaster seemed to be coming down around her. Failure had been unthinkable to the Eleventh Edition's staff. After all, in the previous dozen years, through the end of Victoria's reign and into the opulence of Edward's era, the *Britannica*'s latest owner, a brash American, had pumped millions into promoting first the Ninth and then the Tenth Editions. Improbable success had been the result. To understand the creation of the Eleventh, it is necessary to understand the huge gamble each of those earlier editions represented, how each played its part in inflating the significance of the *Britannica* as a brand, and how the tireless marketing efforts on behalf of the Ninth and the Tenth editions shaped anticipation for the Eleventh.

The Ninth Edition had been sold as the ultimate tool for those parents who wanted the pursuit of education to be given a place of prominence in their homes; it was steeped in Victorian erudition, and seemed to possess the received wisdom of all bearded grandfathers; it was all that had been, all that was. To give the *Britannica* an added portion of authority, the proprietor had fashioned a deeply entangled relationship with the English-speaking world's most credible newspaper, *The Times*. Under its new, American-led ownership, the Ninth Edition had been reissued in partnership with *The Times* and advertised relentlessly in the paper's columns.

The Tenth Edition had been sold as all that *is*—the "supplemental volumes" that in 1902 brought the world's greatest encyclopedia current; it was sold by *The Times*, marketed with astonishing (some would say alienating) fervor, as an end-of-reign update of the Ninth a year after Victoria's death.

Then came the twentieth century, and with it came the Eleventh Edition, the first truly British-American encyclopedia, organized around the unassailable assumption of limitless progress and as forward looking as possible. The Eleventh, with its shorter entries and slightly modern, American sensibility, told you all that the world had become and seemed to suggest where progress might be able to take us next.

The three great *Britannica*s: past, present, future. The Eleventh Edition wasn't just another new reference book. It was perfectly positioned as the logical consequence of earlier *Britannica*s. It would be the latest word on everything, and the most famous of the great editions of the world's most famous encyclopedia. It seemed all but certain that future *Britannica*s would be somehow less—and, sure enough, a 1933 or a 1985 *Britannica* might be much more up-to-date, but, ironically, that wouldn't make either of them better, more august, more *authoritative*. To a modern reader, then as now, the Eleventh was the edition to own.

For two months, Hogarth had seen the encyclopedia's editor, Hugh Chisholm, her friend since their days at Oxford, herald the Eleventh as he presided over these impressive public banquets, rising to toast the army of well-known explorers, scholars, statesmen, scientists, painters, and writers who had helped fill the Eleventh's twenty-eight volumes as a way of building the already elevated reputation of "the monarch of encyclopædias." Each banquet was held at one of the capital's most expensive hotels, and each of them was a promotional triumph, generating a great deal of press attention, with a focus on the invited lists of the "brightest intellects" contributing to the exalted tone of everything associated with the project.

Indeed, many felt that tone had reached an almost offensively hyperbolic pitch, taking scholarly authority and making it vulgar and ostentatious through mass marketing and aggressive advertising. When the first in the 1910 series of great banquets to celebrate the incipient publication of the Eleventh Edition was convened at Claridge's on October 21, 1910, by Cambridge University's chancellor, Lord Rayleigh, a substantial number of Cambridge dons recoiled in horror, just as they had a few months before, when Cambridge had offered its omophorion to the *Britannica*'s audacious American proprietor, Horace Everett ("H.E.") Hooper, a man in a hurry, with caterpillar eyebrows, TR's mustache, and a millionaire's pockets. The Cambridge crowd had conveniently forgotten the celebration banquet for the Ninth Edition held at Cambridge University just twenty-two years and two days before. Now, thousands of volumes of the Eleventh were being shipped all over the world with Cambridge's seal on the cover of each, promoted with all those exclamation points in the newspapers.

The banquets had a predictably glorious aura: each one feted a sizable cohort of what the *Britannica* promised were the world's "great leaders of thought, pioneers of discovery, and men of practical experience in every field," and many column inches of newsprint were filled with those great names, giving each banquet a halo of unparalleled significance. The series of dinners together created the sense that launching a new encyclopedia was a monumental event, something even greater and more significant than all the individual great and significant people, places, and things it described. As *The Daily Telegraph* put it, the very appearance of the Eleventh "attains the dignity of a historical incident, full of national importance"– and this, in the capital of the world's most important empire. If to today's reader this sounds like press-fired hoopla, well, it was: the public dinners were not intended to feed guests, after all; they were intended to stir public interest in the great project and associate it with all the best people. Publicity was essential, and on behalf of the *Britannica* London's journalists and editors were glad to be of service–since many of them had contributed to the new edition and almost all of them knew well its affable editor.

Hugh Chisholm was one of Clubland's leading citizens, a past editor of *The St. James's Gazette* and a *Times* insider. He may have started out to be an academic or a lawyer, but that was years earlier. He was a journalist, and although the Eleventh Edition may have decorated itself in scholarly pretension, it was above all a product of journalism. Chisholm's approach to editing the Eleventh was to tell a coherent story: the *Britannica* promised to explain everything, including where we are and how we got here, where we were going, and what it all might mean. It was not a story with a traditional arc, of course, and it certainly wasn't a work of fiction. But it was a work of editorial creativity; Chisholm knew–or perhaps intuited–that the most effective way of building authority was to link pieces of information in such a way that it would create a logical set of assumptions that validated readers' own best instincts. Hogarth understood this perfectly, as her index to the Eleventh shows: 500,000 items, each pretty much where a sensible reader would expect to find it– and, finding it, murmur, "*Ah*, that's what I thought . . . ," even if the thought had never furrowed a brow. Chisholm's "story" was about the primacy of progress as a foundational, informing belief of the new, modern world. That faith was woven through the whole work. Those leaders of thought and pioneers of discovery? Academics and experts, as every editor knows, often make the most useful sources. Hogarth marveled at Chisholm's editorial rigor, describing how he templated these sometimes ornamental entries–outlined and pre-written by him, then shaped carefully to fit into his vision of "making the work as a whole representative of the best thought." Or, put another way, what everybody Chisholm knew thought. This tight, parochial, class-based view of things was inevitable and perhaps essential when so much had been turned so upside down.

This final London banquet (there would be more speeches and toasts in New York later) brought together a group of very well-known women writers, activists, and academics—all of them acquainted with each other, some of them personal friends, many of them enemies, and most of those present not actually "women contributors," but certainly celebrated women, attracting reporters everywhere they gathered.

Hogarth was no doubt aware of the multiple layers of the promotion involved. She had been selected to address the dinner because she herself was one of those celebrated women contributors. Not only had she written and edited hundreds of unsigned articles for the work, she was the editor responsible for compiling the half-million entries of the extraordinary index published as the twenty-ninth volume of the Eleventh Edition. Her work had been important and, given the significance of the index to Chisholm's "systematic" editorial approach, remarkable.

Her role on the staff made her presence, and that of the women she celebrated, an essential part of the *Britannica*'s modern preoccupation, something the guest list made obvious. Crowded around the tables were some of Britain's most famous women. A table filled with journalists took notes. Together, they all made an evening that could only bring happiness to the *Britannica*'s happy owner. "'H.E.' had taken infinite pains with the menu," Hogarth observed, "the music, the lighting which was softened to make us look our best, and the gift boxes of cigars or bonbons like miniature volumes of the 'E.B.'."

Chisholm introduced the evening's program, rising to announce, a bit slyly, "Ladies and gentlemen, you may smoke"—and Hogarth, taking her turn to speak, obliged by immediately lighting a cigarette, and consuming several more in the short span of her praise of the women contributors.

"This," said Hogarth, "was the first occasion on which the share of women in producing a great work of learning had received public recognition." She admitted that there had been "women contributors to the Ninth Edition, but if any one had suggested to the then editors and proprietors that women's share of the work should not only be acknowledged, but proclaimed on the housetops, the suggestion would have been regarded as revolutionary." Women, Hogarth pointed out to the applauding guests, "were even in the most conservative of all institutions"–the Bank of England. "They have been there for 16 years, and there have been none of those terrible results foretold by aged men who had grown grey in the service of the bank. I well remember–for I was the first woman to go there–how they taught us for a few hours a day to sort banknotes, while discoursing pleasantly with us on such innocent and suitable subjects as the growing of polyanthuses. There are 60 women in the bank now and they have learned to economize the bank's time better than by talking of polyanthuses." This prim irony was greeted with cheers. The best answer she had ever heard, she said, to the question "What are women put into this world for?" was "To keep the men's heads straight."

Women, in those days of controversy, were in the news, and, as the proprietor had hoped, the next day *The Illustrated London News* would show Hogarth holding forth while *Punch* would enlist "Miss Fluffy Frou-Frou" to respond to her idea that women serve to keep the men's heads straight by reminding "Miss Janet" that "We . . . just live to turn them!!" More importantly, all the major newspapers carried an account of the evening written by the tableful of well-fed reporters who were seated off to the side of the room, where Arthur Croxton, a loyal *Britannica* marketer who would soon go on to promote Sarah Bernhardt's remarkable London performances, kept the champagne flowing. The reporters would record the presence of dozens of august persons, ensuring that those not present would talk about it. It would all go according to a plan that would result in the Eleventh Edition becoming the first encyclopedia in history to sell 1 million sets.

The next morning's *Times* proclaimed the banquet "one of the most remarkable events in the world of women for many years."

But *Punch*–and the others–may have missed the young woman

with the long, sad face sitting at the head table stage left, alone, like a neglected child, sandwiched between a septuagenarian church historian and the lord lieutenant of Wigtown, her eyes perhaps dulled a bit by the polite conversation. On the seating chart, she was simply "Miss Stephen," there as the daughter of the late Sir Leslie Stephen, the most preeminent editor of his day. To most of the guests, she would perhaps have been as well known that evening for her blackface part in the Dreadnought Hoax as for any literary skills. But in her 1923 essay "Mr. Bennett and Mrs. Brown," the future Virginia Woolf looked back and famously said, "On or about December 1910, human character changed." And certainly lost in all the publicity would be the fact that not only had the Eleventh Edition two *fewer* women contributors than the Ninth, but that for all her anxiety, Janet Hogarth should have enjoyed a much easier time: as she later admitted, "we made up the speech amongst us . . . and I learned it by heart." Her Yankee boss, "H.E.," felt it had to be pitch perfect. "I have made many after-dinner speeches since, but I have never dared to repeat that experiment. It was too risky, for if I had lost my place or forgotten my cue, I should have had no chance to recover."

How Hooper, an American with little formal education, came to possess the book with all the wisdom in the world is a roundabout story, one that started more than fourteen years earlier.

EVERYTHING EXPLAINED THAT IS EXPLAINABLE

CHAPTER I

PLYMOUTH 1896

HOOPER, HORACE EVERETT (1859–1922), American publisher and book distributor, joined the other passengers on the first-class deck as his steamer passed the lighthouses of the treacherous south coast of England. First, the Wolf Rock light, standing alone on its sea-level stone perch, then the distant Lizard light, said to be the equal of a million candles, and visible from sixty miles away. To transatlantic passengers, such as our man, lately of Chicago, the long journey was nearly over. Just a few miles ahead was Rame Head, the light and marker for Plymouth harbor.

From what we know about him, it's easy to imagine a man like Hooper—a square, solid man, with a walrus mustache and thick, theatrical eyebrows—anxiously pacing a little square of the deck as other passengers, participating in a time-honored traveler's tradition, gathered quietly for a sunrise view of the Old World. Distant steeples, churchyards crowded with the bodies of storm-wrecked sailors, white-sand arcs below the green cliffs of the shore—none of these would have interested him. He was the worst kind of tourist. He was a man in a hurry. He was thirty-seven years old and he had lived his entire life in a rush. He walked quickly, thought as he walked, talked as he thought, his voice pitched high in the syncopated, sharply chipped rat-a-tat-tat of mid-Massachusetts—Worcester, "*Whista*," to be exact—where he had been born and raised. He wanted to get to London and he was sick of the sea. He had boarded his ship in New York with more ideas than he needed. During the weeklong crossing, they had multiplied crazily, creating a wild architecture for a plan he was eager to put in play.

His ship was filled with Americans rich and poor. Even in the depths of the depression that gripped America in 1896, jumping on a steamer to cross the Atlantic was a mainstream indulgence; a ticket to Europe cost about as much as an average bicycle. Thousands of passengers boarded these ships every week, gladly paying £10 for a first-class passage (and only half that for steerage). American wealth in those days wasn't deep; many of those wealthy enough to ride in a cabin next to Hooper's were the recent descendants of European immigrants who had struck it rich selling groceries or hardware. They were returning to a continent their families had forsworn only a few decades earlier. Now their children and grandchildren were coming back by the boatload, literally, to lord it over the unfortunate uncles and cousins who had opted to remain behind.

Hooper may not have been the richest man on board. But it's likely that the upper decks of Hooper's ship were filled with those whose own American pedigree might not have come close to his, descended as he was from Joan Beaufort, the fifteenth-century queen of Scotland. John Leverett, who had been born in England in 1616 but

died in office as governor of Massachusetts in 1679, was an ancestor on Hooper's mother's side; the Leverett name is still potent in New England. Hooper's father, William Robert, was descended from Robert "King" Hooper, a hard-selling merchant born in Marblehead in 1709 to a candlemaker. For at least one early part of his life, Horace was called Horace Leverett Hooper.

Although born in Massachusetts, Horace's own father, an attorney and sometime journalist and editor at the *Worcester Spy*, was an important member of pre–Civil War Yan-

Governor John Leverett of Massachusetts
(1616–1679), Hooper's ancestor

kee society. William planned for his children—six in all, including the three boys, Horace, Franklin, and Louis—to be educated properly and launched in the professions. Horace, the oldest, was secured a place at Princeton Preparatory School, where he did well, but only during baseball season and even then only as shortstop. When the family moved to Washington, D.C., to join his father, who had taken up a clerk's position in the Lincoln administration, young Horace went too and took a job in a bookstore. Instead of pursuing his father's somewhat conventional ambitions for him—university, the law, perhaps government service—he took an unexpected turn, for he had fallen in love with books, if not with the conventional means of gaining an education from them. After a year or so selling books in Washington, he and a friend, Sam Alexander, another boy from Worcester, headed west. It was 1876, the year of the Battle of the Little Bighorn. Hooper was seventeen years old. Hooper and Alexander traveled across the plains to Colorado and took up lodging in Denver City, the county seat of Arapahoe County.

Hooper was a young New Englander a long way from home with little to his name but a bona fide genealogy, a lot of ambition, and a sincere passion for books and bookselling. Barely out of his teens in 1881, he met and married Mary Alice Woodbury, the daughter of Roger Williams Woodbury, the New Hampshire–born founder of the *Denver Daily Times*, and settled comfortably into the community. Twin boys, William Everett Hooper and Roger Woodbury Hooper, were born in 1884.

For a young man leaving the East Coast during the Indian Wars and traveling west, the anticipation of meeting a new kind of American would surely have been great. In the imaginations of boys like Hooper, western Americans were completely unlike

Roger Williams Woodbury, ca. 1880

the people one would encounter in Worcester or Washington. They would be big, rough, perhaps justifiably disliked by the original inhabitants, at home on a horse, with a professional interest in cattle.

Cowpoke dreams notwithstanding, the western American a boy would be most likely to encounter first would be a salesman. Door to door and town to town was the preferred means of marketing and distribution in the years following the Civil War. Preachers, judges, doctors, and dentists all rode circuits making regular visits to communities far and wide; far more ubiquitous were the missionaries of mercantilism—men, almost exclusively, young and old, who carried western America's retail sector in black suitcases and in small order books, making elaborate pitches for very simple objects, and especially books.

Soon, Hooper had established a distribution business called Western Book and Stationery, making books available not only to other agents but also to retail counters in various western towns. For himself, he set up a business pushing a line of books that would seem almost comically unsuited to his clientele, who were not city-dwelling book browsers but settler families living in harsh conditions in remote areas and for whom a distant post office was the only, tenuous, link with the wider world. Hooper's starting inventory included reference works abandoned by their publishers—dictionaries and

GET YOUR

School Books and Supplies

AT THE OLD PLACE

The Western Book & Stationery Co.

1126-1128-16th Street,

DENVER, COLO.

HIS FIRST CIGAR

"His first cigar"—how Hooper sold books to schoolboys

The Woodbury mansion, Denver

encyclopedias, republished classics, including "unauthorized" versions of books published in Great Britain left unprotected by the copyright laws then in effect.

Although it beggars many modern imaginations, publishing and selling books was very good business back then, highly profitable on the publisher's part, and for readers an essential part of life. In the western states, the postwar settlement pattern was everywhere the same: wherever the railway passed, small communities were built that took as their civic models the big cities in the East. Thus, small towns featured not only homes, shops, and churches but also schools, colleges, opera houses, and libraries. Literary circles were everywhere books could be found. Public education had been ubiquitous since the 1850s—in fact, by 1890 America's literacy rate was among the world's highest. Social aspirations required even the poorest settlers to seek cultural equality by owning one of the badges of literacy—a bound set of Dickens or Shakespeare, Mark Twain's latest book, or an imposing shelf of encyclopedias, atlases, and dictionaries.

While many traveling salesmen included a few handy books

Horace Everett Hooper, ca. 1900

among their wares, book agents were specialized characters. They brought to the most isolated hamlet news of what was then the most important part of the entertainment industry. Hooper and his agents, for example, carried more than just a catalog of books. They arrived with complete literary entertainment often centered on a promoted title, including an elaborate presentation prepared by the publisher, a recitation of the featured work, and a beautifully bound set of prospectuses for other books that might or might not have already been published.

He and his agents sold these books, often on credit, leaving the first volume of one endless set or another with customers on trust: the payment of an initial deposit was enough to guarantee future deliveries.

The publishing business adapted to this exploding market of readers. The American Publishing Company of Hartford, Connecticut, for example, prepared detailed presentation "kits" to sell subscriptions to the work of their most popular author, Samuel Clemens, and thousands of customers responded by ordering Twain's books as quickly as they could. A new Twain was a significant event. For agents representing books such as *Life on the Mississippi* or *Roughing It*, Twain added text, some of it not very good, to ensure that salesmen had a book of sufficient thickness to command a decent price. Other Twain prospectus books, such as that for his unlucky *Tom Sawyer*, offered readers not only passages of out-of-sequence text but also huge spoilers that made the outcome of the story obvious.

There was more than a touch of multilevel marketing in all this. Good book salesmen became local distributors, and Hooper was one. He opened shops and stalls, but he also employed sub-agents and collected proceeds based on those sales, as well as his own. "Subscription publishing" was a tremendously savvy way for publishers (who, in those days, were also sometimes printers and booksellers) to finance the publication of a work in advance or to augment the sales of existing titles by manufacturing only the number of books actually committed for sale.

The *Century Dictionary and Cyclopedia*, available in as many as ten volumes, was a very popular set of books among readers, booksellers, and sales agents. It appealed to a very basic instinct to possess some knowledge of a world that seemed to have expanded enormously in the space of a lifetime. Denver, for example, was on the high ridge of an entire continent that was still being discovered, mapped, and culturally defined even as new theories raced across oceans and around the world. Contending with traditional pieties were scientific theories and astonishing claims—mankind, some said, was descended from apes! Emerson and the transcendentalists were preaching the Romantic gospel of divine Nature, while new inventions were altering such fundamental enterprises as transportation and communication—not to mention the domestic life of families. Behind all of this was the phenomenally powerful locomotive of public education. Literacy not only opened minds, it also opened pocketbooks. Who could be surprised that in many homes, the icon of enlightenment was a collection of bound reference volumes on a shelf?

Hooper grew rich. He organized campaigns around the sales of the *Century Dictionary*. He prepared his own "specimen books" for use by his salesmen in making their pitches and paved the way for the door-to-door men by offering titles as premiums for newspapers that used them in circulation drives. He sold all kinds of books, of course, but the reference set appealed most to his belief in the improving qualities of books, in autodidactism as the preferred means of pedagogy, and in the profit to be found placing information in the living rooms of working Americans. He also had a family example: his younger brother, Franklin, who had recently graduated with honors from Harvard, already was working for the *Century* as a junior editor.

Hooper's belief was a sincere and lifelong one. He may have lacked the patience for classrooms, but he had all the time in the world for books. He had an organized mind, one that saw connections in business and culture that others sometimes had difficulty seeing. Not surprisingly, his commercial specialization was the multivolume cyclopedia-dictionaries of which the *Century* and the *Britannica* were then the best known. He loved these compendia the way his father wished he had loved Princeton, and he read them the way others read adventure stories or books about agriculture, science, and religion. There were dozens of multivolume reference titles being sold as quickly as they could be produced. These ubiquitous sets appealed to his appetite to easily learn what he needed to know—which, in his case, was nearly everything. It was "education" as it seemed it should be to Hooper—practical, self-directed, easy to access, responsive to passing needs and new information and classless in every way. Everything a man could know could be put in those sets of books. After that, it was just a matter of looking it all up and reading it. That simple enthusiasm for finding what you felt you needed to know to be successful at whatever you were doing—blacksmithing, banking, surveying, preaching—was one that made complete good sense to western Americans.

Books from the entire English-speaking world outside the U.S.—England, Ireland, Scotland, and all the publishers in all the colonies of the empire—were fair game for American bookmen, who often took an original work and, without a profitless regard for integrity, "Americanized" it to give it a more obvious sales appeal. It was a legal practice, but obviously not an ethical one. Foreign authors and publishers saw works changed without consultation; few of them saw a penny of profit on these sales. American copyright law not only permitted this, it encouraged it.

The *Encyclopædia Britannica* was a very lucrative target; A & C Black, who had held the copyright since 1827, published the Sixth, Seventh, and Eighth Editions to disappointing results in the UK, but to a much warmer, if less profitable, reception in the U.S., where the sets were treated as raw material, something to be harvested then refashioned into more desirable products in the workshops of American publishers. Entries were edited, omitted, and added at will, and sometimes without much regard for quality. Publishing derivatives of the *Britannica* was easy money. Publishing the *Britannica* itself was much more daunting.

This was not a new development. In Britain, the *Britannica* had brought prestige, but not much profit, to every proprietor and publisher who had touched it since its first appearance in 1768. That year, the first of three volumes of the 1771 first edition of the *Britannica*—subtitled "A dictionary of arts and sciences, compiled upon a new plan"—was launched by Andrew Bell and Colin Macfarquhar, two Edinburgh printers, and William Smellie, an editor and friend of Robert Burns. Of course, the first *Britannica* was far from being the first encyclopedia; Robert Collison traces the idea of creating a comprehensive reference back to Greece, to Plato's nephew, c. 350 B.C. It wasn't even the first modern encyclopedia—the first *Chambers Cyclopedia* (two volumes, 1728) had a good claim to that—nor was it the most celebrated: Denis Diderot's famous and controversial *Encyclopédie*, assembled in Paris by "A Society of Men of Letters," was seen as a revolutionary set of books, literally. Diderot's last volume appeared in 1766. Two years later came the *Britannica*, and through a series of relatively frequent revisions, it gained and held a prominent position among reference works as it passed from one proprietor to another, each brought to the brink of financial ruin by trying to publish and sell the thing to a British public that couldn't afford to buy it even if they could be persuaded to want it.

But that certainly wasn't the case in America, where many thousands of sets were sold cheaply because many of them had been pirated. Of all the sets of books Hooper sold, the various versions of the *Britannica* were especially important to him. The Ninth Edition, especially, published serially in individual volumes between 1875 and 1889, and in assorted configurations by American publishers afterward, was a remarkable thing—beautifully illustrated with engravings and maps and containing long, erudite articles written by the most celebrated men (and, as we've seen, even a very few women) of the time. British admirers called the Ninth "the scholar's edition," a useful sales slogan for those selling social and self-improvement in the American West.

Hooper read it all, and in it he saw a world in which he needed to live, one in which big ideas were illuminated by confident expertise and polished with scholarly dignity. In its light, he saw the value of unassailable intellectual authority, cultural refinement, a thoroughly British sense of continuity with the past, a mastery of the ideas that were shaping the future, an admiration for fair order, and a hierarchy based mostly on merit and logic. It was an American view—

specifically, a New Englander's view—of a world many Americans worried they might be missing or might have left behind.

The last volume of the Eighth Edition, a fairly comprehensive revision edited by Thomas Stewart Traill, appeared in 1860. It was out of date immediately: in 1859, the two books that were to change the way men and women saw themselves in relation to both God and country appeared—John Stuart Mill's *On Liberty*, which articulated the rights of the individual against the claims of the state, and Charles Darwin's *Origin of Species*, which changed the way in which both believers and skeptics understood the emergence of humankind. In fact, 1859 was a great year for readers; the books by Mill and Darwin were published in a rush of new publications tapping a new and growing market of readers. In 1859, in London alone, 115 periodicals made their first appearances. The Eighth Edition could have reported on early information about, say, evolution, but something so novel might have appeared speculative, so it missed all this and therefore missed the birth of modern understanding, a decided weakness in an encyclopedia. Besides, these kinds of reference works, appearing in "new editions" separated sometimes by decades, are themselves products of evolution. The Eighth may not have had an entry on evolution, but it soon evolved into the Ninth, which did.

The Ninth ably reflected the era and its controversies. It was edited by Thomas Spencer Baynes, a philosopher and scholar, a professor of English literature at St. Andrews, a logician, an expert in Shakespeare's works, a sometime journalist and essayist, and, after a long line of Scots, the *Britannica*'s first English editor. In 1881, when his health began to fail, Baynes was joined by William Robertson Smith, a philologist, physicist, archaeologist, and biblical scholar, and the professor of Oriental languages and Old Testament exegesis at the Free Church College in Aberdeen. He wrote several important entries on biblical subjects, starting in the "A" volume ("Angel," "Ark of the Covenant"). The third volume, containing Robertson Smith's article on the Bible, appeared on December 7, 1875. Its confident assertions—including, especially, the relatively benign observation that the authorship (Moses', for example) and chronology of some of the Old Testament books (Deuteronomy, for example) couldn't jibe with known facts—infuriated the Free Church's leaders. Beginning the following year, Smith was subjected to a series of church disciplinary hearings that in 1881 finally resulted in his dismissal from his academic post. He was immediately named coeditor of the encyclopedia, joining as the twelfth volume was in production. In 1883, he was given a professorship of Arabic at Cambridge, a post he held until his death in 1894.

The Ninth Edition was a collection of unrelated but authoritative essays by scholars so undeniably expert that it went far beyond all other dictionary-encyclopedias up to that time and achieved a status among its readers that had little to do with its awkward form—huge, thick, heavy volumes, book-length entries—or its obscured function—a practical reference work. Both Baynes and Robertson Smith erred on the side of definitiveness; this contributed to its perceived value but robbed it of easy use, and, in the UK at least, of many individual buyers. Institutions were the principal buyers of the thing.

For those who could pay, however, bringing the *Britannica* into one's home became the ultimate validation of a family's intellectual health. Just as the Eleventh Edition captured the cheerful character of the Edwardian Age, so the Ninth was a mirror of the high Victorian era. Mill, Darwin, Huxley, Comte and the Positivists, the "apologetic

Dearborn and Monroe Streets in Chicago, October 1871

agnosticism" of men such as Leslie Stephen and John Morley, had transformed intellectual life in Great Britain. Literacy was on the rise and traditional religion was everywhere being redefined, and where it was not able to adapt to the evolving claims of the new scientific culture—Darwin and evolution, for example, made perfect sense to many important Victorian Christians—it was on the defensive. The intellectually vacant efforts by biblical literalists, including Robertson Smith's tormentors, to capture and restrain the imaginative soul of religion reduced God to a primitive deity and transformed secularism to the status of elite faith.

From the first, American sales of the Ninth Edition had been brisk, the reception was encouraging, and demand was high. In 1879, only two years after the first volumes of the Ninth had begun to appear, Scribner's already had accepted subscriptions for eighteen thousand sets (Little, Brown sold the trade edition), and it did so in the face of stiff competition from legitimate salesman-publishers like Alvin J. Johnson, whose *New Universal Cyclopaedia*, edited by no less august a figure than Frederick A. P. Barnard, the president of New York's Columbia College, appeared in 1875. A number of others quickly followed.

But the promising success of the *Britannica*'s Ninth Edition cheered not only A & C Black and their American partners, but also a vibrant, rambunctious sub-species of publishers, many of them based in Chicago, who successfully offered a bewildering variety of bootleg versions of the Ninth, often reduced in size to make an easier sell, sometimes containing a notice on the title page to indicate the addition of some American content, but sometimes given a new title entirely. No reputable publisher or author was immune to this. Even Samuel Clemens railed against the pirates after they captured an early foreign edition of *Tom Sawyer*. Entrepreneurs such as James Clarke and Alexander Belford, a Canadian, plundered foreign catalogs and lists, looking for new books to print. From their headquarters in Chicago, they published hundreds of titles without paying a cent in royalties.

James Clarke was an especially ambitious publisher. He often visited Canada and Britain to see what new books were on the shelves, while his lieutenants were dispatched to encourage jobbers and to measure the changes in the book market. On one such trip, to Denver, Clarke's brother, George, met Horace Hooper, whose Western Book and Stationery Company was already well known to the Chicago pirates. Hooper's small army of book agents was deployed throughout the western plains and the Rockies. Hooper backed them up with newspaper ads, helping give urgency to his agents' ingenious presentations, which resembled entertainment more than salesmanship.

But after a full decade of economic growth, in the 1890s the economy began to disintegrate. Panics, such as that in 1893, had a pronounced effect in places like Denver, but all across the American West communities built only a decade earlier were beginning the slow process of depopulation. As credit collapsed, farmers began repacking and giving up, railroads went broke, banks failed, shops (and whole towns) closed, and subscription publishing salesmen grew increasingly desperate. Some of the worst began cheating their customers. Word spread that unscrupulous agents were collecting deposits for books that were never delivered. Whatever small market was left for subscription salesmen was further undermined by conventional retail shops selling both pirated and authorized books.

Hooper, of course, grew worried. But not as worried as Mary Alice, who soon was living in her father's mansion in Woodbury Place ("The barn itself is a fine enough establishment for anybody to reside in," reported one of Woodbury's competitors, the *Rocky Mountain News*) with her stepmother and her twin boys, because her husband had left town.

He had found a new home with the brothers Clarke. In 1893, James Clarke convinced Hooper to move his operation to Chicago, promising him the book department in the Fair, a major Chicago department store, along with a secure position at James Clarke & Co. Hooper seized the opportunity.

For a time, Hooper, the Clarkes, Paul Werner, Belford, and a half-dozen other rough-and-ready publishers made Chicago an important center of that uniquely American kind of publishing, one that was only coincidentally literary, when it was literary at all, and certainly different from the kind of publishing done in New York and Boston, where lists were carefully cultivated and the reputations of the

Alexander Belford

great publishing houses were carefully burnished.

Chicago still had a frontier sensibility. The city had grown from a middling-sized cow town to a major American metropolis in half the lifetime of an average man. The late 1800s, especially, were years of tremendous growth; the population grew from 30,000 in 1850 to 150,000 in 1860. The great fire of 1871 put a third of the population—about 100,000 people—into the streets, but in a rebuilding frenzy perhaps unparalleled in American history, the city housed a half-million peo-

The Fair department store, Chicago

The Chicago Exposition of 1893: Court of Honor and the Grand Basin

ple by 1880, and in 1890 it passed the million mark. The huge World's Columbian Exposition of 1893 attracted nearly 26 million visitors in six months despite the massive depression.

It's hard for an inquirer to track the surprising changes in Chicago publishing during that period. Hooper, one Clarke or another, Belford, Andrew McNally, and any of a dozen other publishers were putting together partnerships and companies and quickly collapsing them again. Variations on a theme of reference works were numberless. The *Century*, the *Britannica*, the *New International*, and many others provided content for many other improvisational, pop-up encyclopedia publishers. Other reference works, made from similarly recycled material, along with instant books (books on the Chicago fire of 1871, for example, began appearing before the embers cooled), popular fiction, and reprinted biographies of famous people all found publishers in Chicago. And, of course, newspapers and magazines popped up without warning, and reporters came and went in great numbers. One such journalist was Henry R. Haxton, a flamboyant star reporter for William Randolph Hearst's *San Francisco Examiner*.

CHAPTER 2

THE ADMAN

HAXTON, HENRY R. (1860–1924?), an American journalist, a favorite of William Randolph Hearst, a bohemian writer, and an advertising genius, was on the docks at Plymouth waiting for Horace Hooper's ship to come in. Haxton was a slightly unsettling person, a tall, lean, unpredictable, edgy, stuttering man with a broad nose and a triangular goatee.

He was the proximate cause of a voyage that, for Hooper, grew painfully longer by the second. When the two men had first met—possibly in New York, when Hooper was there setting up one of his effervescent businesses, or, more likely, a few years earlier in San Francisco—is uncertain, but in Hooper, Haxton had found a friend and a lifelong meal ticket, and Hooper had found one of the most peculiar marketing men imaginable.

They were a pair, their skills perfectly matched, as they discovered early on when collaborating for the first time on the problem of what Belford, Clarke could do with a warehouse full of outdated *Century* dictionaries. It was urgent: the dictionaries were aging quickly, and if they were going to be sold at all, it would have to be immediately, with only a few weeks remaining before Christmas 1895. Unemployment had eased a bit that year, but the market for the *Century* had long been tapped by agents and salesmen. Finding new buyers would be tough, and even if they were flushed from the tall grass, Hooper thought there wouldn't be sufficient time to sell them the *Century* through the subscription method. He opted instead for a series of newspaper ads. He asked Haxton to develop the campaign and write the ad copy. As Clarke left on one of his occasional trips to Britain to scour London for new titles, Hooper and Haxton set about launching a last-minute newspaper ad blitz designed to clear the Clarke warehouse of *Century* dictionaries. The great prize of this campaign was Hooper's discovery of Haxton's remarkable ability to generate prose—and lots of it—that was effective not just as ad copy but also as a way of creating interest in a fairly dull product with an urgency that was difficult to deny or resist. Haxton was quick to learn that he could convince readers that not to buy a set of encyclopedias was to accept less than the full portion of the life of the age. It was an act of subversive art. Over the next two decades, Hooper would turn to him again and again as his advertising and marketing weapon. Without his inspired work on behalf of the Ninth and Tenth Editions, it's doubtful there would have been an Eleventh, at least under Hooper's proprietorship.

Haxton by 1895 was a popular Hearst journalist, with a wide circle of artistic friends, including James McNeill Whistler. He was also a bohemian writer of odd novellas and an intelligent, often alarmingly chronic drifter. Born in 1860 in East Orange, New Jersey, he

"Fancy Jim" Whistler

was an ostentatious chap who affected Britishisms so well that as he passed through their lives, everyone assumed him to be English—in fact, Hearst, who knew him very well, later remarked that Haxton had gone on to become a member of Parliament. (A century later, Hugh Cudlipp, a British press baron in every possible way, thinking back on Haxton, assumed the same thing.)

He never was an MP, of course, but he was recklessly athletic and possessed an appetite for perilous adventure that attracted the attention of women, and a stammer his friends found amusing, sometimes cruelly. In London, during visits in the late 1880s, he was a frequent visitor to 21 Cheyne Walk, where Whistler entertained, and where he mixed with Whistler's army of regulars, including Walter Sickert, Sidney Starr, S. S. McClure, William Heinemann, and other younger cultural celebrities. Haxton taunted Whistler for his constant socializing, calling him "Fancy Jim," while Whistler would mimic Haxton's stutter, outrageously (although, as a couple of Whistler's friends noted, Haxton "never could manage the last stage when words that refused to be spoken had to be spelled"). When Whistler decided to move to Paris in 1890, Haxton was there to enjoy the artist's famous garden behind the big, arched porch at 110 rue du Bac. In early 1894, Haxton's book *Hippolyte and Golden-Beak: Two Stories* was published under the pseudonym "George Bassett" and was dedicated to Whistler: "[T]o you whose brush renders your friends immortal, and whose pen reduces to their last mortality the enemies it is your gentle art to make perceptible." The book betrays a little of the flamboyant style that would later make Haxton so vital to Hooper's success. The two stories are stylishly bohemian and brisk and sometimes witty. "Hippolyte" is a kind of swank little tale of gallant sacrifice (valet dies nobly) set in Monaco; "Golden-Beak" involves a vengeful young shogun prince skilled with a garrote. The best a callous reviewer in *The New York Times* could say was, "Mr. Bassett is nothing if not bizarre, and to be bizarre is not much."

The years leading up to Christmas 1895 had been extremely busy for Haxton. He had run away to sea before turning twenty and arrived in Chicago by way of Europe, Australia, and New Zealand, and then New York, where he had been serving Hearst as an editor at the *New York Journal*, a brash and sensationalist paper. Hearst bought it from Albert Pulitzer, Joseph's estranged and neurasthenic brother, in 1895; Haxton was assigned to work with Stephen Crane and other, often disgruntled, Hearst hangers-on.

The brazen publisher and the anything-goes journalist first met in San Francisco, where, after a brief stint on *The San Francisco Call*, Haxton in the late 1880s crossed over to become the star reporter of Hearst's *Examiner*. He gained even greater fame with a series of spectacularly daredevil page-one stunts, each staged melodramatically and played grandly by Hearst, and written by Haxton in a breathless, overwrought style.

For example, when Hearst decided to do a story about lifeboat safety on the bay ferry services operated by the SP—a favorite target of the city's papers—Haxton was sent to do an investigative piece. It turned out like this:

OVERBOARD

AN "EXAMINER" MAN TESTS
THE LIFE-SAVING GEAR OF THE FERRY.

INVISIBLE LIFE BUOYS.

THE GENERAL PUBLIC ARE RECOMMENDED
NOT TO FALL OVERBOARD TOO OFTEN.

One day last week the Sad Sub-Editor, whose task it is to gather literary roses from thorny manuscripts for the adornment of the EXAMINER'S Sunday supplement, was assailed by a persistent poet. All ordinary methods of defense proved unavailing and, in his anguish, the Sad Sub-Editor devised a new formula. "I regret, sir," he said, "that your 'Ode Inspired by the Approach of Admission Day' is not available for publication in our columns, but there is something else you might do for the Sunday supplement."

"Is it fiction you want?" asked the poet. "I have in hand a love story based upon tariff reform which would make a good newspaper serial."

"No," said the sufferer, "but it occurs to me that if you would accidentally fall overboard from an Oakland ferryboat, in order to test the life-saving appliances furnished by the company, you might make a readable story out of the incident." And the speaker chuckled within himself, thinking that he had found the panacea for poets at last.

"Mr.," said the poet, "my life has a certain value. I am a bard. I have a gap in literature to fill. Why don't you do it yourself?"

For a poet, this was not bad; and as the author of the ode bowed himself out the Editorial Fifth Wheel realized that the gun of flippancy had kicked him in its recoil. He didn't want to catch cold, spoil his clothes and be jeered at. On the other hand he didn't want to be bluffed. And at 9 o'clock the next morning, accompanied by two artists, a time keeper, an old sailor and a sinking sensation at the pit of his stomach, he boarded the good ship Oakland at the foot of Market street. . . .

The boat struck the Oakland slip with a dull, sickening thud—or what would have been a dull, sickening thud if the executions reporter had been present—and then started on its return journey. The Sad Sub-Editor seated himself on the rail and prepared for accidents. He knew that it would not be right to jump overboard with malice aforethought, but if he could Fill a Long-felt Public Want, and experiment on the ferryboat's ability to pick up a man, by *falling* overboard, he was ready to assist chance to any reasonable extent. He had provided himself with one of his own manuscripts—a pleasant idyll of summer resort life which he hopes some day to publish—and after reading over a few sheets of it he felt a delicious drowsiness steal over him. He dreamed that an organ-grinder, a proof-reader and the baby at his boarding-house were being burned at the stake, and was preparing to add to the company a Carson man who writes illegibly, when he awoke with a distinct impression that he was under water. The next discovery he made was that the wake of a steamboat does not afford desirable swimming-water. The keel when it has passed leaves a hole in the water (not to be too scientific), and the water behind rushes into the hole, carrying down with it empty bottles, orange peel, sub-editors, or other refuse matter with which it is encumbered. It took pretty solid swimming to overcome this undertow, and by the time he reached the surface he was so indifferent about the niceties of decorum that he took off his coat and kicked off his shoes. They sank. This is the only tragic incident of the affair, and it is to be regretted that the sub-editor cannot write verse; the coat deserves an epitaph.

By this time the boat was half a mile off (or so the old salt says—the sad-eyed one had forgotten his tape measure), and he looked round for a life buoy, not because he wanted it, of course, but because it seemed the conventional thing to do, and then he made his first Note. The life buoys are not much use, because they cannot readily be seen. The foam in the wake of the boat and the light and water in the swimmer's eyes make it almost impossible to find a small flat object on the surface of the water. Each buoy should carry a little stick with a flag on it. The writer saw one buoy and swam toward it, but subsequently saw another one nearer. The average "faller-overboard" would probably not have seen either of them, because he would have been confused and bewildered.

The ferry's lifeboat took three minutes and forty seconds to reach Haxton—a long time for an elderly passenger or a child or, really, any commuter less fit than Haxton, an accomplished swimmer and oarsman. He pointed out that "the boat davits are so rusty that it requires a sharp effort to turn them" and the tackle in such disrepair that "the boat could not have been lowered at all . . . if a wet day had swollen it, it would be sticking there yet." Chastened, the ferry operator made the necessary changes.

Readers loved the high adventure, and Hearst enjoyed the success of the gambit. Death-in-the-bay exposés were a staple of San Francisco newspaper sales, and Haxton figured in more than one such story. One stormy day a little over a year after the ferry incident, word reached the *Examiner*'s newsroom that a fisherman, one Antonio Nicholas, had fallen into the bay and was clinging to a rock at Bonita Point. The local Coast Guard station had pronounced a rescue of Nicholas far too risky because of the rough weather and refused to go to the man's aid. So Hearst hired the *Sea Queen*, a tug, and sent Haxton and another reporter off to save the man. When they found him, Haxton jumped into the sea with a line and tied it around the terrified man, who was then pulled into the boat. The story ridiculed the Coast Guard rescue team, who wanted to wait for calm weather to come out to save the poor man. The *Examiner*'s coverage of its own stunt humiliated the Coast Guard, of course, and eventually a new rescue station was built.

Haxton moved easily among the city's bohemian set of the

1880s and became a member of a cohort of celebrity journalists that included Ambrose Bierce, Frank Unger, H. D. "Petrie" Bigelow, and Lloyd Osbourne, Robert Louis Stevenson's stepson. In 1888, Stevenson arrived to spend some time in San Francisco before setting sail for the South Pacific and was introduced to Haxton by Osbourne. The night of June 27, 1888, Haxton joined the others at a "hilarious" farewell party on board the *Casco*, the schooner Stevenson hired to take him to Samoa, where he eventually died. The day after the party, his *Examiner* "interview" with Stevenson appeared—a pastiche of notes taken during the course of two or three long conversations. "Mr. Stevenson has early this morning weighed anchor for a long cruise in the South Seas," wrote Haxton, "so that it is permissible to add a word of prose . . . [and] with his reluctant permission, I have made some semblance of the thing he most abhors—an 'interview.'" Fortunately, the *Casco* sailed under the Golden Gate at 5 a.m., before the morning papers appeared.

At some point in the 1880s, Haxton married a passing British actress, Agnes Thomas, who was said to dote on him. But they weren't married for long, apparently, since by 1891 Haxton was married yet again, this time to Sara "Sallie" Thibault, a tall, thin, often sickly member of California's "400"—the descendants of the state's settler families whose social circle was the most exclusive in western America. He had met her through Bierce, who described her to Gertrude Atherton as "intelligent, receptive, sympathetic"—traits Bierce found appealing.

Sallie was part of a coterie of self-described "intellectual women" who gathered around artists and writers, including Helen Hunt Jackson, whose papers she helped destroy the night of August 12, 1885, after Jackson's death, only months after publication of *Ramona*, her most famous work. Thibault and her friends called themselves "The Salon," and dabbled in the spiritualism that was fashionable at the time, often meeting to discuss what *The San Francisco Call* said were "obstruse [sic] and occult topics."

In 1891, the *Call* ran a snide springtime story announcing Sallie Thibault's marriage to Haxton. In addition to her musical talent— "perhaps the finest pianist in local society"—the paper also observed archly that Sallie was "somewhat original in thought," such as when

ON THE WAY.

Haxton's leap

she nurtured her skill at organizing her "pleasant little parties in the [family's] house on Hyde Street," where she "was the moving spirit" behind her favorite sort of soirée–"ghost parties," melancholy, atmosphere-rich evenings in which "each depressed young person in turn narrated the most gruesome tale that recurred to his memory or that he could invent upon the spur of the moment," while servants draped in sheets shuffled through the gloom and the guests all shrieked.

She was extremely popular, but when she went to Europe, "her friends were . . . thunderstruck at receiving the news of her marriage to the youthful H. R. Haxton, who gained fame and fortune as a jour-

Agnes Thomas (right), the first Mrs. Haxton,
in an undated publicity still

nalist." How had it happened? "To the initiated, the event was not so entirely a surprise, for more than two years ago, the newspaper scribe had succumbed to the charms of the talented lady." He was deliberate in his courtship, leaving his rooms in the Baldwin on the northeast corner of Market and Powell to visit the Thibault house at 1317 Hyde Street at least once a week. There he had lunch with Sallie and "overwhelmed her with flowers and worshipped at her shrine," while the boy next door, her constant admirer, Winston Jones—known to Sallie's friends as "Our Winnie" and "Safely Jones"—watched in distress. For Jones, Sallie was a life-long love. For Haxton, it was her "matured mind" that appealed so strongly and her knowledge not only of the aristocratic types who burned their cares every year at the Bohemian Club's annual outing, but also of everyone in what the *Call* said was "the social swim of to-day." Haxton in particular.

Meanwhile, Agnes Thomas, said the paper, "had never had the pleasure of meeting the lady who had so befriended her husband." And when news of the marriage started circulating in San Francisco, "a few who had remembered the first Mrs. Haxton's devotion to the man asked, 'What has become of his wife?'"

MRS. H. R. HAXTON is a lady whose name has been the subject of much discussion of late in San Francisco society, where for many years she belonged to one of the most exclusive and inner circles of the "four hundred." As Miss Sallie Thibault she will be better known than by her newer appellation of Mrs. H. R. Haxton. The Thibaults are a part of the early California history. The family was always exclusive, always members of the Southern set, of which the leaders were as now—the Haggins, Tevises and Gwins. For many years her father, the late Mr. Thibault, was an honored and respected notary public. But for some time before his death, a long and lingering sickness had forced him to abandon the practice of his profession. In his latter days he was even taller and thinner in appearance than he had been while in the enjoyment of better health. Mrs. Haxton resembles him, both as regards figure and general appearance, far more than she does her late mother.

Sallie Thibault, the second Mrs. Haxton, in the gossip pages of The San Francisco Call

Not that it really mattered—except to one lonely chap. "Miss Thibault is now Mrs. H. R. Haxton, and her friends are anxiously awaiting the return of the happy couple in order to receive them into the sacred precincts of the social circles of the elect." As for Safely Jones, "[R]umor says he is disconsolate over her marriage."

The Haxtons went to Europe several times over the next few years doing some life-as-art touring, and in October 1892 a son, Frederic Gerald Haxton, was born in Paris. Soon thereafter, they settled in London. But eventually, the Thibault money ran out, and with it, Henry R. Haxton.

By the time Haxton met Hooper, he was looking for a little quick cash. He took on the job of writing ad copy for the *Century* campaign he devised for Hooper and excelled at it. His style at first was merely abrasive and repetitive, flailing readers harshly with the threat of losing out on a great, once-in-a-lifetime chance to own the perfect gift and the one thing that they needed, but, until this very moment, could never have hoped to afford, namely a *Century Dictionary and*

Cyclopedia of their very own, all those volumes at one low price. But there were only ten days left to get it! Nine! Eight! Seven! And, well, so on.

The result was a surprising success. However hysterical, Haxton's compelling narrative, counting down the days till Christmas and building suspense around the question of whether or not a customer would be able to get a copy of the perfect gift—a *Century Dictionary and Cyclopedia*—in time for the holiday, worked impeccably. Nobody—Clarke and Hooper, and quite possibly Haxton, included—expected it to do as well as it did.

The *Cyclopedia*s all sold, Haxton then set off for England. Hooper, stunned at the easy way Haxton had created a market out of thin air for an out-of-date reference work, thought he knew where one of the most famous out-of-date reference works in the world could be had. And he had an idea what to do with it.

For Hooper, it must have been excruciating as he watched the apparently stationary shoreline, pacing the deck as the steamer slowly came round to port and into the harbor, contemplating his coming meeting with Clarke in London. Slowly, an indistinct tangle of debris along the docks resolved into a massive collection of needle-masted fishing boats, with a fleet of larger steamers dwarfing some small coastal vessels. At last the passenger gangway was lowered into place and secured. Haxton stepped forward a bit and looked along the railing until he found his friend.

The two men immediately set off—on horseback, heading out over the moors, following the map to London and ultimately to here:

CHAPTER 3

PRINTING HOUSE SQUARE

B ELL, CHARLES FREDERICK MOBERLY (1847–1911), *The Times*'s Alexandrian-born Egyptian correspondent, understood clearly the limitations of his employer, Arthur Walter, a newspaper proprietor who had very little interest in journalism or publishing. By 1896, that much was very obvious.

In the glorious project of building a convincing center of gravity for Britain's planetary Empire, certain important businesses and institutions grew to the status of cherished national emblems intrinsic to the nation's self-identity. Language was, of course, the crucial component of this identity. But oddly, among the great institutions of the English language—including the *Oxford English Dictionary*, Cambridge's magnificent *History*s, and, some would argue, the BBC—only two existed before 1900: *Encyclopædia Britannica* and *The Times*.

But barely, because by the mid-1890s, both were broke. The *Britannica* wasn't profitable, at least to its legitimate publishers. It had never met Black's expectations, just as it had never met any previous publisher's expectations, so there was no longer any prospect of investing more money into newer profitless editions. The simple solution there: stop publishing big encyclopedias. *The Times*, however, was bleeding money on a daily basis. It was a dilemma familiar to newspaper proprietors today: every day the paper was published, it lost more money. Yet the only hope for survival was to keep publishing and hope something would happen.

The proprietors of *The Times*, perhaps happily for them, had no precise sense of the precariousness of their business. They owned

*John Walter I, with Printing House Square
in the background*

a newspaper that had been around for more than a century, grown as an instrument of imperial sensibility, and, like the empire it chronicled, they saw no reason why it should not continue on for more than another century, if only because—well, it had been around for more than a century. After *The Times* was founded in 1769 by John Walter, a bookseller, the paper's ownership had passed in an unbroken line of successive Walters, all eldest sons and all named John, and had continually grown in scope and influence despite increasing competition from less exalted papers, so their confidence was perhaps understandable. To many Britons, everything about it spoke to the institutional credibility of the thing: in the long history of the paper, there had been only four owners and four editors. It had become a paradigm of journalistic consistency and integrity, sometimes undeservedly.

The Times, at the peak of its influence, was influential the way the Bible is influential. Even if you didn't read it or believe everything in it, you couldn't possibly pretend it didn't matter, at least if you were a sophisticated person engaged in the world. "The London *Times* is one of the greatest powers in the world," said Abraham Lincoln. "In fact, I don't know anything which has more power—except perhaps the Mississippi." To read *The Times* at the end of the nineteenth century was to self-identify as a serious person with sufficient culture, education, and wherewithal to be interested in the things unknown, or at least not enjoyed, by the lower classes—especially money and power. The paper mainstreamed snobbery, swelling the number of swells, adding a greater number of noses down which one

John Walter II

might look at those who were unwashed and poorly educated. A penny press reader might be interested in murdered harlots and the latest in the local music halls. But a *Times* reader was a person whose interests spanned the upper crust of the globe–literally, since *The Times* was read wherever the empress ruled, and in 1896, that meant a quarter of the planet's surface.

By the time Hooper and Haxton arrived in London, the paper was just completing a transition from one Walter to another. There were problems. The third John Walter, who had assumed the proprietorship in 1847, had died in 1894, and for most of the forty-seven years of his ownership he had closely observed the traditional processes by which *The Times* operated, which emphasized exploiting the paper for the profit of the press.

As a rule, one John Walter groomed the next John Walter by having the boy serve as an assistant manager, looking after the day-to-day. But in 1870, John IV drowned in an accident at Bear Wood, the vast family estate. That left two sons, Arthur Fraser Walter and Arthur's younger half brother, Godfrey Walter. Arthur and Godfrey were amateurs in both business and journalism; their principal interests were gardening and hunting. Arthur was appointed assistant manager in 1885 and ignored completely by his father for the next four years. For Arthur, that was a wonderful thing.

The complacency of Arthur was understandable. Discovering the details that could describe the grim realities faced by *The Times* was impossible in any case. The newspaper was an extremely expensive, complicated proposition. Yet the firm's bookkeeping was entirely improvisational and the proprietors and the staff, like the public, simply assumed that *The Times* was as imperishable a part of national

John Walter III

life as the Church of England, though more widely believed.

But a confluence of events intervened in the last decade of the century to put all that at risk—and to provide an opportunity for Hooper, who saw in *The Times*'s travails a way to combine these two institutions into a single, great monument to the English language. *The Times* and the *Britannica* would become one, combining American energy and ingenuity with British credibility and authority. Together, they would describe a powerful vision of a modern, progressive, Anglo-Saxon world at the moment of its greatest importance.

Moreover, Hooper's affection for *The Times*, while perhaps a little sentimental, was completely genuine. He could rattle off the names of past editors and principal correspondents the way other Americans could cite batting lineups; he saw the paper as a literary product formed by intellectual minds. And he was outspoken in his view that both the newspaper and the encyclopedia should find common cause if only because of their emblematic values—*The Times* as the active mind of the English-speaking world, and the *Britannica* as the repository of the accumulated wisdom of that world. He saw both the *Britannica* and *The Times* as the great stone lions guarding the entrance to an edifice that was the product of applied Anglophilia. His belief was deep and sincere. If he could bind them together tightly, Hooper felt certain that *The Times* and the *Britannica* would be strong enough to support his vision, for Hooper understood that his business wasn't just publishing reference books. It was monetizing authority. What could be more credible and permanent than the newspaper known throughout the world as "The Thunderer"? So he moved quickly to push *The Times* and the *Britannica* closer together, completely confident that his vision and his energetic strategies would be sufficient to support them both.

But Hooper was blind to the rickety underpinnings of the great newspaper, and for much of the next decade, his work and capital would be devoted to shoring up the great pillar on which his publishing dreams relied. The *Britannica* depended on *The Times*, and, as our story will show, he would be dedicated to buttressing the newspaper as a way of saving the encyclopedia. Yet even then, and invisible to Hooper, *The Times* as a business was rotting away. First, the long-standing contractual arrangement that permitted the paper to be printed only by the Walter family presses at Printing House Square had become unbearably costly, not least because while the press remained autonomous, the previous Walters, and especially Walter II, had divided ownership of *The Times* itself into sixteen shares and then developed the confusing habit of giving these away to faithful employees and family members. Over time, those faithful people produced many squabbling offspring, among whom the one-sixteenth shares were divided during the course of a century. It was necessary to distinguish the managerial Walter of the day, each of whom was styled the "chief proprietor," from all the annoying minor stakeholders, of whom there were many. By the time Walter III died, the Walter family owned half of *The Times* and the other half was the property of around a hundred people, all of whom habitually realized handsome profits from their holdings. But as the paper fought increased competition, and as its once-vaunted technology grew geriatric, dividends grew smaller, and some of the stakeholders grew restive. Unfortunately for *The Times*, the terms of the proprietorship agreement required that even the holder of the smallest slice of the paper could insist on exercising the full rights of an owner.

So the buildings and the presses were owned entirely by the Walters, while *The Times* paid rent as a tenant at Printing House Square, was run by a manager—usually the Walter-in-charge—and was owned by many proprietors, large and small.

A third entity was the printing contract, which was a perpetual

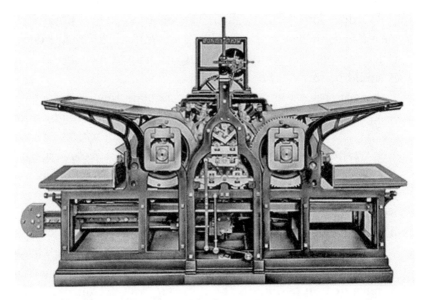

Koenig Cylinder Press. In the first decade of the nineteenth century, The Times's revolutionary steam-powered cylinder press could produce a little more than a thousand pages per hour. By 1860, the presses were printing twelve thousand sheets per hour.

agreement controlled by the two principal Walter heirs—at the time, Arthur and Godfrey. *The Times* was bound by this contract to be printed on the Walter press, which, by 1860, could run twelve thousand sheets per hour. At first, this arrangement had been logical, a more or less conventional way for a printer to demonstrate his printing capabilities. But after a century or so, it had the effect of removing from the newspaper the ability to control the cost of its production. *The Times*'s printer's bill was nonnegotiable, unlike those of other papers, including papers sometimes printed at Printing House Square—*The Daily News*, *The Scotsman*, and *The Birmingham Daily Post* among them.

The result of all this made Printing House Square a circle of confusion, and created a business that resembled Trinitarian theology more than newspaper publishing. The Walter family may have owned the pressroom and the presses, but many, many people owned the newspaper that had to be printed on them under the terms of an ironclad contract owned by a third entity, which was a partnership. Even small tremors made the whole absurd structure sway.

For example, at one point, the proprietor with one of the smallest slices of ownership—Clara Sibley, a granddaughter of Walter I through her mother's line—sued the chief proprietor and largest stakeholder, John Walter himself. Sibley, who owned $3/25$ of $3/16$ *and* $1/25$ of $1/16$, was irritated that other London newspapers, unlike *The Times*, were making a profit, especially *The Evening News*. The *News* was an upstart paper published by a very ambitious man, Alfred Harmsworth (later Lord Northcliffe), and edited by his unsentimental lieutenant and sometime coconspirator, a man named Kennedy Jones. In 1885, Sibley expressed her frustration by refusing to sign a routine agreement making Arthur a joint manager of the paper with his father, Walter III. Under the terms of the arrangement, such senior appointments required the unanimous signed assent of all proprietors, large and small, and Mrs. Sibley wouldn't be moved. So Arthur simply became "assistant manager" (an awkward title that the subsequent manager, Charles Moberly Bell, had to carry until near the end of his thirty-six-year tenure at the newspaper), Mrs. Sibley's objection was shrugged off, and everyone carried on.

That was the incorrect response, however. Over time, Sibley's complaint expanded to include a revolt against necessary changes at *The Times* and demands to see the company's books to determine why dividends were declining. The case cost thousands, took years to settle, brought the operation of the business to unexpected standstills—and, as we shall see, finally led to a surprising turn of events that involved everyone with a stake in the success of *The Times*, including, eventually, even Horace Hooper.

At about the same time Clara Sibley was developing her plot, the paper decided to cover what it perceived as the propensity toward violence of Charles Stewart Parnell, the Irish nationalist. Parnell offended the British establishment in a number of ways, the least of which was being Irish. The paper—that is, Walter—was convinced, not unreasonably, that Parnell was a ringleader in a conspiracy to assert Irish home rule by force. It was a chance for Walter to bring his influence and leadership to the editorial workings of the paper. Everyone Walter knew thought that Parnell was a villain. So there was no doubt in Walter's mind that Parnell must be exposed.

During March and April 1887, *The Times* dedicated itself to un-

Richard Pigott, the journalist–con man

covering the plotters in a series of pieces running under the incendiary title "Parnellism and Crime." The proof linking Parnell with criminality was a document that clearly tied him to a trio of political murders that had taken place in Phoenix Park in Dublin in 1882. Among those killed had been Lord Frederick Cavendish, chief secretary for Ireland. In a deal orchestrated by the chief proprietor, Walter III, and *The Times*'s notoriously Machiavellian solicitor, Joseph Soames, the document was purchased by *The Times* and duly published. Parnell sued, and it quickly became apparent that the document was a forgery, and a very bad one at that. It was something cooked up by a journalist named Richard Pigott in an Amsterdam hotel room. *The Times* had purchased and run the forgery because they wanted it to be true and couldn't allow themselves to think otherwise. Parnell, of course, won the lawsuit.

The loss not only cost the paper a great deal of money—more than £200,000 in legal fees and a settlement paid to Parnell—but also a large measure of *The Times*'s carefully nourished prestige, independence, and credibility. How could the world's greatest newspaper have been taken in by a petty con man? Circulation quickly declined; readers turned to other newspapers; George Earle Buckle, the editor, and John Cameron Macdonald, the manager, both submitted their resignations, since they had been privy to the fact that the authenticity of the letters had been untested. (Soames, the lawyer, didn't resign.) In any case, Walter refused to accept the resignations. Although Walter took responsibility for the decision to buy and print the letters, Macdonald was broken by the affair and died shortly thereafter–but not before Pigott, who granted a final interview to a fellow journalist in Madrid before hanging himself.

The paper was poised on the brink of bankruptcy, its chief proprietor an old, tired man who, after the death of his oldest son–who had drowned saving his younger brother–had given his dull and uninterested second son, Arthur, the job of manager in Printing House Square. However, he had been unwilling to instruct the boy how to do the work, creating a necessary indolence that Arthur, an avid gardener, embraced with gusto.

But by 1890, Arthur realized that the growing mountain of work on his desk was not a problem his father would be able to solve. He had no idea of the paper's precarious position, and he would have been unable to do anything about it if he had.

Looking perhaps as much for friendly collegiality as practical assistance, he summoned Charles Frederic Moberly Bell, the paper's longtime correspondent in Egypt, to come and help on a temporary basis. This unlikely choice came as a surprise to many–but to none more than Moberly Bell.

Already forty-three years old, Moberly Bell (he was always called this, even when discussed by members of his family–never "Charles" and rarely even plain "Bell") had been born in Alexandria on April 2, 1847, just a few months before Walter II died, and, except for time at school in the UK, had spent almost his entire adult life there.

C. F. Moberly Bell, 1908

His father, Thomas, was a partner at Peel & Co., brokers in cotton and Egyptian wheat. But he was not successful; a granddaughter later described him as "a man of integrity rather than of any brilliant intellectual attainments or business acumen." She may have meant more integrity than attainments, since his successes were small, and he did have an eccentricity or two. For example, Thomas's first love had been a cousin named Moberly, and he gave this as a second name to his children in honor of the woman.

Hester Louisa was the name of his apparently tolerant wife, a beautiful and vivacious woman, an accomplished Greek scholar, and the widow of the chaplain aboard HMS *Madagascar*, a man named Charles William Dodd. Hester was very well known in Malta, where she was the admired daughter of John David, the local administrator of hospitals, and in Alexandria, where she was immediately suspect: the British expatriate community frowned upon any indication of nonconformity, especially among women, and Hester was double cursed, socially, since women were not typically scholars and Britons did not typically speak Greek. When Charles Frederic, her youngest child, was only five, she died, along with two of his brothers, in a poisoning episode, circumstances unknown. She was only thirty-nine. A third brother, James, older than the others, survived.

With one of his two surviving sisters, Louisa, Moberly Bell was sent to England, where an impoverished relative took in the pair for pay, instilling in them an early conviction that they were destined for hell because of their many childhood offenses. The children never saw their father again, even after he remarried and had two more boys.

In 1859, when word came to England that their father had died, Moberly Bell and his sister were playing in the garden. Summoned inside to be given the terrible news, the newly orphaned pair listened attentively, silently. It was awkward. Finally, Moberly Bell tugged at Louisa's dress and said, "Let's go and finish our game." This detachment never disappeared. Far from becoming embittered by his childhood, Moberly Bell became amused by it. Affable, intelligent, sometimes self-deprecating, he was sent off to a small school run by a country vicar and at eighteen began looking for work.

He found it back where he started, in Alexandria, at Peel & Co., now grown prosperous under the careful management of his older brother, James. The firm's principal commodity was cotton, and in the mid-nineteenth century, cotton, especially Egyptian cotton, enjoyed rising prices, supporting not only companies like Peel and traders like James Bell but also a significant part of the Khedive's political establishment. Peel was in the middle of the cotton boom, shipping cotton to clients all over Europe and as far away as Japan. Drawn perhaps more by easy opportunity than by nostalgia for the family firm, Moberly Bell persuaded James to offer him a job as a clerk. In the middle of 1865, he left England for home.

CHAPTER 4

THE CAIRO CORRESPONDENT

Cholera in rural Egypt, 1883

Charles Moberly Bell arrived back in Alexandria to a scene of unimaginable fear and chaos. Some 35,000 terrified Europeans and other foreigners were jamming every outgoing vessel of every possible kind, trying desperately to escape Egypt to Malta, Trieste, Marseilles, southern Italy—or anywhere in the Mediterranean, so long as it was far from Egypt. They jammed the docks, holding weakened children and pleading in hoarse whispers to weary, sickened police, who turned them away roughly and left many collapsed on

Scenes from the Hajj of 1865 as reported by Harper's Weekly

The Hajj of 1865: "The dead were everywhere . . . escaping was nearly impossible."

the spot. They were all fleeing one of the region's terrible epidemics, another of the cholera outbreaks that had become common since the disease first escaped from the Indian subcontinent in the early 1800s.

The first great cholera epidemic devastated Egypt in 1831 before spreading to Europe. But the disease had returned every few years since—in 1838, 1840, 1850, and 1855—each time killing thousands of the poor clustered around the mouth of the Nile and in Cairo's narrow alleys. At first, these outbreaks were attributed to the low, yellowish fog that often engulfed the Nile Delta at the height of the annual flood, but the outbreak in 1865 after the Hajj was a particularly virulent one. By April, nearly twenty thousand were dead in Mecca, and the fleeing pilgrims traveled on the improved railroads and ships up the Red Sea to the Mediterranean, leaving sixty thousand more dead in Egypt in June and July. By August, the dead were everywhere; commerce and society effectively collapsed.

Escape was nearly impossible. Every Ottoman port was suspect; every ship was impounded on the slightest suspicion of having been contaminated. The entire Mediterranean, each harbor, vessel, and dock, was gripped by fear. As Moberly Bell discovered walking from the docks, the streets were empty—except for the bodies. Those still in the city were hidden away from each other behind closed shutters. Every Alexandrian waited, terrified the first signs might at any moment appear. Employers gave their workers leave or abandoned business altogether. The city, hot, humid, fetid, and aroused by fear, froze.

At the offices of Peel & Co., James Bell sat alone in an office that had once been filled with clerks. For a time he had been able to watch them arrive every morning, but every morning there had been fewer and fewer of them, until one morning there were none. So he worked alone until Moberly Bell walked in. James looked up and said, "So you've come."

"Yes. I said I was coming."

"Well, you'll probably die of cholera, but I'm very short-handed so sit down and work."

So he did, almost nonstop through the rest of that decade and halfway into the next.

. . .

Thomas Bell had been a senior partner at Peel & Co., and had made nothing of it beyond a modest living. Under his more ambitious son, James, however, the company grew rapidly, and by the time of the epidemic it had already become one of Egypt's most active cotton traders. James was deeply involved in the life of the city; he not only moved among its rich and powerful merchants, he also occasionally drafted reports on the events in the city for *The Times*. The use of informal correspondents was a very common practice at the time; many of the nineteenth-century amateur dispatches published by *The Times* and others read somewhat prosaically because they were written by amateur journalists who saw and reported the world in matter-of-fact terms.

The access his brother enjoyed to the manager of *The Times* impressed Moberly Bell, and with such an easy and useful accomplice to help him, he navigated Alexandria and Cairo easily. Many people wrongly assumed by his appearance that he was an Anglo-Egyptian. He was swarthy; his features were heavy; he had the eyes of a hypnotist. Behind his back, he was called "the pirate." But he was enormously energetic; even as a teenager, his play was his work. If he wasn't sleeping, he was working. And in working, he was brisk and active, appearing to be vastly overextended and always writing furiously. Despite having been away from Egypt during most of his childhood, it took him less than a year to understand most of what was going on in a country that could be frustratingly confusing to foreigners.

Moberly Bell came across an idea that he felt would ingratiate him with *The Times*. The newspaper had taken great interest in the development of a foreign reporting corps. Often *The Times* carried news, often including reports from the government's own representatives, that proved invaluable in making decisions that affected the lives of many. Sometimes, these made their way into the pages of *The Times* even before they appeared on the desks of the bureaucrats in London. Foreign news in those days ran in two distinct varieties: "official" correspondents wrote authoritative dispatches behind which *The Times* stood completely. But the informal correspondents— the amateurs and the letter writers, and there were many—were often used by newspapers as a far-flung web of stringers. Letters from all over the world competed for space, and *The Times* made no effort to check the assertions made by these writers (although some, like James Bell, eventually grew to be trusted enough to merit the description "occasional correspondent"), relying instead on corrections supplied, sometimes heatedly, by other readers.

The Times was unique in the amount of overseas news it provided Londoners, and news from India was especially prized. But while letters traveled from the subcontinent by post and courier, and sometimes by private wire—a very expensive alternative—the paper still needed the useful context provided by newspapers in India. Those traveled with the parcel post around the Cape, adding three or four weeks to the delivery.

Moberly Bell wrote to Mowbray Morris, at the time the manager of *The Times*, proposing to intercept these shipments at the Gulf, bring them overland to his post in Alexandria, and then forward them on to London. The offer was quickly accepted, and by November 1865, the eighteen-year-old Bell found himself in the extraordinary position of corresponding directly every week with the manager of the most powerful newspaper in the world. To his routine collection of journals and packets, he began including a commentary on current events in Egypt. These were read with interest in London, and Morris began sending queries back to Moberly Bell asking, among other things, whether Ismail Pasha's attempted negotiation of a huge loan was a wise thing for London financiers to entertain. The teenager compiled a memo containing a good deal of insightful information about the viceroy's inept attempt to play

The reviled Ismail Pasha, ca. 1878

"The Censor on Duty"

two sets of European bankers against one another, and his failure
to secure the loans he needed: "Thus between the two stools, Ismail
fell to the ground," he wrote.

Moberly Bell realized the value of the information he so easily
harvested. By 1866, he was writing a weekly letter from Egypt for
The Levant Herald, an influential Constantinopolitan newspaper published in English and French for readers all over the Middle East. To
help Bell in his work on behalf of the *Herald*, the editor supplied his
Egyptian columnist with a steady stream of political news from the
Ottoman capital, which Moberly Bell used judiciously. Newspaper
publishing was a quick way to wealth, but not a very tranquil one,
especially in Constantinople in the 1860s.

To stay ahead of the competition was risky business. The news
had to be appealing enough to interest readers, but it also had to
appear to be innocuous enough to pass the scrutiny of the Ottoman secret police. In distant Alexandria, where the viceroy had often
to suffer the humiliation of begging to European banks in order to
buy enough popular affection to ensure his survival, it was a bit
easier. Moberly Bell enjoyed a relative degree of safety, and his letters reflected no particular difficulty. The fact that Peel & Co. were

vital to the cotton trade that constituted one of Ismail's few reliable sources of income helped further ensure his independence. The information he gleaned from his close ties to the Middle Eastern and European trading communities was combined with the news sent to him from Constantinople and used for two purposes: to write the *Levant Herald* column, and to insinuate himself further into the good opinion of the manager of *The Times* in London.

He soon grew comfortable using the columns of *The Times* to settle scores, pursue personal interests, and, apparently, indulge in a guerrilla-journalism campaign against the hated viceroy, who, for some reason, liked and trusted Moberly Bell and sought to curry his favor in influencing European opinion. Ismail was spectacularly misguided in this. Moberly Bell used *The Times* as a kind of truncheon, pulverizing Ismail again and again, while also using his reports to ensure that Mowbray Morris remembered his man on the Nile. It worked brilliantly; in 1875, Bell finally became an official part of the staff of the paper he would serve until just before lunch on April 5, 1911.

From Cairo and from Alexandria, Moberly Bell covered his part of *The Times*'s immense waterfront for twenty-three years, reporting on Napier's 1868 expedition into Abyssinia to free hostages taken in Magdala; the opening of the Suez Canal in 1869; the acquisition of Ismail's shares in the canal by the British government; the nationalist uprising in 1882 and the arrival of British troops to protect the canal; the bombardment and burning of Alexandria; and the return of cholera the next year. Bell was there to see off Ismail and to greet the new viceroy, Nubar. He was in Egypt to meet "Chinese" Gordon as he passed through Cairo on his way to Khartoum, and pushed very hard

General Charles George "Chinese" Gordon Pasha, Britain's hero killed by Muslim fanatics in 1885

C. F. Moberly Bell, ca. 1910

for William Gladstone's government to send relief to Gordon after he was besieged by the Mahdi's army of zealots. When Mowbray Morris became ill in 1873, he was sent to Egypt for his health, and Moberly Bell was there to receive him.

At the same time, his financial interests grew and he drifted off the staff of *The Times*, but he continued his unofficial correspondence for the paper. Moberly Bell became a senior partner of his father's old firm, but when he was unexpectedly fired by Peel and Company in the middle of his marriage preparations in 1875, he immediately returned to work in another firm, managing grain exports, and building up his own business as a broker and insurer as well.

And he'd done something else: he'd built a life for himself, meeting, courting, and winning the hand of Miss Ethel Chataway, in 1875. Raised in a rural rectory, she was the eldest of fifteen children and therefore a highly competent person who accompanied a friend on a family visit to Egypt. There, she met Moberly Bell, who appeared on the railway platform having just returned from fighting a fire at an establishment insured by his firm. He looked like what he at the moment was: a filthy, swarthy, and disheveled fire survivor. He succeeded in making himself memorable to a repulsed Miss Chataway, who joked with her friend about various unsuitable men she encountered in Egypt afterward by saying she'd "just as soon marry Mr. Bell." *Et voilà*. Her features were as delicate as Bell's were rough. "She took from her husband all the responsibility of their domestic life," wrote her daughter, Enid, in what seems to read like a job description: "She kept the accounts, she brought up the children, she managed men-servants and maid-servants and the strangers within his gates, not only without fuss, but with positive enjoyment."

With Suez open, and Egypt now a busy link to India, Moberly Bell could see the wide ribbon of empire tying together the British globe from his perch on the Nile. Britain's growing involvement in Egypt was encouraged by Bell—not so much as a way of bringing home comforts to a far-off outpost; Egypt, not England, was Moberly Bell's home, after all—but because he was a true imperialist, convinced that Britain's mission to bring the civilizing consequences of commerce and settlement were consistent with his view of a moral planet. By 1882, he was again the official *Times* correspon-

John Cameron Macdonald, ca. 1885

dent, happy with the part he had to play in it all.

In 1885, after losing the battle to provoke the dithering government to save Gordon in Khartoum—a crime for which *The Times* helped Gladstone pay with his job—Moberly Bell went to London. His tireless work on behalf of Gordon had earned him the animosity of some but the friendship of others, and during his visit he found himself welcomed as a familiar name by those he had never before seen, including *The Times*'s legendary Henri Stefan Opper de Blowitz and John Cameron Macdonald, who had taken over as manager from Mowbray Morris after the latter's retirement. He was entertained by John Walter III at Bear Wood and struck up a friendship with Arthur Walter, a man of Bell's age but very inexperienced in publishing—and indeed in anything not related to gardening.

John and Arthur Walter and their families wintered that year in

John Thadeus Delane, ca. 1890

Egypt, and Moberly Bell was in constant attendance, making sure the chief proprietor and his son met those they wished to meet and saw all that they wished to see. As the Parnell case began to unravel for *The Times* over the course of 1888 and 1889, Arthur Walter relied on Moberly Bell's good business sense and journalistic judgment not only for advice but also for sympathy. In doing so, he learned to trust Bell's plainspoken, clear-headed views.

CHAPTER 5

THE ASSISTANT MANAGER

Moberly Bell and Arthur Walter both at first thought that the invitation, sent out by Arthur on February 2, 1890, for Bell to "come over here for a few months" was exactly what it seemed to be. After the disaster of the Parnell trial and the business and other legal reversals of the paper, Arthur Walter needed somebody he could trust, somebody who knew *The Times*—but not somebody who had close associations with others in Printing House Square, since the small proprietors seemed to have allies everywhere. He knew they were eager to reduce printing costs, yet the paper had been forced to support the by now antiquated production machinery of Printing House Square. Arthur and his younger half brother, Godfrey, resolved to rely on their unlikely ability to work well together and to resist the demands of their noisy coproprietors until the finances of the paper could be stabilized.

But how to do that while circulation continued to decline, and with it advertising and revenue, and while the competition from the penny press grew? The emergence of wildly successful throwaways, such as those published by Alfred Harmsworth and Cyril Arthur Pearson—who had won his job in publishing literally by entering a contest in Harmsworth's *Tit-Bits* and collecting the prize, a job as a clerk on the weekly paper—provided no model for *The Times*. The very person of these entrepreneurs was foreign at *The Times*—an egomaniac and a low-ranking fluke? Not exactly the kind of person found behind the drafty windows of Walter's old brick building. Besides, success as a "popular" newspaper would have been seen as failure in Printing House Square, where scoops and sensation were dismissed as trivial vulgarities. Walter II more than once had to take the trouble to explain slowly to his employees that more readers meant more advertisers and more advertisers meant more money for good journalism and good journalism would attract more readers. But that exotic formulation was habitually forgotten. By the 1890s, what constituted "good journalism" increasingly meant journalism of interest to a certain narrow class of interested people, including other journalists, not only those at Printing House Square but also at other newspapers that emulated *The Times.* After nearly a full generation of institutionalized elitism, concerns about readers and advertisers were as distant from the lofty editorial and journalistic minds of *The Times* as London was from, say, Egypt. The world had gotten smaller, but so had *The Times*'s market share.

Walter made no pretense of having the ability to understand either the editorial problems or the detailed and complex financial situation of *The Times,* nor did he very much want to. The editor of *The Times,* George Earle Buckle, was, aside from his penchant for lashing out at "papists," a very knowl-edgeable man, insightful in the coverage of political and domestic news, and, if uninterested in, at least respectful of the foreign coverage that was generally the responsibility of the manager, who was also responsible for the general running of the enter-prise. It was all a bit much for Arthur, the man with the mind of a gardener. He needed some-body who could help him make order of the chaos that was rising around him. He may not have been sure where his newspaper stood, exactly, but the growing pile of papers on his desk sug-gested peril.

Arthur Walter's own role had

George Earle Buckle

changed since John Cameron Macdonald's death on December 10, 1889, only a few months after the Parnell decision. Arthur himself had been the target of the small proprietors when Walter III tried to name him manager in 1885; recall, he instead was, formally anyway, the assistant manager, a titular distance from authority that suggested a real one and therefore suited him fine. But as his father grew older, the need for somebody to maintain the family's authoritative leadership grew. John Walter was less and less in attendance at Printing House Square, but the staff—from editor Buckle to the lowliest copy boy—were all fiercely loyal to the Walter family, the monarchs of their small kingdom; indeed, many of the noneditorial employees in Printing House Square lived in a model village on the Bear Wood estate, which also provided the trees from which *The Times*'s newsprint was made. As Walter III faded from view, they instinctively turned to Arthur Walter for answers. He, in turn, instinctively turned to look behind him, where he was quite alarmed to see no one. So the assistant manager of *The Times* decided to hire himself an assistant, temporarily, and Moberly Bell was just the man.

Moberly Bell had two small children and a wife, and as comfortable as he was in Egypt he knew how dangerous the crowded banks of the Nile and its delta could be. Every year saw a fresh threat of cholera; indeed, the 1884 outbreak was one he and his wife and children had faced together. He was also a little nervous; he knew nothing of printing, and while business, generally, was his non-journalistic forte, the London newspaper business, with its clubby intrigues and incestuous quarrels, was far outside his own interests.

When he arrived in London, he took a room at the Devonshire Club and reported that, at least ostensibly, the job was as he thought: "Mr Arthur Walter is sole manager, and if I am to have any position at all, I am *pro tem.* honorary secretary," he wrote to Ethel. But the real work was navigating entry into a chummy, closely knit company of men who were egotistical, powerful, and insecure. It was also an awkward position, being assistant to the assistant manager. Everyone was quite clear that the assistant manager, after all, was also the next chief proprietor. So his immediate job was smoothing ruffled feathers. Printing House Square old-timers, "who," he wrote, "have been born on the premises and who dread any change," were stirred to disdainful irritation. They were annoyed and slightly fearful at the presence of an outsider who had been invited to stand so close to Arthur Walter. When de Blowitz complained that he had not been properly consulted before Moberly Bell's invitation was sent, for example, the latter sent a note explaining, "I am come simply as a friend to help Mr Walter for a few months."

At the same time, Arthur Walter was aware of his own inadequacies. He preferred that they remain hidden, however, especially from himself, and therefore he sought to protect himself from the competencies of his new man. He gave him many responsibilities but little authority and no useful consultation or advice. At first, Bell was relegated merely to writing apologetic notes to creditors explaining that it was impossible to sign checks owing to the proprietor's absence. But every day, Walter transferred a portion of the pile of paper on his desk to the surface of Moberly Bell's. The days grew longer.

On March 11, 1890, Bell again wrote home.

> We are little by little beginning to go on wheels in this department. I tell Arthur Walter the only person I can't reduce to order is himself, for, with the well-meant intention of lending a hand, he gets hold of my papers and loses them. He arrives about 12 noon, and by lunch time is half-way through a stray letter which, as he says, he has been allowed to play with because it happens to have been addressed to himself personally. I generally have to finish it. He declares that I come down and have occasional raids on his room and snatch up whatever I can—which is about true. The more I see of him the more I like him. He is also very straightforward and thoroughly honourable, and is also free from any petty jealousy. The other day we were negotiating a certain document. Discussing its value with me, Arthur Walter said he thought we could afford to pay £20 for it—that it was worth that to the paper. When the man came, I suggested £10, which he agreed to take "if we thought it fair." Arthur Walter at once said: "Well—no, I was prepared to pay £20 so I will pay it."

The task Moberly Bell faced was insurmountable, of course. Both he and Walter were limited in their range of options. They each worked cautiously, since they could control little. They only knew they could make no more mistakes. One more Parnell-type fiasco and *The Times* would vanish.

In fact, it looked close to vanishing anyway. Moberly Bell later recalled the situation for the benefit of the small proprietors, who were always demanding their dividends. "When I came to England . . . to assume my present office," he told them, "I found *The Times* insolvent. The entire assets (exclusive of good-will) were £61,000, and the liabilities were at least £102,000—we could not, in fact, have paid 12s. in the £, and while the revenue was falling, and had . . . for fifteen years been falling at the rate of £9000 a year, there was a growing tendency to increase the size of the paper and to increase the relative expenditure, and there was no capital whatever from which we could pay our debts or expend in developing the resources of the business."

Moreover, the business department over which Bell presided—when he was permitted to do so—was in ruins. Macdonald had left the accounts in complete disarray; letters from creditors had gone unanswered, payments had been made haphazardly, the company's books had not been looked at for at least three years, and correspondence to *The Times* had been allowed to accumulate in towering piles. Many of the letters were so old their writers no doubt had long abandoned any hope of a reply. Bell was shocked to see that wildly improbable expense accounts had been filed by foreign correspondents with only the sketchiest of documentation. The advertising department was run with an indifference to customers that appalled Bell: when advertisers would arrive with their copy, the staff collected the fees, but proudly refused to divulge a date when the ad might run. Not surprisingly, advertising was declining even faster than readership, which was in a steady, apparently irreversible decline. In 1852, eleven years after one of *The Times*'s most influential editors, John Thadeus Delane, assumed his role at Printing House Square, the daily circulation of the paper was 40,000. In 1877, when Delane finally retired, it was 65,000. By the time Moberly Bell arrived, it was 40,000 again. And there was no money. Meanwhile, rivals, like *The Daily Telegraph* and *The Morning Post*, were flourishing under energetic, entrepreneurial management.

Walter and Bell were men about the same age. They had that much in common. The rest was lucky harmony. Where Walter was dapper, quiet, slightly diffident, and distracted, Moberly Bell was bull-like, rumpled, argumentative, focused, intense, constantly working, and vaguely foreign: the denizens of Printing House Square called him "the Assyrian." He loved to talk and viewed contentious discussions about religion and politics as a kind of sporting event—lots of volume, fight to the death, no hard feelings, buy you a drink. Arthur Walter, on the other hand, loved to listen, but only to a phrase or two. He was abstemious, restrained, uninterested. He disliked reading. Moberly Bell read everything—starting with that stack of back correspondence, methodically answering every single person who had written to *The Times* but not yet had a reply. And he wrote as he spoke—at length, combatively, entertaining trivial but volatile readers until he had the last, precious word.

Not surprisingly, the pair became first true friends, then true colleagues, Arthur Walter a retiring Bertie to Moberly Bell's rough Jeeves. Arthur viewed his work as a strange object obviously having nothing to do with him, yet he was not graceful in yielding to Moberly Bell the authority he needed to get the work done. However, he did very much like the sympathetic company of an intelligent, optimistic, energetic man, and then came to appreciate that Moberly Bell actually enjoyed doing all the things Arthur Walter found not just boring, but incomprehensible—like all those letters from wherever. Moberly Bell was blindly persistent and terrifically busy. Arthur Walter was merely blind.

As Moberly Bell's confidence grew, so did his imagination. This, too, caused friction with some of the staff who had come to venerate *The Times*, cherished its traditions and unaltered practices, especially those that camouflaged their incompetence, and saw every innovation as an assault, every improvement a kind of heresy. Nearly the entire staff, for example, was infuriated by Moberly Bell's introduction of typewriters and *telephones*. To many, these things were secular novelties in a place as sacrosanct as a newspaper office. And Moberly Bell's interruption of Buckle's obsessively detailed political coverage to allow a few columns to cover literature and the book trade—book publishers were eager advertisers, after all—provoked sullen anger as well. In the newsroom, the manager, far from becoming a shadowy figure from the business side, was often a familiar participant, and when a story captured his attention, he didn't walk away until the denouement was clear. The American presidential election for 1896, for example, fascinated him. Moberly Bell hoped that William McKinley's defeat of William Jennings Bryan would signal the end of American isolationism, despite the Republican's high-tariff policies. No matter who won, Bell was aware that the increasing insinuation of American money, culture, and personalities into British life made the outcome of the election important for readers of *The Times*. As the votes were being counted in the U.S., Moberly Bell was at his desk, watching the story of McKinley's massive victory slowly unfold over thirty-six straight hours, taking only a single, one-hour nap, and not leaving until the California votes were in and counted.

He saw Walter less and less. All the questions that would normally have gone to the chief proprietor were now entrusted to Moberly Bell. It may have started as a temporary assignment for "a few months," but Bell was now firmly and permanently in place at *The Times*, title uncertain but manager in fact, dining with political leaders and jousting with *The Times*'s many irritated readers, for British readers did not like advertising—at least, not the intrusive kind. The front page with its hundreds of small ads had become invisible to them. They simply went past it to the news. Increasingly, under Moberly Bell, when they did so, they were greeted by yet more advertisements. *That* was offensive to the many readers who did not understand that even though they had paid for news, they also had to pay again through distractions if the paper were to stay in business.

Moberly Bell's family was by now safely in London, but he was always at his desk, his door always open. "For him, his work was all-sufficient," his admiring daughter later wrote. He was always working, always writing, always looking for a way to keep *The Times* afloat, occasionally interrupting his days with a visit to his home, where Ethel and his six children happily received whatever guests he had brought along for dinner. The next morning would find him back at Printing House Square, ordering more infernal typewriters and personally instructing *The Times*'s dwindling number of noisy readers on the business of newspaper publishing. His life was full of trouble— that is to say, *The Times* was in trouble, and *The Times* was his life.

.   .   .

Into it, on the morning of February 23, 1897, walked James Clarke and Horace E. Hooper.

From where Bell and Walter stood at the end of 1896, 1897 did not look like it would be a very happy new year. Although they were only beginning to understand how difficult their position was, they both knew they were running out of time. John Walter III, Arthur Walter's father, had died in 1894, leaving disorder as his principal bequest. Arthur himself had become even more frail, more confused. The small proprietors, at first minor annoyances around the cuff, had become larger and more snarling. It was the talk of Fleet Street: the great paper could cease publication at any time, and every morning's edition might be the last. Something had to change.

But Walter and the other proprietors would never countenance changing the tone, perspective, or even the fundamental appearance of the paper, let alone the unique social role that both made failure seem impossible and success improbable. Moberly Bell's challenge, then, was to find an alternative. He couldn't lower the editorial quality of the paper that went through the press, and he couldn't lower the price of the paper on the street. Doing the former wouldn't have attracted the readers advertisers most wanted to reach anyway, nor would it have guaranteed increased circulation, especially in the face of competition from other papers that were decidedly popular in every way readers of *The Times* would not have understood. Dropping the price to 2d might have increased circulation, but to whom? Capitalization through investors was out of the question; the small proprietors were trouble enough.

The strategy devised by Moberly Bell was to find other sources of revenue that would not involve any alteration at all to the character of *The Times*. His hands were tied, so he used his head: he was sitting in a large brick building filled with printing presses. He would publish books and supplements that would reflect favorably on *The Times*'s reputation, give readers a little more of what they expected from the newspaper, and create revenue without touching any significant aspect of the thing.

He had already launched a digest, *The Times Weekly Edition*, in 1893. It had grown, slowly at first, then more quickly, but it had always made a profit—although, he feared, at the expense of *The Times*, since many readers were happy to settle for a weekly summary for a frac-

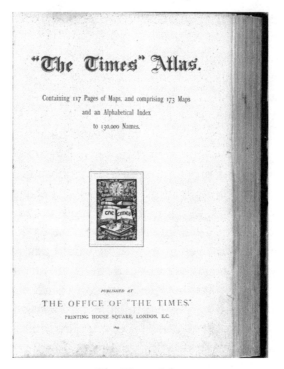

"The Times" Atlas.

Containing 117 Pages of Maps, and comprising 173 Maps
and an Alphabetical Index
to 130,000 Names.

PUBLISHED AT
THE OFFICE OF "THE TIMES."
PRINTING HOUSE SQUARE, LONDON, E.C.

The Times Atlas

tion of the price of a daily update. It was the same with *The Times Law Reports*. So Moberly Bell decided to try books. In 1895, he took a full page to straightforwardly announce the publication of *The Times Atlas*. It was a reprint of a book published by a German firm in an English translation, with 117 maps showing the more exotic corners of Victoria's vast empire and bringing the great age of African exploration right up to date; the very wide scope of the empire seemed to support *The Times*'s own authority. Bell offered it in fifteen weekly installments for a shilling each, and in 1896 it was sold as a bound volume for a pound. It wasn't a newspaper, but it did make money. Or, given *The Times*'s problems, it made money because it wasn't the newspaper.

It also attracted the attention of a certain type of book merchant. James Clarke and Horace Hooper both saw and understood how *The Times* had been able to leverage its authoritative reputation by creating other publications and books—especially reference works—that drew on the strengths of *The Times* and all it had come to represent, while also validating the paper's credibility. Moberly Bell understood that what *The Times* had to sell wasn't just news, or periodicals or books, or, least of all, printing. *The Times* was selling what is now called its "brand," which in the case of *The Times* was something far greater than the sum of its parts. It was selling the aspirational quality of British self-perception. It was selling the middle class a mirror that reflected their social and cultural superiority. It was, in the words of Matthew Arnold, "an organ of the common, satisfied, well-to-do Englishman." Clarke, Hooper, and Haxton saw all this and understood it perfectly.

When Hooper and Haxton arrived from Plymouth, they took rooms at the Savoy and began putting substance to their plan. From their own investigations, and from Clarke's intelligence, they knew that the Ninth Edition of the *Encyclopædia Britannica* had long ago exhausted its market in the UK. At £37 per set, it was far more than most people could afford to pay for a reference set, and it was getting more and more difficult to convince average Britons of the value of a set of reference volumes some of which were already twenty-five years old. It was, of course, the same problem Clarke, Hooper, and Haxton had just faced in Chicago with the *Century*.

While Clarke and Hooper understood Americans and their susceptibility to salesmen with an entertaining or engaging line—all those amply illustrated pitches made by Hooper's book agents, for example—the marketing of books in Britain was a grim and uninteresting business. In most newspapers and periodicals, advertisements for books looked exactly like death notices—the same minimal, matter-of-fact text, the same low-key typography, the same tombstone-like boxes. That the announcement of the birth of a book should so closely resemble an announcement of the death of a reader was an irony that apparently had never occurred to British publishers. Few industries in the United Kingdom were as restrained in their public offerings and as bound to tradition in their business practices as the publishing and selling of books.

Hooper had options about how to proceed. He didn't want to approach A & C Black directly; not only would Adam Black not be inclined to discuss his publishing problems with unknown

American salesmen, but given their background, he might bring up some unpleasant copyright issues. What Hooper needed to do was to discover the production cost of the encyclopedia. The selling price—books had rarely been discounted in Britain, even as they sat gathering dust in warehouses—seemed to him to be arbitrary, since the encyclopedia had been in print long enough to make irrelevant any additional editorial expenses. Hooper finally decided he didn't need to meet the publisher. He needed to meet the printer.

Haxton and Hooper traveled to Edinburgh for an interview with Edward Clark, the proprietor of R & R Clark. Clark had been the Blacks' printer for many years and understood the company's circumstances well: the encyclopedia had hobbled the firm, preventing the development of a robust list of titles—and at the worst possible time. Hooper thought James Clarke might be interested in making a deal to obtain copies of the *Britannica* at discount, since he had plans under way to sell an augmented edition of the Ninth Edition in America, and, for a change, he wanted to use legitimate copies. By 1896, it had been seven years since the appearance of the last volume, and American sales at the price charged by Scribner's and Little, Brown were rapidly ebbing. The official encyclopedia at a bootleg price might be just the thing.

A & C Black had been founded in 1807, when the twenty-three-year-old Adam Black, the son of a builder, opened a bookshop in Edinburgh on South Bridge. (Adam was the "A" in the name of the firm; the "C" was nephew Charles, brought into the company some years later.) Adam was freshly returned from London, where he had eagerly and optimistically sought success in the book trade. But the intervention of reality limited his choices, and instead of working in one of London's elegant bookshops, he instead ended up at Lackington, Allen, & Co. As bookselling and publishing went, Lackington's was at the bottom of the food chain, a boneyard of books. The five-floor Finsbury shop was styled "The Temple of the Muses" and was walled in by large signs that boasted of being "the cheapest booksellers in the world"—mostly, as Black discovered, because the books were secondhand and ragged or unsalable stock discarded by more reputable publishers. Of course, selling only remainders is a wonderful way to learn how not to publish a book, so after three years, Black, responding to the twin calls of parents and common sense, returned to Scotland and to Edinburgh, where so much was going on in the city's bustling literary and academic community.

As in London, the publishers in Edinburgh were also the booksellers in Edinburgh, and Black started slowly, publishing books that he thought would sell quickly and easily, gradually building a list featuring a heavy dose of medicine and lots of science. In 1826, Archibald Constable & Co., at the time one of Britain's greatest publishers, well fattened by the phenomenal sales of Sir Walter Scott's historical tales of Scottish derring-do, fell into default. Among the assets: the rights to the *Encyclopædia Britannica*, by then in the Sixth Edition, the last volume of which had appeared in 1823. In 1827, Black snatched the copyright for £6,510, less than a third what Constable had paid for it in 1812.

Black appointed Macvey Napier, the scholarly editor of *The Edinburgh Review* (another Constable property that had fallen into Black's hands), to edit the work and began planning the Seventh Edition, with twenty-one volumes, eight hundred pages to the volume. Advertisements in *The Edinburgh Literary Journal* and elsewhere began appearing early in 1830 offering a subscription to the set at £36 per volume. The first volume appeared on March 30, 1830. Sales were satisfactory, aided by the work previously done to broaden the encyclopedia and make updates an anticipated aspect of encyclopedia publishing, something that reflected the eager mood of the day. Napier had already made an important contribution by soliciting experts as entry writers and, for the first time, by creating a supplement to the previous three editions, the last volume of which appeared in 1824, just two years before Constable's bankruptcy.

By the time the Seventh Edition appeared, well-known experts, including Humphry Davy, Walter Scott, Thomas Malthus, John Playfair, Dugald Stewart, Francis Jeffrey, John Stuart Mill, William Hazlitt, David Ricardo, Thomas Young, and the French physicists Dominique François Jean Arago and Jean-Baptiste Biot, had become associated with articles in the *Britannica*. Some, like Young, became habitual contributors; he contributed sixty-three articles between 1816 and 1823. Others wrote exhaustively; Stewart's "A General View of the Progress of Metaphysical, Ethical and Political Philosophy, Since the Revival of Letters in Europe" came in at 423 pages.

Over the next twelve years, Black would spend £100,000 on

NEW EDITION OF THE ENCYCLOPÆDIA
BRITANNICA.
On the 31st of March, 1830, will be published,
PART FIRST,
Price Six Shillings, of a new, greatly improved, and cheap Edition
of the
ENCYCLOPÆDIA BRITANNICA, being the
SEVENTH, including the recent Supplement to that Work :
with Preliminary Dissertations on the History of the Sciences. By
the late Professors STEWART and PLAYFAIR, and by the Right
Hon. Sir JAMES MACKINTOSH and Professor LESLIE. Illus-
trated with a new set of Engravings on Steel. To be published in
Monthly Parts, and completed in Twenty Volumes quarto.
Edited by Professor NAPIER.
MODE AND TERMS OF PUBLICATION.
I. By augmenting the contents of the page, but without decrea-
sing the size of the type, the work, while much improved in appearance, will be comprised, notwithstanding the great extension of its

Selling the Britannica *in the pages of* The Edinburgh Literary Journal, *1830*

the twenty-one-volume set, along the way publishing at least one
additional book a year with the contents harvested from the encyclopedia. In 1842, Black published an extensive atlas, putting all
of the encyclopedia's famous maps between the covers of a single
volume. The inventory of scholars writing in the three editions and
supplements—the Fifth, Sixth, and Seventh—not only enhanced the
Encyclopædia Britannica's already exalted reputation but also created
a kind of impediment to competition by other, aspiring encyclopedia publishers, of which there were many. Publishers were naturally
attracted to the idea of subscribed series of books, greatly reducing
the unpredictable nature of the business. But encyclopedias were
expensive and complicated to edit and manage. Still, by the 1890s,
the production of a new encyclopedia every half generation or so
under one or another Adam Black—by the time Hooper arrived, a
third Adam Black (the grandson of Adam Black and son of Adam W.
Black) was running the firm—seemed almost routine.

The Ninth Edition—edited by Baynes, the metaphysician with
a scholarly appreciation of Shakespeare, and Robertson Smith, the
academic with an interest in the Middle East—represented an unex-

pectedly large and therefore paralytic investment by A & C Black. Adam W. Black was the "moving spirit" behind what was clearly an impossible project undertaken despite his father's disapproval. It had tapped the company's finances dramatically, while the American copyright issue grew worse. (Black made four transatlantic journeys in search of a remedy.) It had taken more than two decades to sell a mere ten thousand sets in Britain, and the possibility of expanding those sales diminished with every passing month as the edition grew more and more out of date, and as the publisher's health grew more and more precarious. In 1891, Adam W. Black retired, and at age sixty-two he took to his bed to await death. His son took control of the company.

To the latest Adam Black, Hooper presented his survey and produced his plan. It would require Haxton's ad-writing skills and his own marketing genius. It would also require a brace of deep pockets. These he found on James Clarke and on a book-man both he and Clarke knew and admired—Walter Montgomery Jackson, yet another high school dropout. Jackson had lifted himself out of the stockroom of a Boston bookshop to run the Grolier Society, an upmarket subscription publisher. The society sold overpriced, limited-edition reprints of many of the same books that Hooper's book agents were selling, in less luxurious bindings, at a fraction of the price. Collectors snapped them up, comforted by Jackson's public personality, to the extent such a thing existed: he was a careful, thoughtful, self-styled man of letters and patron of poets and other writers whose books had a commercial appeal that was not immediately apparent to Hooper. But Jackson knew how to sell to affluent readers. His success couldn't be disputed, as his wealth proved.

Only a year after selling out of those *Century Dictionary and Cyclopedia*s in Chicago, Hooper and Haxton thought they had their pieces in place.

So, in 1896, James Clarke appeared with Horace Everett Hooper in the offices of A & C Black and made an offer to obtain the exclusive publishing rights to the Ninth Edition until January 1, 1904, along with the old plates. The company quickly accepted £6,500 for five thousand sets, the plates, and the right to any remaindered stock still on hand. How Hooper and Clarke proposed selling more than five thousand nearly quaint encyclopedias was a question the latest Adam Black apparently didn't ask.

It's not entirely clear if a response given by Clarke, Jackson, Hooper, or Haxton would have made sense in any case. Clarke had said he wanted to sell legitimate copies of the Ninth Edition in the U.S., and, as we shall see, they did. It was growing more apparent to Hooper that a far larger untapped potential existed right where they stood, while Clarke's sometime business partner, Alexander Belford, was preparing to flog the Ninth to American buyers once again—this time under the Werner imprint.

However, it was clear to Hooper that the British had no idea how badly they needed a set of the Ninth Edition of the *Encyclopædia Britannica*, with its nostalgic, mid-century views of all things that started with the letters A, B, and C, and its charming maps of a more exciting Africa, where the terra was still incognita, and where Stanley still searched for Livingstone. The British didn't know they wanted and needed this—but Hooper felt he should tell them, and with Haxton on hand, and Jackson and Clarke by his side, he felt he couldn't fail.

And so the parallel lives of the two men who believed most fervently in *The Times*, one a product of empire and the other a self-made man out of the American West, now crossed in a small office in Printing House Square.

CHAPTER 6

THE AMERICAN SCHEME

On February 26, 1897, Clarke and Hooper made their way to the City of London and into Printing House Square to keep their second appointment with Moberly Bell. Only a few days earlier, the hurried conversation between the three men had gone badly, perhaps because Hooper's idea of selling a Ninth Edition of the *Encyclopædia Britannica* emblazoned with *The Times*'s proud logo had been too preposterous for Bell to grasp, just as Haxton had found it improbable that so august an institution as *The Times* would want to play on the same side as a bunch of reprint men from Chicago. A letter of introduction from Adam Black had been no help. Earlier, Hooper had written to Clarke that he had "found out things since I've been here. We need someone on this project, and we surely need *The Times*. But I think *The Times* needs us even more than we need *The Times*."

It didn't seem so, gauging by Moberly Bell's dubious reaction. As he understood it, Hooper and Clarke wanted to buy a substantial amount of advertising space from *The Times* to convince readers to buy an old set of encyclopedias on credit—a guinea down and then a guinea each month for thirteen months. It was a very good price for a set of books that normally sold for £37 each, but it was a mostly untested way of collecting it. The books, Hooper said, would be sent on receipt of the initial payment, but with nothing but a promise to pay the balance. And even though Hooper and Clarke said they would stand for any bad debts, they expected *The Times* to act as publisher and put its name on the project. This would be *The Times Edition of the Encyclopædia Britannica*! For the use of the brand, *The Times* would receive a guinea for each copy sold? Ludicrous.

Until Moberly Bell thought about it. The Americans may have been onto an ingenious plan after all. As far as he could tell, the advanced age of the encyclopedia was the main thing, and one would think that, barring an extraordinary advertising effort, it was an insurmountable obstacle. But the advertising effort had a definite appeal, too: the Americans offered to pay cash for the advertising space required in addition to the sales commission. It was found money for doing nothing more than lending the name of *The Times* and forwarding the paperwork for each order on to the Americans—that didn't seem like such a bad idea. And the Americans had said they thought they could sell *thousands* of copies. But wait: What if *The Times* offered the books, collected the money—but had no books to send? A print run of the Ninth Edition was no small thing, after all.

So from his home the night after the meeting, Moberly Bell wrote to Adam Black to see if this farfetched idea was even a remote possibility. "I have had much pleasure in seeing Mr James Clarke, who presented your letter of introduction, and discussing it with him and another gentleman whose name I must apologise for forgetting, the proposal as to the reissue of the *Encyclopædia Britannica*. The proposal is a somewhat novel one."

Black must have replied in an effort to reassure Moberly Bell (and to remind him of Hooper's name), for two days later, Bell wrote again:

> Before we publish advertisements inducing people to send one guinea to this office we must have some guarantee that the E.B. *will be delivered as promised*. This guarantee must be given by you or some responsible firm in this country. . . . We have no control over the *Encyclopædia Britannica*. Who guarantees that it *will* be delivered? If your firm does so, we know where we are—but we know nothing of Messrs Clarke or Hooper or of the printer, binder or others through whose hands the book will pass. . . . Before we enter into a contract which may involve a liability of 200,000 pounds we must be covered by some responsible, well-known signature.

> Black duly guaranteed the sets.

So now, seeing the pair again—one, the forgettable chap chirping along in a high-pitched nasally whine, the other muttering belligerently—he began to pick out some interesting noises, and the more he listened, the more they sounded like money, and money was something *The Times* needed very, very badly.

When the men left, he tried to gather his thoughts, but instead decided to put it all down quickly on paper. If it made sense to him, he'd send the note along to Arthur Walter, who would be surprised to receive it, no doubt, since only three days before Bell had written to him to say the American idea, whatever it was, wasn't practical. As he wrote, carefully explaining Hooper's plan, the idea became more and more clear to him and its appeal irresistible, until finally, near the end, Moberly Bell made a leap of . . . well, not faith, exactly, but certainly hope.

My dear Walter,

After a two hours talk with the two Americans, at which Dawson was also present, I have come to a conclusion favourable to the *Encyclopædia Britannica* project provided we can get our terms.

Those terms I have drawn up on enclosed rough draft of contract. In sending it to the Americans I have explained that it is merely a project to form a basis of discussion and that it binds us to absolutely nothing—we being still at perfect liberty to decline to have anything to do with it even if they accept unreservedly all we suggest. . . .

It is impossible to write fully the reasons which induce me to recommend it now when, as you know, I had abandoned the idea last Tuesday but I can tell you the reasons when I see you—but the figures mentioned in the subsidiary agreement of [A & C] Black's are the main cause.

I have read over this suggested contract to [*Times* solicitor Joseph] Soames who agrees that with verbal alterations we should run no risk. Of course we should have it properly drawn out if ever we come to terms.

Warmly
C Moberly Bell

The "memorandum of agreement" between "Arthur Fraser Walter for and on behalf of the Proprietors of *The Times* newspaper . . . and Messrs Clarke & Hooper" was attached, although it was quickly amended to read "Hooper & Jackson" to reflect Jackson's contribution to the pool of capital, and Clarke's expressed wish to attend also to his own encyclopedia project in America.

Clarke & Hooper, Hooper & Jackson, it didn't really matter to Bell & Walter, since their attention was fixed on the idea Hooper had presented and especially on the revenues Hooper had promised. Coming as it did on the heels of his newly discovered source of income—publishing material other than the newspaper—Moberly Bell did not require a great deal of explanation to understand what he thought Hooper wanted. *Times + Britannica* was a simple enough equation for him. And once he had the assurance that the books would actually be provided, he was eager to move ahead.

Happily, he soon found that the man whose name he had once forgotten was a kindred spirit, a man permanently on the job and in whose mind a great plan was taking shape. Hooper gladly gave advice on *The Times Atlas*, donated the copywriting expertise of Henry Haxton, and proved worthy of Moberly Bell's attentiveness. Bell must have appreciated the tag that Printing House Square denizens soon awarded Horace Everett Hooper: "HEH," they said, stood for "Hell Every Hour." They meant it mockingly. But Moberly Bell took solace in it.

The potentially awkward posture of having *The Times* act as publisher on behalf of some unknown Americans must have given Walter pause, as it had Bell. And, of course, neither Bell nor Walter had the slightest idea if an out-of-date encyclopedia actually could be sold on credit to people who had never before demonstrated an interest in it. But that was the last worry on Hooper's mind; his energetic optimism quickly won over Moberly Bell, who so badly needed to believe in what Hooper was doing.

Hooper and Haxton returned to Manhattan and rejoined Clarke. Working under the Werner imprint, and now in possession of five thousand sets of old encyclopedias from A & C Black, they were ready to try their own test of the model Hooper had proposed to Bell. If it played well in New York, it seemed certain to work in London.

For years, *The New York Times* had fulminated against the pirated copies of the *Britannica*'s Ninth Edition sold by men like Clarke, and ridiculed the otherwise reputable companies that dealt in them—especially John Wanamaker and Funk & Wagnalls. Just a few years earlier, in 1893, the paper applauded a federal court injunction "to restrain the pirates who made and undertook to see a cheap reprint of the *Encyclopædia Britannica* in violation of the copyright of the publishers from prosecuting their nefarious traffic. The attempts to pirate this great work in the United States have been of a particularly mean order. . . . [S]tealing by cheap processes of reproduction has been exposed and is liable to be punished. It will henceforth be not only a disreputable business but a risky and, it is to be hoped, an unprofitable one."

The stridency and directness of the paper's campaign against the "reprinted 'Britannica'" grew so shrill that Funk & Wagnalls sought to make their own position very clear:

> In view of the renewed association of the name of our house with the reprint of the *Encyclopædia Britannica* in America, permit us to repeat what we have said again and again: We never set a type of the *Britannica*, we never made a plate of it, we never printed a page of it, nor have we had at any time anything to do, directly or indirectly, with the making of any reprint plates of it. Our whole connection with the *Britannica* is summed up in the following: For six weeks in 1890 we took orders for one of the reprints—the same then and now sold by scores of newspapers as a premium, and by hundreds of leading book and dry goods houses from Maine to California. Since July 1, 1890, we have not booked an order for the work.

The charge against the newspapers mentioned in the letter had special currency at *The New York Times*. The paper had taken a very dim view of newspapers that sold encyclopedias as a way of boosting revenue and circulation. *The New York Times* sniffed in 1890,

> The St. Paul *Pioneer-Press* is usually a careful newspaper, but it errs grievously when it says that "the leading American

newspapers, among them THE NEW-YORK TIMES, . . .
have adopted the plan of distributing the Americanized *Encyclopædia Britannica* among the readers in their respective ter-
ritories." We know nothing whatever of the "Americanized
Encyclopædia Britannica," but without further knowledge
than its title affords we feel free to despise and condemn it as
illegitimate and base. The main point, and to that we invite
the attention of our St. Paul contemporary, is that THE [New
York] TIMES is not in the business of "distributing" pirated or
"Americanized" books or any other kind "among its readers."
The *Tribune*, we believe, is now the only New-York newspaper
of any pretension or standing that keeps up the cross-roads
habit of seeking to procure readers by the bribery and enticement of "premiums."

The Times soon realized that you could hate the piracy but love
the pirate. No sooner had Hooper and Haxton reunited with Clarke
than a new offer began appearing in *The New York Times*, one apparently designed to procure readers by the bribery and enticement of
"premiums": *The New American Supplement to the Latest Edition of the
Encyclopædia Britannica.* Werner had published it in 1897, and now it
was being sold by *The New York Times.* Just clip the coupon and send
it in.

Work on *The New American Supplement* had been under way since
at least 1895, and it represented a significant investment by those
underwriting it–the piratical Chicago bookmen, including Belford
and the Clarke brothers. Whether Hooper was one of the investors
in the edition isn't known. But he and James Clarke had found a
common cause to visit Black's and buy the rights.

The New American Supplement was a rather substantial effort at
an American-oriented revision, one so successful that it virtually
erased its potential for a sale in Britain. In the preface, the editor,
Day Otis Kellogg, DD, a former minister who had become professor of English literature and history at Kansas State University–and
had spent some time before editing a different edition of an "Americanized" Ninth for a Philadelphia publisher–carefully explained the
scope of *The New American Supplement:*

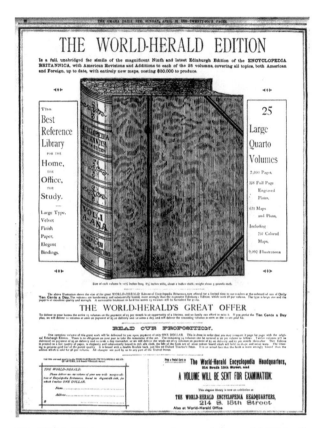

The Ninth Edition was promoted around the world. Virtually every major newspaper had an "edition" of the Ninth to call their own. The Omaha World-Herald's *edition, like the others, was announced with Hooper's characteristic exuberance.*

After some years of experience with the book, having sold it all over the United States, and having learned in the operation what would best adapt it to the needs of the English-speaking world, THE WERNER COMPANY undertook to make this new edition (virtually the TENTH) of the ENCYCLOPÆDIA BRITANNICA. The aims sought are, to supplement the BRITANNICA as to bring all the developments of history, discovery, arts and sciences down to date; to extend biography as to include living men of distinction; to enlarge the view of American interests; and to supply references to the original text, making the whole work available for easy consultation.

The Wichita Eagle *sold "The Kansas City Star Edition,"*
which provided a "University Education for a Song."

The work was entrusted to an editor who had spent twelve
years in the study of the BRITANNICA, about whom was
gathered an office-staff of twenty and a special staff of sixty-
seven persons, including heads of bureaus in Washington,
army and navy officers, eminent theologians, college presidents and professors, women at the head of the best-managed
reforms, educators, statesmen and specialists.

The boast wasn't an idle one. The list of the contributors to the
American edition must have impressed even Haxton. John Sherman, a former secretary of the treasury, wrote about the national

debt; Cardinal Gibbons expounded on the history of the Catholic Church; A. G. Spalding covered baseball; and Walter Camp did the same for football. The government donated the services of a number of experts, including the commanding general of the United States Army, the Navy's chief engineer and constructor, the military man in charge of Arctic exploration, and the nation's foremost expert on Indian affairs, Francis E. Leupp.

The marketing of the encyclopedia to readers used tricks that would soon become familiar to Britain's more innocent readers.

In April 1897, the paper began using its columns to promote the thing. "The highest state officials were applied to for State documents and other trustworthy information," wrote *The New York Times*, in a lavish April 29 review of what it called a "judicious and accurate" work—and, coincidentally, one that was available to readers of *The New York Times*.

> Modern maps, showing the most recently formed countries and provinces, have been inserted in the work. The story of every kingdom has been brought down to date, its ruler's biography written, the lives of its statesmen detailed under their names, and the achievements of its great men described, its history specified, and its progress chronicled. Over 1,500 new illustrations embellish the text. . . . [T]o secure the work in its new form is tantamount to possessing one's-self of the nearest approach to a tenth edition of the work the present generation is likely to see.

Haxton couldn't have said it better. Perhaps he didn't need to. The review was unsigned.

While the business arrangement between Clarke, Werner, Hooper, and Haxton isn't known, the prints of Haxton are all over the 1897 *New York Times* encyclopedia sale. He was still developing his characteristic, run-on pitch that would soon enough entrance, irritate, annoy, and amuse readers in London. And he and Hooper both were honing their skills at insinuating commerce into the columns of *The New York Times*, including the letters page, just as they would at *The Times* itself:

A GRATEFUL SUBSCRIBER

DELIGHTED BY THE RESULTS OF
THE NEW YORK TIMES COUPONS

To the Editor of *The New York Times:*

When I clipped my coupon from your advertisement setting out the superiority and merit of your 1897 or tenth edition of the *Encyclopædia Britannica* I did not for a moment imagine that you had any attending features which connected with the work which rendered the same doubly valuable as a time saver and educator. Your representative called on me during my busy period, but I am amply reimbursed the short interview I granted him, and now I feel that I am obligated to you instead for bringing me full and comprehensive information and the opportunity of subscribing at such remarkably low figures and on such very reasonable terms. When you bring your readers and the public in general such lasting benefits through the instrumentality of your work and its supplementary features, there remains no doubt that you will daily spread your influence, increase your prestige, and multiply your subscriptions. I desire to state, for the benefit of the other readers of your paper, who aim to advance their individual interest, as well as the education of their families, that the features set out in connection with your encyclopedia constitute one of the most laudable and worthy projects that could come within the scope of modern journalism. It is truly American and philanthropic as well, and demonstrates the fact that a reliable newspaper, such as *The* [New York] *Times*, can accomplish no end of good if your readers will but avail themselves of the coupons in your paper before limitation excludes them from a subscription to your remarkable proposition. *The New York Times* has ever been noted as a reliable, clean, and worthy sheet. In its integrity as a great metropolitan newspaper [it] ranks second to none, and it has ever commanded the respect of the most worthy classes.

The New York Times has never degraded its columns with

news unfit to print. Neither has it fallen in self-respect by lend-ing aid to schemes.

If my few remarks will aid in inducing your readers to send in their coupons while they still have the opportunity, I shall feel that I have repaid you in part, at least, for the cour-tesy accorded me by sending me your personal representative, and am,

Thankfully yours,
G.C. Stewart.
No. 1, 109 Washington Street,
Hoboken, N.J., May 17, 1897.

On May 1, a full two-column ad heralded "A 3½ Million Dollar Library." It was, the ad said, a library that "covers everything that has been done by, or that is known to, man," one that "'Twill give you the united wisdom and knowledge of humanity." It came with a bookcase—and, best of all, "You can get it cheap."

The next day, in the Sunday edition, a full-page ad heralded "An Enterprising Offer! From an Enterprising Newspaper!! To an Enter-prising Public!!!" It was the *Britannica*—Clarke's five thousand cop-ies, no doubt—with the Werner volumes added, all available for a small down payment in a deal "accorded only to regular or prospec-tive subscribers to THE NEW YORK TIMES." Included: a subscrip-tion to *Self-Culture*, a magazine about a century ahead of its time, but one launched by Werner in 1897 as a guide for the inwardly bound—mostly autodidacts and self-improvement types—and used as a marketing tool for the encyclopedia. At the bottom of the page, a coupon that appeared in many of the ads: "OUR LIBERAL PROP-OSITION," and a Haxtonian slogan, "Remember: *The Times* Pays the freight." Missing from the ads: a price—neither the down pay-ment nor the purchase price were revealed. The idea seemed to be to elicit sufficient interest that the encyclopedias would sell themselves, and *The New York Times*: those willing to take out a subscription to the paper were told only that they would "secure at wholesale rates the entire set . . . by making a small cash payment," with the rest due over time.

Hooper and Haxton watched the campaign unfold from the deck of a chartered yacht anchored in the Hudson, eager to learn in New York what they needed to know to launch a much bolder marketing strategy in London. Clarke may have been happy enough with the sales of the five thousand copies of the encyclopedia he had bought from Black. For him and the others involved in the Werner edition, it was a tremendous feat to sell five thousand copies of an encyclopedia that had been marketed for more than a decade not only by the British publisher and by the official American distributors but also by a multitude of pirate publishers, each under one version or another of the *"Encyclopædia Britannica"* title. But to Hooper and Haxton, *The New York Times* trial was just proof enough that the Ninth Edition could still be marketed in the UK, where publication had been tightly controlled and was the carefully guarded province only of A & C Black. The Americans just needed the right partner, and the British just needed a little convincing.

On March 23, 1898, Londoners came face-to-face with the first of Haxton's outrageous advertisements for *The Times Edition of the Encyclopædia Britannica.* A full-page announcement covered page 15. Readers were by now accustomed to Moberly Bell's hawking of books in dull full-page advertisements, including *The Times Atlas* and a series called "The Times Biographies," a multivolume collection of obituaries of "EMINENT PERSONS" sold by Macmillan. These notices had been generally understated and straightforward, often containing a rather dull refrain:

FOR THE NORTH POLAR REGIONS,
SEE THE TIMES ATLAS.

FOR THE ATLANTIC OCEAN,
SEE THE TIMES ATLAS.

FOR THE PACIFIC OCEAN,
SEE THE TIMES ATLAS.

And so on, down a full column of type, with sales copy that seemed almost apologetically stiff: "It is a remarkable but undoubted fact that a first-rate Atlas has hitherto been regarded rather as a luxury for the rich than as a necessary possession for every person who takes an intelligent interest in the world about him."

But Haxton's ad was different. It was dense, emphatic, jammed with text; it was so intense, it seemed almost personal—and definitely not British. A reader could be excused for thinking that once the door had been opened the pitch never stopped: "The 1898 impression is now on the presses and will soon be in the binder's hands. The special price is offered only to subscribers whose names are enrolled before the date of publication. Provision has been made for no more than the expected number of prompt applications."

Haxton filled the single page with five thousand words of ad copy. He trumpeted what to those unfamiliar with printing terminology must have seemed to be new work ("The 1898 impression [of a twenty-three-year-old encyclopedia] is now on the presses") while at the same time celebrating the glorious history of the *Encyclopædia Britannica,* from that first impression produced by a "society of gentlemen of Scotland." He elaborated at length on the *Britannica*'s symbolic value, quoted famous men and the unknown, invoked the native wisdom of *sailors* and the acquired intelligence of scholars, and laced the copy with high-pressure bombast followed by leisurely stream-of-conscious amplification. The sentences had a surreal architecture to them; Haxton's labyrinthine corridors took readers past India's northern frontier district and into thirteenth-century China, with pauses for Andrew Lang's love of ghosts, Sir William Jackson's visits with Hottentots and Hindus, and a callout to his friend Robert Louis Stevenson. If James Joyce had sold encyclopedias, this is how he'd have done it, with one thing leading to another and another and another until the coin—actually, a guinea, please—dropped.

When the copy wasn't outrageous, it was preposterous: The *Britannica* was not just a set of books but

the essence of all books, ancient and modern . . . A LIBRARY IN ITSELF, a collection of admirable treatises upon all conceivable subjects. Even the most recondite branches of learning are treated without a trace of pedantry. The volumes are EMINENTLY READABLE.

The pandering was not subtle. The encyclopedia wasn't for just anyone. Instead, "the wonderful story of the nineteenth century" was for "men–and women–who have already enjoyed the fullest opportunities of education, who desire to refresh and clarify the impressions already received."

In Haxton's hands, the *Encyclopædia Britannica* even became a weapon wielded on behalf of the common man in class warfare, and the ad, in places, became a populist manifesto. Once, wrote Haxton, in the dim recesses of time when the first *Britannica* appeared, "superstition and prejudice governed the lives of rich and poor alike; a sort of Chinese respect for the customs and traditions of the past

The "1898 Reprint Edition" of the Ninth Edition originally had been published one volume at a time between 1875 and 1889. The 1898 Times *edition contained no new content–other than the date of the reprint.*

made all attempts at progress appear revolutionary. Cotton and woolen goods were still woven by hand; iron was hammered and not rolled; the alternation of crops was unknown—the farmer grew corn, year after year, until the land was exhausted, and then left it foul with weeds for years. Bone and guano fertilisers had not been introduced, the draining and reclamation of low-lying land was regarded as a visionary project." *The Times Edition of the Encyclopædia Britannica* changed all that:

> [T]he farmer and manufacturer of that day bear the scrutiny of modern criticism better than the classes who were supposed to be vastly their superiors. The professional classes were stubbornly opposed to progress of any sort, and corruption was not uncommon among both the legislative and judicial authorities. At the end of the last century a sudden and irresistible sense of impatience seems to have been born in the nation, and at the cost of strenuous and continued effort all the conditions of life were changed for the better. It is not too much to say that the English are to-day, of all the people of the earth, the best governed and the most law-abiding, the most comfortable and the soundest of body and mind—in all respects, the happiest. There is yet much to be done, and we are doing it.

Ultimately, Haxton claimed, the *Britannica* was more than a set of books, more than the essence of books, more than a wrench for loosening social paralysis. Owning it was an educated English person's *duty*.

The ad, both as it appeared that morning and in more concise and restrained versions appearing in *The Spectator* and elsewhere, offered Britons things that were quite new to most of them: a chance to buy on an installment plan—called "The Times System of Easy Payments"—that guinea-a-month deal—and a true novelty: a *coupon*. Customers merely completed the tiny contract, sent it off with a guinea to Printing House Square, and within days, here is what the customer would find on the doorstep: "Twenty-four massive volumes of about 850 pages each, and a twenty-fifth volume containing an elaborate index to the whole. In addition to the 30,000,000 words which fill its 22,000 pages of letter-press, it contains 33 full-page plates and 671 maps and plans. There are over 9,000 other illustrations. Over 1,100 writers contributed to the work, and a sum of more than £60,000 was paid for the manuscript alone." Haxton boasted about the concision of articles a mere twenty thousand words in length, and he trumpeted the *Britannica*'s unerring choice of experts; they were "not only men of learning . . . but also men of action," for "the Encyclopedia gave no hospitality to the sort of 'harmless drudges' who used to compile works of reference when the world was younger." And not only were they men of action, each of them was a master of the "technique of style" used to illumine "even the least picturesque of sciences." The ad gathered intensity as it went along, hopping this way and that, according to Haxton's mood, until finally it reached a crescendo of endorsements, including one from one important British institution to another: " 'The "Encyclopaedia Britannica" is the one work to which every inquirer first addresses himself, with the certainty of finding firm ground beneath his feet.'– The Times."

It was all new, this form of bombastic, full-page and direct-mail marketing. The ad, and those that followed, along with the pamphlets, booklets, postal solicitations, all of it, became the stuff of adman legend, discussed in universities and lecture halls years later, even if at the time they seemed drug induced. And perhaps they were, since in producing these torrents of advertisements, brochures, sales letters, and fliers, Haxton's methods of copywriting were unusual: he'd work for three days in a row without sleep, madly pacing about his hotel room, his stammer vanished, as he gave dictation to transcriptionists working in shifts and assigned to catch every word. When he reached a frenzy so insanely high-pitched, he'd calm himself by racing downstairs, grabbing a horse, and running the poor beast until it was ready to drop. When he plastered the walls of his room with his own newspaper ads, management complained, and Hooper would have to pay for the damage. In summers, Hooper sent copyists throughout the countryside to one rural inn or another in pursuit of Haxton. More than once, the story went, he would do his monologues from small boats on country lakes, working himself up so intensely that he'd suddenly stop, strip off his clothes, and jump in the water while an astonished secretary shrieked. Thousands and thousands of words—and invoices seeking hundreds of pounds for repairs and damages—arrived in High Holborn. Jackson fumed at all this, but Hooper was dedicated to his ad genius.

Something important was happening, of course; for the first time, a vaunted encyclopedia—really, *the* encyclopedia if you lived in the English-speaking world—intended for only the very rich and for exclusive institutions and clubs was being made available all at once on a mass scale to anyone with a guinea to spare. Literacy and scientific innovations were fueling a craving to just know *everything*—which is precisely what one could find in the pages of the *Encyclopædia Britannica*, the perfect middle-class utility that had become suddenly, beautifully, incredibly cheap, relatively speaking—but only for a limited time! as Haxton urgently warned again and again.

Discount bookselling was not unheard of in the UK—shops like Lackington's "Temple of the Muses" were around, and remaindering books began with Gutenberg, practically. But the very idea of selling the *Encyclopædia Britannica* at a bargain price—well, it seemed almost embarrassing, something that might suggest to a cynical mind that perhaps an outdated set of reference books wasn't worth much, a belief that could easily be used to tarnish the encyclopedia's "brand"—until, that is, one remembered that *The Times* was the publisher. It was *The Times*. It must be all right, then.

It was certainly priced so: marked down from £37, the price of £14 represented a real deal. Even the half-Morocco binding ("which we recommend") was only £18, while a full-Morocco leather set ("a sumptuous binding," Haxton's copy read, "for special purposes") was a song at £25. For those who chose to use "The Times System of Easy Payments," the price was reckoned in guineas—a pound and a shilling, thus giving Hooper and Jackson a bonus for making the credit available.

To thousands of Britons, the combined appeal of *The Times* and the *Encyclopædia Britannica*, the collected wisdom of the age's leading brains—those masters of technique of style and men of action—coupled with a credit purchase plan was just too hard to resist.

The ads ran almost daily (and not just in *The Times*, either—other newspapers and journals were enlisted). They were reinforced with direct-mail pieces and with brochures and presentations made by salesmen in workingmen's halls. It was a relentless campaign. Haxton must have written hundreds of thousands of hyperbolic and outrageous words.

But outrageous language produced outraged readers. These appeared early on, along with the more welcome encyclopedia buyers. The *Britannica* ad was no small tombstone-like notice, no typical book promotion–title, author, blurb, publisher, price. It was ubiquitous and very big. Entire broadsheet pages were loaded with Haxton's hard-driving message, appearing day after day. Hooper swooped on empty ad columns and filled them as quickly as Moberly Bell and other publishers could find them. After just the first week's worth of ads, however, Bell was occupied with complaining mail. The most persistent dissatisfaction was not with the ads themselves–although there were plenty of irritated readers who apparently found it impossible to avoid Haxton's dense and intense ramblings. The real complaint was the one Moberly Bell had foreseen: *The Times* was selling a very old encyclopedia. Readers understood that the general "1898 impression" was of a major newspaper trying to fob off bad goods on unsuspecting people who may have had no business reading *The Times* in the first place.

Moberly Bell's reply, perhaps intentionally conflating "reprinting" with "revision," was always the same: "As stated in every advertisement we have published, the edition we are reprinting is the Ninth, and it is the last edition. Its publication began in 1875, it was completed in 1888, again reprinted in 1894 and again in 1896. It is now being reprinted again in 1898."

Nevertheless, soon a painful joke began to circulate: *The Times* was behind the encyclopedia, but the encyclopedia was behind *The Times*.

This was followed by an outpouring of wounded propriety. As he apparently had done with *The New York Times*, Hooper, now working with Moberly Bell, began insinuating marketing into the news columns–in this case, content from the *Britannica* relevant to the story of the day and added without finesse. How Bell managed to walk over George Buckle to do this isn't clear, but the selling of the encyclopedia had clearly become an important part of every day's *Times*. Meanwhile, Hooper threw in a revolving oak bookcase for an extra £3 for those with mad money to go with their taste in encyclopedias, while Haxton began his ticking-clock conceit, warning readers that the low £14 price might soon be withdrawn for good. August 6th was set as the last-day date, and Haxton set ad copy accordingly. Soon, two more months! became two more days! The orders poured in, *The Times*'s balance sheet lost its redness, and Moberly Bell learned to respect Hooper, despite his volatility and his emotional approach to business in general. The pair settled into guiding their symbiotic interests: Hooper trying to sell encyclopedias, Moberly Bell trying to save his paper. At one point, Bell even chipped in and helped write some ad copy himself, complete with Haxtonian overtones, and ridiculing "the various almanacs and Year Books [which] supply to the public the sort of ephemeral information which is in its way convenient and useful, just as the minute hand of a clock is serviceable when one has a train to catch but for the broader purpose of life it is necessary that men and events should be regarded from a point of view neither too shifting nor in too point-blank a proximity. In the distance, it is interesting to know that Socrates loved better to stroll through the streets than to stride over the fields, but the fact that a man of our day—whose house is just around the corner—prefers billiards to golf hardly fits the scholarly atmosphere of such a work as the *Encyclopædia Britannica*." Just two sentences, but they seem like a thousand.

By the end of the first two months, *The Times* had sold 4,300 sets—nearly half what A & C Black had sold since the *Britannica*'s original publication—and added thousands of pounds to *The Times*'s account. Moberly Bell even offered to let angry customers escape their contracts—not terribly generous, since it was Hooper who would have to absorb those losses—but after two months of sales, Bell was able to note, "We have let off their contract 11 people out of 4300." Although the price of the *Britannica* had increased on August 6, there were still plenty of customers at £16 16s. As the year wound down, so did sales. Nonetheless, by the end of December, *The Times* was £11,830 richer, thanks to the *Britannica*.

Moberly Bell had the zeal of the converted. He had seen the

alchemy of American marketing turn stacks of old books into cash. Writing to Haxton at the end of January 1899, just after Hooper had left for America on one of his frequent visits, Bell needed some help with a reference book he couldn't quite figure out how to sell. So he wrote to "Dear Mr Haxton":

> Before he left Mr Hooper was good enough to say that he would ask you whether you would be good enough to put into shape for us two or three two column and one column advertisements for *Longman's Gazetteer* which we are taking over for sale with *The Times Atlas*. He asked me to let you have the main particulars and I enclose them. I shall be very much obliged if you can do this for us as we have been impressed by the excellence of your EB. work.

The "preliminary announcement" of the *Gazetteer*, a book six years old, appeared on February 4, 1899. It was done up the way books had always been announced in *The Times*, with a style that can only be described as both dignified and ineffective: "On or before February 15th, THE TIMES will be enabled to fill orders for THE TIMES GAZETTEER, a work of reference peculiarly adapted to the wants of purchasers of THE TIMES ATLAS."

Not peculiar enough for Haxton. By the 9th, he had touched the copy: "ONE GOOD BOOK DESERVES ANOTHER," read the headline.

> Many of the purchasers of THE TIMES ATLAS have found that a good dish stimulates the appetite, that the satisfaction of one intellectual need strengthens the habit of investigation and in its turn Creates a further need. An Atlas is, indeed, a good beginning for any library; it is the broadest statement of our broadest knowledge. The bird's view of the world, the relative positions of cities and rivers, Continents and seas— the "Where It Is" as distinguished from the "What It Is" can only be presented in a series of maps. The roughest sketch on the back of an old envelope yields a clearer impression than the most studied phrases that a frontier commissioner ever

put together. When, however, the locality of a geographical unit and its relations to other units has been apprehended, the atlas has done its work. The maps themselves cannot be made to yield any detailed information. The size of a town and the incidence of a watershed can be broadly indicated, but most of the more elaborate descriptive devices which have been attempted in recent years are as useless as the images of elephants and lions which made Africa terrible on a medieval "world napkin." . . . No book of reference can give every sort of information. It is unreasonable to expect an Atlas to tell you that Aarziehlebad is a cold sulphur spring or Zvyerinogo-lovskaya a surveyor's bench-mark.

Sales were brisk; the *Gazetteer* became a staple item in *The Times*'s inventory.

Next, Bell quickly launched a special "Times Edition" of the *Century Dictionary*—where Franklin Hooper, Horace's acerbic younger brother, was still an editor—selling it on the installment plan, and by the end of the following year, book publishing had added yet another £8,000 to the company's accounts. Moberly Bell's newest administrative invention, the Sundry Publications Department, became a very busy place. In 1896, when Bell was desperately trying anything to raise badly needed cash to keep the paper afloat, the *Atlas* experiment had made a profit of £1,846 8s. 3d. The next year, the profits were less than half that. But nearly £12,000 had come in during 1898, thanks to the encyclopedia venture. The next year, that figure dipped to £9,594 15s. Starting in 1898, the *Century Dictionary* and the *Gazetteer* netted £7,556 3s. 6d, bringing the profits from Sundry Publications to more than £17,000. In 1900, Hooper added *Fifty Years of Punch* and some other titles to Moberly Bell's little list, and profits reached £22,449 7s. 1d.

With Hooper lending him confidence and copywriting, Moberly Bell was making money for *The Times* faster than Arthur Walter and *The Times* could lose it. Progress.

CHAPTER 7

TEN

Now that Moberly Bell was setting the pace, Hooper and Jackson found themselves in an awkward business relationship with their sometime partners, James and George Clarke. Hooper and Jackson were eager to move forward in London, but the Clarkes were finding much more to interest them elsewhere. In early 1900, they sold Clarke Company Ltd., the British umbrella they had set up to handle the quartet's various London projects, to Hooper and Jackson. Hooper gave the Clarkes five hundred shares in Western Book and Stationery and Jackson gave the same number of shares in his Standard American Publishing Co. They also paid the Clarkes a stupendous sum–$425,000–and became the sole partners in the encyclopedia project.

The pairing of Hooper and Jackson seemed to have all the benefits of a perfect business match. Hooper's skill was in finding one market after another for even the most unlikely product; Jackson's was in his organizational skills and his ability to come up with ready capital, since most of Hooper's projects needed money to set them in motion. At least at first, Jackson's support was vital and unstinting.

There was also Jackson's demonstrated skill in publishing, evidenced by the success of his upmarket reprint press, the Grolier Society, its name borrowed from the Grolier Club, a lofty nest of bibliophiles in New York, and his less lofty Standard American Publishing, launched in 1894 in Chicago and by 1897 itself the publisher of encyclopedist John Clark Ridpath's multivolume collection of "general knowledge." Hooper also trusted Jackson's New England roots. Estes & Lauriat, where Jackson got his start, was a very famous

Boston establishment that had successfully sold historical and art-related books in monthly parts to wealthy subscribers for years. It's also the place where Jackson learned the value of quality in book-selling, an approach he adopted early on with the Grolier imprint. When Estes & Lauriat's editions of Dickens, Scott, George Eliot, and Alexandre Dumas appeared, beautifully bound and designed, they sold to a waiting clientele. By the time he was twenty-two, the firm's publishing program was in Jackson's hands.

In the early 1890s, he branched out on his own, buying small firms, building an organization of his own, and producing two ten-volume sets of memoirs of French aristocrats, popular because of an inexplicable revival of Napoleonic sentiment. These carried the Grolier Society colophon.

Since James Clarke had introduced Jackson to Hooper in 1897, the encyclopedia project had grown rapidly as various ways of selling the Ninth Edition of the *Encyclopædia Britannica* were tried, usually finding success in some measure. Once the marketing for the *Times* edition had peaked, Hooper and Jackson sold even more copies of the Ninth in temporary partnerships with the *Daily Mail* and the *Evening Standard*, among others, being careful always to keep the price just a few shillings above the price given to *Times* readers, who would soon receive an added incentive to purchase a Ninth before it was to be withdrawn from sale in 1899.

The two men had gotten along well; despite their obvious differences in style, they had quickly moved beyond short-term marketing plans to

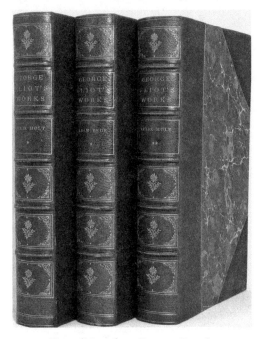

Fine editions from Estes & Lauriat

think about something a little more grand—the creation of an Encyclopædia Britannica company with a business structure built around supporting sales of the encyclopedia. For the first time, the *Britannica* would be its own business and not just a big and expensive item in somebody else's catalog of books.

For Jackson, it was a reasonable business idea, although he mistrusted Hooper's enthusiasm.

For Hooper, it was the beginning of a vision. He was dedicated to the *Britannica* in ways that often confused those around him. He thought the encyclopedia was not just a good business idea but also a tool useful for making the world a better, more civilized place by supporting his romantic vision of an English-speaking elite, and maybe as a means for validating his own experience. His ambition, he told friends and employees, was to make the *Britannica* self-sustaining and give it to Britain as a national trust. To him, the encyclopedia was above all a monument to everything that was good in people with values based on education and knowledge.

Like many visionaries, Hooper was long on broad ideas but a little short on detailed execution. That made fitting into a rigid business structure difficult. It didn't seem to be a problem, however, since for all of Jackson's prowess as a manager, Clarke Company Ltd. was run along extremely informal lines, the partners taking money from the company whenever they liked and making whatever deals they thought worked best. Only the most important decisions required the consent of both partners. New businesses were spun off whenever a new opportunity for distributing the encyclopedia (or any other likely work) appeared, and both men ran these as joint partnerships with as little red tape as possible.

They both traveled often across the Atlantic. The week-long crossing was commonplace; Hooper's name shows up on dozens of passenger lists, often traveling alone—but once, in 1900, he arrived in England in the company of Harriet Meeker Cox, the daughter of a peripatetic civil engineer who worked as a surveyor for the Northern Pacific Railroad; one of seven children, she was exactly ten years younger than Hooper, and was his new wife. They had met in Iowa, on one of Hooper's journeys into the West, and he brought her back to Pendell Court, his semi-stately home in Surrey.

High Holborn, ca. 1900

As for Jackson, his crossings were almost always to Boston and, less often in the beginning, to New York. Their companies were run out of their pockets and their hats; whatever clever skills Jackson possessed with respect to business management apparently were undone by Hooper's optimism and exuberance.

The Times rented the company space to contain the editorial staff Moberly Bell wanted to hire and charged far more for it than a fair price. Hooper and Jackson, meanwhile, took offices for themselves and the business departments at 125 High Holborn, on the other side of St. Paul's.

The idea to create a Tenth Edition of the *Encyclopædia Britannica* is credited to Moberly Bell, but in fact it wasn't much of an idea at all. It was more a consequence, as Moberly Bell no doubt would have acknowledged, of the success of *The Times*'s reprint of the Ninth. Moreover, Hooper, at least, wasn't sure it was going to be a new edition at all.

They both knew that the success of the Ninth had made the creation of an updated set of books an obvious decision. This had been clear to both men within the first few months, as the Ninth Edition began to sell in the thousands—and as its most obvious shortcoming became the butt of jokes. Hooper could see that a market had been created by the investment thousands of people had made in the Ninth, and he and Moberly Bell both thought the best way to capitalize on the demand would be to move as quickly as possible to bring the Ninth up to date—at an extra charge to owners of the Ninth, of course.

Hooper guessed a few volumes—maybe six or seven—would be enough to give currency to the Ninth while harvesting more revenue, while a whole new edition would reduce the Ninth's commercial value to nil. He and Moberly Bell both wanted to roll something out quickly, unveil it artfully, and advertise it heavily garnished with Haxtonian oversell. Although published by A & C Black (the original volumes) with the Encyclopædia Britannica Company of New York, it would also be the first edition advertised under the name of *The Times* in a way that had meaning beyond a marketing gimmick. That doubled the risk, of course. Bell rightly feared that a slipshod update badly marketed would cost *The Times* much more than it would make. Creating it would be more complex than Hooper might have preferred, but both men agreed that whatever was going to be done, they had less than three years in which to do it. Although they had yet to set the price, marketing the supplements would have to begin early in 1899 if they were to be made available by 1902. Hooper and Jackson agreed to assume the costs and happily ceded editorial control to Moberly Bell, who was asked to assemble the staff he thought best suited to protecting *The Times* against criticisms that would surely come, if not from consumers, then from the competition. It required careful maneuvering, since the enormous outlay of cash required to execute whatever editorial plan Bell came up with required sustaining sales of the Ninth as long as possible.

The more Moberly Bell and Hooper discussed the project, the more Hooper and Jackson both realized the scale of the commitment they had made. This would be no repackaging of a pirated book or a resale of a remaindered set. Everyone in Printing House Square watched them closely. Hooper and Jackson reacted by cautiously calling the new project a "supplement." The watchers at *The Times*, however, knew that whatever it was called and whatever form it assumed, this would be a publishing venture requiring enormous editorial skill and significant financial investment. How much of this should be entrusted to Americans was a real question.

To accommodate the business, Hooper and Jackson abandoned Clarke Company Ltd. and formed a new firm–Hooper & Jackson Ltd. Their first task was to set about securing the only real asset they could control: the copyright of the encyclopedia itself. It took very little effort, since A & C Black's proprietor, Adam Rimmer Black, understood that Hooper had certainly tapped whatever market could possibly still exist for the Ninth. He also knew his company would not be underwriting a new edition, and he wasn't particularly attracted to the idea of the supplemental volumes, either. The only question for Black was how much he could get for the rights. A & C Black had so far received £46,500 from Hooper and his various partners. The answer to that question was contingent on the answer to another: If there were ever going to be a Tenth Edition, to what extent would it rely on the proprietary content of the Ninth? And to answer that question, Hooper and Jackson needed Moberly Bell's editorial plan, something that was still in the very early stages.

Assuming they could come to an agreement with Adam Black, Hooper and Jackson would have to face their own concerns with potential copyright problems. Although the 1891 International Copyright Act had solved some of the more obvious dilemmas facing copyright holders, remaining issues–such as where a book was manufactured and where the editorial offices were located–could impact the new protection provisions in the law. Besides, both men understood completely that no matter how successful the selling of the Ninth Edition in the UK had been for them, the total number of sets sold in Britain was dwarfed by the hundreds of thousands of copies of the Ninth (or some variation thereon) that publishers of all kinds had sold in America. American sales, they knew, would make the project profitable.

An American publishing company mirroring the company in London would be essential, even if the main editorial work of the encyclopedia would be done in London–if possible, at Printing House Square–where Moberly Bell could supervise the compilation process.

Bell convinced Sir Donald Mackenzie Wallace, one of *The Times*'s most accomplished editors and correspondents, to direct the editorial side of the project. The appointment suggested just how much importance Moberly Bell and Walter attached to the creation of a distinguished, *Times*-branded supplement. When he needed an editor, Moberly Bell went with what he knew, and to a certain extent, that meant a departure from the *Britannica*'s past. No longer would academic specialists drive the editorial process. The *Britannica* was installed in Printing House Square and run by Moberly Bell just like any other department of *The Times*. Starting with the appointment of Wallace, journalists took over the editorial direction of the project, going to experts for material necessary to add substance to a process that was deadline driven.

At first, Wallace seemed more in the Robertson-Napier tradition. Born in 1841 to an old but not recently distinguished Scottish family in a place called Boghead, Wallace was orphaned by ten and precocious by fifteen, when he announced to his guardians that he would be seeking fulfillment in "a passionate love of study" and a determination to make learning his life's work.

Before he was in his mid-twenties, he had studied ethics and metaphysics at both Glasgow and Edinburgh universities and read law in France, but he settled in Germany, where he studied in both Berlin and Heidelberg, determined to become a professor of comparative law. By then he was twenty-eight and, as *The Times* later reported, "seemed to be settling down into the life of a student and a savant of the German type." A chance invitation to visit Russia changed his course, and, like the encyclopedia he would one day serve, he turned to journalism, remaining in Novgorod for some time and observing the way life was lived by those he saw in the villages and cities. The resulting book, *Russia* (1877), was comprehensive, insightful, and very successful. It landed him the job of *Times* correspondent in St. Petersburg. In 1878, he was given the same position in Berlin.

By the time he was given the encyclopedia assignment, Wallace was well known not just in London literary circles but around the world as an extremely distinguished man, a polymath comfortable wherever he went—he was fluent in twenty languages—an affable companion, an academic without need of affiliation, a diplomatist

Donald Mackenzie Wallace

of the first rank, and a very good journalist.

For a man who had spent a decade in out-of-the-way places, by the end of the 1880s Wallace seemed to know everybody. In a dozen years, he had graduated from wandering student to professor of everything. He hobnobbed with royalty, stayed in great homes throughout Europe, and accompanied the Tsarevich Nicholas on a journey through India in 1890 and 1891. When he finally was given the directorship of the foreign department of *The Times*, he ingratiated himself to Arthur Walter's new assistant, Moberly Bell, by giving him invaluable help while lounging large in London society as a frequent houseguest of the prince of Wales and his circle. He was, *The Times* dryly noted, obviously the right man to edit the new supplements to the *Britannica* because "his knowledge was so encyclopedic."

He'd need it all, because compiling the volumes Hooper and Bell wanted was going to be a huge job—in fact, it was still being formulated even as it was being announced. The initial idea had been straightforward enough: create a half-dozen new volumes that, when published with the existing volumes of the Ninth, would give the work some pretense of timeliness. Moberly Bell saw this as an imperative to justify *The Times*'s participation in selling the out-of-date encyclopedias, and his appointment of Wallace signaled that conviction. Hooper, on the other hand, saw it as an opportunity to sell a lot of books while squeezing additional sales for the Ninth out of the British market. This certainly reflected Bell's wish as well.

But as the months passed, the project grew, and by early 1899, while no one may have wanted to admit that the supplement constituted a new edition, it obviously was not going to be a simple update of the collection of scholarly monographs that characterized the Ninth Edition, either. It would contain about 10,000 new entries by more than 1,000 contributors. There would also be 125 colored maps, 150 full-page engravings, and 2,300 illustrations. The contents of the volumes, reported *The New York Times*, would all be "dealing with recent history and recent progress in all departments of knowledge."

And all of this was to be done almost instantly, since the first books were scheduled to appear in the spring of 1902. Always in a hurry, and hoping to avoid costly delays, Hooper had Haxton create a campaign that committed the *Britannica*—and *The Times*—not only to meet the impossible schedule but to do so by first sustaining or even increasing sales of the Ninth Edition. The money for the supplements would come from Hooper and Jackson, and they had no interest in bankrolling an open-ended project without any guarantees. Sales of the Ninth were essential to controlling their risk.

So on February 23, 1899, the following announcement was spread up and down a half page of the newspaper:

NOTICE OF DISCONTINUANCE.

THE SALE OF "THE TIMES" REPRINT OF THE *ENCYCLOPÆDIA BRITANNICA* AT THE PRESENT PRICES TO CEASE NEXT MONTH.

Prices must rise! The reasons, as Haxton explained, were simple to understand. The ticking clock would soon tick no more. The time had come to act.

In accordance with arrangements made by THE TIMES and by Messrs. A. and C. Black, Publishers of the ENCYCLOPÆDIA BRITANNICA, THE TIMES Reprint of the 9th Edition has, for some time, been sold by THE TIMES at a reduction of 55 per cent. from the price originally named by the Publishers. These arrangements will, on March 23rd (one year from the day on which THE TIMES Reprint was first offered to the public) cease to be operative and the sale will be discontinued on that day. This early intimation is given so that readers who desire to procure a copy of the ENCYCLOPÆDIA on the present terms may send in their orders promptly. It will be impossible to accept belated applications, and if more orders are received than can be filled, those which reach THE TIMES office will have priority.

In its way, the ad was even more bizarre than the *Britannica*'s first ad had been. That initial announcement had been useful in describing the encyclopedia to people who may never have used one, and needed to know what was in the thing. Haxton's rambling overview had served that end admirably.

Eleven months later, Haxton's prose had taken on an even more surreal quality. The rambling text in the ad moved from confusion and fear, through urgency and need, to a promise of comfort—only to wind up lost on the Nile, where France and Britain had just marked the zenith of imperial expansion at a small village called Fashoda, a name that had become familiar to everyone, even if few could say exactly why (or where, without the *Britannica*'s help). The advertisement ended with the sincere promise always implicit in the sale of the *Encyclopædia Britannica*, namely that owning the *Britannica* would make the world a better place, one filled with more intelligent people. One of them could be you—but only if you acted *now*! To Haxton, the *Britannica* was not just a book, it was a cure:

Nothing can be more pernicious than to live in a sort of mental fog, perpetually blinking and turning aside when a bright train of thought suggests itself. Yet it is not easy to keep the mind alert, to look questions fairly in the face, unless one has the right kind of books at hand. An excellent library may be only a mile away, but it is too far away to answer questions promptly. The wet morning in the country, the quiet evening by the fireside in town, offer to most of us the only opportunity for reading, and then the book that is not instantly available is of no use at all. Of how many private libraries can it be fairly said that they are so comprehensive that one may turn to them with confidence? Unless the ENCYCLOPÆDIA

BRITANNICA stands on the shelves, how many books must one have in order to cover all the range of modern thought? The editorial page of any morning's TIMES will make any but the most careless reader desire to refresh his recollection of at least one or two branches of knowledge. The regeneration of the Sudan inevitably recalls his hazy impressions of the extraordinary struggle between the wealth of the Nile and the poverty of the desert, which has been waged since the world began. In the pages of the ENCYCLOPÆDIA BRITANNICA he finds all that the greatest Egyptologists know about the marvellous public works executed, thousands of years ago, by a people who had none of our modern engineering appliances to assist them. The history of France, from day to day, is only an added chapter of the story of revolution and distrust and discontent which began more than a hundred years ago. . . . And now that the present opportunity approaches its end it may confidently be expected that a great number of persons who have been hesitating over the matter will arrive at a con-clusion, and procure copies of THE TIMES reprint of the ENCYCLOPÆDIA BRITANNICA.

Having announced the end of the run, Hooper now began to preview the sequel. Only a week after the end of sales of the Ninth Edition was announced, readers were given another opportunity. *The Times* of March 4, 1899, contained three ingenious demonstrations of book marketing.

The first was an official-looking notice appearing on page 10:

THE *ENCYCLOPÆDIA BRITANNICA.*

The *Encyclopædia Britannica,* since the publication of its first edition in 1771, has taken the position of the leading work of reference in the English language, if not in the world. The Ninth Edition was prepared under the editorship of Dr. Rob-ertson Smith. The first volume was published in 1875, but it was not till 14 years later, in 1889, that this edition was completed by the issue of the 25th volume. The reprint by *The Times* of this edition last year has shown that, though all of it necessarily ignored the events of the last ten years and much of it those of the last quarter of a century, there was a very large public who regarded it as an indispensable adjunct to a library. The articles up to the date at which each was written gave a compendium of information on every subject in a form more easily available and more completely trustworthy than any, similar publication; but the world moves fast, and the necessity of remedying its one defect has become daily more apparent. By an arrangement made with Messrs. Adam and Charles Black, the proprietors of the *Encyclopædia Britannica*, *The Times* has acquired the right of publishing a supplement to the Ninth Edition. This supplement is now in course of preparation, and will be offered to the purchasers of *The Times* reprint of the Ninth Edition at a much lower price than to the general public. Each article treated of in the Ninth Edition will be brought up to date, biographical notices of eminent persons deceased since the publication of the Ninth Edition will be added, as also special articles on countries and subjects which have come into prominence during the interval. It will be edited by Sir Donald Mackenzie Wallace, K.C.I.E., assisted by a competent staff and by the leading specialists on the different subjects which will require treatment. It is hoped that the publication of *The Times Supplement* will be completed before the end of the century.

The notice was intended to be as much a sales pitch as insurance against the effects of gossip, especially in publishing circles, where rumor had it that the belated success of the Ninth Edition had encouraged A & C Black to move forward with a Tenth Edition, making future purchases of the Ninth pointless.

The effect these rumors were having on sales was significant. Hence, the notice about the supplemental volumes always avoided characterizing them as a "Tenth" edition.

To drive the point home, a letter to the editor appeared immediately below the notice, in the same column:

To the Editor of The Times

Sir,–

Our attention has been called to a paragraph which seems to imply that we are making preparations for the issue, in about four years, of a tenth edition of the *Encyclopædia Britannica*. We think it only fair to the public to state definitively that no steps of the sort have been taken, and that, under our existing arrangement with *The Times*, we cannot commence taking any for many years to come.

Believe us, Sir, yours very truly,

A. and C. Black.

And if that weren't enough, the same day's paper also contained an extended explanation of the supplements by a subdued Haxton writing in a public-spirited frame of mind:

IMPORTANT INTELLIGENCE FOR BOOKBUYERS.

FORTHCOMING SUPPLEMENT TO THE *ENCYCLOPÆDIA BRITANNICA.*

DISCONTINUANCE OF THE SALE OF THE TIMES REPRINT OF THE NINTH EDITION.

On the 23rd of March, nearly a year ago, THE TIMES announced the issue of its reprint of the Ninth Edition of the ENCYCLOPÆDIA BRITANNICA. Since that time more than 10,000 copies of this standard library of reference have been delivered to purchasers in the United Kingdom, and a large number of copies have also been sold on the Continent, in India, and the Colonies. The announcements made by THE TIMES and by Messrs. A. and C. Black, publishers of the ENCYCLOPÆDIA BRITANNICA, will on the 23rd of the present month render it necessary to bring to a conclusion the sale of THE TIMES Reprint at the existing prices and on the existing terms. The effect of this news, which first appeared in THE TIMES of February 23rd, has been greatly to stimulate the public demand for the work. Many persons who had for one reason or another postponed sending in their orders perceived that if they did not promptly avail themselves of the offer they would lose once and for all a very remarkable opportunity.

"One reason or another"? Haxton, of course, knew perfectly well why readers had not yet sent along their guineas, and he told them so:

The words "Ninth Edition" on the cover of each volume inevitably suggested the possibility that there would sooner or later be a Tenth Edition. Since the First Edition was published in 1771, the ENCYCLOPÆDIA BRITANNICA has been reconstructed from time to time, and many persons who contemplated the purchase of the Ninth Edition asked themselves whether by waiting a year or two they could not procure a Tenth Edition. There were indeed rumours and newspaper paragraphs in circulation which seemed calculated to suggest doubts of this sort. The general public, however, knew very well that the work would not have been offered for sale by THE TIMES if there had been the slightest chance that those who purchased it might in a year or two be confronted with a Tenth Edition.

. . . and all the berating ads that would come with it.

Who could blame skeptical readers? Over the past two centuries the pattern that had begun to emerge was not very subtle, after all: the First Edition, then a Second Edition, then a Third and so on. Now the Ninth. What next? *Not* a Tenth? No. Instead, *The Times Supplement*, which, as Haxton admitted, would cost a bit extra over the price of the Ninth. Of course, that added expense was not an added burden. It was, he explained, "a sort of bonus":

The announcement which may now be made conveys to purchasers of THE TIMES Reprint the gratifying assurance that they made even a better bargain than they supposed when they purchased the work. A Supplement to the Ninth Edition is now in course of preparation, and will, as soon as possible, be offered for sale by THE TIMES. It is primarily designed for the benefit of purchasers of THE TIMES Reprint, and it will be supplied to them at a lower price than that at which it will be obtainable by the public at large . . . to those also who shall promptly avail themselves of the opportunity which is still open, THE TIMES SUPPLEMENT of the ENCY-CLOPÆDIA BRITANNICA will be supplied at a special price, and upon special terms of payment, so that in addition to the great saving which they effect by purchasing THE TIMES Reprint of the Ninth Edition at a great reduction from the original price they will now receive a sort of bonus in the form of a preferential price for the forthcoming Supplement.

Haxton's train was always leaving Hooper's station; of course there was a limit to the patience of *The Times* in filling these advance orders for the augmented Ninth.

It must, however, be remembered that the present offer will very shortly be withdrawn, and that persons who fail to secure copies of THE TIMES Reprint of the Ninth Edition will also forfeit the privilege of participating on the best terms in the approaching distribution of the Supplement. On the 23rd of this month, only a fort-night from Thursday next, the present offer so far as, at any rate, it affects the sale of the work in Great Britain will be definitely withdrawn. There is no time for delay or hesitation, and in order to avoid all chance of disappointment it is advisable to make prompt use of the order form which appears at the foot of this column.

Readers who wanted the Ninth Edition at a good price had been warned. But nobody warned them of Haxton's next ad barrage, one that would make the marketing of the Tenth Edition something that would live in the hearts of admen for decades.

Finding an American editor was Hooper's responsibility. No journalists for him. As an editorial leader, he needed a man of peerless academic credibility, able to give suggestions when needed and to

Arthur Twining Hadley, president of Yale University, was chosen to be the coeditor of the Tenth Edition

speak for him when necessary. The economist Arthur Twining Hadley, the president of Yale University, was Hooper and Jackson's choice. Hadley's expertise was railways and bons mots. Once, looking out a window in lower Manhattan at the street below, he spied the financier Jay Gould, a man perhaps unfairly renowned for his greed, standing on the sidewalk opposite. "Well, what do you think of that?" Hadley said. "There's Jay Gould standing across the street, and for once he has his hands in his own pockets." His role was frankly ceremonial, useful in talking to the press and in attracting qualified American contributors. In Hadley's biographical notes, his association with the *Britannica* is almost a footnote.

But the other American editor—nominally an assistant editor, but functionally the managing editor for American entries—was perfectly suited to the task and therefore much more involved in the daily work of the encyclopedia.

Franklin Henry Hooper was Horace Everett's younger brother, and in his way as remarkable a man. Historians of the *Britannica* have given him short shrift; the current *Britannica*, for example, describes him as a man "undaunted by his own lack of scholarship." That may be an unfair appraisal. Franklin was three years younger than Horace, and he may have lacked his brother's romantic vision and real-life adventurousness. Nevertheless, he was a magna cum laude graduate of Harvard, and, by the time of his appointment, he was an experienced and valuable senior member of the staff of the *Century Diction-*

ary and Cyclopedia, an early rival to the *Britannica*, where he had gone immediately after graduation in 1883. He often played down his own mental capacities. But the *Century*, when he was there, was also an institution in its own right, and as an editor through several revisions he had cultivated not only many useful contacts and reliable contributors but also a sense of how a reference work was put together.

In Britain, Wallace also needed a competent assistant, since tying the great socializer down to the detailed task of alphabetizing the universe was not very likely. The position was given to a former editor of the influential *St. James's Gazette*, now an editorial writer for the somewhat more pedestrian *Standard*.

CHAPTER 8

A DINNER FOR MR. CHISHOLM

Hugh Chisholm at age thirty-seven

For those who knew CHISHOLM, HUGH (1866–1924), Oxford-educated journalist and editor, the invitation to a celebratory dinner in his honor at Limmer's Hotel on Conduit Street that appeared in letterboxes and on office desks just before Christmas 1899 was an announcement, simple and straightforward. On December 30, 1899, the capital's new generation of literary journalists would gather to welcome him to the ranks of Victorian literary gentlemen.

But it also revealed a great deal about the man Hooper would choose to guide the *Britannica* the following year. Even the date–two days before the numbers rolled on another century–signifies, for those invited were the sort of men who would have to make room for one more dinner on a schedule already heavily laden with these very frequent professional obligations, as well as other holiday events and gatherings.

Certainly the venue expressed a set of inferences about the affair, for Limmer's was one of the most popular banqueting halls in London. Unlike the Savoy, the newly reopened Claridge's, and other newer banqueting venues popular with the new rich, Limmer's very notoriety suggested a kind of upper-crust bad-boy sentiment, since for most of the nineteenth century it had been known for its ability to reliably host the aristocratic end of the sporting crowd, who would put up at Limmer's and leave their stable boys to the Coach & Horses, a much more down-market inn adjacent. For decades, Limmer's had been the scene of outrages, arguments, and offenses. As Bernard Blackmantle, the "English Spy," observed in 1825, "many a little milliner's girl has had cause to regret the seductive notes of . . . Limmer's Hotel."

As the guests at Chisholm's dinner strolled in off the street and wandered up and down the long tables arranged like a giant horseshoe to find their places, some must have been amused by the seating of the guests.

It was wry, for example, to separate Britain's two most celebrated fencers—Egerton Castle and Theodore Andrea Cook—with the likes of Max Beerbohm and George Percy Jacomb-Hood. Beerbohm had already been dubbed, to his eternal profit, the "incomparable Max" by George Bernard Shaw. His arch cartoon lampooning the press—"Globe: pink paper for pale people"—decorated one side of Chisholm's dinner program, while Jacomb-Hood's drawing of a *St. James's Gazette* newsboy scooping a rival with news of the "Very Special Extra Dinner to Hugh Chisholm" was printed on the other. Near the end, next to Cook, was George Street, an essayist hired to write amusing editorials for the *Gazette*. The young John Walter IV, the relatively gregarious son of *The Times*'s withdrawn proprietor, must have felt slightly overmatched at his distant post, surrounded by fencers and wits—in Cook's case, both.

It was by any measure an interesting gathering, but a modest one in its way. Not all of the guests are familiar names today, and—aside from some very notable exceptions—perhaps some of them weren't household names at the time, either. But all of them were well known to each other; the cliquishness of the affair was the point. From this guest list, and others similar, Chisholm would find the talent he needed for his next assignment.

Edmund Gosse, certainly one of the most ubiquitous cultural figures of the nineteenth century, presided over things, which made sense, since he presided, by a resigned acclamation won by sheer persistence, over the business of literary journalism and editing generally. Gosse was a man of somewhat limited formal education but limitless energy; as a scholar, he was a lecturer at Trinity, Cambridge, for two years before the university awarded him an honorary master's degree in 1886; as a literary entrepreneur, he was unmatched by any of his time. His profession was that of what we would now call the public intellectual, so he is now mostly unread. On either side of him, John Alfred Spender and Norman MacColl, the editors of *The Westminster Gazette* and *The Athenæum*, respectively; on the right flank, with Chisholm, Sir George Armstrong, the proprietor of *The Globe* and *The People*; on the left, a famous chronicler of royalty, James Edmund Vincent, sitting next to Sir Douglas Straight, a name at the top of many high Victorian A-lists.

Near the top of the right-hand table was William Heinemann, the publisher who first perfected the art of despising literary agents. *The Art Journal*'s Lewis Hind was put between two of London's most powerful newspapermen, Ernest Parke, whose sensational reporting of the Jack the Ripper cases had led to him being given the editorship of *The Star*, and James Nicol Dunn, the editor of *The Morning Post*. Arthur Shadwell, who wrote often about the shortcomings of the press, was put next to Montague Horatio Mostyn Turtle Pigott, the barrister and parodist. And on the far side of *The Pall Mall Gazette*'s cartoonist, F. C. Gould, and Caldwell Lipsett, the chronicler of melancholy Celts, and just beyond the popular playwright Henry Arthur Jones, sat Gerald Duckworth, publisher of Henry James, August Strindberg, and John Galsworthy, alleged by his stepsister, Virginia Stephen (later Woolf), his victim, to have been a pedophile.

On the other, more sedate wing were Clement Shorter, a terrifically prolific editor and writer; Edward Goulding; Arthur Waugh; and the prolific writer and publisher (of Shaw and Housman, among many others) Grant Richards, whose jousts with Joyce over the libertine content of *Dubliners* had not yet taken place. Opposite Richards: John Lane, an antiquarian bookseller under the sign of the Bodley Head, and then also the womanizing publisher of the slightly scandalous *Yellow Book*. Next to Lane, Thomas Seccombe, the influential assistant at the *Dictionary of National Biography*. Far down the table were Gerald Campbell, J. P. Brodhurst, Pett Ridge, the *St. James's Gazette* subeditor Frank Cana, and Richardson Evans, all journalistic personalities. Holding up the table's end was mad Ronald McNeill, the volatile Irish Unionist who, a dozen years later—while both a member of Parliament and an editorial assistant at the *Britannica*—would drop a book on Churchill's hairless head as a gesture of disagreement with his views on Home Rule. Among the "absent hosts"—the honorary patrons of the occasion—were Alfred Harmsworth, John St Loe Strachey, and Rudyard Kipling.

In all, there were more than fifty guests at Mr. Chisholm's din-

The menus for Hugh Chisholm's "Very Special Extra Dinner"
at Limmer's Hotel, with annotations by Chisholm and illustrations
by Max Beerbohm and George Percy Jacomb-Hood

ner, and, thanks partly to the abandonment of anonymous journalism, all of them were influential and important practitioners of what was then called, by Matthew Arnold, "New Journalism," with its emphasis on sentimentality, outrage, sensationalism, and partisan political views. Late Victorian newspaper and periodical publishing was driven mostly by politics and the financial support of political parties and personalities, but by the end of the second half of the nineteenth century a second, more self-consciously superior kind of higher journalism had come into fashion. Liberalism, Toryism, all those earthling concerns were easily pushed aside by the rush of well-known intellectuals eager to express views that they hoped would be seen as bohemian, eccentric, modernist.

Dinners "to" one person (or thing) or another were frequent at the time, and every man present would have no doubt been to at least one in the week preceding and the week following this one. The ostensible occasion was to commemorate the official finale of Chisholm's competent editorship of the influential *St. James's Gazette,* despite the fact that he had been absent from the office for much of the previous year, and that Cook had been left to run the *Gazette*'s show. For Cook, the dinner may have been a truer fete, since, as he later remarked, the next day he became the editor of the *Gazette*, while for his "scholarly and chivalrous" friend Chisholm, the future seemed to be not so clear. He apparently was moving on to become an editorial writer for *The Standard*, a sort of backward lateral in the career of a chap who could now officially be called a celebrated man of letters.

Hugh Chisholm was born on February 22, 1866, into a vast Highland tribe of people descended from Danish pirates and planted like heather all over the northern half of their chilly island. The Chisholm tree is filled with the requisite Scottish warriors riding into halls on horseback and many representatives of the suffering poor. It also boasts a number of difficult but intelligent men. Hugh was along one of those limbs, a bit of a literary exception in a family that usually combined a talent for organization with an unconventional affection for things numerical.

His grandfather Henry was a transplanted Scot whose own grand-father "left the paternal glen and walked up to London," according to Hugh's father. He was a tall man—all of the Chisholms on Hugh's branch were—standing over six foot four in his stocking feet. His height was his talent, and it landed him the luxurious post of porter and night watchman at St. James's Palace, which came with rooms near the foot of the grand staircase near the entrance from the Ambassador's Court. "The duties," noted his great-grandson, "were almost nominal." Hence, he had a son, William, who inherited the job and its leisurely pace. William soon met a woman named Eliza Dixon and married her. A son, Henry, was born in 1769.

The porter's sinecure had passed to an uncle, but Henry was given a job near the palace with a "Mr. K.," a bookseller with a shop near St. James's. The shop sent him off to organize the library of a Buckinghamshire aristocrat, Sir William Young, and this launched him into genteel employment in the homes of wealthy English families, usually as a secretary, and he was often owed money by his employers. He eventually came to the attention of William Wyndham Grenville, a very rich and powerful man and the perfect patron in the

Dickensian sense. Grenville, then on his way up, hired Chisholm to be both his private secretary and his personal librarian, and as Grenville's fortunes rose, so did Henry's in proportion. In 1790, Grenville was raised to the peerage and named the auditor of the Exchequer—a title that paid him £3,000 a year for doing very little. Henry was given a position of responsibility in the Exchequer, running the Bill Office and writing out speeches for the king; finally, in 1807, he was made king's agent for Sierra Leone.

It was a job with a salary sufficient to support a family, and it came with some unusual perks. For example, he was able to use his stationery allotment to purchase a set of the Fifth Edition of the *Encyclopædia Britannica*, Hume and Smollett's *History of England*, and a set of Gibbon, along with more conventional supplies (the books ended up filling one of grandson Hugh's bookshelves). In 1803, Henry married a Welsh woman named Gwen Williams. The following year, the couple had a daughter, Harriet. In 1809, a son, Henry Williams Chisholm, was born, followed by two more girls.

For more than twenty years, Henry worked organizing the revenues of the colony and was able to augment his £200 per annum salary by means of a conventional form of bonus: he took the colony's yearly parliamentary grant, some £30,000, and invested it for thirty-day periods in Exchequer bills, which paid a daily interest of 5 percent. But in 1829, he reached the limit of his health and his intelligence and was caught up in an Indian stock scam: Chisholm, it appears, had taken the parliamentary grant and put it in what his great-grandson later called "one of the most barefaced Stock Exchange swindles of even those extraordinary years" and lost badly. Half the revenues of the two colonies were gone, and Henry Chisholm was ruined, with nothing else to do but follow the well-marked path of all ruined English people and flee to France, where he died in 1832 in a global cholera epidemic. He left behind Gwen, the Welsh widow, their four children, and some £3,000 in debts—some of which was covered by insurance, some by Grenville and his associates, thus saving the family from complete disaster, although the government seized most of the family's furniture and possessions and forced them from their home and into rented rooms.

Henry Williams Chisholm was then twenty-three, and to him fell the task of supporting his mother and three sisters on his salary, which was still that of a lowly clerk. Although on Grenville's recommendation he had started at the Exchequer in 1824 as a fifteen-year-old, by the time his father died eight years later he was still making no more than £10 a month. His father's financial misadventure obviously had done him no good, and his position in the civil service was being threatened by a government reorganization that was shoe-horning the Treasury into a ministry under the chancellor.

But Henry Williams Chisholm came to be appreciated for his reliable competency and so managed to survive those years of bureaucratic turmoil in relative obscurity and eventually even began to flourish a bit. In 1841, he helped untangle another financial scandal, one that reminded him so much of his father's problems—not in detail, since this one involved forgeries of Treasury bills, but in the emotional impact on the man's family—that after he helped unmask the culprit, he then turned to trying to have the man's wife's pension restored.

At home, he took care of his mother long after his sisters left the house. When she died at age eighty-three, he felt liberated from his past—but only gradually, apparently, since it took him two years, until 1859, to marry.

Henry's new wife was a very patient woman named Anna Louisa Bell. She was not a new acquaintance: the wedding came after a courtship of nearly twenty years. He was fifty; she was thirty-five. In 1862, a daughter, Marion Elizabeth, was born. She was brain damaged, and lived in an institution for her twenty years. A year later came Helen Augusta; "crippled from childhood [by polio] but of the sunniest disposition and undaunted courage," she went on to become a poet favored by *The Spectator* and a translator of note. Hugh Chisholm was born in 1866, and another sister, Grace Emily, followed two years later. Henry Williams was an attentive father, eager to impress on his son, especially, the high Victorian virtues of his class. He didn't waste time, either. Once, writing from Edinburgh when Hugh—called by his father "the chick"—was not quite nine months old, he tried to encourage his "dearest Anna" to give the baby boy a little starch. After laughing about "little Hellie" becoming a "flirt," he wrote, "As for little Hugh, the little mannie must begin

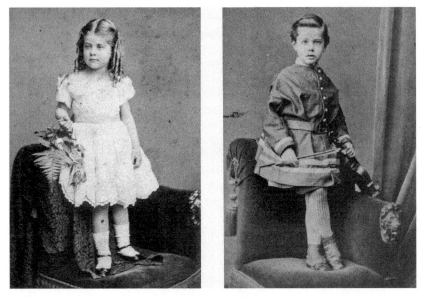

Grace and Hugh Chisholm

to submit to some discipline though I don't wonder that he doesn't quite approve of it."

The Exchequer and Audit Act of 1866 had permitted Henry Chisholm to take up a new post in the Board of Trade with a much-improved salary. He became known for the precision of his numbers, and to honor his skills he was made warden of the standards, an office that hadn't existed before him and didn't exist after. His job was to make sure all that could be quantified was quantified accurately, that an inch was an inch and a foot was a foot, and to recommend and study all things measurable. On the northern side of Trafalgar Square he had an official brass measure mounted so that all of London could come and see just how long a yard was, exactly, provided that the outside temperature was 62°F. (It's still there, moved a bit.) He was sent abroad to monitor the implementation of the new standards then being propounded in Paris by the International Metric Commission and came back a convinced *metre* man. In 1869, his three-volume *Great Account of Annual Public Income and Expenditure from 1688 to 1869*, the product of a decade of research, was given to Parliament and published to a kind of narrow, specialized acclaim.

At the Board of Trade, the revered work was called simply "the Chisholms." Perhaps understandably, it was the first such history ever published.

In 1876, after more than a half century as a civil servant, he retired to the village of Haslemere in Surrey, where Tennyson, Conan Doyle, and William Morris all lived. The Chisholms moved into Church Lane House, which was surrounded by trees and gardens wrapping around a church and churchyard at a crossroads. Henry Williams learned to entertain, and according to his great-grandson, the house was often filled with guests of an artistic sort and lots of music—the warden of the standards was an avid violinist and his wife an accomplished pianist. In 1891, he wrote a memoir of his days spent measuring things. The title: "Recollections of an Octogenarian Civil Servant."

As his retirement grew closer, Chisholm spent increasing amounts of time with his children. He celebrated his sixtieth birthday holding his newborn daughter, and as she grew, Grace's passions, especially, appealed to him. She loved math, and the pair would sit in the garden for hours talking about numbers and what they could be made to

Anna Louisa Bell Chisholm with
Eliza Beatrice Harrison Chisholm, ca. 1907

do. She was treated as a fragile survivor, the only unimpaired daughter, but soon she began demonstrating symptoms that distressed her parents. She suffered from severe headaches, and she was a somnambulist. Her mother would be terrified by her daughter's nocturnal screams. When she was five, the village doctor was summoned in the middle of one difficult night. Her son later reported that when the doctor arrived at the house, Grace seemed disoriented, so he asked her name. She replied, "I'm John of Gaunt, time-honoured Lancaster!" The doctor promptly decided she mustn't attend school, and thus she was educated by governesses and by her parents, who indulged her passion for music and sums.

Not so Hugh.

At age eleven, the boy was sent to Felsted School in Essex, a traditional public school founded in the sixteenth century by Richard Rich, a lord chamberlain under Edward VI, with money made suppressing monasteries for Thomas Cromwell. Hugh, who was a tall and powerful boy, excelled at Felsted, academically and in sports, and demonstrated a talent for leadership and oratory. He was captain of his school for three years in a row, and from there went up to Oxford. He fit perfectly into life at Corpus Christi College, one of the university's smallest and at the time most selective colleges. The closed quadrangle at Corpus, with its famous pelican sundial, had a distinctly monastic feel to it; most of its two-hundred-odd undergraduates read Classics, debated politics, and rowed boats.

When he arrived at Oxford, women undergraduates were still somewhat a novelty. Lady Margaret Hall had been founded in 1878 (the same year University College London began awarding degrees to women). The women enrolled there could study and, if permitted and chaperoned properly, attend lectures at some of the colleges nearby. They could not, however, be awarded Oxford degrees, and they were not at all encouraged to mingle with the young men at the university, although there were exceptional circumstances that allowed a young woman to make new friends.

For example, a young woman from Lincolnshire, a vicar's daughter and a student at LMH, Janet Hogarth, was once invited to the rooms of a student at Corpus. It was an unusual event, for, as she later wrote, "Our social rules were a little strict, and some of them were a little absurd. We [women] might walk alone on the outskirts of Oxford, but only two together in the High or Broad [streets]. If we went to the Cathedral on Sunday, or to the University Church, we must always have a companion, and a very carefully selected and altogether unexceptionable chaperon was required for any visit to men's rooms."

Hogarth's immensely responsible chaperone that day was her friend Edith Langridge, a young woman from a family of impeccable propriety; Edith would later devote her life to the poor in rough places. Langridge asked Hogarth to come along on a visit to see her brother. It was a cup of tea that Hogarth would remember for a very long time. Although, in writing about it later, she doesn't say much about the no-doubt virtuous brother, she does have something to say about one of the boys she met that day at Corpus.

> There for the first time I met Hugh Chisholm ... a fine-looking young man, who had already got his "first" in Mods and was spoken of with some certainty as a probable "first" in Greats. He had won a scholarship in 1884, after seven brilliant years at Felsted, whither he had gone at the early age of eleven and where for no less than three years [1881–1884] had been Captain of the School. No wonder he was the darling of masters and a young god to the rank and file. On speech days, so an old-school fellow of his once told me, he was wont to be referred to as "the flower of the School," and he so far out-distanced all competitors as to be only too *facile princeps*.

Hogarth wrote this in 1931, after knowing Hugh Chisholm for years, first as a somewhat obvious admirer, but then as a fast family friend. That transformation of admirer to trusted friend may have been what allowed her to turn her glowing description on a sisterly pivot:

> This, perhaps, was not very good for him, especially as he had no brothers to take it out of him at home. In the small but distinguished College he went to at Oxford, he certainly met and mingled with his equals, but they were not a large

enough company. Lack of contradiction may have fostered in him that confidence of statement and assumption of superior knowledge which clung to him through life and did injustice to a personality essentially simple and far from arrogant. Combined with his fine features and commanding inches this manner gave him, now and again, the air of a Mussolini.

Normally, Chisholm exuded self-assuredness. His height, physique, erudition, and muscular intellect even made some of his friends fear that more success than he had already had throughout his academic career would make him unbearable. He had gained entry to Oxford on a scholarship to read *Literae Humaniores*, the demanding undergraduate Classics course. By 1886, he had already gained the First Class in Honour Moderations—the "Mods" exams. The Mods stressed Greek and Latin and required producing a dozen exhaustive papers over a very limited number of days.

Having passed his exams, and with two firsts and a waiting fellowship, he considered a career in teaching, but finally settled on the law. He did not embrace this future, but rather resigned himself to it. He began reading for the bar and entered the Middle Temple, intending to begin practice when he was called in 1892.

There's little doubt Chisholm would have been as successful a lawyer as he had been a student. So if he was so clever, why did he end up becoming a journalist? Chisholm's family was not wealthy enough to give their boy a living, so to find income he did what was easiest. He wrote, and he wrote about the easiest of all topics: politics. Soon, he had become a familiar name in London reviews, newspapers, and periodicals, and he enjoyed the work very much. He hit it off especially well with Sidney Low, the editor of *The St. James's Gazette*, under whom the paper had risen to its maximum influence, without disturbing for a moment the downward spiral of its profitability. Working as Low's assistant had been a very useful apprenticeship.

Now the dinner at Limmer's demonstrated how effectively Chisholm had used his position at "the Jimmy" (as Rudyard Kipling had dubbed it), working with some of the country's best-known writers to encourage the manufacture of stylish journalism which employed

Sidney Low, editor of
The St. James's Gazette

(mostly) men from Oxford, Cambridge, and Trinity College Dublin who were asked to not only report events but to inject into their reportage commentary wrapped in literary style. Journalism was barely a recognized profession in the middle of the nineteenth century. But the rapid growth of a reading public had lifted journalism out of tawdriness and up to a higher intellectual respectability that gave criticism and polemics greater power than ever. Chisholm had conformed to that fashion and commissioned pieces that were very much like those ordered by Low. Soon, his network of writers was far-reaching, a valuable asset for a man who would soon have forty thousand articles to assign.

Low was at Limmer's that night, recall, sitting at the very top of the left table, just across the glasses from Chisholm. It was a signal appearance, since as many there knew, Chisholm's relationship with Low had not always gone smoothly. Chisholm had come to the attention of most of the people in the room only after Low had left the *Gazette* in July 1897 when he failed to persuade the proprietor, Edward Steinkopff, the German son of a Lutheran preacher, to accept his suggestion of "further expenditure on the *St. James's*" along with "a new arrangement" for himself. When he resigned, Low accepted Steinkopff's suggestion that he take a month or two to visit America at the proprietor's expense, but when Low returned several weeks later and mentioned that he would have no problem writing for Chisholm, he was told, inexplicably, that his contributions were not required. Steinkopff must have tried to blame this petty behavior on his young editor, since Chisholm quickly sent Low a note assuring him that his exclusion from the journal had been Steinkopff's decision, not his. It was an obvious embarrassment to Chisholm.

For men with strong opinions based on political principles and moral convictions, it was an extremely interesting time. For publishers of newspapers and magazines—then, as now—it was difficult; a growing number of "serious" publications contested for the loyalties of a steady number of readers, while a growing number of readers rushed to the popular press.

Chisholm was of his time in this respect. Although he was, as he himself said, a consummate Conservative "publicist"—the word more closely equates to "pundit" now—as much as a critic and a literary journalist, he was also a lifetime champion of tariff reform and a firm believer in the beneficial effects of British rule in the poorer quarters of the planet, a conviction shared across the political spectrum. He believed it was Britain's duty to make those benefits as widely available as possible. For Chisholm, the answer to social ills was straightforward: education. Perhaps he was convinced of the elevating qualities of education because, at least in his mind, it certainly had elevated him.

In fact, belief in education and scientific progress were twin public faiths among all high-minded Victorians. It stirred many to action, including an Anglican clergyman, Canon Samuel Augustus Barnett, Anglican vicar of St. Jude's in the East End, and his very energetic and dedicated wife, Henrietta, who launched the University Settlements Association in July 1884 and opened the first settlement house—called Toynbee Hall after Arnold Toynbee, then a young advocate for the poor—in Whitechapel. The hall's first "settlers" arrived on December 24, 1884, when Chisholm's tutor, Henry Devenish Leigh, and another Oxford man, C. H. Grinling, went inside Barnett's building at 28 Commercial Street with a collection of bedding, joined the Barnetts and a few well-wishers in toasting the Nativity of Our Lord, closed the door, and went to sleep.

It was the beginning of a movement that encouraged educated

young men and women to move to the poorest parts of the city and there establish a colony of light, learning, and leisure. The social settlement campaign captured the imagination of the young and the idealistic, much as the civil rights movement would sixty years later in the American South. The Barnetts' call to university students to come and live with the working-class poor and imbue them with the benefits of education and culture was met with sudden and passionate support. It quickly spread through London, across the Atlantic, then around the world. Toynbee Hall is still open, and still busy.

The idea, a kind of domestic version of the same zealous, well-intentioned impulse that fueled colonization—in fact, Whitechapel was often called "the darkest East End" by people who rarely went there—reflected perfectly the elitist optimism of the age. Surely, the workingman of London would rather discuss algebra and Confucius than militate and complain and turn angrily toward communism, if only he were given the benefit of Cambridge and Oxford tutors? And for those bright young chaps, what better duty could one have than to climb down the ladder and look an honest man straight in the eye and show him how to stand on a stack of books so high he could reach the bottom rung?

In practice, it treated the East End as a place where the missionaries of the upper middle class could go and spread their faith in the transforming qualities of education among the unwashed of the street corner, the shop floor, and the brickyard. This heartfelt progressivism—though Chisholm might not call it such—exerted a very strong influence on Oxford men, and Chisholm was among the true believers, moving to Toynbee for a time and becoming a part of its lively intellectual and social milieu.

His plan was to live and work at Toynbee while reading law, writing for *St. James's* and other publications. So in October 1889, he went down to Aldgate station, where street urchins eager for a porter's tip hung about waiting for Oxford and Cambridge types to show up with their suitcases. Everyone, it seemed, was moving into Toynbee to spend some time among the poor. At one point, even Clement Attlee passed through.

After being shown around the place and given tea, Chisholm was set to work doing dull things. He sent his first impression home in a letter to his mother: "[Subwarden Ernest] Aves made me do some uninteresting work for him after tea, in entering a lot of names with subscriptions and addresses into a book which already contained a lot of them, with different addresses,–the differences and the agreements having to be squared somehow. This took me till dinner time 6.30. At dinner I found two old Corpus men, H.Ll. [Hubert Llewellyn] Smith and Worthington, and another man Spender whom I knew at Oxford, a journalist."

That evening, Smith, a great friend of Hobhouse, invited Chisholm around to his place in Beaumont Square, a mile or so from Toynbee Hall. He didn't remain with Smith long. The visit left Chisholm a bit unsettled by the homoerotic atmosphere. "We were accompanied there by three of his boys," he wrote, "who seem fond of him. Their talk is rather bewildering, all about Clubs and other intimacies and ties and esoteric jokes. I came back to the hall and went to bed before 11. My bed was too short, but comfortable." By the end of the next day, he was worried that he had made a mistake. After a minor misunderstanding with Aves, he wrote, "I began to feel rather like a fish out of water, in being thrust into something I had no inclination for. I told him I had come here to look around, not to attack anything straight off. I think I made him see it, but I begin to feel a little out of my element. Still I want to understand matters here, so will endure a certain amount of discomfort. On the whole however I expect I shan't make this my future headquarters. Still it is a great thing even to have settled once for all that a thing you have felt drawn towards was not all your fancy painted it."

But eventually, the lectures, meetings, and, to Chisholm, peculiar inmates of the hall began to interest him more and more, as did the general buzz of political and social activity and the unusual collection of visitors that gathered in the dining room, under its distant ceiling, surrounded by statuary and ornate furniture, including a substantial collection of overstuffed chairs and gilt mirrors.

Yesterday evening was full of things, and one feels how annoying it is not to be able to be in more than one place at one time. [The historian] S. K. Gardiner's lecture was going on, for one thing: and he is exceedingly interesting. But I had to resign him, and also a meeting to discuss the draft scheme of the Charity Commissioners for subsidizing Peoples Palace and buying open spaces,–a scheme admirable on many points, but which–as *The Times* pointed out last month in an excellent criticism–has several points which want alteration. Barnett–who was a trustee of the Peoples Palace, but has resigned owing to things being done with which he will not associate himself–had sent invitations to representatives of workmen's clubs and other societies interested in what the Commissioners were trying to do–as being the people affected, and they had a very successful meeting. A great point is that on the Central Governing Body. The School Board and the working men are all directly represented: and if any more in opposition to them is to be made, the opposition should know exactly what they want, and discuss it among themselves and arrive at a conclusion before making any definite agitation. Hence the importance of such a conference. They seem to have been quite satisfied with their meeting.–But I had to give it up in order to attend a meeting of Fellowship Porters, who had asked and been allowed to have a room here in which to hold a meeting to air what their call they "grievyances." What "Fellowship Porters" are exactly, I don't know.

Eventually, Chisholm settled into the routines of Toynbee well enough to want to stay.

Indeed I am not sure that if I had to find some lodging in town I should do much better than here, for the life is bound to be invigorating and suggestive. Of course it is different if we have a house in London.

Naturally a new comer here has much to get over: it is like going to school or college for the first time; you are in a new atmosphere, new surroundings. But life is much more naked and so more real than the more civilized, artificial, sophisticated life of the west. I think–which Barnett assures me–that it is quite possible to insulate oneself for one's own work, and to return to take part in any definite line of life and work more peculiarly connected with the east-ender. One can comfort oneself with watching and finding things out: and very interesting is the civilization in the making, as it is down here; a growth, not the day by day repetition of old fashions, old thoughts.

As his work began appearing more and more frequently in the *National Observer*, the *National Review*, and other mostly Tory publications, he started to lose interest in the law—if in fact he had any interest in it to begin with. He moved out of Toynbee, and by the next time Janet Hogarth ran into him—again with Edith Langridge, this time at a dance being given by the Langridges, under the supervision of Edith's uncle, a celebrated "professor of dancing" named Philpot—he told her he was still reading for the bar. But in 1892, only a few months into his editorship of the Jimmy, Low hired Chisolm as assistant editor. And in 1893, Chisholm got married.

The bride was Eliza Beatrix, and she was one of the three very tall daughters of Henry Harrison, a well-known JP from Hollywood,

Eliza Beatrix Harrison Chisholm

Ireland. She was as musically talented as his mother, five years older than her new husband, the sister of the second Henry Harrison—a champion of Parnell and an undivided Ireland—and very good as a welcoming hostess for the soirées the Chisholms would stage at their home in Cheyne Row. Sometimes musical, sometimes argumentative, sometimes both, evenings at the Chisholm house became familiar for those in his circle. By the time Low resigned and Chisholm ascended to the editorship of *The St. James's Gazette* in 1897, the confusion and insecurity he had felt at Oxford seemed a lifetime away. He had become a Freemason and joined the Union Club and had begun to make a place for himself.

It was his affection for performance, honed at Felsted and polished at Oxford, that was given substantial encouragement in London. He was not shy, especially in aid of what he considered a good cause. In fact, he was a member of the amateur theatrical society presided over by Henry Irving, the first actor to receive a knighthood (for his work with Ellen Terry and others). To help the Actors' Benevolent Fund, he performed in *Henry IV* at the Lyceum in 1890, and the next year in a staged version of Frank Stockton's *Transferred Ghost* in the role of George Handsomebody, invented for the performance, to benefit the Anthroposophical Society. For each of these performances, he saved a program, sometimes marking it with notes.

To his education, Chisholm by now had added important experience; he had defined for himself the way the world ought to look. He used his newspaper to spread his gospel of tariff reform, universal access to education, and the firm belief in British destiny. For investors, *The St. James's Gazette*'s only dividend was influence. And during his tenure, its influence was due in no small part to Chisholm's veneration of the unchangeable criterion, and curse of all journalists: once he said a thing, it was believed, and once it was believed, it could not be changed. So when William Ewart Gladstone, to some the epitome of the late Victorian public man—and to others, the cynical betrayer of empire and murderer of Gordon in Khartoum—finally died in 1898, the London press fell over the corpse in a collective fawn. All of the editors and editorial writers who had been critical of Gladstone in the past now doted on his lifetime of what is called "public service" and which had earned him a great deal of money and a pleasant home in the country. But Chisholm was not among the mourners. "The *St. James's Gazette* had always seen in Gladstone a national danger," he wrote in an editorial. "The danger had been nonetheless real because it was now removed. Therefore why gloss over the past?" It was a principled stand, but not a popular one. A year later, with the *Gazette* still straining under Steinkopff, he was looking for someplace else to work. So he turned to a familiar mentor.

Low, his old boss, had gone on to become an editorial writer for *The Standard* under the editorship of the reclusive William Haseltine Mudford, and he quickly found a place for Chisholm. Still, to go from editing the *Gazette*'s ruminations on prosody to writing leading articles about the inadvisability of horror and slaughter normally wouldn't be an occasion for celebration, such as that at Limmer's. He was at *The Standard* for only a very short time. His wife was finally pregnant, with the first of three sons, and he had grown impatient at *The Standard*, where the hint that Cyril Arthur Pearson might buy the paper was the only motive for staying at a place that seemed likely to go bust at any moment.

It was a stopgap. Weeks after his dinner, Chisholm was continuing a correspondence with Moberly Bell concerning employment at *The Times*. It seemed there was an encyclopedia project under way at Printing House Square.

CHAPTER 9

THE SUPPLEMENTAL VOLUMES

Hugh Chisholm's three sons: Archie (left), John (with Eliza), and Hugh (1907)

Mackenzie Wallace had barely started his work in 1900 when word came from Moberly Bell that Hugh Chisholm was casting about for a job. He was looking for something more suitable than editorial writing at *The Standard*, and though *The Times* had courted him, nothing much seemed to be happening.

Wallace let the thought slip for a week or two, busy with the growing staff of editorial workers and the frequent requests for progress reports from Hooper and Jackson brought to him by Moberly Bell. Finally he replied that he'd be happy to meet Chisholm.

Moberly Bell—generally a diffident man, but, when working with Wallace, positively secretarial—wrote to Chisholm the morning of February 27. "Should you be still, owing to our wickedness, at a loose rope's end—would you care to come & see Sir Donald Mackenzie Wallace who is editing the Supplement to the *Encyclopædia Britannica* and might be glad of your help. I don't know exactly what he wants but it might at all events be worth your while to see him—He is here pretty well all day."

Chisholm replied that he had no experience in encyclopedias, but Moberly Bell rushed to assure him that couldn't be an impediment. "Sir Donald Wallace is very anxious to secure your assistance for the E.B. Supplement," Bell wrote. "He *recognizes* that you have had no experience of the particular work, that it may not prove congenial to you." Moberly Bell didn't need to point out that Wallace had no experience editing encyclopedias either, but he passed along Wallace's suggestion to give it a try for a month, "with of course a view to it being continued provided that you were satisfied with each other & the work." Then, at the bottom, a postscript: "Come see me if you like."

But as Chisholm was arriving, Wallace was departing, first for reasons of health, then for travel, barely to be seen again until the work was nearly done and leaving behind unclear assignments, an impossible deadline, and entries unfinished and in some cases not even outlined. Chisholm was now a *Times* employee—but working in a department Moberly Bell had formally established as the Encyclopædia Britannica Supplement Department. The new department and its activities were viewed warily by the "old gang," as the dinosaurs at Printing House Square were known. And even in his own department, Chisholm found that he'd walked in long after opinions on both Hooper and Jackson—and the *Britannica*—had formed.

Perhaps more accurately, opinions had jelled on Hooper. On Jackson, the jury wasn't out because there was little interest in a trial. Jackson revealed little of himself; his taciturn demeanor, Sydney

Greenstreet appearance, uninteresting goals, and expressionless face gave no opportunity for office analysis, nor provided much basis for wanting one.

Hooper, on the other hand, was an inside-out man, completely straightforward, absolutely frank, voluble, and obviously passionate about a project he had come to see more and more as a personal mission. He demanded that others have an opinion of him, and he made it quite clear that he had opinions of them, too.

As work on the volumes proceeded, Moberly Bell and Hooper began turning what had been a tentative working relationship into a close alliance based on nicely balanced needs and expectations. Moberly Bell found Hooper an inspiration, not least because the American understood Bell's dilemma instantly—something others claimed to be able to do, while unable to provide any helpful advice. But Hooper seemed full of promise. His optimism encouraged Moberly Bell's necessary belief that the character of *The Times* must be protected at all costs, and he had already demonstrated to Bell the way in which the *Britannica* could be used to add revenue to Printing House Square without affecting *The Times* in the least, unless you counted the way advertising looked in the thing. Moreover, Hooper had shown Moberly Bell that he was willing to invest in his own beliefs. The work on the *Britannica*'s Tenth Edition was being paid for by Hooper and Jackson, not by Bell and Walter.

The announcement of the supplement in March 1899 had been greeted with great suspicion in Printing House Square. Those opposed to Hooper's American ways assumed that the reason for moving a foreign project into the top floor of Printing House Square was less to do with saving *The Times* than with making the Americans wealthier, since the British proceeds, they felt, could amount to very little, while the American sales of the *Britannica* had already far outstripped UK sales. Linking *The Times* to an important British scholarly work was obviously being done to increase its value to Americans, unschooled though they might be, and those sales wouldn't benefit *The Times* at all.* "Messrs. Hooper and Jackson could well afford to

---

* Interestingly, the American prospectus does not put the *Times* on the cover or title pages, and in the text, the words "Tenth Edition" appear only on the cover; elsewhere

pay *The Times* very handsome terms for the use of its name, seeing that Printing House Square drew commission only on the British sale and not on the much greater American sales," wrote one critic, indifferent to the fact that Hooper's ideas had saved the paper from extinction.

The supplementary volumes now began to occupy both Hooper and Moberly Bell more and more. With the reputation of *The Times* at stake, Bell managed the editorial operation and seamlessly integrated it into the daily life of *The Times*, treating it as a separate department but part of the whole enterprise of the newspaper. His control was absolute, and neither Jackson nor Hooper attempted even the slightest interference, not with the selection of editors and contributors or even with the amounts they were paid or with the expenses they accumulated or how they accomplished their task. Chisholm had never met Hooper and didn't meet him while the work was proceeding; the encyclopedia department, to the people who worked in it, was just another bin full of bodies working for *The Times*. In fact, Hooper encouraged the arrangement, sensing perhaps that *The Times*, as a sponsor, was most useful when it seemed most aloof from the Americans. So every month, Moberly Bell paid everyone promptly, then just as promptly sent on a demand for reimbursement to Hooper. Hooper paid attention to the business, and left Moberly Bell to meet his side of the bargain. It was a tremendous gesture of trust on Hooper's part.

Moberly Bell reciprocated. He thought Hooper was "both shrewd and trustworthy." He was aware enough of what he thought were Hooper's shortcomings—including "some of his American methods . . . his large ideas and optimistic forecasts," all of which nonetheless ultimately proved valid. And he very much approved of "Hooper's capacity and his integrity, though not always his judgment." On balance, Bell thought Hooper was "good company and very stimulating . . . and a man who was direct in all his methods, outspoken almost to the point of brutality, who said exactly what he meant, and who expected a like frankness from others."

---

they are called simply "The New Volumes." A loose envelope, however, is addressed to "The Manager, The Times London, 225–233 Fourth Avenue, New York, N.Y."

That was an understatement. As time passed, the formality of conventional correspondence, always observed by Moberly Bell even when dashing off a short note, was abandoned by Hooper, whose typewritten letters to Bell were full of handwritten emphases, such as double underscores and inked-in exclamation points. Hooper clearly had a temper and wasn't afraid to lose it in writing. He assumed Moberly Bell's friendship with a kind of innocence that was engaging. After one of his impatient letters to Bell demanding that a man be fired or insisting on a change in the way paperwork was done would come another hastily written note with some friendly banter. Hooper had very little tolerance for the alienating, class-conscious proprieties of Edwardian society, and he brought Moberly Bell around, slowly, sometimes worriedly, sometimes outrageously, playing Mr. Toad to Moberly Bell's Badger and challenging his friend to a little derring-do.

GATLEY PARK

KINGSLAND, HEREFORD

Dear Mr Bell,

My machine has arrived and I have taken two "runs" on it. I can assure you that it is not like Sir Frederick Vincent's as a sleep disturber . . . if you will arrange to have dry roads I will take you at the rate of 25 miles an hour if the police don't object.

But not everyone found Hooper such interesting company. F. Harcourt Kitchin, an ambitious young Oxford graduate with an interest in finance and a disapproving word for all those he felt beneath him, which was a large number, was typical. Moberly Bell had hired him in 1895 because, Kitchin later claimed, he had been clever enough to fashion an employment application that appealed to Bell's vanity. "He liked to be thought business-like, though in reality he was one of the least business-like of men with whom I have worked," wrote Kitchin of the man who had brought *The Times* back from the brink of bankruptcy. He took advantage of Bell's trust in Hooper by befriending Hooper, the easiest of men to befriend. "He was pleased to form from the first a high opinion of me," Kitchin recalled, "and was constantly cracking me up to Moberly Bell. This was extremely useful to me, for Moberly Bell used to profess the greatest respect for Hooper's opinion of men and things."

It was an opinion Kitchin, like many of those at Printing House Square at the time, did not share. Kitchin, however, went one step further and used words—and an opinion—never voiced by Moberly Bell to calumny Hooper.

> He was, I believe, one of those men who have a very high sense of honour when they are trusted, and very little, if any, sense of honour when they are distrusted. A man of this type is the despair of lawyers because they cannot understand him; but those who do understand him, and treat him as he wishes to be treated, receive from him faith and generosity. Moberly Bell, no mean judge, sized up Horace Hooper from the first. He was a ranker who loved to be accepted as a gentleman. Treat him as a gentleman and one had no trouble with him; treat him as a ranker and one got all the trouble there was to get.

"A ranker": it was a kind of condescension that knew no particular logic, a peculiarly defensive form of anti-Americanism, known well to Americans doing business abroad, in which a certain kind of Briton, often slightly unsure of himself in confronting some unrelated shortcoming, laced references with trivial insults—"alien" was a favorite, but so was "noisy" and "rag time"—until he felt his meaningless point had been made.

It was not, however, the way Moberly Bell, or, for that matter, Chisholm felt toward Hooper; Chisholm was an especially vocal supporter of Anglo-American collaboration in all things, a view not formed by an acquaintance with Hooper—they had not yet met—but by practical consideration. Nor was Kitchin's condescension a view shared, at least aloud, by many of those toiling away in the space given to the *Britannica* on the top floor, where a hastily assembled staff was already very interested in discovering exactly how one went about making an encyclopedia, and where Jackson would appear to quietly survey the expenses from behind a cloud of corona smoke, while Hooper, offstage, excitedly encouraged the work.

Books like the supplements were not created from scratch, of course. By 1900, it wasn't necessary to build an encyclopedia from the ground up in any case; categories had to respond to a reader's conventional expectations, and if those expectations were then even slightly exceeded on discovering the information sought, the editor had succeeded. In any case, the mission of Chisholm and his colleagues was limited to addressing the complaints of buyers of the Ninth Edition and doing so in a way that would encourage more sales of the Ninth by adding to it new volumes and charging more for the whole collection. "There are special difficulties in organizing a Supplement to an existing work," Chisholm observed later, "if by that is meant an adequate filling of only the gaps left in the earlier portion. If subjects cannot be treated *ab avo*, something in the nature of a compromise is inevitable."

Since Jackson wanted to do no more than was minimally necessary to sustain sales of the Ninth, and since Hooper was still unsure of what shape the new work would assume, those compromises all fell on Chisholm and Moberly Bell, whose interests were not always the same as their American partners'. They both wanted volumes that would reflect well on *The Times* by representing an obvious improvement on the earlier work. The preparations Hooper and Bell had made were careful, but the project was nevertheless overwhelming— not just because of the amount of work, but also because of the terrific time pressure to get the books out soon. Delay meant disaster. The promise had been made earlier that the supplements would be available by the end of the century, but that was obviously not possible. So the question now became, how soon?

Chisholm set about working quickly. Many of the entries from the Ninth Edition were sent off to new contributors with instructions for making revisions or creating new entries. With Franklin Hooper in New York, experienced as he was from his years with the *Century Dictionary and Cyclopedia*, the list of entries for the supplements was given some balance to add topics of interest to Americans. But executing the required revisions meant reviewing *all* of the entries in the Ninth Edition and discovering which entries needed updating and which should be commissioned anew. Chisholm was walking into something far removed from editing the elegant pages of *The St. James's Gazette.*

And there were other maps to follow, in addition to the Ninth. The last decade of the 1800s and the first of the 1900s saw the appearance of many new encyclopedias. Moreover, there was the already published "Tenth Edition" of the *Britannica* to work from, the American one that was well known to Haxton, the Hooper brothers, and many readers of *The New York Times.*

So by 1900, the pressure to create an "official" *Times* supplement updating the Ninth Edition quickly was enormous, and Chisholm was on his own. But in the spring of that year, Wallace fell ill, and Chisholm moved swiftly to marshal his forces as best he could and issued a call of sorts. "The combination of *The Times* with the 'Encyclopædia Britannica' enabled the editors to appeal with special force to the most eminent experts on all sorts of subjects, not only in the United Kingdom, but also in America," he later wrote.

But even before Chisholm and his staff began work on the supplemental volumes, Hooper, Jackson, and Moberly Bell began searching for ways to supplement the revenues of the Ninth Edition (and therefore *The Times*) with whatever was at hand. Although critics called them "minor shows," these were not occasional campaigns, either; Haxton's exhausting advertisements for one series of books or another appeared routinely.

The idea, as one full-page ad on May 8, 1899, explained, was to establish a "Times Library" for the common man, one that happened to include every book *The Times* had ever sold. Together, these books

> round out a complete library of reference. *The Times Atlas* and *The Times Gazetteer* present, in concert, an exhaustive summary of physical and economic geography. *The Times Reprint of the Encyclopædia Britannica* (Ninth Edition) is the most comprehensive and the most exhaustive collection of treatises in the English language, consisting of sixteen thousand [sic] articles, each one of which is an authoritative and final exposition of its subject. *The Times Supplement to the Encyclopædia Britannica,*

now in preparation, will bring up to date such of these treatises as need enlargement in view of recent progress in the arts
and sciences. To these enterprises *The Times* now adds the issue
of "The Century Dictionary, an Encyclopædic Lexicon of the
English Language."

"The Century Dictionary"! Was it a mere dictionary? Ask Haxton:
Only "The best Dictionary ever published." But was it a dictionary
like all other dictionaries? Well, no. The *Century Dictionary* was "so
much more than a mere dictionary that it is called a dictionary only
because no other word has yet been coined to describe the functions, infinitely larger than those of a dictionary, which it performs."
And was it British? Up to a point. "For the first time a great international work of reference has been planned and executed in America;
and English scholarship is materially enriched by this fruiting of the
branch. The energy of the cadet race is peculiarly manifest in the
originality of the CENTURY DICTIONARY, for this vast work is
based upon an altogether modern conception of the processes by
which knowledge is to be acquired and recuperated." A guinea sent
to Mr. H. E. Hooper would get you the entire set for thirteen additional payments of a pound each. For those still paying on their sets
of the Ninth, the guinea would reserve a set of *Century*s.

On New Year's Day 1900, "the complete library of reference" was
expanded in an unlikely direction. *The Times* was no longer involved
just in "the publication of a daily newspaper and its weekly edition,
of a weekly journal of literature, of a series of law reports and their
digest, of a quarterly summary of the new issues which offer employment to surplus capital, of an atlas, a gazetteer, and the successive editions of a [Boer] war map which afford a key to the military history
of the day, of a Reprint of the *Encyclopædia Britannica* (a supplement
to which *The Times* is now preparing), of the *Century Dictionary*," but
now *The Times* "adds the sale of a Collection of Literature, Art, and
History, which to many of the younger generation is known only by
repute—*The First Fifty Years of Punch, 1841–1891*."

Haxton could explain why a *Times* reader needed a collection of
magazines containing sixty-year-old political satire. "Humour, if it
be anything better than mere drollery, is a vehicle of expression, a

means rather than an end. The men who make the nation's jests, like those who make its songs, wield a strenuous influence for good or evil. Philosophers tell us that we cherish verse because the lilt of the metre is an aid to the memory as well as a gratification to the dance-sense that lurks in the staidest mind, and the Power of the Jest, surviving all the changes of race and environment, no doubt depends on some such subtle law of association." That's why—although many readers might have been just as happy with the laughs alone.

Through these and other campaigns—Jackson's twenty-volume "Library of Famous Literature" was marketed through *The Standard*, but also sold through full-page ads in the pages of *The Times*—"Moberly Bell," wrote Kitchin, his disapproving assistant, "entered into a new stage in his career as a seller of books on behalf of *The Times*." He was right. Bell was selling anything he could think of selling in order to make it possible for the newspaper to continue. *The Times* was fast becoming one of Britain's biggest booksellers—a phenomenon that had unintended consequences in a country where newspaper distribution was often done through agents, such as W. H. Smith, whose retail establishments sold books as well as newspapers and magazines. The suspicion that booksellers and publishers felt toward *The Times* had its origins here, but its consequences wouldn't be felt until later.

In some ways, the feat of creating eleven new volumes from start to bindery in little more than two years was the most impressive editorial accomplishment in Chisholm's long association with Hooper. He would do even more a few years later, and stacked against the august accomplishment that was the Ninth Edition, the Tenth is modest enough. But considering Chisholm's experience, the chaotic start, the quality of the work, the amount of it, and the very brief period permitted to do it all, the supplemental volumes must be considered a brilliant achievement of administration, compilation, and editing. Just producing the index volume, which cross-referenced all of the entries in the Ninth and in the supplemental volumes, would have been work enough.

Chisholm immediately cast a net to find editors either to work at Printing House Square under his supervision or to work independently. The latter group proved surprisingly reliable, although things easily got lost in the rush to get the volumes out. Moberly Bell was deeply involved in the details of managing the editorial work, giving Chisholm regular advice, guidance, and support, especially in dealing with difficult contributors whose erratic approach to deadlines threatened the project's tight schedule.

In early 1902, as Chisholm was finishing his work, the two Hooper brothers, joined by Jackson and Haxton, were meeting in Paris, where they decided, no doubt with advice from Moberly Bell, to set the price of the supplemental volumes at £20. Although the intention was to publish all ten volumes simultaneously, it wasn't going to be possible; it's likely that Jackson wanted to recoup some of his investment as quickly as he could, and besides, the technology and the logistics associated with manufacturing such a difficult work in great quantity in very little time were not up to it. So the first volume appeared in May 1902 to appreciative reviews and uncharacteristically modest promotion.

Of course, selling encyclopedias the old-fashioned way–a volume at a time–didn't appeal to Hooper; that method had driven other encyclopedia publishers into bankruptcy. Besides, he didn't want to bring any of the perceived disadvantages of the Ninth forward to contaminate the supplements. Understandably, he didn't want to spend the time and money necessary to produce a set of books the first one of which would be older than the last by a year or so.

Still, publishing ten volumes over eleven months was quite impressive, and when the last volume appeared the following spring Chisholm wrote, "[T]he whole work had been so carefully organized that, instead of the long intervals which had characterized the appearance of the several volumes of the Ninth Edition, all the eleven supplementary volumes, including a volume of Maps and an Index of unprecedented minuteness to both the old and the new portions, were issued to the public by April, 1903. Purely as a matter of speed in publishing, this feat is unexampled."

The preliminary marketing of the supplemental volumes–as the set was still called–proceeded in an almost stately manner compared to most Hooper-Haxton ventures. Moberly Bell kept a wary eye on these early advertisements, especially when he suspected that an overlooked detail might cause him trouble. "We must get out of the difficulty of addressing [inquiry forms] simply to the Manager *The Times*," he wrote to Haxton, remembering what had happened when the adman used Printing House Square as a reply address when selling the Ninth Edition. "I have a lively recollection of 20,000 letters coming to that address in one day!"

Only the generous mentions of the volumes in *The Athenæum* and other journals, punctuated by a few ads in *The Times* and elsewhere, suggested anything like the advertising carnival that would soon come to Britain.

To celebrate the end of the work done by Chisholm and the rest of the staff, Hooper embraced the idea of staging a huge public dinner to which all of the contributors were invited. It was held at the Hotel Cecil on a Friday night, November 21, 1902. It's not possible to know what the tab was for the hundreds of servings of chicken, lamb, and filets de sole Valeska served that night, or for the many bottles of Moët et Chandon '93 and Mouton Rothschild '70 drunk, or for the boxes of Murias cigars smoked, but the resulting publicity more than covered it.

The press was not just drawn by the guest list, which included five hundred of the most eminent scholars and experts in the country, and the top representatives of *The Times*, including George Buckle, Moberly Bell, and Godfrey Walter. The real fascination was the presence of Arthur Balfour, the prime minister, and virtually the entire cabinet; the Opposition leader, James Bryce, and many of his shadow ministers; and even the speaker of the House of Commons, William Court Gully, who aptly proposed a toast to both the government and the opposition. The political personalities alone were those who normally only met in Parliament. The list was no doubt the work of Wallace, who was propped up, in a commemorative booklet created by Haxton and published for the dinner, as the editor who "had gathered round him the men who, from every quarter of the world's activities, had combined under his direction to present a complete picture of contemporary life; and fitly there came to meet them other guests, representing public interests no less varied, and especially capable of appreciating the utility of the laborious task successfully accomplished." (If Chisholm perceived this celebration of Wallace as a slight, no evidence of it remains.)

It was an unusually august group that crowded into the Cecil's Great Hall to hear Wallace propose a toast to the king and the royal family, followed by Viscount Peel's salute to "The Imperial Forces," which was given a reply by the first lord of the admiralty, Lord Selborne, and by Field Marshal Viscount Garnet Joseph Wolseley, the hero of Ashanti and the very model of a modern major general himself. The toasts to "Science" and "Literature and Art" were given by Lord Avebury, for science, and, of course, Edmund Gosse, who spoke for literature and for art both, and at some length. Chisholm proposed the toast to "the guests"—and to the lord chancellor, who responded in kind. The evening ended just before midnight, when Wallace, chatting amiably in French with Yves Guyot, an influential Parisian journalist, "bade in English a friendly good-bye to the guests who had met together on this occasion in a single interest, that of the perfected *Encyclopædia Britannica*."

To say it was a publicity success is to understate it a bit. At least in journalistic and academic circles, it was the talk of the planet. In Manhattan the next morning, *The New York Times*'s correspondent

The Hotel Cecil, scene of the 1902 dinner to celebrate the Tenth Edition

Wolseley, the modern major general

William Palmer,
the earl of Selborne

was giving his American readers his impression, which was glowing: "I have had many years' experience of great London banquets, but this one was the most interesting and brilliant I have ever attended."

"I suppose," wrote *The Tatler*'s man, "that in the history of dining there have been few public dinners with quite such an array of distinguished names as that given by the proprietors of *The Times* newspaper and Sir Donald Mackenzie Wallace at the Hotel Cecil on behalf of the *Encyclopædia Britannica*. To have at one time the Prime Minister, the Lord Chancellor, the Speaker, Lord Wolseley, Sir Evelyn Wood, Lord Charles Beresford, the Bishop of Ripon, and some 500 representatives of literature and art under one roof was an achievement. . . . [T]he gathering was a great triumph for *The Times* newspaper, for Sir Mackenzie Wallace, and for his colleague, Mr. Hugh Chisholm."

"No more remarkable gathering has, in all probability, ever been seen than that which honoured the dinner of the *Encyclopædia Britannica* last night," said *The Daily Telegraph*. "The very names of the guests were significant of the highest thought of the country on every conceivable subject. The occupants of the high table . . . formed a microcosm of genius exercised in various fields such as have not often sat under one roof."

Commentators of the time enjoyed the spectacle for the political personalities alone. "The gathering was an Articles Club of a kind entirely to be commended," wrote *The Westminster Gazette*.

The Speaker, in a true Britannic spirit, proposed "His Majesty's Ministers and His Majesty's Opposition." And he blessed this combination in the words of Tennyson:

> *Let Whig and Tory stir their blood,*
> *It must be stormy weather;*
> *But for one true result of good,*
> *All parties work together.*

He applied this as a comfortable and true doctrine to the political athlete, but it reads as if it applied more particularly to the *Encyclopædia Britannica*.

The new pages hadn't been seen by anyone other than Moberly Bell and Chisholm and his staff. Nevertheless, *The Globe*, on the authority of the prime minister, was certain that "The *Encyclopædia Britannica* is the result of a great combination of specialists in every department of learning. Its publishers, editors, and contributors all alike deserve the thanks both of students and of those who only casually consult its pages, for the admirable way in which they have done their work. They have made it possible, as Mr. Balfour put it, for all the English-speaking peoples of the earth to obtain, with the least possible exertion, all that the best intellect and research have been able to produce."

Even Buckle himself succumbed to the occasion. Normally, the editorial department of *The Times* remained distant from making comment on the work of the *Britannica*'s noisy crew. But the editor in chief seemed mollified by the presence of so many celebrated guests and took it as proof that "the supplementary volumes of the *Encyclopædia Britannica* have been kept up to the highest mark of modern progress in science, research, and criticism. In what temper this great task has been carried through, how impartial it has been, how free from sectional and party bitterness, how admirable in its large and generous treatment of controversial subjects, the speeches, delivered last night, at the Hotel Cecil bear the most emphatic testimony."

These would be the most restrained words to appear in *The Times* on the subject of the *Encyclopædia Britannica* for quite some time.

CHAPTER 10

HALF A MILLION GOATS

"THE TIMES COMPETITION," read a banner across page 4 of the newspaper the morning of March 31, 1903. It seemed quite official; even the distinctive typography of the paper's logo was used to draw readers' attention to something obviously very important, an announcement covering an entire broadsheet page the size of a small tablecloth.

But what was it, exactly? It was enigmatic, as Haxton explained: "In this limited space it is obviously impossible to describe in full the purpose and scope of the Competition."

Obviously? That's a Haxtonian truth if ever there were one, because if the edition of supplemental volumes was Hooper's veined block of marble, the thing he hoped would support his larger vision of Anglo-American books and newspapers and culture, it was Haxton's Hercules, something he crafted into an extended metaphor about life at the dawn of the twentieth century, filled with peril and mystery, against which a mere mortal unarmed with the wisdom of the world could not hope to prevail. And because of its ubiquity and extensive publicity, it also had a very large impact on the popular perception of the *Britannica* and its unusual marketing efforts. The Eleventh Edition would eventually pay for it all.

Despite Haxton's disclaimer, there were some details about the ostensible "purpose and scope of the Competition" as given in the large type occupying the top quarter of the page: "This novel competition is designed to afford recreation as well as instruction. Young and old, men and women, can compete on equal terms. The first award will be a scholarship of £1,200 (£300 per annum for four years), tenable at Oxford or Cambridge (if the first be a woman, at Girton), or a payment of £1,000 IN MONEY. There are ninety-three awards, amounting in the aggregate to £3,585. No award will be divided as there can be no ties. There is no entrance fee."

There was a big, boxed list of "AWARDS," surrounded by copy with the Haxton open-brain-pour-forth sensibility: long, rambling analogies ending with a demand for commitment *now*. The stated reasons for the newspaper's involvement were narrowly therapeutic: the Competition was

> especially calculated to attract the interest of the class who regularly read THE TIMES. To many the awards offered may not be great inducements, but there are other advantages which will appeal to all intelligent people. Those who love good books and can spare an hour or two, on two or three evenings a week, will find that the competition gives a new zest to the best reading. The concentrated attention which the competitor must devote to it will bring real recreation in the sense that it will effectually divert the mind from business or other affairs, while it acts as a stimulus to mental activity. . . .
>
> The competition, therefore, offers advantages of which the awards are by no means the most important. The less material, but no less substantial, inducements presented to the competitor may be conveniently summarized under five heads. Every competitor will gain increased power of mental concentration, will receive an admirable mental exercise in following a train of reasoning, will learn exactly where to look for particular facts, will find a new form of recreation, and will gain a fund of general information. Underlying each of these five statements there is the same idea that the competition will make one think.

Maybe, but not too hard, especially about some of the copy at the bottom of the page's many paragraphs. Haxton's five pillars of benefit nearly obscured these.

For example: "IT IS USELESS TO CALL. THE TIMES will send, post free, Specimen Questions and full particulars of the Competition to every one who uses the Inquiry Form opposite, no matter how many thousand persons inquire, but in order that The Times Office may not be blocked and the ordinary business obstructed, neither information nor copies of the questions will be supplied to any one who calls in person." The *uselessness* of doing anything other than filling out the form was a standard feature of these.

And what about this? "No one need be deterred from entering the competition by the fact that he does not enjoy convenient access to a large collection of miscellaneous books; a standard work of reference so widely distributed that every one can easily use it, the *Encyclopædia Britannica*, will yield all the information required for the answers, nor is it necessary that the competitor should own even that one book. The competition is within the reach of all, the information needed is accessible to all, and every competitor will be the better for the mental discipline involved in answering the questions."

Nothing else about the *Britannica* appeared that day, or for the following fortnight as the Times Competition was wound tight.

The response was immediate and overwhelming. From his home, a forty-five-year-old former schoolmaster, H. W. Fowler, MA Oxon., stopped his work on *The King's English* long enough to fill out the small form registering for the contest and requesting that the specimen questions be sent to him in Guernsey, where he was living with his brother in a duplex of lexicographers. He was contestant number 15. Within days, he had joined a list of members of Parliament, bishops and clergy, housewives, professors, headmasters, tutors, students, barristers and solicitors and magistrates, physicians, scholars, scientists, and a rear admiral, all of whom had eagerly clipped the little triangular coupon, giving their name, address, preferred honorific, and profession to the Times Publication Department, who were obviously untroubled by the kinds of privacy policies in place today. If you entered the Times Competition, you did it in the full light of day, after day.

Some of the competition ads were simple reminders to the reader why he or she should bother:

A TOURNAMENT FOR READERS
FIVE REASONS FOR ENTERING THE COMPETITION

Every Competitor will acquire:–
Closer concentration of mind,
Practice in ready reasoning,
Quickness in finding facts,
A new form of recreation,
An invaluable fund
of general
information.

. . . followed by a thousand words or so of further details ("The strongest inducement offered to him is that he will improve his mind by taking part in this novel tournament for readers").

As Haxton defaced hotel rooms and trashed country inns, the ads grew increasingly intense. Some days, the competition announcement took on a scolding, hectoring, how-many-times-do-we-have-to-tell-you tone:

URGENT NOTICE.

It becomes necessary, in view of the interest excited by the announcement of THE TIMES Competition, to remind the public that, although the conditions are such that any one who desires to take part in it may easily do so, it is nevertheless expected that those who enter their names should comply with the very simple stipulations which THE TIMES has made.

IT IS USELESS

To ask how many copies of THE TIMES must be purchased or cut from by competitors. No one need cut anything out of any newspaper or buy any newspaper in order to compete. The questions to be answered will not be printed in any newspaper, will not be sold as part of any newspaper, or in any other form, but will be sent gratis post free to every competitor. Subscribers to, and habitual readers of, THE TIMES have, in respect of the competition, no advantage over readers of any other newspaper.

IT IS USELESS

to seek information about the competition by any other method than that of inquiring by post for a copy of the pamphlet describing the competition, which is sent gratis and post free to all applicants.

IT IS USELESS

to call at The Times Office for a copy of the pamphlet . . .

and so on, repeating the phrase "it is useless" again and again, twelve times, almost every statement pointing to the absolute necessity of sending in the "inquiry form" at the bottom of the page. Nearly every installment of this epic campaign implored readers not to call in at *The Times*'s "Publication Department," now housed coincidentally in Hooper's relatively modest office in High Holborn instead of in Printing House Square.

The competition seemed to have a kind of plot, useful in engaging readers. For example, some days, the focus was on criminal masterminds seeking to exploit those uncertain of their own intellectual prowess.

WARNING:

ATTEMPED FRAUD

UPON COMPETITORS

Certain persons are offering to supply, for consideration, sets of answers which persons who have entered The Times Competition are advised to purchase with the idea that a prize may in this way be secured . . . those who are in good faith carrying into effect the purpose of the competition may rest assured that any one who attempts to purchase answers instead of honestly preparing them will be disappointed. The prizes will go to those who exercise their own minds and acquire information by independent effort, not to those who speculate most rashly in purchasing answers.

And from time to time, Haxton took the competition down a Gothic passageway, instilling distress in those who saw modern technology breaking in upon their cozy Edwardian lives every morning in the headlines of the day:

A mass of black mineral is manipulated; no incantations are intoned, no rites observed; a man and his wife are busy with phials and tubes, boiling a pot or mixing a mess, to all appearances playing with chemicals like two children. At last a pinch of something we call radium is produced—costing, by the way, at the rate of something like £180,000 per pound. Put it in your waistcoat pocket, cool, inert, apparently innocuous, and it will gnaw your flesh; test it with a thermometer, and apparently it defies the elementary maxims of physics; controverts the law of the conservation of force; justifies the reasoning of men in lunatic asylums who babble to contemptuous ears their dreams of perpetual motion. That is one of the miracles of this age, one of the miracles that must make the drowsiest of us open his eyes and try to learn. A gaunt pole reared on a tower dangles in the wind an end of wire, pitiably purposeless. Three thousand miles away, on the other side of the Atlantic, another folly of beams supports another strand of wire ending in nothing, the very picture of futility. While the country yokels jeer, an uncomprehended thing called electricity leaps from one wire to the other, and the word written in Cornwall is read in America. . . . A screen, as commonplace as a slab of the pavement we walk on in Piccadilly, stands in an ordinary room. A switch is turned, and you see the bones in your hand and foot as plainly as if the flesh had fallen from them. The grave awaiting you has been violated before it was occupied; your bewitched eyes gaze upon the framework which should not, you know, be bared while you live; you have seen the invisible, pierced opacity.

The *Times* Competition lasted into the summer. Then another strange fortnight of silence—until the new volumes were officially published—before the *Encyclopædia Britannica* was mentioned again, other than infrequently and in passing, at first to reassure prospective contestants that it wasn't necessary to own a set of the *Britannica* to win, but then more and more directly, finally making it clear that every question in the contest could be answered by those who owned a set. For those who didn't, a set could be rented. Only two guineas, delivered, and it could be kept until the competition closed. And in every ad, an escalating demand to send for the specimen questions. The repeated reminders that the competition could be entered, sample questions obtained, information given *only* to those who sent their names and addresses by post to Hooper's office—"all other forms of inquiry will be fruitless"—became an adamant refrain. Finally, on July 8, the last chance. "The list of entries closes to-day, and unless you sign and post this form immediately, you will be too late."

Too late for the competition, maybe, but never too late to give Haxton your name and address, which was then forwarded to Bell and Hooper. Five days after the competition ended, Moberly Bell sent off a note to Haxton: "Your advt on the 8th July was imperative. *'To night the List of Entries Closes'* [sic] I have had complaints that we have broken our word. There can be no single entry after those dated 8th (postmark)." The next day, another, longer message. Bell again explained that no entries should be accepted after the deadline on the 8th, yet

> on that day you returned [i.e., sent on to Bell and Hooper] "270" as the number of entries and the total up to noon 8th was 9,992. On the 9th you returned 119 more entries and I assumed that those had been posted on 8th & reached you on 9th. That made a total of 10,111. Next day came 72 entries & on Saturday 64. Well it was possible to suppose that there were some that you had overlooked or had come from Paris. But when you began adding more for Monday it seemed obvious that you were paying no attention whatever to the notice. From what you now tell me it would appear that you received very many more entries on the 8th than you returned to me. Your daily list has evidently been incorrect. Why? Either they

entered on or before the 8th or they didn't. In no case can you have entries going on to the 10th and the 14th.

Haxton's glib, American, second-person "voice," with its breezy, conversational accessibility and its air of casual erudition–"Since Euclid told the first Ptolemy that 'There is no royal road to geometry'"–became famous among the advertising men of the time. He had succeeded in creating not only an engaging challenge to readers but also a harvest of thousands of names and addresses and personal details that would soon find a use even more annoying than the competition: as fodder for a massive direct-mail campaign that covered the British Isles from top to bottom.

The sixty questions put to Fowler and the others were not simple. Haxton as a quizmaster was even more irritating than Haxton as a pitchman. The competition involved three sets of "papers." The first set comprised questions that could be answered briefly and without much need for explanation: "A poem for centuries attributed to Chaucer, imitated by Milton, and rewritten by Wordsworth, was in fact the work of a poet who was first brought to the notice of modern readers in 1895. The title of the Poem begins with the name of a parasitic bird. Who wrote it?"

The second set required answers that were more analytical. For example, question number 40:

The origin of the anti-Jewish agitation, which played so important a part in European politics during the concluding quarter of the last century, is generally explained, either as a revival of the religious prejudices of the Middle Ages, or as a racial struggle. Neither of these explanations accounts for the comparatively recent date of the agitation.

Give very briefly in each case (A) a purely political reason why the movement could not have started before the revolution of '48; (B) a financial reason why the agitation did not pronounce itself in the country of its birth before '71; (C) connect the movement with the origin of the Franco-Russian Alliance; and (D) give evidence showing that the fully-developed, anti-Dreyfus agitation was not (a) merely a question of race persecution, nor (b) merely anti-republican nor yet (c) merely anti-capitalist.

The third paper was the most diabolical because the questions, such as number 57, functioned more like clues: "When in 1888 Australia was isolated from telegraphic communication with the outside world—when the little ray of light no longer quivered—the colonists in alarm called out the military and naval reserves, thinking that the sudden break might be the outcome of war. The possession of a certain instrument would have assured the authorities from this panic, for it would have unerringly traced the true cause of the interruption. What is that instrument?"

When Haxton was done sending on coupons, 11,080 had entered the competition—more than 1,000 of them among Haxton's latecomers—and an astonishing percentage of those had stayed to the end: 5,646. Of the 93 prizewinners, 26 used the loaner *Britannica*s. And of all the entrants, none got all the answers right.

The winner was an army tutor from Acton, Leslie Ashe, BA, the 557th entrant. By December 8, the news was in the hands of his family in Bournemouth:

Our last bit of family news reached us in a telegram from Sally, "Encyclopædia Competition out. Ashe first." Yes, Leslie Ashe has won the prize of £1,000! It was offered by the Publishers of the *Encyclopædia Britannica* for the best answers to a series of questions on the contents of the said *Encyclopædia*—of course very difficult and elaborate. 11,080 competitors entered, and 5,000 persevered. There were 93 prizes in all, ranging from the £1,000 to £10. We all hoped Leslie would get something, but did not dare to dream of his coming out on the top! He took up the thing when he came home so out of health and unable for ordinary work, finding it a great interest, and, as he said, to save himself "from a nervous breakdown." It is a grand thing for him, and likely to make his name as a Tutor. He is being interviewed by newspapers, and getting congratulated on all sides. Of course it is a wonderful cheer to Sally, and one is very thankful for that, she has had so much to try and depress her.

Ashe did his best to capitalize on his victory. Not only did he pocket the £1,000, but he and the second-place winner, Arthur Carson Roberts, one of Haxton's under-the-wire contestants, irritated by *The Times*'s refusal to publish the full set of questions and answers, published their submissions in a little book in 1904.

Ashe and Roberts finished ahead of some runners-up who must have been embarrassed to see their names so far down the list published in *The Times* that first morning in December 1903. There's W. A. Cox, a senior fellow at St. John's, Cambridge, with his name next to his £25 prize, and William Blaine, the principal clerk in HM Treasury, who got a mere £10 for all his trouble. Of the top ten, four were women. Fowler finished what must have been a mortifying fifth. In *The King's English*, Fowler noted that while the word "intellectual" was "already familiar to all who gave any time to observing continental politics . . . the index to the [*Britannica*] knows it not."

The ads continued month after month through 1903 and into the next year, with one novelty replacing another. The ads still lend themselves well to analysis of a type, and reading them all in a stream is a dizzying experience. As Herman Kogan observed, Haxton had a true skill in drawing lessons from the entries in the encyclopedia and extending them into vignette-like dramas. Kogan cites the mini campaign pitting "A Man Who Missed His Moment" against "A Man Who Took Time by the Forelock." The former was Georges Ernest Boulanger, "who [Kogan wrote] in January, 1899 [sic], could have become dictator of France had he acted in time." The latter: one of the Rothschilds (Nathan) "who had used advance information of the results at Waterloo to make tremendous profits in stock transactions." Readers were invited to choose where they wished to stand—with a French ditherer or a clever inside trader, or, as Haxton put it, under "the column of success or the column of failure." Other themed campaigns stressed the *Britannica*'s value as an equalizing influence both socially and politically or as a source of information about health and well-being. To prove its practical value in daily life, Moberly Bell often augmented news stories with entries from the *Britannica* placed on the page nearby. Occasionally, Haxton would drop small billboard ads inside larger ads, like sidebars, but unrelated to the text. Often the theme was quantified value.

If newspaper ads were the only marketing devices Haxton had used to sell the books, the appearance of the Tenth Edition would have been just another interesting event in a busy empire's life. But simple advertising was a slight sketch of what would become Haxton's most celebrated work: the annoyance of a nation.

The overriding virtue of the ads and the pamphlets was the quality of the copy. They were amusing to read, perhaps because they were so often outrageous, and advertising experts found them to be exemplary. In a series of lectures on mail-order advertising at the London School of Economics, Thomas Russell, the advertising manager of *The Times* under Northcliffe, used Haxton's campaign to sell the Tenth Edition as his 1920 case study of "the greatest single mail-order transaction ever carried out" in the UK. The "object [of the campaign] was to obtain a list of names. It was done by means of newspaper advertisements of very extraordinary merit, written by the greatest literary genius who ever adopted Advertising as a career, my friend Mr. H. R. Haxton and directed by the greatest director of Advertising I have ever known, Mr. Hooper."

By the time the winners of the competition were listed in *The Times*, every person who had requested the specimen questions—and many thousands of others—had been inundated with pamphlets, booklets, samples, letters, even telegrams instructing them to order the Tenth Edition, especially if they already had invested in the Ninth. This seems almost benign to a modern person, surrounded, as we all are, with spam, junk mail, leaflets, phone bots, skywriting. But to a Briton of the late Victorian–early Edwardian period, and especially one who would be expected to read *The Times*, the activity on behalf of the encyclopedia and the advertising in *The Times* itself stirred both passions and fear. The warning-laden ads, filled with deadlines that must be met in order to assure a life lived in wisdom and happiness, worried pensioners and caused maiden aunts to order encyclopedias they didn't want. Max Pemberton, faithful member of the Sette of Odd Volumes, an adventure novelist and flamboyant dandy who would later become the biographer of Alfred Harmsworth, had a vivid memory of the campaign.

Well do I recollect being startled at eleven o'clock at night by a telegram which met me in a lonely part of Suffolk. The reply to it was paid, and the messenger despatched by the courtesy of the local post office believed that it was mightily urgent. I found in it an intimation that my last chance of obtaining the *Encyclopædia Britannica* expired at noon on the following day. It was signed "Manager of The Times, Printing House Square, London." Many thousands of these telegrams had gone over the wires that night, scaring invalids in their beds, and the source of alarm to many innocent people. Not only this, but those who lived in remote districts often had to pay a heavy surcharge for the delivery of the far from exciting tidings.

In *The Irish Times*, in *The Scotsman*, in newspapers all around the empire, ads for the *Britannica* filled pages while Hooper's pamphlets filled mailboxes.

The advertising department, with Haxton at its head, had a decidedly Bohemian quality. One of the luckiest hires was Oswald Sickert, a thirty-two-year-old Cambridge-educated journalist, the brother of the painter Walter Sickert, and, like virtually every other writer and artist in London, another acquaintance of Whistler's, under whom Walter Sickert had worked, studied, and anguished. Haxton's "Fancy Jim" had just died in 1903, but Whistler's network of friends and former-friends-turned-adversaries, such as Walter and Oswald Sickert, comprised a roster of artistic types all of whom knew each other well.

The Sickert family was a complicated little troupe. The father, Oswald Adalbert, a melancholic Danish-born painter, and his wife, Nelly, produced a girl and five boys—only two of whom were ultimately unemployable, and one of whom—Leonard, called Leo—made a living as a singer. Walter was the famous painter, and a daughter, Maria Helena, who, as Maria Helena Swanwick, was the famous suffragist. Oswald was by far the most conventional Sickert. The family made a second home in Dieppe, where Walter painted on the beach while his brothers walked along the shore or spent slow afternoons under the arcades facing the harbor.

He was an almost ironic counterpart to Haxton. Haxton might terrorize the secretarial staff and ruin the wallpaper while creating ads, but Sickert, according to his sister, was simply "much the best of us all. . . . [E]ven as a young man he had much the better and more considerate manners than any that I knew"—if no gift for hard work. "He was a terrible worker," his sister admitted, "and he used to excuse himself by saying that he had to be, because he was slow," not in his thinking, but in his preferred manner. He once told her that his idea of a perfect vacation "was to do what he usually did, but take ten times as long in doing it."

There were a few odd parallels. While Haxton was doing stunts for Hearst in San Francisco Bay and lounging in the city's Press Club with Ambrose Bierce and Petrie Bigelow, Oswald was at Cambridge launching a weekly newspaper, chumming with Bertrand Russell, pursuing women chastely, and socializing on the margins of the Apostles, although he was never a member. His best friends were Lowes Dickinson, the composer Dalhousie Young, Eddie Marsh, and, especially, Roger Fry, who became a close friend of all the Sickerts, and stayed with the family when his wife became mentally unstable. Fry called Oswald "the most entirely beautiful character I have ever known." The paper, the *Cambridge Observer*, was a project by Oswald and a few friends—identified by Russell, who was among them, as "a clique of high-brow and extremely literary Cambridge undergraduates." Oswald gave Russell his first appearance in print. And in 1894, when Haxton's *Two Stories* was appearing under his Barrett pseudonym, Oswald's *Helen*, published by Fisher Unwin's "Pseudonym Library" under the name Oswald Valentine, appeared and was even more quickly forgotten than Haxton's little book, which apparently was not even a personal success. Their lives all intersected in Whistler's famous garden.

"This sensitive and exquisite creature," to use Marsh's description, had been hired in the typical Hooper manner—they met at lunch, where Hooper persuaded young Sickert to leave the staff of *The Saturday Review*, where he had found work after university, to help Hooper with selling and Haxton with advertisements. Soon, he was circling the globe, his sister wrote: the Orient and India, the U.S., southern and central Africa—"even in Spain." Sickert was a missionary for the project, and, as Marsh recalled, "spent years of his life as a 'traveler' in the Dominions for the new edition of the *Encyclopædia Britannica*," often delegated to survey the Asian and imperial market for the set. After one such sales journey to China and Japan, he contributed a very thoughtful and well-researched collection of letters that eventually were published in Arthur Waley's *Nō Plays of Japan*. While working on advertising and sales, he loved to tell office visitors the story of an Australian sheep farmer he had discovered somewhere in the great outback who had excitedly responded to one of the circulars he received by mailing a guinea off to London. He finally received word that his package had arrived, so he rode his horse miles into town, eager to fetch the shipment. When he saw the huge stack waiting for him, he was appalled. "Books! I ain't bought *books*, have I?"

In 1904, when he returned from one of his lengthy voyages, he devoted himself to helping his brother Bernard, a nearly incapacitated alcoholic with pretensions to a writing and artistic career, like his brother Walter. He was asked to help Janet Hogarth at the Times Book Club, and proved to be a lively, gregarious collaborator who worked hard to help Hogarth, even as he turned what his sister said a friend called "the finest monosyllabic style in Cambridge" to adopting Haxton's use of avalanche language in ad copy. "It was one of the oddest appointments and oddest successes which I have known," his sister recalled.

Selling the Tenth Edition of the *Encyclopædia Britannica* was one of the most famous episodes in the then admittedly short and dull history of British advertising, something as widely discussed in Britain as war or royalty, and something that had a lasting influence on how the *Britannica* was perceived, especially by the elites in academia and publishing. What had once been a dignified, if only occasionally successful, publishing venture had been transformed by Haxton's suspenseful exuberance into a *consumer item*, a thing that had to appeal to a broad market of middle-class people with aspirations. The Tenth was something else.

For example, in the middle of Haxton's campaign, Clement Shorter presided over a dinner at Madame Tussaud's with a long and distinguished list of diners, including Max Pemberton, Conan Doyle, and Harold Harmsworth—the more reclusive brother of the man who in 1905 would become Lord Northcliffe. Halfway through, George Sims, the journalist and playwright, rose to give an impromptu speech. "With a voice choked with emotion [and] a manner of thrilling intensity," recalled the impresario Arthur Crox-

Max Pemberton

ton, another guest, "he held out in his right hand a telegram, which he dramatically read to the company, who were keyed up for a catastrophe. . . . 'Ladies and gentlemen,' he said, 'I have a message here that demands your immediate attention. . . . It reads as follows: "The sands are running out—only one day more—and one of them the shortest. Send in your order for the *Encyclopædia Britannica* now." ' "

Long after the marketing blitz ended, the aftertaste remained. Kitchin was mortified to see *The Times*'s logo on so many pieces of ephemera—well, ephemera that wasn't specifically a newspaper—that he surrendered: "Flight was useless. The whole country from Land's End to John o' Groats and from Yarmouth to Dunmore Head was pervaded by the *Encyclopædia Britannica*. It loaded the breakfast table with the morning coffee, and lay, hard and knobby, under British pillows throughout uneasy nights. There was no escape from the torrents of 'follow ups' save by the despatch of a firm order to purchase accompanied by an installment of one guinea." William Heinemann, the publisher, was appalled that *The Times* would adopt such "alien" methods as those used by the Americans on the loose in Printing House Square. One former MP became so exasperated that he sent a letter: "You have made a damnable hubbub, sir, and an assault upon my privacy with your American tactics."

The Americans who were familiar with the competition and sales push weren't that crazy about it, either. The *New York Times* book columnist W. L. Alden was in London that spring of 1903. "Perhaps nothing has attracted more attention during the last week than the announcement that the London *Times* has instituted a 'competition,'" he wrote. "It was the last thing the public expected. That *The Times*, the Leading Journal, the incarnation of British propriety and conservatism, should follow the methods of the weekly papers that rely upon their 'competitions' for their success was astonishing. But *The Times* assures the public its competition is unlike any other. It is to be improving to the mind of the competitors."

It took very little time for parodists to circle and pounce. *The Outlook*, discovered Alden, had launched a competition for its readers, too. The first prize, he reported, "is 'Free Board for Life' at Colony Hatch, the chief lunatic asylum. The character of this competition may be judged by the first question. . . . 'Who was what, and when, at the time his brother was which?' The avowed object of the competition is to stimulate the growth of lunacy."

Punch was quick to ridicule the whole Horace Hooper–Moberly Bell axis of Americanism:

> *"You are old, Father Thunderer, old and austere,*
> *Where learnt you such juvenile capers?"*
> *"It's part of the Yankee Invasion, my dear,*
> *To galvanise threepenny papers."*

The doggerel was picked up and used by E. V. Lucas and Charles Larcom Graves, two of the most prolific and deadly parodists of that and most other times. Both men were *Punch* regulars—Lucas was an assistant editor, and Graves's work, often unsigned, appeared in *Punch* for more than twenty years, even as he was serving as *The Spectator*'s assistant editor. By the time good fortune delivered to them Hooper and Moberly Bell, the pair had already feasted on H. G. Wells and most of the nations of earth. In little booklets, such as *Wisdom While You Wait, Being a Foretaste of the Glories of the "Insidecompletuar Britanniaware" and Twentieth Century Dictionary*, they skewered the *Encyclopædia Britannica* and perfectly captured the distinctively American style Haxton brought to selling it.

The
Insidecompletuar Britanniaware.
TERMS, MECHANICAL

DEVICES, AND WARNINGS.
To Intending Purchasers of our
Casket of Jewels.
THE instalment system as applied to this stupendous work
has been so carefully arranged, as to bring the volumes
WITHIN REACH OF THE HUMBLEST,
if anybody after reading our Preface is humble any longer.
To those who are so eccentric as to prefer to pay for the
INSIDECOMPLETUAR in the lump,
THE PRICE IS A COOL "THOU." . . .

When the campaign for *Britannica*'s Tenth Edition finally came
to an end, it became necessary to stop selling the Ninth. Chisholm's
"Retrospect" in *The Times* tried to add some context, not just to Haxton's book-barker routines but also to the work he had done for both
the *Britannica* and *The Times*. If he observed only one beneficiary—
well, the account was for readers of *The Times*, after all, who may have
preferred not to know about the way in which their newspaper had
been saved from oblivion by an American "ranker" such as Hooper.

The end comes to-morrow to a remarkable episode in the history of British publishing. It was on March 23, 1898, that *The
Times* first invited subscriptions to its reprint of the Ninth Edition of the "Encyclopædia Britannica," and after tomorrow—
December 19, 1903—the special facilities then started for
obtaining that work (which in the meantime *The Times* has
supplemented with its new volumes, and so converted into
the Tenth Edition) will cease to be available to the book-
buying public. This withdrawal by *The Times* from a venture
which, as I propose to show, has been successful beyond all
expectation or precedent, invites something in the nature of a
retrospect. The intervention of *The Times* has had an influence,
which must be lasting, on the fortunes of the "Encyclopædia
Britannica"; and the public at large have taken advantage so
widely of the novel methods adopted for bringing that valuable but necessarily costly book within the reach of purses of
moderate dimensions, that it can hardly fail to be interesting,

at the conclusion of the enterprise, to show, in the light of the actual facts and figures, what *The Times* set out to do and what it has accomplished.

Chisholm wasn't immune to the controversy stirred up by Haxton, Sickert, and Hooper and their "alien" methods. Like Moberly Bell, Walter, Buckle, and even Kitchin, he understood the risk such marketing tactics represented to a brand so indelibly marked by restraint. But in a long passage at once assertive and defensive, he gave readers a lesson in publishing economics, including a billboard paragraph designed to close the discussion.

> The actual results [of the campaign] prove that, while the efforts made to stimulate the public into equipping themselves with the "Encyclopædia Britannica" have been unexampled, the response has been also on an unprecedented scale in the history of publishing. In the course of the 300 weeks during which the sale has lasted more than 1,500,000 volumes weighing more than 5,500 tons have been sold and will have been delivered on an average of more than 5,500 a week during the whole period of 5¾ years. The largest sales on any one day exceeded £30,000, and in any one week £100,000. . . . From time to time there have been great difficulties in getting binders to bind the sets fast enough to meet the demand, and also in obtaining leather for the full morocco three quarter levant and half morocco bindings. Suffice it to say that altogether over 500,000 goats have been requisitioned, while the amount paid by binders for gold leaf alone for the lettering and edges has been more than £50,000.

In his preface to the Tenth Edition, written in early 1902, Chisholm said he felt he had created an encyclopedia to last for "the present generation." It exceeded in scope and execution anything done on either side of the Atlantic since the Ninth Edition, with 212 contributors from Cambridge, 178 from Oxford, 43 from Harvard, 39 from Yale, and more from universities throughout Europe and North America—more than a thousand contributors altogether.

Their work filled ten volumes, all compiled and published in a year, with 10,000 new articles, 150 full-page plates, 25 colored maps, and 2,300 additional illustrations.

By the end of the following year, Chisholm had already started work on the Eleventh Edition.

CHAPTER II

ANGLOSPHERE

Less than three weeks after the dinner at the Cecil, Hugh Chisholm was in New York, encamped at the Waldorf at the start of a four-month American tour. It would be the first of five visits he made to the city. He was playing up leisure and playing down business. "All the work [on the Tenth Edition] is finished," he told a *New York Times* reporter, "and of the ten volumes in the supplement seven have been printed. The other three will follow in about a month. I am very glad, too, for I have been steadily at work for ten years, and now am going to have a vacation." He seemed to appreciate that ambiguity, for he never corrected it. Ten long years—with the *Britannica* compressed into twenty-one months, the Jimmy and freelance journalism occupying the rest.

"I may write a book when I get through seeing America, but whether I do or not, I expect to have a good time, and hope to meet all the fine people to whom I have letters of introduction." He was expansive, ebullient, talking up Cecil Rhodes and his new scholarships ("[M]y one regret is that some of your American millionaires have not seen fit to do the same for us. As an Oxford man, I will say that I believe that this influx of Americans will result in great good . . . and at the same time won't do you any harm") and President Theodore Roosevelt ("He is what you may term a real man, and is very popular in England. I have read his books and was greatly entertained. I look forward with great pleasure to taking him by the hand"). His plan for his American holiday, he said, was to take "the northern route to California" and return through the South, thus taking in "all of the most interesting things from the Canadian border to New Orleans and from Boston to San Francisco."

But one of the first things he wanted to take in was the New Haven office of Arthur T. Hadley, where he spent the day on December 16, 1902.

Chisholm was happy as a pitchman for Hooper's *Britannica*, and he had an understandable wish to get a sense of the country. He knew that any future updates to the *Britannica* were going to have to cater much more to the American market. That was something he relished; his view of the world was based as much as Rhodes's or Chamberlain's—or Hooper's—on the assumption of a vast cultural empire beneath a grand, starry Anglo-American firmament.

But all anybody wanted to talk to him about was Venezuela. The then-volatile border dispute itself apparently had no limits, since it remained in the news for years—largely as a simple England vs. America narrative for dull editors confronting slow news days. It's extremely unlikely to have engaged much popular notice other than in such broad strokes; the status of the Essequibo River or the unpaid debt Britain claimed Venezuela owed faded into the background of larger, simple-to-understand issues, like the Monroe Doctrine, which was a concept easy to deck out in jingo for the average man. Chisholm had no official standing, of course, but he felt confident answering *The New York Times*'s questions by simply reflecting the common wisdom of the political class in England, where it was generally accepted that the Monroe Doctrine was an overall advantage to Britain's global strategies, except when it wasn't. "England does not have any intention of violating the Monroe Doctrine," he would say firmly—before going on to praise TR and the Rhodes scholarships from one end of the country to the other.

Giving little talks along the way, Chisholm came to know America and Americans and the things they thought were important. The speech he gave at Boston's Victorian Club on January 20, 1903, was typical. "I may tell you," he said, "that I have this very good feeling between England and America always very much at heart. Ever since I have had the honor of having a small share, as a writer and an editor in London, in leading public opinion, I have done my best to make people in England understand the enormous importance of keeping friendly with America and Americans. Up to a very recent period English public opinion was very little alive to the growing importance of the United States in general politics. As a matter of fact American policy did not touch us at many points. We only came into contact with America, as a rule, when a little tail-twisting was indulged in, which we recognized as being purely for political purposes, when, for instance, a Presidential election was coming on."

The importance of the relationship between the two countries, he said, was not merely a matter of sentiment. It was something bigger. As the world grew more complex and as other nations, now struggling, grew in economic strength, Chisholm said, "it is the English-speaking race which is going to have the most say in the development of those countries, and therefore of the whole world. The more interests the United States gets outside of this country, the more America will have to come into contact with the rest of the world. In the meanwhile we have to look to keep things going, and try to cultivate a better opinion of things English in this country."

At this point, Chisholm had been a journalist for little more than a dozen years—and had yet to even meet Hooper.

While Chisholm was touring America in 1903, Hooper and Jackson were working to protect their American flank. Although the Encyclopædia Britannica Company maintained an address in New York—at 120 West Thirty-second Street, also used by Haxton as his personal address—both men felt they needed a Chicago office as well, perhaps to keep an eye on all those semi-reformed rogue publishers. The copyright law was still being tested, and the old habits that had helped the Ninth Edition find such a phenomenally large American market were ones that could as easily be turned on the Tenth. But now, of course, the *Britannica* was owned by one of their own, and neither he nor Jackson were inclined to see their substantial investment in the Tenth disappear in the book carts of the unscrupulous. Jackson especially was very disinclined to slight the American end of things. Besides, from America, Hooper and Jackson were better able to track sales overseas, in South America, Australia, India, and elsewhere. Thousands of sets were being offered abroad, often through the same newspaper-driven marketing effort; *The Times* wasn't the only needy newspaper in the world, after all. The *Britannica* name even helped sell the books in Latin America and the Far East.

And they were making money—lots of it. The records aren't available, of course—in fact, they probably were never available, owing to Hooper's and Jackson's improvisational business style—but one estimate suggested that they made a million dollars between them. *The Times* did even better. Printing House Square's take for turning bookseller: almost £110,000—today worth around £6.5 million.

In 1902, Chisholm had given no more than a passing thought to a new edition of the *Britannica*, one to replace the supplemental volumes. After all, he'd just completed a revision that he had publicly pronounced sufficient for the age. By 1903, a new strategy was becoming more apparent. Of course, updating the *Britannica* was important to Moberly Bell and the two Americans, who saw an endless sale of "supplements" stretching into the future, providing a steady stream of income for as long as there was knowledge to be gathered.

Remarkably, it wasn't until 1903 that Chisholm and Hooper met for the first time. Although Chisholm had just finished work on the supplemental volumes, Hooper arranged for a meeting and asked his editor to survey all the volumes that together made up the Tenth Edition and report on how extensive a revision would be necessary to meet the terms of a contract Hooper and Jackson had made with *The Times* to lend its name to the next edition of the *Britannica*.

It must have been difficult to go back through a work that had just been exhaustively overhauled. To help him—and to bring some much-needed academic ballast to the ongoing development of the *Britannica*—Chisholm enlisted the help of a cousin, Walter Alison Phillips.

Walter Alison Phillips,
Chisholm's cousin and loyal assistant

Phillips's involvement with the *Britannica* would last for years, but it's interesting to see the kind of man Chisholm picked as his second—because of what it says about the kind of people who were, as Chisholm had been, at "a rope's loose end" at the last century's loose end.

Two years older than Chisholm, Phillips was a graduate of Oxford's Merton College. He had been president of the Oxford Union and a senior scholar at St. John's. By the time he came to work with his cousin he was already well known as a prolific and important historian, as well as for his translations of German verse—his godfather was Goethe's grandson. His illustrations done for an 1896 translation of Schiller's *Lay of the Bell* were extremely fine. His study of the Greek war of independence had been published in 1897, his (still) highly readable survey, *Modern Europe, 1815–1899,* had already gone into its second edition. In 1902, at the time he joined Chisholm and began poring over the work, Phillips's biography of former prime minister George Canning and Chisholm's final volume of the Tenth Edition were both barely off the press.

The result of Chisholm's and Phillips's audit surprised everyone but Hooper and Moberly Bell. Only a paltry 10 percent of the *Britannica*, they said, could be used in going forward.

So much for the encyclopedia for the "present generation." The startling discovery that 90 percent of their work might not have been suitable for modern readers after all may have had less to do with the work they had done than with Hooper's ambitions for the future. In any case, his reported response—"Now we can start from scratch and have a completely new edition! Completely rewritten! Knowledge has moved too fast and we must catch up with it"—differed from the unreported response by Jackson, which, judging from subsequent events, was rather the opposite.

Hooper's exclamation must have been pretty well rehearsed, for, in fact, he and Moberly Bell had been discussing an Eleventh Edition for quite some time. Hooper spent part of the winter of 1903 in Cannes in the Villa Clémentine, a very posh seaside mansion; the prince of Wales, among others, was a sometime resident of that house. A couple of weeks into the new year, he received a letter from Moberly Bell proposing a forward-looking plan for putting an Eleventh Edition on sale, using proceeds from the Tenth to provide part of the working budget. There was, however, some haggling left to do, something Hooper clearly relished. On January 19, 1903, Hooper wrote,

> Your letter of the 17th just at hand. The time to sell the "11th Edition" in England is all right and I think well chosen. I really think my figures of £2.10, £1.10 and £1. are fair to you and ought to go through with out the least trouble but the figures you suggest are not fair to me in my opinion. If you like the £2.15 for the U.K. I have no objections if you will make the rest of the world £1. This ought to pay you £100,000 with out any expense on your part and even if it did not you would have nothing. Looking at it from this point dont you think I am absolutely fair towards you when I say £2.15 & £1.? Now as to an agreement, I have no objection to a definite agreement but I dont want one so absolutely one sided as the last one Then I feel that you did not know us and as the agreement was to be carried out at once practically and I knew that I wanted the best of work in every way as of course you also did, that I could afford to sign any kind of an agreement that you asked me to. But now it is diferent as you say others may have to carry out the business and any agreement made should be fair to my successors as well as yours. Of course as I have always said I want to be fair to you as well as my self and I have never made you a proposition that I did not think was fair to you and the above is no exception.

In 1903 and '04, Hooper was back and forth across the Atlantic, working to encourage an increasingly dubious Jackson in America, and cement an even bigger deal with Moberly Bell and *The Times* in London. The focus of all Hooper's activity—and everything else that would ensue over much of the rest of the decade—was to bolster the financial health of *The Times*, for without that, everything would collapse.

The Times, not the *Britannica*, remember, was the center of Hooper's imaginary empire. It was as monumental as the *Britannica*, and also appeared anew every single day. Hooper had convinced himself that without it, everything else would collapse. Fortunately for him, he had convinced Moberly Bell that without the *Britannica*—and hence without Hooper—*The Times* would come crashing down. The two men thus learned to lean against each other for support, and every scratch or sneeze produced a momentary pause.

Hooper and Bell weren't the only active players, of course. Arthur Walter, and even Godfrey Walter, were also scrambling for ideas that might add a little to the accounts—without doing anything to change the essential character of *The Times*, of course. With that, the marketing of the Tenth Edition was not an unqualified success.

The agreement Hooper finally worked out was a product of the American's confident optimism. In May 1904, after consulting with Haxton, Hooper and Moberly Bell contrived an arrangement that made Hooper the advertising director of *The Times* and Haxton his lieutenant. It wasn't a job so much as a wager: under the terms of the agreement, a baseline of £200,000 in ad revenue was set and half of anything above that over the course of a year was Hooper's wage. However, if advertising revenues dipped below the baseline figure, Hooper *and* Jackson would have to make up half the loss out of the partnership's cash box. Jackson knew nothing of the arrangement.

The strategy Hooper formulated might be familiar to publishers today, but in those days it was thought almost nonsensical, especially when applied to the Leading Journal. Most of the revenue of *The Times* came from sales through news vendors who sold subscriptions in a local area, then delivered the newspapers to their customers and kept a bit back as a commission. The advertising revenue was based on "smalls"—the classified-type ads that filled *The Times*'s front pages and provided an opportunity for the kind of voyeurism familiar to readers of the old personals ads in *The New York Review of Books* or visitors to match.com today. As for display advertising, unless Hooper and *The Times* were flogging an out-of-date book, it was almost nonexistent in the paper. If an advertiser wanted to make a grand splash, the solution was to repeat a small ad down a column for a few inches.

Hooper explained to Moberly Bell that the key to success was to increase circulation. By doing that, he could sell large display-type ads that would command a premium fee, one based not only on the space they occupied but also on the number of readers who might see them. To increase circulation would require reducing the subscription cost from £3 18s. to £3, but he hurriedly added that the loss in sales revenue would be more than balanced by the added revenue from circulation-based advertising. Bell agreed to take the plan to Walter. Hooper took it to Jackson.

When he told his partner about the arrangement—and told him, no doubt to his surprise, that it had been arranged to make Jackson the circulation manager—Jackson was noncommittal. Whether this was caused by a genuine sense of pessimism or by a recent personal tragedy can't be known. Mary Chapin Jackson was a charming antidote to Jackson's lugubrious inscrutability; she was much younger than Jackson—only twenty-eight when she died of a heart attack on February 27, 1904, in St. Moritz, where she had gone to seek relief from nephritis.

Jackson took her home to Boston to bury her, and from there wrote to Hooper dismissing the whole scheme. Arthur Walter, he told Hooper, would have to be jolted into accepting the kind of modern advertising Hooper envisioned by inserting many large ads at once, otherwise he would simply never find the courage to run them at all. Hooper disagreed, but more than that, he thought Jackson's own reluctance to become more actively involved was caused by ambivalence no different than the indecision he attributed to Walter, and what he needed was a good jolt himself.

> In one of your letters to me you said you wanted to start out with big advertising, because they were very weak-kneed at *The Times*. I want you to understand that they are not and have not been weak-kneed in any way, shape or manner. I arrived [after signing the agreement] on Thursday at 1 o'clock, and that same afternoon at 3 o'clock the enthusiasm in *The Times* office was as great as it has ever been since I have known them. They are all delighted and willing to do everything that I ask them. You can imagine how delighted they are when you look at this first page of *The Times* which I am sending you.
>
> I am taking dinner with the editor tonight to explain to

him my wishes in regard to supplements. A financial supplement has been decided on, and I am now taking dinner with [*Times* editor George Earle] Buckle to explain to him how I want the sport supplement to run. However, all joking aside, everything possible is being done by *The Times* office that we can possibly wish for. They are willing to let us say anything in our advertisements, do anything that we want, and make everything as we suggest.

To Jackson's well-founded worry that increasing circulation dramatically would require working with, or around, Britain's newsagents, key players in any distribution plan, Hooper had some good news. He had sent out a "bright young Englishman" named Heath to canvass fifty or so newsagents. None of them saw a problem with playing a role as delivery agents, but they did worry about the loss of revenue many of them had customarily received from the practice of "renting" copies of *The Times* for a few hours, and putting unsold copies of the paper on sale at a penny off the price late in the day.

They thought it was splendid. They'd do everything they could to further it, and all said that it would increase the circulation of *The Times* very largely, with two exceptions. These two, however, they said would hurt them, because the people to whom they now rented *The Times* or sent it away in the afternoon for 2d. would then subscribe; in other words, their only criticism was that it would increase the circulation of *The Times*. They all offered to deliver anywhere from a mile to two miles away from their newsstands, and one man actually said seven miles.

Jackson might have been forgiven for thinking display ads would represent a change in *The Times* of which Walter would never approve. This view wasn't entirely sentimental. Other than a very occasional book announcement—and of course the obnoxious ads spawned by Haxton to sell the books that had kept *The Times* afloat—there didn't seem to be much of a market for large empty spaces in the paper. *The Times*'s issues in early May certainly contained no foreshadowing of what Hooper hoped would come by June. Hooper started hiring ad salesmen to bring in business, and set Haxton loose with some of the men he had hired to help him write the copy that would be needed.

The new circulation-and-ad effort also brought both of them more closely under the scrutiny of not only Moberly Bell but also Godfrey and Arthur Walter. The pamphlets and ad copy Haxton wrote for *The Times* became a constant worry for Bell, who found himself in the unenviable position of trying to restrain the man. The gently persuasive and flattering notes he had written several years earlier to get Haxton's help selling books such as the gazetteer had been eroded not only by Haxton's intense zaniness and Moberly Bell's impatience but especially by Walter's undisguised exasperation expressed to Bell.

"I return you the proofs of the pamphlet," Bell wrote to him on April 21, 1904, as Haxton was gearing up for what would become *The Times*'s first mass-market circulation campaign. "The main objections of Mr. Walter are these . . . ," and there followed a catalog of complaints including "exaggeration . . . deception–eg, telling them we will only take a limited number of subscribers when we will take all we can get . . . depreciation of other papers [and] expressions which make inanimate objects do things."

A few days later, Bell was still deciphering Haxton.

I find that Mr. Walter has returned to Bear Wood and will not be in town this week. Before sending him the pamphlet, there are certain small amendments I would suggest. . . . I doubt the advisability of the reference to the practice of reselling *The Times*. . . . I don't know of any club taking 25 copies. I know of some clubs that don't succeed in selling all their copies and I don't want to encourage them to try. . . . [Some of the copy] is Hebrew to me & I erase it. . . .

I now come to the subscriptions form which is the only badly conceived part of the whole thing. I hope the unknown author will forgive me if I say that it has two vices–it is too long and doesn't say enough. For instance, it is of the essence that it should record the dates of the beginning and end of the term. Yet these essentials are left out. . . .

Now though I have been thinking of this subject for the last three months I should really have found a difficulty in knowing how to fill up your form.

The "unknown author" was Haxton, of course. At the bottom of the page, a hastily scribbled postscript: "Mr. Godfrey Walter, reading the whole thing, stopped at once at [the] order form & said it was unintelligible!" Moberly Bell dummied a new form for him to follow.

On May 21, 1904, a week or so after Hooper's agreement had been signed, the ads Bell and Haxton had been selling began to run. The first one was a dense page that Haxton had filled with five thousand words of closely set type explaining how to subscribe to a newspaper. It was a phenomenally complicated procedure detouring through advertising issues, the relationship between readers and advertisers, the elaborate safeguards in place to "protect the newsvendor," paragraph after paragraph addressed to "intermittent purchasers," and a whole middle column of the page titled "THE NEW SYSTEM IN BRIEF."

The principal headline was devoted to "A NEW AND ORIGINAL PLAN OF NEWSPAPER DISTRIBUTION." The main idea was to provide readers with *The Times* "Delivered Daily by Newsvendors or by Post at any house in the United Kingdom." The announcement had several of the usual Haxton touches, including the limited-time-only warning, but it also made a remarkable offer. Readers who had been paying the standard rate would now receive the paper for only £3 instead of £3 18s., the rate that had been in place since 1861, even though the costs associated with publication had risen dramatically and the paper itself had been quantitatively improved: *The Times* in 1904 contained on average seventy news columns each day, against forty columns four decades earlier. Yet the new subscription rate offered a savings of nearly 25 percent. The profit made by the news vendor, the ad made clear, would be protected.

In Britain, maintaining the goodwill of the corner newspaper shop was supremely important, since that's how most people received their papers. Without the newsagents' support, *The Times* would have to rely extensively on the post office, along with private delivery-men, a costly solution. So a great deal was riding on their loyalty to *The Times*. The campaign would only run until July 4, 1904. Hooper needed tens of thousands of new readers by the time it ended. He pinned his hopes on Haxton to deliver them.

But Haxton's health was beginning to suffer—anxiety and a kind of growing frailty seemed to be the symptoms. It had been five years since he first sent *Times* readers scurrying to buy an old encyclopedia, and there had been a lot of Haxton in *The Times* since. But he loyally did what he could to find new *Times* readers, and sometimes the old lunatic reappeared. One of Haxton's favorite conceits, for example, was to invent a complaining customer as a stand-in for all customers everywhere who might one day also complain, from Arthur Walter to the man on the Strand, then use a full page in *The Times* to eviscerate him. For example, on June 23, a clearly make-believe crank wrote, "I fail to see any reason for the dictatorial position you assume in declining to receive subscriptions for 'The Times' after 'a few days more.' I am disposed to take 'The Times' but it would suit me better to subscribe in August. Why am I not at liberty to choose my own time? The currency of the realm is not depreciating and my subscription for a twelvemonth has the same value for you whether it begins July 4th or August 4th."

Haxton answered, as only he could:

In an advertisement published yesterday we endeavoured to explain why the offer of our new system of newspaper distribution is extensively advertised. Such a letter as that from which we quote the passage above would seem to indicate that our offer has not been sufficiently advertised.

(1) He imagines that he is at liberty to subscribe at any time.
    He is mistaken . . .
(2) He conceives that any limitation of date is "dictatorial."
    He is mistaken . . .
(3) He asserts that his subscription would be as useful to us
    in August as it is now.
    He is mistaken . . .
(4) He overlooks the fact that "The Times" has explicitly
    pledged itself to withdraw the offer on July 4th.
    This is the most serious mistake he makes.

The offer will be withdrawn on July 4th with great satisfaction, as it has been a success. . . . But even if it had been an absolute failure, we should have withdrawn it on July 4th, because we had determined to do so. "The Times" has, in the course of hundred and twenty years, made its reputation by endeavoring to report the news with absolute accuracy and fidelity, but telling its readers the exact truth about the events of the day; and we fail to see how the writer of this letter can have supposed that we could under any circumstances depart from an arrangement to which the good faith of "The Times" had been distinctly pledged. But the reason for its withdrawal is that we said it would be withdrawn on that day.

As Haxton was working on circulation, Hooper was pushing for advertising revenue. The large ads he wanted were important, since they would represent advertising revenue above the normal flow of cash that always accompanied the smaller ads. Those had long been the staple of *The Times*; their front-page position starting with birth notices in the upper left corner not only defined what the newspaper looked like but also reinforced its reserved and aloof image. To find new advertisers—and to calm their fears about advertising generally—Hooper hired some salesmen, told them to polish their shoes and look their best, and sent them out to represent *The Times*.

As July 4 approached, further incentives appeared. Subscribers to *The Times*, it was announced, could also take advantage of an offer to receive *National Review*, a magazine of political and cultural commentary, for only £1, instead of the customary £30. Or subscribers could receive a huge, canvas-backed map showing the principal battles of the Russo-Japanese War—at a steep discount. Finally, a large square ad by Haxton began appearing at the top of page one warning that the days were counting down on the New and Original Plan of Newspaper Distribution, and that *The Times* would never again be available so inexpensively.

July 2 was a Saturday, and, other than Haxton's "last day" ad on the front page, the paper that day looked like it always had: sixteen slate-gray pages filled with tiny type. On Monday, July 4, *The Times* appeared in such a way that no matter what Moberly Bell or Arthur Walter thought they were going to get, what the readers of *The Times* got was a twenty-page paper that, once they got past the usual front page filled with small ads, was *foreign*, unlike anything they had seen before. Huge ads for Martell, Dewar's, and Rose's lime juice spilled across the pages. Large square ads for insurance companies and grocers crowded the outer columns of the pages. A carpet dealer went wall to wall with page 6. Whiteleys, Peter Robinson, and other big shops rushed in, some displaying Haxton's *huh?* touch with the display copy: "The rearing of infants by hand becomes more and more necessary among civilized races and so much attention has been directed to this subject during recent years that the question of infant feeding has ceased to be a purely empirical one." Counting the small ads, the space taken up by advertising looked certain to reach 50 percent. On July 4, 1904, *The Times* looked like a fairly modern newspaper, and the change had happened literally overnight.

There was a very strong reaction by readers, especially the geriatric cohort. One group of seven elderly men wrote jointly to cancel their lifelong subscriptions. Bell worked overtime patiently writing lengthy letters to subscribers explaining the economics of newspaper publishing—although Haxton had explained it all in detail already in ad after ad. And some advertisers seemed worried about what they had done. One grocer's large display advertisement didn't even try to sell a tin of beans. Instead it was devoted to an explanation of why the ad was there.

The circulation plan had obvious problems. News vendors balked, convinced that they were underwriting *The Times* unwillingly, while the cost of acquiring advertisers and the expense of delivering papers to crofters dwelling at the end of a path on an island off the coast of another island kept increasing. Soon, Haxton had added more than thirty thousand readers to *The Times*'s circulation lists. "It led to so large an increase in our circulation that our revenue from advertisements rose by more than one-half of the former amount," reported one circulation ad in *The Times*. "It cost us a large sum, but the money was well-invested." The trick became how to give subscribers their daily paper without going broke doing it. Jackson, nominally the circulation manager of *The Times* by now, had no solution for it, and neither did anyone else, if only because *The Times*'s own circulation and advertising departments were so inept. A man named Stephenson, a fixture in circulation, hated the marketing Hooper and Haxton were doing, and in the advertising department, Messrs. Wright and Plumbridge, two offended employees who actively sought to dissuade potential advertisers from placing ads, were especially difficult. All three men, no doubt abetted by others who emerged from various closets and corners of Printing House Square, worked to sabotage Hooper's efforts, and their duplicity, combined with their habitual ineptness, drew Hooper into angry discussions with Moberly Bell more than once.

Dear Mr. Bell,

It is now three days since I lost my temper in your office, and talked pretty plain, and I am quite sure that I am angry no longer.

However, let me first say that I should not have lost my temper in your office, as it wasn't a very gentlemanly thing to do, but as I look back on all I said, there is not one word that I wish to take back. It was all true. What I am sorry for is that I said it when I was angry instead of saying it coolly.

Now I want to point out one or two little things to you. First, you said that Mr. Plumbridge, in opening a letter which was marked "personal" (knowing that it was marked "personal" before he opened it, and then sending it to me) was doing nothing but what my office had done to you. You went on, however, and said that my man always wrote you and apologised. I am very glad to hear that, because I should discharge any man in my employ who did not write and apologise when he had done such a thing as this, but "The Times" man didn't apologise . . . quite a different thing in my mind.

Now let me point out two things which I might have said but did not. First, the behaviour of Mr. Wright, Mr. Plumbridge and Mr. Stephenson has in the past cost you almost half your circulation, and about £130,000 per annum in your advertising receipts.

I have no right to object to that at all, for this year their behaviour and action doesn't cost you anything, but does cost me something.

Second. When we started the circulation scheme and I

agreed to take all the risk, and spend at least £25,000 (which I might add that I not only did but increased it by over £13,000) "The Times," through you, agreed to do everything in their power to make not only the circulation scheme a success, but also to do everything to increase advertising receipts, so that I might get my money back. This I claim you are not doing when you allow such things to happen as that the printer can say at 1 o'clock at night that he won't put in a correction that the advertiser wants because the paper might not go to press in time. This statement on the part of Mr. Wright is absolutely untrue, and Mr. Wright knew it when he made the statement, as is proved by the fact that two or three nights previous to that an advertisement was written by Mr. Haxton, and he wished to correct something at almost 11.30, and the printer stated that it was too late, that the page had gone down. Mr. Haxton insinuated that he might go down and get that page and fix it, or they could leave the advertisement out, as they preferred. It was fixed. If Mr. Wright had told the exact truth he would have said "I don't care to take the trouble."

You also said that all I said was true, but that it took time to accomplish what I wanted to accomplish at once; but, again, you forget that time costs *me* money, and costs *you* nothing. You have a perfect right to take all the time you want when you are the only sufferer, but in this case *I* am the *only* sufferer. I have now spent seven months on either "The Times" circulation scheme or trying to increase the advertising receipts, with the result that instead of losing a few thousand circulation each year you have gained quite a number of thousand, and your advertising receipts are for the first five months £4,000 larger, and I have in hand advertising to increase it certainly to £6,000 if not £7,000. Your advertising receipts ought to be increased by at least £100,000 per annum, but to do so you have got to change your methods, and you say to make changes takes time. Alright, take the time, and meanwhile I will go to work and try and make up my losses in "The Times" scheme by working at my own business, (which I can assure you I am very sorry I ever left.)

Now let us get down to my real business. You told me that Mr. Walter did not wish to take up the History, but suggested that we have another talk with him. I would like to know whether you wish to take this matter up again or whether you wish to consider it settled. I am perfectly satisfied to let it remain settled where it is, but I think it only fair to you to say that last winter when I was in New York, I arranged with a New York publication to bring it out. Before coming to terms they had six of the editorial men read different sections of the work, so that all of the first 16 volumes were read over by these six men. All of these men said that it had some faults here and there, but as a whole was a first-class book. Since coming back here I have had it examined very carefully by two or three men here. All of them say that the book (with some slight exceptions, and these exceptions are being fixed) is a first-class book. Now if you'd like to take this matter up again, I should be very glad to do so, but if you don't care to do it, don't do it. Frankly, I believe you will be throwing away a great many thousand pounds, but that is your part of the business, not mine. I wish, however, you'd take the matter up at once and give me a decided answer, because I want to start the sale of this History here by the 1st December, and then after it is well started, about the 1st January, I want to go away for a couple of months or so.

I hope that you will feel that I am not acting in this matter in any way, shape nor manner angrily, and especially would I not have you think that I was angry with you. I hope that the friendship that you seem to feel towards me for the last few years, and certainly my friendship for you, will not be broken because I can't see men at "The Times" office throwing away my money without losing my temper.

Yours sincerely,
H. E. Hooper

P.S. Of course it is needless for me to say to you that I will write up for you all the £4,000 worth of advertising that I have in hand, and as in the past will not charge you the time of my own men.

Other schemes followed. Jackson's interest was rekindled by the publication of *The Historians' History of the World*, a project he had overseen, giving to the young historian James Thomson Shotwell the duty of helping Henry Smith Williams, an attorney, physician, and science historian, provide a wider view of things. The twenty-five-volume set, pushed in 1904 by an advertising effort so relatively restrained it could not have been done by the already overworked Haxton, was selling steadily. Moberly Bell had launched a "Literary Supplement" in 1902 and added an "Engineering Supplement" soon after. F. Harcourt Kitchin, seeing a chance, appealed to Bell to let him create a "Financial and Commercial Supplement," and Bell passed it off to Hooper for an opinion. It was Kitchin's first outing as an editor. It was also the beginning of his "relations with Hooper and with an extraordinary creature called Haxton who was Hooper's chief advertisement writer," as Kitchin wrote later.

Hooper and Haxton, Kitchin recalled with some fright, descended on him to flail him with optimism. "This is the finest thing which has been produced by any newspaper since the world began," Hooper said.

Haxton, whose high-pitched voice and sustained drawl made his manner of speech resemble the neighing of a horse, said ditto to his boss, and added that he saw splendid advertising matter in my scheme. Both of these experts in publicity fastened upon the proposed reports from the principal business centres of the Empire and foreign countries. . . . Hooper assured me he would support my scheme with Bell for all that his influence was worth, and Haxton declared that he would instantly embark upon the preparation of startling advertisements. His genius for publicity had, it appeared, taken fire. I was serious alarmed. . . . My first editorial cockle-shell looked like being swamped in a raging torrent of American advertising. . . . If Haxton were to let loose his American pen and write as he had talked, no effort . . . of mine could keep him within the limits of approximate veracity. And so it proved.... I blushed and felt shame at the very sight of them in the pages of *The Times*.

Kitchin survived. "The curious thing was that after I began publication of the Supplement no one called me to account for not achieving the impossible level of performance 'promised and vowed' for me by my godfather Haxton."

His supplement, however, disappeared shortly after it appeared during the circulation drive, on July 18, 1904, and was replaced by more robust City coverage in *The Times* itself.

At Printing House Square, Hooper was met by condescension, resentment, a passive refusal to help, and sometimes outright sabotage. In the advertising and circulation department, now under Hooper's supervision, many of the older employees of *The Times*, men who had been doing their jobs faithlessly and badly for decades, greatly resented taking orders from a very tactless American and went to both Walter and Moberly Bell to complain—especially Stephenson. Hooper remarked on this more than once, and when Bell mildly came to the defense of the man, Hooper fired back a colorful reply, defending the success of his circulation and advertising schemes, and any criticism of his efforts as both unjust and ungrateful:

I don't think you are quite just to Mr. Stephenson and the men in our employment.

Now let us see whether it is Mr. Stephenson and his men or myself and my men to whom injustice is done. I believe that you will admit that the business methods of Mr. Stephenson and his men, Mr. Plumbridge and his men, and Mr. Wright and his men for the last 20 years has resulted in "The Times" having less than half its former circulation, receipts and profits. We came along and paid "The Times" about £100,000 in profits on sales of books which you would not have received without us. This profit was received by you not by your pushing us but by our pushing you to let us make it for you. Then came up the question in regard to circulation. I drew up a scheme which I believed would help you increase your circulation, and offered to loan you Haxton and our entire organization to carry it out, and help make a success. You didn't undertake this, so that finally we offered to take the entire risk, so that if failure came, you, "The Times" didn't lose anything. The scheme was carried out with the result that you increased your circulation 30%. Your advertising, however, didn't increase, and I saw that while you had a larger circulation without the expense of a penny on your part, we who had advanced the £40,000 had to stand a loss of £12,000 per annum because Mr. Plumbridge and his men, and Mr. Wright and his men (through stupidity I will admit) actually did all they could to prevent advertising coming in. I personally then went to work on the advertising, and in six months increased your advertising receipts by £35,000, or at the rate of over 50%. . . .

I might easily add a good many pages to this letter showing where the *justice* or *injustice* comes in, but if you can read the above and prove to me that any of it is wrong in the slightest detail or insinuation, I will be most happy to apologise to anyone you want me to.

But was it a success? Judging by some accounts, no—or at least not successful enough. Kitchin dismissed it, and Harmsworth, speaking through Max Pemberton, thought it was useless. "For all his efforts, Hooper's project was a failure," wrote Herman Kogan. But Moberly Bell certainly thought it worthwhile, and in the official *History of "The Times,"* the chronicler—probably Stanley Morison—provides a more satisfactory appraisal.

The revenue for 1903–1904, it has been seen, was £200,000. The continuous tendency to fall in previous years was at the rate of £9,000 a year. The revenue for 1904–1905 might, therefore, reasonably have been expected to fall to £191,000. Equally, but for the Hooper and Jackson agreement, the revenue for 1905–1906 might reasonably have been expected to fall another £9,000 to £182,000. Actually the revenue for 1905–1906 was £295,539 19s 3d. Similarly, without the Hooper and Jackson agreement, the revenue of *The Times* for 1906–1907 might reasonably have been expected to fall to £173,000; but actually it was £285,258 5s 3d. The figures prove not only that the Hooper and Jackson agreement covering the forthcoming new tenth edition of the *Encyclopædia Britannica* was a valuable asset but that the new advertising and circulation schemes by which *The Times* and Hooper and Jackson provided against the cessation of profits on the old ninth edition were justified.

These crowded events that shaped the immediate future of the encyclopedia project all unfolded while the editorial staff of the *Britannica* beavered away, building their book. Chisholm would not be distracted.

CHAPTER 12

PLAN B: A BOOK WAR

Janet Hogarth, the no-longer-quite-young woman who years before had met Hugh Chisholm one memorable day at Oxford, was on her way up the steps leading to the offices of Hooper and Jackson at 125 High Holborn. It was just before Christmas 1905.

She was a tall, striking, but perhaps not classically beautiful forty-year-old spinster living at the time with one of her sisters, Mildred, a schoolteacher who was ten years her junior, in a new housing development called Lauderdale Mansions in Maida Vale. She was making her way as an unmarried professional woman in a world that had almost no professions to which women could easily be admitted. Oxford had not helped, at least in a practical sense: studying philosophy was not much in the way of vocational training for a single woman. She traveled in Chisholm's circle at a middle-distance orbit, but her days at Oxford must have seemed even more far removed from her present life than Chisholm's did.

Oxford had been her defining experience, of course, if only because it had been so unexpected. Her family home was a vicarage heavily populated by her mother, Jane, the daughter of John Uppleby, Scarborough's town clerk, and a crowd of sisters and a solitary brother. Jane Uppleby Hogarth "bore fourteen children in seventeen years," wrote Hogarth in a memoir, "and no twins amongst them [and] lived to the age of eighty-six, a fine upstanding specimen of North-country womanhood." But of those fourteen, only eight had survived childhood. Janet was the second daughter, born on November 27, 1865. One round of diphtheria alone wiped out three little girls when Janet was but eight. Most of the boys died, leaving only one brother for seven sisters.

Her father, Reverend George Hogarth, had been born into a family of Scottish Presbyterians; his father was a minister, and his cousin was Charles Dickens's greatest muse. Orphaned by age fourteen, George was moved south in the care of a sister and finally found his way to Cambridge. When he came out the other end, he was the vicar of Barton-on-Humber. It would be his only job; he held it for thirty-one years, using kindness and efficiency to bring a slightly High Church aesthetic to a decidedly low church. "My father was, I think, liked," Hogarth recalled; "most assuredly he was respected. He treated all alike, gentle or simple; he never went into any cottage uninvited, or sat down until he was asked. As a result he was seldom excluded." But often consulted: you can still see him in some of the parish's old records, presiding over one meeting or another, convening this or that, making decisions that had a very narrow, but very deep, significance to the four thousand souls then living in Barton.

Janet (Hogarth) Courtney in 1916

His son he encouraged. David Hogarth went on to become one of Britain's greatest archaeologists, a true adventurer, navigating close calls and narrow escapes all over the Middle East and half of Araby. His exploits gave him a fine sense of history, both ancient and immediate, for along with all his excavations and discoveries, he was not only the British Museum's premier Egyptologist but also the mentor of T. E. Lawrence.

His daughters he protected more, trying to guide them into a traditional narrative, but fecund wives often produce solitary and independent daughters, and the vicar was forced to yield on more than one occasion. His oldest girl, Mary, demonstrated

T. E. Lawrence, David Hogarth, and Alan Dawnay in a photo by Lowell Thomas, ca. 1914

some artistic skills, so he allowed her to pursue painting, which she did successfully as a member of Walter Sickert's circle, her exhibitions routinely generating critical praise and enough sales to make a living. Janet's skills were academic, strong, and impressive enough that Oxford wanted her, but Reverend Hogarth resisted mightily until it was demonstrated to him that Elizabeth Wordsworth, the principal of Lady Margaret Hall, a women's college then barely five years old and embracing only a very small cluster of students, was not only the grandniece of the poet but in fact also the eldest daughter of the bishop of Lincoln. This soothed his opposition, so off to Oxford went Janet.

After more than a decade as the first female clerk hired by the Bank of England, where she amused herself by regarding her coworkers as "psychological instances," Hogarth finally realized one day that her fantasy that "a bomb would explode and wreck the Bank" meant that she should think about making a change. She looked around, and saw a career dead end in an ancient building in which almost no women worked, but was filled instead with "almost human gold-weighing machines, which spat out light sovereigns sideways as let the rest fall in a steady stream unto copper vessels like coal pans— all the significant evidence of Britain's wealth and British solidity, so picturesque, so historic, so reassuring and, in the long run, so unbearably tedious."

She tried moonlighting; she went to the offices of *The Fortnightly Review*, where W. L. Courtney, her tutor-turned-suitor, was editor; he gave her a job as a reader. She considered herself a knowing free-

Canal della Salute, Venice, by Mary Hogarth

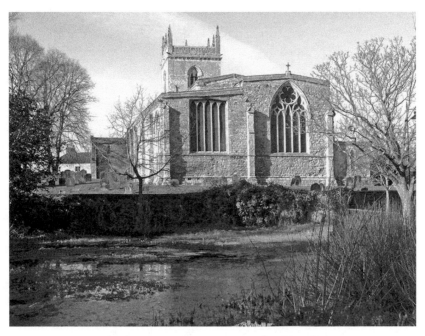

St. Mary's Church, Barton-on-Humber, Lincolnshire

W. L. Courtney, the tutor-suitor

thinker, and the *Fortnightly* was just the place for that. She tried her hand at writing a few things, but keeping her day job at the bank for security's sake. Her occasional attempts at finding a regular staff position at a serious periodical were futile; as an editor at *Murray's Magazine* told her as he escorted her from the building, "A lady and a scholar. No, no, no."

Finally, one November weekend, she went down to Bournemouth—a destination for depression any time, but especially in late autumn. To make the point, on Sunday it rained. She must have taken refuge in one of the seaside arcades, for there she recognized "an interesting and 'psychical' woman," a local eccentric she had known when she was a child in Barton. "She had always been given to telling fortunes; up in North Lincolnshire she had got an almost sinister reputation for notable predictions." Hogarth asked the woman to tell her fortune. "She said I was on the eve of a big change."

When she returned to London, there was a letter on her desk from a friend, perhaps Chisholm. *The Times*, the note said, was looking for a librarian, and she had been proposed.

She had little idea what that might mean, since archival work wasn't something in her immediate experience, but she was game to see what was up and so climbed the stairs with a certain degree of expectation. Whatever it was, it would be more interesting than what she had been doing all those years leading up to 1905's winter and that staircase.

What it was was not a library. It was a "book club."

It was a fatal idea Hooper and Bell had come up with to boost circulation by giving readers free access to a subscribers-only bookshop filled with all the books they could possibly want and priced at a discount—certainly a novelty in English bookselling. *The Times*, which was already operating a theater ticket bureau, would buy books in large numbers, and sell them in a grand, clubby bookshop, making publishers into happy advertisers.

Describing it to a friend in India, Moberly Bell wrote,

> The scheme—so far as the poor, unfledged thing can be called a scheme—is, briefly, to open a large West End office of *The Times* well stocked with books, some 25,000 volumes of that sort of quality likely to be asked for by readers of *The Times*. . . . Of the more recent books and of the more alive books there will be many copies; of the older books and of dying books there will be less. This will be the nucleus on which we build. But the main stock will be new books as they come out, and these we propose to buy in large quantities. (1) They will be for sale to anyone at ordinary lowest price. (2) Any subscriber to *The Times* may have any three on loan. With each book they will have a card telling them that if they like to keep the book they may do so on remitting $x-x$ being the ordinary price with discount at which they could buy it elsewhere. Or they may return it when they have read it and say that they will have it one month hence at, say, 10% reduction, or two months at 20%, or three months at 30% reduction (these figures are merely imaginary), but at the increasing reduction according to age.

There were already lending libraries all over Britain—Mudie's and Boots, among many others. But they charged a fee; renting out books for so much at a time, just as would be done with films a century later. "[Subscribers] will have a right to three volumes at one time," explained *The Times* in an article, "and a right to change any, or all, of these volumes, as often as they please. They will have a right, if they reside within the London postal district, to have these three volumes, or any of them, changed, at their addresses, carriage free not oftener than once a week."

To the kind of person who read *The Times*, the offer was irresistible. Other than going out to a theater, entertainment meant reading. And readers, the story said, "will have a choice, which will be practically unlimited, amongst all new books and all standard books published in the United Kingdom which are reasonably suited for circulation, and a wide choice amongst books published abroad." It was, *The Times* said, a better deal than they could find at "the best circulating libraries for a yearly payment of £2 2s," and all included in a normal subscription to *The Times*. Of particular interest to Hogarth, if she was paying attention, was this little bonus: "At the Library there will gradually be established a staff of trained experts; whose advice and assistance [readers] may command in the selection of books on any subject which they may wish to study, or in the choice of lighter books according to their tastes. A catalogue of over 800 pages is in preparation: it will shortly be supplied gratis and post free to subscribers, and to others."

There was no attempt to hide the rationale for this remarkable plan. In fact, the motives for all this were spelled out clearly: "*The Times* . . . does not expect to make money out of The Times Book Club. . . . We are prepared to spend £100,000 on the scheme. We expect to be remunerated for that large expenditure, of course, but to be remunerated, not by the additional subscriptions we shall receive, on which we shall make little or no profit, but by the additional advertisements which those subscriptions are sure to bring."

Jackson, who should have played a role in a project that had a big impact on the business of selling books, especially since it was done in the name of boosting circulation—nominally his bailiwick under the new deal Hooper had struck—was a mere shadow. As Hooper rushed about plastering one plan over another, with Moberly Bell, desperate to replace the revenue that the encyclopedia sales had reliably provided, he wasn't unaware that of all the partners in all the various plans and schemes he had going, he was often the only moving part. Hooper saw it all of a carefully engineered piece: circulation, advertising, and ancillary schemes all support *The Times*, and in turn, *The Times* supports the *Britannica*. No *Times*, no *Britannica*, in other words. Hooper had no conception that the *Britannica* would be as profitable without *The Times* as with it. He considered it essential to his success; he had built his empire on the rickety foundation of *The Times*, and now he was trying to repair that foundation. So doing whatever it took to add a subscriber was, to Hooper, the same as turning up a lead for an encyclopedia sale. That thinking animated all that Hooper would do for the next several years. To him, it was all perfectly obvious: make people want what they didn't know they needed. It worked for the *Britannica*; it would work for books.

But he didn't understand Jackson's increasing passivity. Although sympathetic toward Jackson for the loss of his wife, Hooper had work to do, and he grew more and more exasperated with his partner, finally sending him an impatient update on June 6, 1905:

> I got your long letter of May 20, in regard to the book scheme. Before I got this, however, all matters had been arranged here, so your advice in regard to *The Times* scheme was useless. The state of the case is something like this: After a conference with Mr. Walter, chief owner of *The Times*, and Bell—Moberly Bell, manager, &c.—they wanted to go into the book scheme, were very enthusiastic over it, but they wanted the same guarantee that we had this year: that is that their receipts should not go below £200,000.
>
> I told Mr. Bell last Friday that I'd think of it till Monday. On Monday, I came in and said to him: "Look here, I have come in downtown to this office and put my shoulder underneath you—and you are a good heavy man—and it takes me two or three weeks to push you around into a place. Then you and I have to push Mr. Walter into a place, and that takes a week or so. Then I have to go up to High Holborn and push my partner, Mr. W. M. Jackson, into a place, and then I have to go out and enthuse the public." Needless to say,

Bell was scared out of his boots, and he turned and asked me what I wanted to arrange, I said that without waiting for you I would make the arrangement that we'd guarantee him that his receipts should not be below £200,000, but that any profit from the selling of books must come to us.

The Times Book Club would benefit *The Times*, of course, but Hooper was footing the bill, certain that in the long run, the profits would be there. He thought the club would be slow to return a profit on its own, but he had little doubt that the entire house of cards, from bookstore to *Britannica*, would eventually strengthen and become a steady source of revenue.

It was not a model Jackson understood. For him, finding somebody to subscribe to a newspaper had no logical connection with selling a book. Where Hooper saw many smaller ventures leading to a big payoff, Jackson was a one-project-at-a-time man, taking the profits from each deal, pocketing some of them, investing the rest in the next deal. He had made his reputation by investing wisely, not by dreaming wildly. The idea of pouring hundreds of thousands into an untried bookstore experiment in the hope that somehow, someday, a profit would appear on the bottom line of an encyclopedia sale was a fairly artistic notion to him. Jackson knew what he liked, and these kinds of majestic, conceptual experiments weren't on that list.

Besides, putting together what would amount to the country's largest bookstore over the space of a few weeks was risky business in more ways than one. First, the publishers had to be dealt with. Obviously, anything that was going to increase the circulation and purchase of their books was going to interest them. But bookselling was far from a straightforward line connecting a manufacturer—the publisher—with an end user. For as long as anyone could remember, publishers had tried to control the prices paid by readers for books. The "net price"—the price below which no new book could be sold—had been an inviolate proposition since 1852, when a group of publishers acting together against a smaller group of publishers who thought it was right to let the market determine the best price for their books sought to prevent "underselling" of books at less than their cover price. They were unsuccessful. Most publishers felt that their products should be immune from the normal operations of commerce—that is, when they offered a book for sale, they should retain a power to set the price even after the purchase had been made. Underselling, many of them felt, was an "evil," because it held the promise of lowering the prices they could charge for the books they made and marketed.

Miraculously, book publishing continued to operate quite profitably. In 1890, a new system, formulated by Sir Frederick Macmillan, was put in place to guarantee publishers and booksellers a special status in the kingdom of commerce. Macmillan's plan established two classes of books—"net" books, which could never be sold new for less than the cover price, and "subject" books, which could be sold without any regard for the published price. Publishers were asked to sign this "net book agreement"—really, just a scheme for simple price fixing and the protection of retail distribution.

Sir Frederick Macmillan
(Image: British Museum)

Moberly Bell and Hooper were aware of the potential problem their plan for selling "used" books posed for Macmillan and the others. In a series of meetings with publishers, they set forth a complicated pricing policy: subject books would be sold at a 25 percent discount; net books would be sold at their cover price until either they had become so used by readers that they could not be sold as a new product or until six months after publication, whichever came first. Books that had circulated on loan for a month or so but were still in like-new condition would be sold at a 35 percent discount, except net books, which would sell at a price 20 percent lower than their cover price. Once books reached a state of use that made impossible their sale as anything but a used book, they would be discounted to whatever price made a sale possible.

On July 29, 1905, Moberly Bell had an update for his Indian friend:

> I have taken my premises—93 Bond Street. I am getting together the people necessary to begin with, and by a very vague circular addressed to about 20,000 subscribers I have got over 10,000 people, who, as they have paid in advance exactly the same price as they might have paid daily, are presumably anxious to take books. There, for the moment, or for one month, I mean to rest on my oars—for various reasons, but chiefly because I think it is well to go slowly and to try how it will work with 10,000 for one month before spending money in getting more, also because I think that those 10,000 may themselves bring in more without expense of advertising, also because it is hot and I don't want to have more than enough to do. . . .
>
> On the 15th September or thereabouts we blow our trumpets, send out about 700,000 circulars, prospectuses, catalogues, etc., and shall see the result to a certain extent—not to its full extent, for many have already their subscriptions with their libraries to the end of the year, and they will wait till then both to see how it works and to save their pence. Before the end of the year we attack again those of the 700,000 that have not fallen victims, and shall, I hope, reap in a few more. Meanwhile we shall have all the booksellers in arms against us, and a battle royal between libraries, booksellers, publishers and *The Times*.

The Times Book Club actually opened on Monday, September 11, 1905, but long before that, Hooper had been sending staff down to the club and put them to work creating a huge index of books of every kind, from Tacitus to Tom Brown, some in special decorative bindings, and organizing the shelving and the counter area for the clerks. After a few weeks, Jackson arrived, and tried to catch up with

Hooper. The men were often seen in tandem, Hooper talking madly, Jackson at first a placid somnambulant, gradually becoming more engaged.

In the frantic weeks before and after the club opened to the public, according to the club clerk Ethel Jeanes, "Messrs Hooper and Jackson were much in evidence, bristling with ideas for recording entries and exchanges and so on and at first were very disturbing as we were compelled to change the original system shortly after opening—I would get memo after memo asking for figures or demanding fresh ideas."

The excitement leading up to the opening was contagious. Young John Walter was in and out of the place frequently, and every morning a delegation from High Holborn led by Oswald Sickert, then working as Haxton's assistant, would appear to convene a meeting to lay out plans for the day. It was a mammoth, complex retail operation run by enthusiastic amateurs.

But as soon as the club opened, the place was swamped with *Times* subscribers wanting to get their free books or buy the deeply discounted titles available. "The first few days were one continuous crush of celebrities—and others—but with the exception of the King everyone of note seemed to come in," Jeanes recalled. "The majority were delighted to be getting such a Book Service but the outrageous demands of the few were Colossal. Mr. Hooper said nothing must be refused so the buying was very interesting, many unsuitable editions, etc. had to be supplied only to be returned unread!"

Sickert provided intelligence for Hooper and Haxton. The club was so busy, and so understaffed, wrote Jeanes, that Sickert "kept his hat on in self defense as anyone without one [thus suggesting a staff member] was almost mobbed."

Full-page ads continued in *The Times*, especially in the *Literary Supplement*, and the following week a full page of endorsements culled from "among the hundreds of appreciative letters sent to *The Times* by delighted subscribers"—including one from a Guernsey resident saying that, after calculating his costs for books and the paper, he could "save 12s. and get *The Times* for nothing. Number of books unlimited and latest publications. How *The Times* is going to make its library pay is a mystery." Indeed.

The reception far exceeded Hooper's expectations; the club outgrew its premises almost overnight. It took very little time for the publishers, who at first had been delighted at the idea of selling *The Times* thousands of books, to grow nervous—especially about what constituted a new book and one that looked new but wasn't, and was therefore subject to discount. And a surprising number of visitors were there to buy, not borrow, books. The tills literally overflowed with cash: "The money problem was tiresome at first," Ethel Jeanes remembered. "I had only a little table with a very frail drawer so a system had to be devised to come and empty it more frequently."

Almost immediately, a complaint was made to the Publishers Association by the Booksellers Association, and a meeting was convened to reiterate and settle once and for all what constituted a "used" book. It was this: "One which has been used by more than two subscribers, and is returned in such a state that it cannot be sold as a new book." The Publishers Association and Moberly Bell both signed a document certifying their agreement. But the booksellers, with whom the Times Book Club was in obvious competition, were not calmed. Their attitude toward *The Times*, as Bell later said, was "[t]hat of the rat to the ferret."

Plans were soon announced to move around the corner to a larger, newly built premises at 376–384 Oxford Street, a small block by itself on the busiest shopping street in England. Hooper was satisfied that the immense investment in the club would soon pay out.

When Hogarth walked into the office on High Holborn that morning, she was surprised to find that she was meeting not only with the American who had invited her, H. E. Hooper, but also with Moberly Bell, the manager of *The Times*. The "librarian" job was clearly something more.

She left the office feeling, as she put it later, more than a little thoughtful. "To go straight from the seclusion of the Bank [of England] to the almost startling publicity of a great shop in Oxford Street with little or nothing in its plate-glass windows to obscure the view of the crowds on the pavement, was a change so abrupt as to be almost subversive, especially to a woman of my age." She knew she didn't want to stay at the bank, but now, in addition to visions of violence, she also added to her reasons for taking up the job of running the club the very real consideration that even if she stayed where she was, she wasn't going any higher than clerk.

"So far as I could see," she wrote, "no further extension of the Women's department was possible, hardly even desirable, as it would have only resulted in displacing men from positions which had been theirs for many decades. At best it would have meant taking over for inferior grades of work in one or other department. For myself, there was no prospect of rising. Had I been a man, I might have aspired to the glories of the Chief Accountancy. . . . As a woman, I could only look to security, consideration, and a pension. It was not enough." She could not, she complained, even look for "a set of fresh interests in marriage, or, if she does, she must in Government and other pensioned service do so by the surrender of her profession."

Working for *The Times*, she thought, came as close as she was likely to come to making a living by feeding her interest in literature. Hooper had told her he needed somebody who could talk about books and somebody who could manage a large staff, most of whom were women. "I happened to fill the double bill," she recalled. She decided to take a few days to think it over and consulted "my best friend in journalism"—W. L. Courtney, her former tutor and now the editor of *The Fortnightly Review*. He told her *The Times* was engaging in "wild-cat schemes" and that he thought the paper and the schemes would both soon fail.

"I dare say all that is true," she replied. "But I should have most to do with that American. He's quite unlike anything I have ever met before; but I like him and I trust him, and I am going to work with him."

Hooper had at least tried to prepare her for her new job, noting that her background was considerably different from those who would work under her supervision. "You will have a hard job," he told her. "They won't like you coming in; they don't want a lady about; and they will know I want to find out what they are after."

Hogarth joined as Hooper was still planning the book club's move to Oxford Street. She was overwhelmed; the crowds and the frenetic pace threw her into a deep depression. "Hooper saw the signs of this," she recalled, "and, with characteristic kindness, sent for me and explained that his schemes were not quite so far advanced as he had expected . . . and he would be glad for me to take a holiday abroad at his expense until he was ready to install me as librarian in the new premises on Oxford Street."

When Hogarth returned, it was to the Oxford Street premises, where she marveled at "the club-room and the tea-room, a scheme for servants' registry, and other methods of obtaining for *The Times* the revenue from advertisements which it so sorely needed." Over time, she and Sickert worked up a friendly convivial enjoyment of the shop, its customers, and the fascinating effect of retail on the human mind.

> To sit all day in a big book-shop is a glorious opportunity for a study of the reading public. . . . I sat out in the open shop, a prey to all and sundry, answering questions, soothing complaints, pacifying petulant authors, flattering fashionable dilettanti. It was no uncommon experience to be asked in one breath to recommend the chief works of philosophy in the last ten years, or the latest thing on door-knockers. . . . [I]n a big shop you come up daily against the shifty and the unscrupulous. Sometimes they are merely stupid, like the subscribers who took out a new copy of a book, kept it a month and then claimed the privilege of buying it at a reduction "after one month's circulation."

"Clergy," she added, "were very frequent offenders; I think they get into a habit of being dictatorial to women-folk." Those, of course, Hogarth could spot a mile off, but she seemed to enjoy more and more the flow of theatrical types, the Harley Street doctors, the leisured ladies, and a fair share of the upper crust. "My name's Curzon," one of them, the celebrated viceroy of India, announced imperiously. "You worry me to death with your little bills!" Hogarth quickly set him up with an account.

She and Sickert discovered what today might be called the art of the endcap when they found that if they displayed their books not singly, but in "battalions," they sold well. "It is astonishing what books you can induce the public to take out, and even to read, by a judicious use of these methods," she wrote. "Translations, for instance, are more often than not a drug in the market for our insular reading public. Yet when we displayed Fogazzaro's *The Saint* we sold out an entire edition."

To call attention to the Oxford Street location, Hooper came up with a lavishly advertised book sale promotion, one that would remind readers of the value of a subscription and draw people's attention to the new premises. The ads had all the Haxtonian flourishes, including one remarkable virtue Hogarth appreciated as "insinuation"–although by now many of them were being written by his able student and protégé, Sickert. The result was extraordinary. On the morning of May 1, 1906, "The Greatest Sale Of Books that has ever been held" was announced, with "600,000 books of all kinds–fiction, biography, travel, &c. of which the published prices amount to a total of £222,000, to be sold for less than £25,000." Having drawn readers' attention to the book club, now *The Times* laid into the publishing industry, telling readers to end "The 'Vicious Circle' of high prices":

It is the opinion of *The Times* that books have always been sold at too high a figure, and that if their prices were reduced to a scale more in correspondence, for example, with the price of a newspaper, books would circulate in correspondingly large numbers. In the course of only two days, for instance, *The Times* itself prints in its columns, and sells for 6d. (the price of two issues of *The Times*), as much news matter as is contained in an important biography published at 21s. net. The cost of paper, printing, and binding in the case of such a book may amount to 1s. 6d. The enormous balance of its price goes in profits to the publisher, author, and booksellers, wholesale and retail–an enormous balance indeed, but by no means an enormous profit, because the quantity sold is small. At our great sale such books will be sold for twenty-eight and thirty PENCE! As a consequence of the low prices, we believe that the whole of the enormous stock of 600,000 books will be sold off in a very short time, and we shall have thus obtained our object of bringing to the favourable notice of all book lovers in the United Kingdom the great advantages offered by *The Times* through its Book Club. Fixing the prices of the books which we offer at our sale, it is not their cost that *The Times* has considered. We name prices which are lower than anybody has ever seen, in order that no one can fail to be attracted, and in order that, in the future, no purchaser can help remembering and saying to his friends, of the Sale, "It was The Times Book Club that gave me this bargain!" Indeed, our ultimate object is to create, by means of this extraordinary sale, so close a connexion between the ideas represented by the two expressions "book" and "The Times Book Club" that, whenever the thought of a book crosses your mind, you will also think of The Times Book Club. Hitherto book-buyers have been accustomed to see books of the kind which we are selling priced in shillings. At our sale you will notice that the prices of books are marked in pence, a proceeding which fairly suggests the extent to which prices have been reduced.

The result, that May Day 1906, was madness. The club was completely overrun by a "mob in Oxford Street, which rushed the doors, climbed over all the barriers, swarmed up the staircase and obliged us in less than an hour to send for the police," Hogarth wrote. "Books vanished like magic; we had to rush in fresh supplies; library subscribers fighting their way in through side-doors to change their books stood amazed and remained amused to watch the surging multitudes. Hooper promptly had the crowds photographed and the advertisements recast."

People bought books in bulk: one thousand assorted books, all kinds, for £80, payable in monthly installments. Subscribers too busy to come face the crushing crowd could send a note expressing a general area of interest and the staff of the best lending library in existence would "select books for you[,] books of which the value will amaze you."

But, as Moberly Bell had predicted, the booksellers were up in arms and the publishers were beginning to suspect that net books were being sold at a discount too early, and that simply circulating a book once or twice wasn't sufficient to merit selling it at a cut price, and that in any case, the Times Book Club was declaring books as remainders when they weren't.

The Publishers Association swooped down on the club. The president of the association, Edward Bell, and the vice president, E. J. Longman, went to Printing House Square on May 9, 1906, along with the president of the Associated Booksellers, to have a word with Moberly Bell and Horace Hooper. Moberly Bell had a stenographer present, and so did the representatives of the publishers. Edward Bell later recounted his impression of Moberly Bell and Hooper:

> As this was the first occasion on which I had seen Mr. Bell and the only one on which I met Mr. Hooper I may as well describe the personality of each as it impressed me. Mr. Moberly Bell, who holds the position of business manager of *The Times*, is a large and powerful-looking man with a singular face—dark-complexioned, colourless and smooth-shaven, with a prominent nose and upper jaw. His features are decidedly oriental, and though he is described in books of reference (presumably on his own authority) as the son of "Mr. Henry Bell of Egypt," his real name is variously given. Mr. Wilfrid Blunt, who was brought into contact with him at the time of the Arabi's military rebellion and is not a friendly critic, has recorded that he was "a commission agent on the Alexandrian Stock Exchange (his real name being Benjamin Moss), who acted first as Scott's assistant when Scott was *Times* correspondent at Alexandria, and then got Scott's place," which eventually led to his obtaining the important position which he now holds. A well-known author who knows him told me, however, that his name is Moses Abel. In some conversations which I had with Mr. Bell, in which I made some reference to the identity of our surnames, he told me that he belonged to the Bells of Cumberland or Westmoreland, I forgot which. . . . Mr. H. E. Hooper was a very different looking man of slighter build with hair on the upper lip. He had a bright eye and intelligent-looking face, with small features, hands and feet, but there was a certain duskiness of complexion which suggests a tinge of foreign blood—possibly Indian or Mexican. He spoke little, but in a positive manner, and his voice and pronunciation were of an extreme American type.

Edward Bell demanded that the club "agree to a limit of time—which we put at six months—within which surplus copies of new books, or 'dead stock,' should not be offered to the public. To this they [Hooper and Bell] refused to bind themselves formally, though they stated that—except in one case in which the publisher had sold copies at a low price—they had not yet done anything of the kind."

Moberly Bell and Hooper wouldn't budge. A couple of weeks later, the club infuriated the Publishers Association by announcing a big sale of remaindered books—and some new titles, as well—that had been supplied by various publishers eager to empty their warehouses.

Moberly Bell heard nothing more until after the association met on July 4, 1906. At that meeting, the group decided to boycott *The Times*. Advertisements disappeared off the book pages and revenues began to drop, but Moberly Bell refused to sign. Instead, he sent a note to the association explaining *The Times*'s point of view:

> You do not refer to the fact that at no time between 9th May and 30th July was there any communication with us, though it is admitted that you were consulting all the branches of the trade. . . . I must leave the public to judge between our conduct and that of the Publishers' Association, which condescends to retaliate by withdrawing its advertisements and boycotting one bookseller in order to enforce a regulation carried behind that back of that bookseller and avowedly directed against him alone.

In response, the publishers blacklisted the book club and refused to ship new titles to Oxford Street. Moberly Bell went to Rudyard Kipling, who had sided so far with the publishers, and asked him to do a fact-finding study. *The Times*, he said, would publish the findings verbatim. Kipling refused.

So *The Times* retaliated by finding other sources for inventory and by launching a series of articles branding the publishers as price-fixers trying to dictate terms to its most influential customer at the expense of the reading public. Otherwise, *The Times* continued its book coverage unaffected by the book war, as it was now being called, although when appropriate a notice was appended to reviews telling readers that the publisher of the book under review was not cooperating with the Times Book Club and should therefore be avoided. A little book called *The History of the Book War: Fair Book Prices Versus Publish-*

ers' Trust Prices, written anonymously, but almost certainly by Sickert, with help from Haxton, perhaps unwisely noted that the book club's approach to business was purely American. "Inefficient distribution [i.e., through the book trade only] has already led in the United States to a very remarkable displacement of business," he wrote. "At least sixty per cent. of the retail trade in books has passed out of the hands of booksellers into those of other retail traders who have shops open for general business, and find no difficulty in adding books to their list of articles." *The History of the Book War* went on to explain how wider streams of distribution, "whether they begin or end with books," would lead to "the emancipation of the retail book-trade from the bondage in which it is now held by the publishers."

But it was far too early for a history; the war was still raging, with skirmishes breaking out everywhere. When John Murray published a long-anticipated collection of Queen Victoria's letters in October 1906, Moberly Bell wrote to Murray to ask about buying a large quantity of the books, to be discounted by the book club, suggesting that if the very high net price of £3 3s. were reduced slightly to club members, the compensating increase in sales would also increase Murray's profits. Bell even appealed to Murray's sense of loyalty to the crown: "The book is, of course, of interest, but the price is such that it can only have an official, and a circulating library, sale. We are willing to lose a little money on it if you care to meet us half-way, and would take a very large number if you are disposed in this one case to deal with us direct. . . . For the sake of the late Queen we should like to give the book as good a send-off as possible."

Murray replied, "Nothing would give me greater pleasure than to do business with you again, not only with regard to one book, but all along the line. Can't you reconsider your decision as to the six-months limit for the new books? If this were done, I think I could answer for it that not only mine but all the other doors would be opened. I cannot, however, make an exception."

It must have been quite an effort just to have the conversation. Murray had been among the most intransigent of the publishers and had broadened his attack on the book club to include *The Times* and the *Encyclopædia Britannica*. When Moberly Bell refused to change the book club's policy, Murray declined to sell the Victoria letters collection to the club at a discounted price. When the book was reviewed in *The Times Literary Supplement*–by John Bailey, the editor of *The Quarterly Review*, a periodical published by John Murray–it was full of praise, except for one paragraph inserted by *The Times Literary Supplement's* editor, Bruce Richmond: "But a grave mistake has been committed in the name of publication. This book is one that will create very wide interest–in one form or another it will appeal to every reader in the Empire, and it is difficult to overestimate its educational value if it were accessible to the classes who are apt to believe that wisdom lies only in a democracy. But the three volumes which might, one would imagine, have been produced at ten shillings, and which at a reasonable figure would have sold by hundred of thousands are offered to a privileged few at £3 3s."

The paragraph was written by Moberly Bell at Hooper's urging. Richmond had told Bailey he was free to remark on the cost of the book, and sure enough, when the review came in, Bailey had written after a very laudatory passage, "Alas! that we should have to add, 'if he can afford to buy it.'"

The review was followed by a letter to the editor of *The Times*, on October 19, from "Artifex," reading, "Sir,–Your reviewer of 'The Letters of Queen Victoria' has observed that the three volumes could probably have been produced for 10s and sold at a reasonable price, instead of being priced at £3 3s net, and thus rendered inaccessible to all but a privileged few." After a projected breakdown of costs, Artifex concluded, "Now, Sir, these figures in any case spell simple extortion. . . . [Murray] has exploited the great personality of Queen Victoria for his own ends and carried the national interest in her doings for his own enrichment into 32 piece of silver, to be precise." Other letters castigated Murray's "plunder" of the queen's letters and his "extortion . . . [of] luckless victims." "Artifex," Latin for "a cunning inventor," was one of Hooper's employees, a certain Mr. Ross, and Hooper had supplied him with the cost breakdown. Murray sued *The Times* for libel.

It was a big story, widely discussed. Popular opinion was overwhelmingly on the side of *The Times*, of course; once the boycott and blacklist were known, business at the book club doubled, then tripled. A sympathetic member of Parliament, Henniker Heaton, organized a massive petition drive against the publishers, and over the course of several days before Christmas 1906 some ten thousand names appeared in *The Times* day after day, ordered by social rank, with the aristocracy at the top of each list, then descending through military leaders, bishops and other clerics, legal practitioners, doctors and scientists, on to the average *Times* reader. Virtually every *Times* subscriber of note was on the list, from the lord mayor of London to the duke of Hamilton, but neither would the publishers yield, so with the lines well trenched in the great book war, and as work on the *Britannica* calmly proceeded, both sides settled back to see who would be forced to surrender.

CHAPTER 13

CHAOS

Opening bookstores and reinventing the retail model in publishing was an unusual way of supporting the publication of an encyclopedia. It must have been impossible for Hooper or anyone else to foresee what effect all these events would ultimately have.

In fact, the book war's collateral damage was felt most keenly by the small proprietors, the dozens of distant relatives of people who benefited handsomely from a gift given by somebody they didn't know to somebody else they didn't know long before they were born. Many of the proprietors were docile; at least in the beginning, they supported whatever was being done in Printing House Square to keep their dividends flowing.

But two of the small proprietors decided to open a new front in the war that was being fought around *The Times* and its activities, and the opening of the Times Book Club in September 1905 spurred them to action. They were certain that *The Times* was being controlled by an unpredictable chief proprietor who had hired Egyptians and Americans and had turned the paper into a sheet dedicated to selling reprints of old books. The leader of this revolt of the heirs was an extremely contentious Harley Street doctor, William Knowsley Sibley, the son of Clara Fanny Sibley, the small proprietor who, twenty years earlier, had objected to the appointment of Arthur Walter as comanager. Demanding access to the accounts at Printing House Square was by now a family tradition with the Sibleys. In this pursuit, they had gone to Harmsworth in the spring of 1902.

Harmsworth had been watching *The Times* closely. Owning it was a cherished dream. Understanding the potential problem represented by dissident coproprietors, he cordially sought Arthur Walter's advice on how to deal with "a Dr. Sibley, who has been bothering me a great deal lately," but also used the exchange as an opportunity to renew his offer to buy *The Times*. Walter had brushed it off.

Now, three years later, the Sibleys, who owned one-seventh of one-third of one-fifth of three-sixteenths of *The Times*, were back, and this time they came armed with lawyers. In their wake came another cohort of proprietors, this one led by a very persistent great-granddaughter, Wilhelmina Lydia Brodie-Hall, proud owner of one-half of one-ninth of two-sixteenths of the paper.

This was a turn of events Moberly Bell had foreseen; he had written a lengthy memo to Arthur Walter outlining this very scenario and proposing a reorganization—or even an outright sale, back to themselves, if necessary—of the paper seven years earlier. Walter had ignored it. That option was now gone.

The repeated reminders that the profits of the printing operation were out of reach of the small proprietors excited their sense of entitlement, and more and more of them became sensitized to the issues surrounding Walter's management of the paper. Though divided by often unreconciled individual interests, the small proprietors were united in one thing: they despised the presence of "alien" influences at *The Times*—meaning Moberly Bell and Hooper. The Times Book Club and the war it spawned, the vulgar encyclopedia campaigns, the up-all-night competitions, the books and maps and telegrams, all these filled the proprietors with nostalgia for *The Times* that had once quietly piped them income, as water from a miraculous spring. It also filled them with loathing, not just for the Americans, Hooper and Jackson, but for their enablers. Moberly Bell appeared to the proprietors to grow swarthier by the moment, but for Sibley and Brodie-Hall the real villains were their cousins, those Walter boys at Printing House Square—who, it might be added by both major camps of dissident proprietors, were making much more money than they needed to make by the charges they made against the newspaper for printing. Most importantly, it seemed that the amounts being doled out in dividends to the small proprietors were in an apparently unstoppable decline, the sums growing smaller year after year. Their wish: for *The Times* to be organized like a business, in which there would be accountability and an end to the disruption Hooper, Jackson, and Moberly Bell had brought in saving the newspaper from extinction. The only way to get what they wanted, Sibley and Brodie-Hall decided, was through the courts.

So Sibley, with several other proprietors, went to Chancery Court on September 12, 1905–the day after the opening of the Times Book Club–and brought suit against Arthur Walter demanding "an account of the assets, debts and liabilities, the manner of dividing the profits; a declaration that the property be transferred to a limited-liability company and that the necessary direct be given to this effect. Finally it was asked that the court direct that Walter was not entitled to employ the assets for the establishment of a Book Club, or the maintenance of any library." Never mind that Hooper had sported the investment for the club. It must cease, they said. Walter, in response, gardened.

After a year of seclusion from the noisy coproprietors, Walter convened a meeting of them all on November 12, 1906, at Printing House Square, at which the "alien book schemes of Messrs. Hooper and Jackson" were singled out for angry criticism. Finally, it was decided unanimously that the "friendly" action "for the purpose of forming the partnership into a private company with limited liability–the details to be worked out between the plaintiffs and Walter"–be undertaken as soon as possible. The proprietors left happy, and the court, by consent, ordered the articles of association for the new business to be drawn up.

But Walter did two things that would renew the anger of the dissident proprietors: first, he forgot to mention that in October 1906 he had renewed the contracts of the despised Hooper and Jackson. He had no choice, really. Hooper and Jackson had invested £124,665 9s. 8d. in the book club with very little as yet recouped, and The Times owed Hooper money–more than £20,000. The paper didn't have it. While Hooper didn't mind waiting, he would have minded being fired.

Second, Arthur Walter had amended the articles to make sure that he was recognized always as the "Governing Director of The Times Limited" and to "be so styled." He didn't seem to quite understand that one of the ambitions of the proprietors was to get rid of him, so anointing him "governing director" for life was out of the question. "One of the very objects of this action was to do away with Mr. Walter's autocratic powers of management which he has hitherto exercised," one of the solicitors representing the now-even-more-furious dissident proprietors wrote. "This will never be agreed to by our Clients and those supporting them now, the large majority of the Proprietors."

It was the perceived infection of *The Times* by the Americans—and especially Hooper—that had always been at the crux of this conflict. The unusual business activities at Printing House Square—the book club and especially the encyclopedia project—had always been a source of irritation, even anger, and now these moved to the foreground. Arthur Walter found himself unable to explain how the *Britannica* sales had buoyed *The Times* and how valuable had been the association with Hooper and Jackson. His inability was caused not by an absence of information but by a surplus of complexity.

Besides, as Stanley Morison's *History of "The Times"* put it, "The objection of this set [of proprietors] was to Hooper and all his profits as well as to Walter and all his autocracy." A new cohort of proprietors swung against Walter, this time blaming the advertisements for the book club for their decision. In June 1907, Brodie-Hall's lawyer succeeded in making Soames, the *Times* lawyer, reveal the renewed contract with Hooper. Reading that, Brodie-Hall said, was the last straw; by not revealing all that he knew, Arthur Walter, she said, "forfeited the last shred of forbearance with him on the part of the proprietors and of all indeed who know about it." Thus galvanized, Sibley and Brodie-Hall made common cause to get the support of other proprietors to go to court to get Hooper's contract nullified.

In response, Arthur Walter immediately called for a meeting of the proprietors. Patiently, and with Moberly Bell's help, he explained that the revenues brought in by Hooper and Jackson from 1898 until the previous year, 1906, had alone been responsible for supporting the continued publication of *The Times*. Sibley and Brodie-Hall stayed away, but many others attended and declared themselves satisfied. The result was the formation of yet another faction of proprietors, one that stood in opposition to both Brodie-Hall and Sibley, and for Arthur Walter.

Hooper and Moberly Bell understood clearly where they fit in all this. Moberly Bell knew he had been tattooed by his active involvement with Hooper. The schemes and innovations that had saved the paper were now seen by those who profited from it as evidence of a kind of descent into barbarism. Moberly Bell may have feared for his position, but even more he feared for *The Times*, for he truly believed that only he could safeguard the paper for its chief proprietor. Hooper—and to an almost equal extent, Jackson, preoccupied though he was with an impending marriage, this time to a dark-haired, beautiful painter from Connecticut named Eloise Carpenter—had another concern. They had a great deal of money invested in various activities, the *Britannica* especially, associated with *The Times*, and the idea that the business of the paper should cease to be closely influenced by them filled them both with dread. They would lose everything.

For Arthur Walter, the small proprietors were a tremendous threat. But to Hooper, they were a distraction. He wasn't concerned with printing contracts and dividends. In fact, he realized the turmoil caused by Sibley et al. might be a useful opportunity to implement a plan that would deliver both *The Times* and the *Britannica* into the same lifeboat, one that he would navigate into safe waters. It was a pivotal moment for Hooper, a golden opportunity, and he knew it.

He and Moberly Bell spent much of the summer of 1907 in Hooper's Grosvenor Square home giving his plan shape. The idea was to combine *The Times*, the Times Book Club, the Walters press, the *Encyclopædia Britannica*, and Hooper and Jackson's business into one big, Anglophone conglomerate, the GM of English, except solvent. Everything would turn on the events of that busy summer.

Since first learning of *The Times*'s financial problems ten years earlier, the goal had always seemed to Hooper to find a way to support a newspaper that cost a lot of money to publish, shouldn't be allowed to perish, but didn't make enough to survive. But of course, it was more than just a practical solution to a problem, more than a winning play. For Hooper, it was the object of the game. Hooper's dream was to level Babel and pave it with English, and combining all of his interests was the logical way to do this.

The thought of merging his interests in the *Britannica* with Walter's interest in *The Times* had been discussed before by Hooper and Moberly Bell. Once before, in 1900, when Hooper was in New York, the *New-York Tribune* had carried a story erroneously reporting Harmsworth's purchase of *The Times*. "If Mr. Walter wants to sell," Hooper had quickly written to Moberly Bell, "why can't we buy *The Times*?" The idea must have stayed with Bell, too. He and Hooper had by now tried everything—he had raised circulation and driven revenue and advertising up, but it was now clear that under the rickety business structure at Printing House Square, it would never be enough. Hooper's Anglophone plan, Moberly Bell was now certain, would allow for ongoing financial health, not only for the newspaper, but also for *Times*-branded publications, including atlases, gazetteers, anthologies—and especially encyclopedias.

The two men shared the same sentimental convictions about the paper. In fact, Hooper's reverence for *The Times* was, if possible, even greater than Moberly Bell's. Bell had been raised with *The Times*, while Hooper came to it with the zeal of the convert, all, as Janet Hogarth wrote, "part and parcel of his great reverence for what was the best in English life and English scholarship. It was this," she said, "which made him buy the 'E.B.' and devote his life to its development, and it was this which first drew him to *The Times*." Not only did he revere the office of the editor of *The Times*, "he knew this history of *The Times* backwards and forwards, the characteristics of every member of the Walter dynasty, the qualities and demerits of Delane, Chenery and all the other editors; and . . . he was full of great plans for improving its news service, its machinery, its print and paper, but always with the object of maintaining its great name and prestige."

He had felt the same way about the *Britannica*, said Hogarth. "There again he knew the history, the character and much of the contents of all the editions right back to the first and was never weary of reading them. He believed that in that one book alone lay an educational heritage which should be brought within the reach of every English reading person." Left to his own devices, he would "found a great educational trust, which should forever preserve this great property, be always seeking to improve it, and undertake its distribution throughout the English-speaking world."

Hooper later told others how he thought the business side of publishing shouldn't intrude in the workings of such important cultural institutions. They should be trusts. He would buy them and give them to the nation—to the English-speaking world. For Hooper, the *Times-Britannica* combination not only cornered the market on authority, it was the fulfillment of his dearly held ambition, one he was coming closer to realizing than he had ever imagined. This winning gambit with *The Times*, he was sure, would make it all possible.

For Moberly Bell, it was perhaps an ambition less exalted, but one that had the added advantages of securing the Walters' interests and his own job, dealing with the proprietors—who would simply become irritating stockholders, rather than a tribe of volatile and unpredictable co-owners—and, above all, protecting the character of *The Times* and the fortunes of those who worked for it. But Bell wanted to be certain that he was not being swayed by the emotional appeal Hooper's plan held, so, like a good manager, he vetted the plan carefully and sought advice from those he trusted, and he began including Arthur Walter in his thoughts.

Walter understood clearly the importance of Hooper's participation, as well as the difficulties it involved. Like Moberly Bell, Walter was appreciative of Hooper's demonstrated skills, but he was also completely aware of Hooper's role as a lightning rod for the animosity of his tormentors. He certainly didn't want to scotch Bell and Hooper's plan; indeed, the more he learned of it, the more appeal it had. He just couldn't think of a way to convince the angry crowd of Lilliputian proprietors shouting at the gates of Bear Wood that their salvation was to be found in a lifetime of ads that counted down all remaining days. They were unwilling to relent in their drive to oust the ruling Walter. Finally, he acquiesced to them: on July 18, 1907, the court dissolved the partnership and ordered the sale of *The Times*. Walter was appointed receiver. It would be up to him to come up with a plan everyone could accept.

He didn't have much to work with in that respect, and of course he was incompetent to do any work at all. All he knew for certain that the one thing *all* of the proprietors agreed on—and there really was only one thing—was that a public sale of *The Times* would be a disaster. It would destroy the paper, and all their six-tenths of one-fifty-fourth of one-half of a sixteenth, or whatever, would be worthless. They each knew they were all better off holding shares in a company that was in business than in holding fractional ownership of a company that was defunct. So whatever happened, everyone understood that it all must be dealt with quietly.

This restraint had a limit, however. It was essential to the small proprietors that *The Times* be separated from the influences of Moberly Bell and especially of Hooper and his ragtime band of admen and mini tycoons. Readers persistently complained of all the bookselling and huckstering going on in *The Times*. Moberly Bell must have written his treatise on the value of advertising a thousand times or more in letters to readers who were clever enough to read *The Times*, but not smart enough to see that the paper needed to make a profit. To the proprietors, Hooper was the man in the cheap suit, and nobody, with the obvious exception of Moberly Bell, wanted to be seen standing alongside him. They would, it seems, almost rather see *The Times* die than continue to live with such an "alien" presence in their midst.

Both Moberly Bell and Hooper were quite aware of this animosity, but nevertheless throughout that July and August of 1907, Hooper worked on refining the plan while Bell subjected the details of it to the scrutiny of an accountant, William Plender, a man discovered by Hooper and used by him for years. Then he went over them again and reported on them to Arthur Walter, sending, as the *History* put it, "schedule of figures, memoranda explaining the schedules, letters explaining the memoranda, and notes supplementing the letters." It seemed to be having an effect, like erosion, on the chief proprietor.

On July 25, in a letter sent to Walter from his residence at 22 Park Crescent, Moberly Bell repeated what was now his firm belief: "We cannot do more for two years than

William Plender, the accountant

balance receipts and expenditure." Hooper and Jackson, he said, were "our one chance of escape. . . . [W]e should start with Hooper and Jackson a scheme for floating a company of two millions, as one in which they could take shares in exchange for the present holding." He valued the company at around £400,000. If Walter had a controlling interest, Moberly Bell said, he'd be willing to buy shares in it himself.

Walter said he agreed that *The Times* could never be made to pay a profit by anybody, and he admitted that in any case, without Hooper, there would be no business to restructure. After consideration, Walter told Moberly Bell he thought he could endorse the plan the two men were hatching. He liked the way it would recapitalize the newspaper and retain many of its newer and more profitable relationships, and he was not opposed to securing the energy and expertise of Hooper and Jackson for the new business. By now, both Moberly Bell and Arthur Walter believed that, in view of the fact that nobody was making much money with newspapers, maybe publishing newspapers wasn't a great business to be in. After all, other men, including George Newnes and Philip Gibbs and Edward Steinkopf

Alfred Harmsworth, later Lord Northcliffe

and Cyril Pearson, had all tried and either had failed or were now struggling painfully to survive. The exception was Alfred Harmsworth, Lord Northcliffe, but nobody wanted to sell his soul for whatever salvation the publisher of the *Daily Mail* might provide. In late August, Moberly Bell finally gave Walter a formal proposal and asked for a quick reply.

But he didn't get one. Despite his encouragement of Hooper and Moberly Bell, Arthur Walter was playing two hands at once. He knew that his stepbrother, Godfrey, was at work on a rival scheme, one that would do the opposite of all that Hooper and Bell had proposed. Arthur Walter needed capital quickly and began quietly supporting Godfrey's plan with steps of his own, appealing to various friends, including Lords Lansdowne and Rothschild, while Godfrey worked behind the backs of Hooper and Bell with Plender, whom Hooper continued to trust, and another accountant, a man named Coward, to undermine the Bell-Hooper plan—all while drafting a new set of articles for "The Times Limited," as the new company was to be known.

Unaware of this, Hooper continued a strategy based on overcoming objections to his ways of doing business. He pointed to his string of successes and the money he had brought to *The Times*. And he echoed what Moberly Bell had already told the chief proprietor: "I have no desire here except to straighten out a mess that will simply continue to get worse and worse. I have no wish to interfere editorially—although I do think *The Times* is sometimes too discreet." All he wanted to do, he said, was to safeguard *The Times*—and, he might have added, keep at bay anyone who might threaten all those contracts and agreements.

But Walter said nothing. By October 1907, Hooper's practically nonexistent patience was gone. He went to call on Arthur Walter and delivered an ultimatum: "Look here, Mr. Walter, we have been talking with you almost three months now and have not, so far as we can see, advanced a step."

Walter disappeared for another ten days or so, conferred with his stepbrother, and finally said no. It was a critical moment for Hooper, but perhaps he didn't fully understand it. He didn't realize how defeated he was, and how mercilessly Plender, Godfrey Walter, and the others had treated him. He thought it was just a matter of putting together the pieces in a different way, so he didn't feel defeated. He did feel angry, and Moberly Bell was morose. But together, they were calculating.

Of course Plender didn't have to work very hard to convince Arthur and Godfrey that if *The Times* were just better organized, more subscribers would send in their £3 18s., and that if only Moberly Bell and Hooper could be sent away, the City—and especially the pro-German faction there—would be more forthcoming with investment,

Cyril Arthur Pearson,
contest winner and publisher

since a sacked Bell would mean a reassigned George Saunders, *The Times*'s highly critical Berlin correspondent. A new managing director would be needed, of course, and Godfrey Walter was thus introduced to Cyril Arthur Pearson, the publisher of the *Daily Express* and *The Standard*. The choice of Pearson as managing director of *The Times* would not have pleased the Germans, since he was a Chamberlain supporter and an advocate of tariff reform, but he was a better idea to them than Moberly Bell, and, unlike Hooper, at least he was British, and thus a known quantity; while the *Express* was a suspect newspaper—it ran actual news on its front page, instead of small ads. Pearson had been riding a rocket from obscure contest winner in 1900 to publishing magnate in the span of a small rodent's lifetime.

The acquisition in 1904 for £700,000 of *The Standard* from the Johnstone family had put the final polish on Pearson's reputation as a self-made man. And even though neither newspaper had become hugely profitable, Pearson had personally made lots of money on his way up—and he'd managed to keep most of it. He was also pushing himself; he was going blind and knew that he had little time left for newspapers. Riding out on the greatest English-language newspaper in the world would be a fitting farewell to publishing. Although knowing it would mean the end for Moberly Bell—and for Hooper and Jackson—Arthur Walter privately pronounced himself satisfied with Pearson, and Godfrey opened final negotiations with relief. To Godfrey, who had remained very much in the background until then, the man from *Tit-Bits* was a far better, much more acceptable alternative to those vulgar Americans and their constant, noisy making of money.

The need for absolute secrecy and discretion was paramount. Nobody at *The Times* knew about the Pearson negotiations. Godfrey and Plender hurried things along; the negotiations concluded on December 12, 1907, and for a few weeks things grew calm.

But suddenly the veneered Harmsworth, Lord Northcliffe, Pearson's archrival and a man who aspired to own *The Times* as badly as Pearson did—and who had been trying to acquire it for much longer—reentered the scene through a window left open by pure bad luck. Northcliffe's *Daily Mail* was going head to head against Pearson's *Express*, and winning. However, his purchase in 1905 of *The Observer*, published weekly on Sundays, hadn't yet paid off and had diminished his splendor; the paper was popular among the smarter set in London, but circulation was tiny, well below 7,500 copies a week.

At the end of a damp and chilled holiday season, Northcliffe and his wife had been invited to a post-Christmas dinner given by a peer who was on the board of directors of several companies, including the Great Central Railway. The night was horrible and foggy; Baroness Northcliffe called the hostess at the last minute to say they would be unable to attend, but the woman begged her to try, *begged* her, and so they arrived in mist, were received warmly, and were fed, and after dinner the ladies went into a drawing room while the men sat around and chatted about business, especially the big news of the day: the incipient merger between the Great Central and the Great Northern Railway. The host thought it was a lopsided marriage, almost nonsensical. The amalgamation of the two railroads, he said, resembled another unlikely merger, that of "the unprosperous *Standard* with the prosperous *Times*," an event close at hand.

Northcliffe gave a start. "Are you sure?"

"Quite sure."

Northcliffe knew that his host served on the railway board with Lord Farringdon, the chairman of the Great Central—and he also knew that Farringdon was one of the investors in *The Standard*. As soon as he got home, he called a man whom he knew to be a friend and neighbor of Moberly Bell and asked him to verify the story by asking Bell. But Bell dismissed it as a rumor of the day; laughing, he told his neighbor the joke about what happened when word got out that Lord Rothschild had bought *The Times*. "How much did he give for it?" was the natural question. The answer: "Threepence."

The news and the joke were repeated back to Northcliffe, who didn't laugh. He suspected he was on the brink of being outmaneuvered by his antagonist, and pressed for more information. After a day or so, he finally received confirmation of Pearson's victory from W. T. Stead, who told him it was too late, the deal was good as done.

On Wednesday, January 1, 1908, an agreement was signed quietly by Pearson and Arthur Walter. Circumventing the small proprietors, it ensured the Walters' positions and profits, gave them some additional financial guarantees, and included a handshake understanding that Moberly Bell and Hooper would both have to go. The document had no validity without the approval of Sibley and the others—and the court, of course—but neither Pearson nor Walter thought there would be any difficulty once it was known that Moberly Bell and the Americans would be shown the door. They would be before the judge, presenting the only possible plan moving forward, and out again before anyone could do anything about it.

Unaware of what was going on at Bear Wood, Moberly Bell that day set off for Calais to meet his daughter on her return from India. He would be out of touch and not back in his office again until the following Monday night. On Saturday, January 4, Northcliffe inserted the following paragraph in Sunday's *Observer*: "It is understood that important negotiations are taking place which will place the operations of *The Times* newspaper in the hands of a very capable proprietor of several popular magazines and newspapers."

George Earle Buckle saw the paragraph Sunday afternoon when he arrived at Printing House Square. He thought it was baseless, just some malicious gossip cooked up by Northcliffe to make things more interesting for himself. Arthur Walter wasn't in London—he was at Bear Wood, laid up with the flu—so Buckle sent the clipping down to him with a note saying he hoped Wood might find the enclosed amusing.

It wasn't amusing, of course, and the next morning Godfrey Walter was at Buckle's door. He was excited, having just conferred with the accountant Coward, and needed to compose a brief story. The solicitors for the small proprietors were already filling the Chancery court, and it was too late for Monday's paper in any case, but it should go into type immediately and run Tuesday morning.

Buckle was stunned; the *Observer* paragraph was true, then. He knew Moberly Bell couldn't be back until that evening, so he suggested to Godfrey Walter that the item be written as merely a vague denial. He was rebuffed, and wrote Arthur Walter privately expressing his fear that whatever advantage there might be in selling out to Pearson, Walter should also consider "his association in the public mind with a Press of very different aims and ideals. In other words ... I fear his *name* may do us harm." On Tuesday morning, the 7th, when Moberly Bell arrived in his office, he read this in his paper:

Negotiations are in progress whereby it is contemplated *The Times* newspaper shall be formed into a limited company under the proposed chairmanship of Mr. Walter.

The newspaper, as heretofore, will be published at Printing House Square.

The business management will be reorganized by Mr. C. Arthur Pearson, the proposed managing director.

The editorial character of the paper will remain unchanged, and will be conducted, as in the past, on lines independent of party politics.

The contemplated arrangements will in all probability require the sanction of the Court before they become definitive.

Moberly Bell had been warned, of course—although not by Walter. He had been approached by a *New York Times* correspondent who had, it seems, just interviewed a very pleased Pearson, and had been given the information that both Buckle and Moberly Bell "will shortly retire." In fact, the front-page story that ran in *The New York Times* on the 7th was much more detailed than anything read by readers of *The Times* the same day. It was filled with inside information that could have come from many sources, and certainly not all of it from Pearson, who must have cringed when he read the paragraph that began, "Mr. Pearson, who thus comes into the control of England's historic newspaper, was described by Mr. [Joseph] Chamberlain as 'the greatest hustler I ever knew outside of America.'"

Northcliffe now was enjoying himself too. He and Pearson were perceived, quite accurately, as two competing "yellow" newspaper-men; they were the monsters readers and proprietors of *The Times* conjured when they wanted to imagine the worst for their paper. Northcliffe used this perception to great advantage in praising Pearson. As the *History of "The Times"* put it, "The world was being prepared for the hustling of the historic journal into reorganization, revision and perhaps revolution."

That day, the *Daily Mail* ran a lengthy article on the proposed sale along with a sardonic editorial: "Mr. Pearson is to be warmly congratulated on his great success in securing control of *The Times* at a point relatively early in his career. Our best wishes will follow Mr. C. Arthur Pearson in his newest and greatest enterprise." Northcliffe also wired personal congratulations from Paris, where he was staying, and a surprised Pearson replied, delighted. The next day, the *Daily Mail* ran an extremely flattering profile of Pearson, and the gullible Pearson sent a note to Northcliffe saying, "I trust I may have an opportunity of showing one day how much I appreciate your action." What Northcliffe thought would happen, happened. While for a day, most people—including the nervous proprietors—assumed that, since the initial telltale paragraph had appeared in *The Observer*, Northcliffe was the "capable proprietor" mentioned, now they suspected it was worse. It was Pearson.

It would appear that the *Times* correspondent may also have spoken to Kennedy Jones, Northcliffe's dutiful lieutenant, who had been talking to everybody he could find that Monday, even to Hooper, who had instantly started his own quiet campaign to frighten the small proprietors over the risk Pearson represented to *The Times*'s venerability. Hooper, after all, knew the business of *The Times* better than anyone, except perhaps Moberly Bell—and he understood it much better than either of the feckless Walter brothers, who happily admitted they knew or understood very little about any of it. Pearson wanted to be rid quickly of Moberly Bell, Hooper, and Jackson—it was essential, if the small proprietors were going to agree, or if *The Times* were going to recover ad revenue from the publishers.

But an outright confrontation with them was something he feared, as he revealed in a confidential letter written to Arthur Walter in mid-January 1908, only two weeks after the agreement had been signed:

I hope we shall not have much trouble with Hooper and Jackson. Jackson came round to see me yesterday afternoon and I had a long talk with him. He says they wish to sever their connection with *The Times* as rapidly as possible, and that they do not want to cause any trouble, all they require being a financial basis of settlement shall be arrived at. . . . I am very glad to hear your views of running no risk of an open break with Hooper and Jackson. They are in a position, both with regard to the Book Club and the Advertising Department, of making themselves excessively disagreeable. In fact so far as these two most important departments are concerned, they can really hang things up entirely for six months if they choose. They are very busy over their new book [the Eleventh Edition] and I feel sure they have no desire to fight. Jackson made a great point that the History of the World [Jackson's own multivolume reference set] shall receive every possible assistance from The Times Book Club and I have told him this shall be done. Obviously as it is a publication of *The Times* we must do what we can to help it.

In view of subsequent events, it's clear that either Jackson was strategically prevaricating or he had very little idea of how the Eleventh Edition was going to be published. The editorial costs had by then reached $700,000, and there was still much more to be done.

Northcliffe was quite happy to sit in Paris and lazily fan flames as the Pearson agreement slowly went up in smoke. He knew Pearson was cash-strapped and he knew too that the small proprietors would greet a Pearson regime with all the animosity they previously had directed toward Hooper and Moberly Bell. He also knew Pearson well enough to realize that Pearson was quite capable of simply talking his deal into oblivion. Pearson couldn't keep quiet. With the signed New Year's agreement in his pocket, he suddenly felt comfortable telling everyone who would listen that he was buying *The Times* but really couldn't discuss it.

Northcliffe, meanwhile, directed Kennedy Jones to seek out Hooper and get from him whatever useful information could be obtained. And this, as it happened, would suit Hooper and Moberly Bell perfectly, for they were now furiously working together and in opposition to Pearson—although not on behalf of Northcliffe. For Hooper, defeating Pearson was all that mattered for now. It was a matter of survival. For him, it wasn't just a matter of no *Times*, no encyclopedia. It was now no Moberly Bell, no encyclopedia.

For Moberly Bell, it was a matter of principle. He had written to Arthur Walter immediately after learning of the Pearson plan, badly injured that his friendship with his employer through all those years and through all of the efforts by Bell to keep the Walters' boat afloat should be unceremoniously ditched in some backroom deal reported in another newspaper—a deal that Walter knew would result in Moberly Bell's dismissal. "Forgive me if I say," Bell wrote the day the story about Pearson's purchase ran in *The Times*, "that I cannot help feeling deeply hurt at the want of confidence you have shown in one who has tried to serve you faithfully, and who regarded you as a friend." ("That," his daughter later wrote, "was the only protest on his own behalf that he made to anyone.") A few days later, he wrote again, this time offering to renounce his salary, if not his position, so he could work against the Pearson agreement. "I want you to know as much as I can what I am doing, and I want you to have absolute faith that in all I do I am acting solely in what I believe to be the best interests of *The Times*."

Tuesday, January 7, 1908, had been a busy day for Pearson, what with all the flattery from Northcliffe, the attention of *The New York Times*, the statement in *The Times* itself, requests for interviews (usually granted), and the congratulations from friends and enemies, fulsome on both sides. Pearson needed to keep his own ranks in order, however, so he invited his managers and editors from *The Standard* to meet him at the Savoy Grill so he could reassure them that all was well, that *The Standard* would carry on, and that their jobs were secure.

But also in the Savoy, just a few hours before, Kennedy Jones had come in search of Hooper, found him, and slid into a chair next to him. "I see from the papers, you're going to have a new proprietor at *The Times*."

Hooper smiled. "I guess that even in this country a man cannot sell property which does not belong to him."

Jones told Hooper that he was interested in buying *The Times*

Kennedy Jones, the dutiful lieutenant

himself, but it's not likely that Hooper gave that idea much credence. He knew Jones was merely a puppet and knew who pulled the strings. Hooper must have marveled at his own good fortune, for here was the representative of a man with a great deal of money and interest, obviously directed to accidentally wander in off the cold Strand, into the warmth of the Savoy Grill, where Hooper often lunched, and strike up a not-very-casual conversation. And here am I, thought Hooper, full of useful information. So as Hooper ate, he also fed Jones all that he wanted Northcliffe to know. He ended with a gruff warning: if the proprietors knew that Northcliffe was behind an effort, they would move quickly to oppose it, fearing that they'd get something even worse than what Pearson threatened to give them. Hooper told Jones he had access to as much as £350,000 himself, and would like very much to buy *The Times*, but any idea that he was involved in a purchase, Hooper said, would bring down the curtain instantly, just as it would for the likes of Northcliffe. Moberly Bell, he said, might make the best stalking horse. "See Bell for yourself later," he told Jones. "I will arrange it."

Convincing Moberly Bell to accept Northcliffe, even as an alternative to Pearson, wasn't easy for Hooper. Bell's first reply: "Never." But he knew that he and Hooper really had no other direction in which to go. Hooper might have been able to pull off something, but Moberly Bell's involvement would tip off anyone interested that Hooper was involved, too; the two men, sometimes joined by Jackson, were seen together everywhere. Northcliffe, however, had the

The Savoy

money, and he certainly had the will. But he also needed Moberly Bell, since Bell was the most logical person to front the takeover without arousing the suspicion of either the press or the proprietors, provided he could make it clear that his financial backer wasn't an American, and especially not Hooper. Besides, everybody knew Moberly Bell wanted to buy *The Times*. It was widely known that he had tried to find other backers after Arthur Walter rejected the offer he and Hooper made; he had even gone to the well of free trade financing, to Evelyn Baring, Lord Cromer himself, the highly influential former consul general of Egypt, and from him to others who shared his views. But it had all come to nothing. Hooper promised to find money from a British source, from somebody who would guarantee the independence of *The Times*, and somebody who would guarantee the jobs of those who understood the character of *The Times*, especially Buckle; his assistant, W. F. Moneypenny; the influential Valentine Chirol; and, of course, Moberly Bell.

On January 17, the court heard Godfrey Walter's plan to sell to Pearson. The judge gave the proprietors until March 15, 1908, to consider their acceptance. But the proprietors were already obviously unhappy with the idea of Pearson. In the clubs of London, the idea was ridiculed; one old friend of Walter's sent him a note saying,

"[W]e do not want to see *The Times* trampled in the dirt by the men of the *Tit-Bits* school."

General John Sterling, a descendant of the original Thunderer and the largest stakeholder after the two Walters, withdrew his support. Three days later, the next most powerful proprietor, Sir Edward Tennant, also withdrew, saying to Walter, "It is held on every hand that under the direction of Mr. Pearson *The Times* could not maintain the traditions of the past." Pearson's agreement was quickly turning into old fish stuck in the stylish pocket of Godfrey Walter.

But by then, yet another secret scheme had been hatched. Moberly Bell had revealed to Buckle that he thought he had a backer. Buckle feared it was Hooper—in fact, an article in the *Daily Graphic* had reported as much—but Bell assured him it was a Briton and a wealthy one with an understanding of *The Times*'s problems. Buckle was very apprehensive of the idea of an anonymous backer, but nonetheless began working inside Printing House Square to keep the staff settled and to do whatever he could to diminish Pearson's chances. Hooper, to quell any suspicion that he was the mystery money man, fled to the Continent.

Meanwhile, to check on his own instinctive dislike of Northcliffe—the two had met several times, most recently in 1906, when they argued over the book club—Moberly Bell made a list of all the potential backers *The Times* might find at hand to save it from a public sale. Included on the list was Northcliffe's name. Moberly Bell then sent the list to all those with whom he had been meeting, asking that the name of any unsuitable proprietor of *The Times* be struck off. When the lists came back, no one had drawn a line through Northcliffe's name. So he then went to Arthur Walter to tell him that he might have an idea for a new purchaser of the newspaper.

With Hooper, then Jackson, on one side, and Kennedy Jones on the other, the two sides—Moberly Bell, representing Arthur Walter and *The Times*'s interests, and Northcliffe, representing his own—began working out an agreement that would carry them forward. On February 3, Northcliffe sent Hooper & Jackson Ltd. a letter:

I am desirous of purchasing *The Times* on behalf of myself and others, and I authorize you up to June 30th, 1908, to negotiate for the purchase of the copyright thereof for any sum up to £350,000. I agree to be satisfied with the purchase at that price.

It is understood that I shall not be liable for any litigation between *The Times* shareholders and that my only legal expenses shall be those properly incurred by you in the negotiations, which shall not exceed £10,000.

Kindly acknowledge this.

Jackson went to find Moberly Bell and give him the details of this first definite proposal from Northcliffe. Bell's concern—and it was a question Jackson couldn't answer—concerned the "guarantees": the preservation of *The Times*'s character, the continued employment of the senior editorial staff, and the like. The next day, just as Sterling was announcing his withdrawal from the Pearson agreement, Jackson and Moberly Bell arrived at Northcliffe's accountant's office in Sackville Street and there the two met for the first of many meetings. "Well, Mr. Bell," Northcliffe said, "I am going to buy *The Times* with your assistance, if you will give it; without it, if you will not."

Moberly Bell explained that he had met with Arthur Walter, and felt he had smoothed the way. Walter's agreement, he said, had been based on what Kennedy Jones had said about the guarantees. Northcliffe assured Bell that he had no interest in changing the nature of the paper and offered him the managing directorship of the new company. The meeting ended with both of them congratulating the other for having "saved" *The Times*.

But now Moberly Bell was pushing the issue of control, of wanting his guarantees observed. Nothing was going to make Northcliffe feel friendship for Bell, or vice versa. For a brief moment, Bell had leverage in this, and that moment was passing quickly. Jackson tried to warn Bell that when people like Northcliffe spend a lot of money buying something, they prefer to control things themselves. But this preoccupation by Moberly Bell became such an obsession that when Jackson passed along a message from Northcliffe asking, "Now Mr. Bell what do *you* expect to make out of this?" Bell's response was: "If I could save *The Times* and get it carried on on the lines [you] indicated I should be content even if I lost money on it."

That reply, of course, infuriated Northcliffe. He sent Alfred Sutton, his assistant, around to Bell's home in Park Crescent—on a Sunday, early. It was February 9, 1908. Northcliffe had heard about Bell's guarantees for four days, and that was enough. Moberly Bell came downstairs in robe, unshaven, and looking, Sutton later told Northcliffe, "every inch a Brigand." From a briefcase, Sutton took the long list of "guarantees" Moberly Bell had given to Northcliffe. It was still unsigned by Northcliffe.

Sutton gave it back to Bell, then dictated Northcliffe's simple terms to Bell: managing director for five years, carrying out absolute instructions. The only other "guarantee" was Northcliffe's agreement that the "present policy in Home and Foreign Affairs should be continued under the Editorship of Mr. Buckle and Mr. Valentine Chirol."

Bell signed, and to the document he added a small obsequious footnote: "In my former letter I desired to make *no conditions*. I merely wished to express what I believed to be your ideas." Sutton went, and Moberly Bell was left to shave, dress, and pull together the rest of the deal, anonymous investor included, for Northcliffe. Bell contacted Sterling, and by February 11 he had the most important of the small proprietors to help him carry a banner. The "Bell-Sterling" scheme attracted support from some of the proprietors and further shifted attention away from Hooper as the suspected financier behind Bell.

On February 14, Pearson withdrew his offer, his support by now almost completely gone.

The strategy Northcliffe used was very much like the strategy Pearson used, except Northcliffe didn't talk, but he did add farce. Hooper and Jackson quickly came onto Northcliffe's side, eager to protect their investments. Northcliffe traveled to Boulogne-sur-Mer for meetings with Moberly Bell, Hooper and Jackson, and sometimes Kennedy Jones at the Hotel Christol, a belle epoque establishment filled with palms and rattan and English people; W. S. Gilbert was among the regulars. Northcliffe signed his notes and messages "X" and assigned the others code names—Hooper was "Adelaide" and Jackson was "Demerara," but Northcliffe was "Atlantic," a shortened form of "Admiral of the Atlantic," something the Kaiser also called himself. From the French coast, he sent his orders and received information. From mid-February until mid-March, Bell and Jack-

Hotel Christol, Boulogne

son deployed agents in the City to scout for news from Wilhelmina Brodie-Hall's camp, still out there in the tall grass. Soames, *The Times*'s solicitor, discovered that Brodie-Hall's German backers were going to make an attempt on persuading the court of an alternative plan, but then it was revealed that the German government was associated with her effort, and that undermined her enormously.

On March 2, Moberly Bell put his offer of £320,000 on the table.

As the March 15 decision date approached, there were three contenders: Pearson, who was trying to find more money to rekindle his bid; Brodie-Hall and all her Germans; and Bell and Sterling. The two latter camps preferred each other's offer above Pearson's, whatever it was. Northcliffe had deposited £320,000 into Moberly Bell's bank account; to prevent surprise, Northcliffe told Hooper and Jackson he was prepared to go to £400,000, if necessary.

The Ides was now upon them, but April 15 was a Sunday. On April 16, Brodie-Hall and her backers asked for a two-day delay and were refused. Pearson had withdrawn. That left only one valid offer– Northcliffe's, hidden behind Moberly Bell's name. The judge asked if there were any others, but there were none. *The Times* had been sold. On March 17, 1908, readers of *The Times* learned:

His Lordship Mr. Justice Warrington yesterday made an order sanctioning an agreement under which a company will be

The lobby of the Christol

forthwith formed to take over the business of the publication of *The Times* newspaper and the undertakings carried on in connexion therewith. Mr. Walter will be Chairman of the Board of Directors, which will consist solely of existing members of the Staff—Mr. George Earle Buckle, Mr. Valentine Chirol, Mr. William Flavelle Moneypenny, with Mr. Moberly Bell as Managing Director. No share will be offered to the public.

There will be no change whatever in the political or editorial direction of the paper, which will be conducted by the same Staff on the independent lines pursued uninterruptedly for so many years.

The statement had been approved by the judge, who then sealed the proceedings of the hearing. Moberly Bell sent a discreet telegram to Northcliffe in care of his valet: "Gone through as we wanted," and later that evening, Hooper and Jackson sent another coded note to Northcliffe: "Dear Admiral Atlantic . . . Not only the British public but all friends of Great Britain will some day know what a great good you have done for the nation and it will be appreciated.

Yours sincerely, Adelaide of Demerara." Northcliffe acknowledged the message and assured them that the Times Book Club and the *Britannica* were foremost among all the changes he would not be making.

The next day, congratulations arrived for the apparent victors. John Morley, at the time one of Britain's most eminent "higher" journalists, sent a congratulatory note to Buckle that any man editing a newspaper would love to receive: "I rejoice that the ruinous schemes of a few weeks ago have been frustrated. . . . [A] real public misfortune has been avoided, and you may have been rather gratified at the testimony so universally furnished to the hold your Olympian Organ has upon the world's imagination and esteem."

A single London newspaper, the *Daily Chronicle*, the next day reported that Northcliffe was behind the new company, but the report was ignored.

The insistence on secrecy, on hiding Northcliffe's role, on perpetuating the myth that *The Times* was run by Moberly Bell, Buckle, and the others, persisted for years, even long after Northcliffe's ownership was common knowledge. However, there was great unease among the paper's editors and writers—Buckle especially felt that Northcliffe was barely better than Pearson, and Walter seemed to agree, although Moberly Bell said frankly, and correctly, that *The Times*, and the Walter family, had squandered the loyalty of them all and missed the paper's best chance when Walter betrayed him and refused the Hooper-Bell offer of 1907. But what was done was done. Bell pointed out to Buckle and the others that at least they still had their jobs—something that wouldn't have been true if Pearson had been successful.

Only a dozen people—Moberly Bell, both Walters, Hooper, Jackson, Kennedy Jones, Chirol, Buckle, Soames, Sutton, and Sterling—all going by the bizarre code names invented by Northcliffe, knew the truth. And only three of them knew a further, more troubling truth: Moberly Bell had no guarantees at all.

Now for an explanation of why these details about proprietorship squabbles, book wars, and Northcliffe's maneuvers all mattered to the *Encyclopædia Britannica* project: the unjustified calm that had settled over Printing House Square and its denizens was broken by the convening of a special jury before Mr. Justice Darling, in the King's Bench Division of the High Court. The case: *Murray v. Walter*, with Murray claiming damages for libel because of the "Artifex" letters Hooper had placed in *The Times* in October 1906.

Hooper could not possibly have found a worse court to hear his case. Mr. Justice Darling was Charles John Darling, a delicate, untalented, fifty-eight-year-old judge who longed to look down his nose at others but, because he was thimble sized, required judicial furniture to do so. His appointment, from the Tory backbenches, had been an overtly political one and had caused some outrage, even on the other side of the Atlantic, thanks to *The New York Times*'s acerbic reports. "Mr. Darling ... is the author of an amusing little work entitled 'Scintillae Juris,' small in stature, juvenile in appearance, a dandy in his dress, and addicted to strong adjectives," noted the paper when his judicial appointment was made in 1897. A couple of days later, just to make sure New Yorkers got the (somewhat obscure) point, Darling was elevated to the front page, where he was the subject profiled under the headline reading "Bad Judicial Appointment":

[A] worse piece of jobbery than the appointment of Charles John Darling, Q.C., Conservative, member of Parliament for Deptford, to the judicial bench would be hard to find. When it was first mooted, the strongest protests against the appointment were evoked, and since it has been made, as announced on Thursday last, the leaders of the bench and bar and the public of both parties have severely and openly censured the step taken. . . . [T]his feeling is so strong that the more unruly spirits of the law courts are talking of organizing a demonstration of disapproval, to take place when Mr. Darling is sworn in.

"He is," the London correspondent concluded, "practically briefless"–a comment Mr. Justice Darling might have put to good use, since his chief judicial strength was a ready catalog of not-bad one-liners he used to draw attentive journalists to his courtroom and cheer what to him appeared to be the dull business of a court of law.

NERVOUS WOMAN IN THE WITNESS BOX: *I—er—don't know how to address you, sir. Do I say Your Worship? Your Honor? Your Lordship?*
THE JUDGE: *Just call me darling.*

HOUSE MOVER: *So we raised the house and . . .*
COUNSEL (INTERRUPTING): *What did you raise it with?*
WITNESS: *Four jacks.*
THE JUDGE: *I would have raised with four jacks, too.*

Exchanges like these assured Darling a courtroom packed with journalists waiting for the next witticism to enliven a murder trial—or a libel case.

Murray was represented by Winston Churchill's great friend Frederick Edwin Smith, KC. F. E. Smith was a frequent sparring partner of Darling's. Once, after making a careful but complex explanation in a capital case before Darling, the judge, impatient, said, "Well, after all that, Mr. Smith, I am none the wiser."

Smith calmly replied, "Perhaps none the wiser, m'lud, but certainly better informed." The crack earned him an "Impudent!"—and his client the gallows.

Hooper's trial lasted four days, beginning on May 5, 1908, and a great deal hung on the decision. Hooper was vulnerable; the Times Book Club was being recast as a financial drag; he and Jackson felt the draft from an open window, and if *The Times*—meaning Hooper—lost the case, Hooper and Jackson would almost certainly be asked to leap through it. With them would go a great deal of money and effort and the *Britannica*'s home at *The Times*.

Hogarth went to the court every day to watch the proceedings, as did a reporter from *The Times*. Mr. Justice Darling was his usual bright self. On the first day of the trial, when the defense tried to explain the view of *The Times* that the price of books was kept unreasonably high, Darling broke in to say that the high price of books wasn't relevant. "It might only show that *The Times* are as bad as they say other people are," he cracked. And when Moberly Bell testified concerning the heat generated by the book war, he recalled that *The Times* had "published a letter, from a client of Mr. Murray, Miss Gertrude Atherton, in which she said, 'I can tell the Editor of *The Times*, in my best Californese, to go to the devil.'"

Darling interrupted. "That might increase the circulation of *The Times*," he said to an approving gallery.

The trial focused on the activities of the publishers as much as on the alleged libel. The jury heard how *The Times* in its coverage of the book war "had treated its opponents with extraordinary fairness," as even some of the publishers acknowledged. However, "these publishers, who were doing all they could to injure *The Times*, were yet sending their books to be reviewed by it." Indeed, Bruce Richmond, editor of the *Literary Supplement*, explained how he tried to keep the book war, the book club, and the interests of the publishers apart from the critical coverage the paper gave new books.

The publishers, the court heard, had threatened other publications with an advertising boycott if they supported *The Times*, and Murray himself had worked tirelessly to destroy sales of the *Britannica* and had been among the most aggressive publishers in attacking the book club. At one point in his testimony, Moberly Bell even offered Murray £3,330 "for the use of it only in order to produce 100,000 copies of the book"—a figure that Bell reckoned to be the true cost of production. "I do not want an answer now," he said to Murray. "You can have 24 hours to consider it." *The Times*'s barrister tried to defend the letter, saying, "[I]t was clear that the writer of the letter was referring throughout to gross profit," to which Smith retorted, "What was said now is that Mr. Murray was not a net rogue, but a gross rogue."

The courtroom was diverted by the Smith and Darling show, but not everyone interested in the trial was watching the comedians. Hogarth, who, she said, attended to study "the demeanour of the protagonists in the witness box," was most impressed by Mr. H. E. Hooper.

> With his few words and the slight but most expressive use of gesture habitual to him, he faced both the cross-examination of counsel and the further cross-examination he was subjected to by the Judge. "How long have you been a publisher?" asked Mr Justice Darling in the tone as of one who should say, "How dare you call yourself a publisher?"

"All my life since I was a boy," replied "H.E." quite simply, though quick as a flash an intuition of the Judge's innuendo passed across his face and was gone.

Hooper's testimony, on May 7, was frank and direct. He had indeed provided "Artifex" with the information in the letters and had suggested that they be written and inserted into the paper. Moberly Bell's agreement to do this may have been suspect, but it was not particularly unusual; as we've seen, he was aware of the usefulness of an apparently disinterested witness in constructing a persuasive narrative; he'd used the technique himself more than once. But, Hooper was quick to add, he had not been targeting Murray; rather, he despised Murray's "publishing methods," and those of other publishers: "I am against the excessive profits of publishers generally, not of Mr. Murray." When asked what he expected Ross to do with the information he'd been given, Hooper said simply, "To write a letter on the high price of the book." And the thirty-two pieces of silver? "I think he thought it a bright way of putting it." Do you write your friends like this? "Mr. Murray is not my friend."

Northcliffe wasn't watching Smith or Darling or Hooper. As the testimony continued, he was walking down St. Martin's Street, having just left the office of William Heinemann, and now Heinemann was on the telephone to Frederick Macmillan. Northcliffe, he said, had just been by and was now coming to see you.

The meeting with Macmillan was brief and to the point; Northcliffe had no interest in "the excessive profits of publishers generally" or even in Murray and the other publishers individually. He told Macmillan what he had told Heinemann—that he was the new proprietor of *The Times*, but not to tell a soul, and that one of his first orders of business was to put an end to the book war and return to advertising contracts for *The Times*. Macmillan took notes:

He said Moberly Bell and his circle were absurdly but firmly convinced that publishers were a wicked race of men, who made outrageous profits and committed all sorts of crimes against the reading public, and he said the staff of *The Times* were also so fully imbued with the same idea that he was afraid if he gave in to the publishers too openly they would all resign their positions, as indeed they had threatened to do when it was supposed that C. Arthur Pearson was going to control the paper. Lord Northcliffe said that he himself was in the ridiculous position of having to defend the libel action of *Murray v. Walter*, and of hoping he would lose it, because if *The Times* were successful in the action the staff would be more than ever convinced they would be in the right and "there would be no holding them."

Northcliffe complained that the book club was too expensive, netting a mere £20,000 a year after expenses—although Moberly Bell had put the accounting differently, noting that the club had made £50,000 in ten months and increased the number of subscribers by 27,000, a huge rise. Perhaps Northcliffe was unsure how to calculate lost ad revenues because of the publishers' boycott. In any case, Macmillan told him the book war would end when the Times Book Club accepted the publishers' terms—although, he added, "we might make some minor and unimportant concessions for the purpose of 'saving the face' of the paper." Northcliffe agreed. He had, he said, put his personal secretary to work "at the T.B.C. under the assumed name of 'Mr. Bates' . . . and asked me if I would see this 'Mr. Bates' if he called and discuss the whole matter with him. This I agreed to do and our interview ended."

The next day, May 8, 1908, the final day of the trial, Macmillan and Heinemann contacted other members of the Publishers Association, told them all what Northcliffe had said, and considered what terms to dictate to *The Times*. Among the publishers' nonnegotiable points: the Times Book Club would stop discounting net books and "neither Mr. Moberly Bell nor Mr. Hooper shall be deputed by *The Times* to conduct the present negotiations."

In court, the morning had been given over to Mr. Justice Darling's peppery summation of the case and the conflict that had caused it. The judge didn't care for Hooper and his unorthodox American ways and made him very much the target of the case. It was all Hooper's deceit and manipulation that had led Moberly Bell astray and had caused Murray to be injured. His weapons, the letters he had masterminded, had been designed to cause Murray harm. Hooper, he said, "did not profess to be a literary man." He was merely an American "business man," so he "had gone looking for a letter-writer, some one to do what he could not. He said he did not want to find a prophet who would prophesy for Mr. Murray, but one to prophesy against him. What a pity that the appropriate creature was not there to warn him!"

He droned on, weaving between weak one-liners and glib recapitulation: what good was a "book war," he wondered, when "it was not even regulated by the Geneva Convention." He rambled for over an hour before he finally sent away the jury to deliberate. They returned in thirty-five minutes and awarded Murray £7,500. "There was some applause at the back of the court," *The Times* reported, "which was instantly stopped."

Hooper lost the case, and much more. By the end of the next month, neither Hooper nor Jackson had any affiliation with *The Times*, and had turned on each other. The encyclopedia project would be homeless, near both completion and collapse. The paper had a new advertising manager and a new circulation director—and the book club had a new manager, Kennedy Jones.

A few weeks later, Janet Hogarth encountered Hooper on the street and complained that the staff had been decked out in uniforms, that books were piling up unsold, and, worse, that Jones had instituted a "censorship" policy preventing the availability of books the content of which he did not approve. Rather than acquiesce, she had resigned.

Hogarth: "Think of Kennedy Jones and the purity of literature."

Hooper: "Think of Kennedy Jones and literature, let alone purity!"

CHAPTER 14

HIGH HOLBORN

Hooper struggled to make an orderly retreat. He pulled back his best staffers from the Times Book Club and gave them work at 125 High Holborn, then set about catching up on the encyclopedia project, starting with the features he felt most likely to contribute to sales. The index, Hooper felt, was failing to progress, so he asked Janet Hogarth to look at the methods being used. If she thought the Book Club had been disorderly, she found the *Britannica*'s chaotic quarters even more chaotic. Small wonder the encyclopedia staff had remained aloof from the trials and all the associated distractions. The index, she discovered, was being built as entries arrived. Information was added to index cards that were attached to galleys hung about the rooms. The High Holborn offices had a look of failed festivity. Suddenly, Hooper would appear without warning in an effervescence of rat-a-tat orders, ideas, and comments, then disappear unexpectedly—often to go back to America, mostly to New York, but sometimes much farther west, sending orders back to London from camping sites out in the Rockies. His frequent disappearances at critical moments provoked *Punch* writers to track his movements: "the Judicious Hooper leaves for America in the 'Vitriolic' in a huff," for example.

Jackson's appearances were even more sporadic; his own business dealings with Northcliffe occupied much of his time. Arthur Mee's *Children's Encyclopedia*, Northcliffe's very popular serial publication, had just launched successfully; Jackson was intent on securing the American rights to the thing and organizing its publication and the two men worked to negotiate an arrangement. He had virtually no involvement, other than to create obstacles, with the daily work of building the Eleventh Edition of the *Britannica*.

Indeed, when he could, he ignored it. Jackson's interest in the Eleventh was mostly limited to expressing concerns about expenses and trying to keep Hooper's many empires from being built. He exhausted himself trying to convince Hooper to publish the encyclopedia in parts, thinking to lessen the enormous financial risk the men were taking. Jackson was a businessman, not an artist or a dreamer. He had been skeptical of Hooper's grand Anglophone-monument idea, and any interest he had in Hooper's lofty vision of a cultural institution, a concept that seems to have driven nearly all Hooper's decisions, evaporated along with the collapse of *The Times*'s buyout scheme. Hooper's announcement that he would never subscribe to Jackson's volume-at-a-time strategy and instead would try to raise $1.5 million—either from bonds or from banks—to enable publication of all volumes of the encyclopedia at once filled Jackson with horror.

Through the rest of 1908 and early 1909, relations between Hooper and Jackson grew more and more tense. Rumors circulated in London that the two men were quarreling. This alarmed the banks financing the encyclopedia project—something that pleased Jackson, who thought the encyclopedia should be financed on a pay-as-you-go basis anyway. Hooper's occasional outbursts in High Holborn had been overheard. He was becoming more confrontational in his criticisms of his putative partner's devotion to his private ventures, including the children's set, a project that, after all, would limit the ability to exploit the *Britannica*'s brand appeal. Indeed, Hooper had already outlined a "junior *Britannica*" to be edited by Hogarth.

A month after the *Murray v. Walter* trial, Hooper was railing at Jackson's lackadaisical attitude. "I have had to push you and Bell before I could get your help and co-operation to push the public," he wrote, "and I have no more intention of going on with it than I have of flying. I am perfectly satisfied to close up the business and let it go. I believe there would be no more trouble, that you and I would each not get more than a million dollars out of it, and I shall be quite happy to retire to the United States with that money and live the rest of my life. . . . I certainly think it is fair to point out to you that for 10 years I have certainly done more than half of the work in the business and I think you would also acknowledge that I have made more than half the money."

Hooper took refuge high in the Rockies with William and Roger, his twin sons from his first marriage. "We eat nothing but elk or deer meat all the time and soon hope to have bear steak," he wrote Hogarth in September 1908. A month later, "we chased a bear (or rather two) for 11 hours up and down mountains till finally we lost him, or rather we lost the sound of the dogs and had to give up. For the last hour we rode home on a trail that if the horses made a false step would have gone down 1000 or 1500 feet without stopping. The trail was not over a foot wide and we had to ride in the dark"—impossible unless one trusted completely the instincts of the horse. He told Hogarth he didn't know when he'd be back.

He seemed detached, but he managed to stay in touch with affairs, telling Hogarth in a letter that he felt Northcliffe was "making a fool of himself" in the matter of the book club. And in 1908, when he felt *The Times* was threatening to abridge its agreement—and when Jackson's menacing legal maneuvers finally grew intolerable—"he just walked into his offices one day at High Holborn when he was still thought to be in the Rocky Mountains," wrote Hogarth.

Angry confrontations with Jackson followed for the rest of that year and into 1909, with various insincere buyout offers and unpleasant meetings that often ended leaving Jackson sullen and Hooper furious.

The *Britannica*'s London office was apparently unaffected by Hooper's long absences. Hogarth and Sickert had more than enough to do without "Hell Every Hour" giving them more. Haxton, with, as Hogarth put it, "his nimble brain in his twisted and failing body," was often away in America to rest from the effects of an apparent breakdown, leaving Sickert to carry on in his place.

Chisholm had begun assembling an editorial staff in 1903, immediately after the result of his content audit became known. He built it around those who had helped him with the Tenth Edition, and put Phillips in place as his number two. Soon, the rooms in Printing House Square were once again busier and more crowded than they had been since the hectic compilation of the Tenth.

But High Holborn was the heart of the *Britannica*, especially as the Eleventh Edition entered the frantic final stages. Staffers came from Printing House Square, a mile away, to High Holborn, where Hooper & Jackson Ltd. occupied as many as a dozen rooms. Phillips or Chisholm or Fisher would preside over these luncheons as Sickert, Haxton, Hogarth, Frank Sala, Gosse, Garrett Fisher, John Malcolm Mitchell, friends, and contributors would all crowd around the tables in a large boardroom. An invitation was a much-sought-after ticket. The food was provided daily by Claridge's, and the conversation was always interesting. Contributors, some of whom used High Holborn as a postal address, wandered through, looking for mail and conversation. Sometimes specific problems were discussed with the editors, but often the topics ranged across art, literature, and science, along with the events of the day and the comings and goings of the literary journalists of the day, many of whom had worked for Hugh Chisholm at *The St. James's Gazette* before and for him at the *Britannica* after. It was very much a clublike scene: "There never was an office so gay, so self-confident, so crowded, so uncomfortable, yet so irresistible in its attraction," recalled Hogarth. "Everyone who ever left it drifted back, or clamored to be re-engaged." Salesmen, paper merchants, printers, ad writers, crowded into the *Britannica*'s rooms, where Hooper's audacity was always among the entertainments, the others enjoying, and sometimes imitating, his brittle, American twang—especially the long "*Saaay*" he'd use to launch his sentences.

Although he may have had less formal education than anyone else in the room, he enjoyed and often led the give and take. "He was," wrote Hogarth, "in every detail of book manufacture . . . an expert . . . [and] a great believer in the pooling of ideas [and] never regarded himself as indispensable." He was also as quick as any of the others. Hogarth recalled "discussing index conundrums one day"; the topic was the unpleasant nature of public transportation, specifically New York City's "principal source of pandemonium"—the elevated trains. "Where would you put the 'El'?" one indexer asked. Hooper instantly replied, "Why, under H of course."

How the people in the room came to be members of that "club" varied crazily. Some, like Haxton, were founding members. Others, like Chisholm, enlisted, and he brought with him many more—

Fisher; Phillips; a bit later, Hogarth; and finally virtually anyone who had ever done anything for the Tenth or for the *Jimmy*.

Some were there thanks to Hooper, of course. One newcomer to the staff, Arthur Croxton, had been given the job of managing the Eleventh Edition's business production after only a ten-minute sidewalk interview. Hooper had spotted Croxton, a true bon vivant who had developed a good reputation as an editor for George Newnes at *The Tatler*, as he was leaving Clifford's Inn, just off Fleet Street. Hooper halted him with a *saaay*, chatted briskly about the problems of producing and promoting a set of books the size of the Eleventh, and hired him on the spot. Although he knew Hooper's name, Croxton barely knew anything else about his new employer. "Until one became an associate of his, one knew little of H. E. Hooper and his knowledge of men and affairs, his quiet control of the most diverse elements comprised in those who write for, and those who produce, an Encyclopædia, his honesty, his fairness and (once one got to know him) his charm," Croxton later wrote.

He might also have mentioned Hooper's irascibility, his audacity, and an affection for administrative shortcuts that often shocked others. Once, for example, John Malcolm Mitchell, an editor of the index with additional responsibility for entries on ancient history, archaeology, European anthropology, and biblical history, noticed that the account of the archaeological features of Corsica and Sardinia were out of date and mentioned it to Hooper. Hooper instantly produced a check for £350 and told Mitchell to find an expert someplace and ship him out to the islands.

Another time, Hooper rushed out of the office to meet with the historian James Thomson Shotwell, who had turned up in London, broke and on sabbatical from Columbia University. Unbeknownst to Shotwell, Hooper, in a fit of anger, had just fired Chisholm over a minor dispute and, without any apparent deliberation, impulsively offered Shotwell the *Britannica*'s editorial chair on the spot. "I have had a number of major surprises in my life," Shotwell remarked later, "but nothing compares with this incredible incident." Shotwell met Chisholm, liked him, and turned down Hooper. "I had never lived in that commercial world where such ruthless things are done," he later wrote.

The eruption quickly calmed and the apparently unflappable Chisholm returned to work, golf, club, and lunch-as-usual. It's not clear how serious the breach was; Shotwell's account is the fullest one. In some ways, the feelings of the American and the Briton toward each other mirrored the way the two nations often seem to be connected. "The relationship between High Chisholm and 'H.E.' was a very close one," wrote Hogarth. "Probably neither knew how much each really owed to the other." It was true, as Hogarth observed, that " 'H.E.' had given Hugh Chisholm his chance . . . but Hugh Chisholm could bring to 'H.E.' those traditions of scholarship which he reverenced above everything and could not get on his side of the water." Hooper often made this complaint, too, but surely somebody from Columbia, Harvard, Princeton, or Yale must have been able to measure up, if it came to that. Franklin Hooper was a Harvard graduate and well connected in reference book publishing. Besides, Chisholm may have been a very accomplished student, but his professional output wasn't actually "scholarship"—it was journalism, albeit often of a pronounced scholarly, even literary, character. However, another remark by Hogarth does a much better job of explaining why Chisholm was necessary to Hooper's marketing vision: "A British editor for a great British book of reference was essential."

The American market was never far from Hooper's thoughts; American sales were to be the payday of the project. And Hooper's romantic ideal required an intervening ocean and the associations of history and culture to give luster to his multivolume collection of artifacts of undisputed wisdom received from on high—from, say, a university like Oxford or an imperial capital, like London, and not from Kansas State or Chicago or even Harvard. Certainly, putting an American in charge of the project would have affected perceptions of the *Britannica*, making it much more unabashedly democratic and commonplace, something more American—something Hooper seemed always at pains to disguise.

More than that, it may have had other, unknown consequences (and this kind of speculation is slightly instructive). Because the encyclopedia Chisholm was producing reflected his understanding of the world, and because the Eleventh Edition became so widely accepted as an ultimate authority on all things—an authority that stretched over generations and to a certain extent endures today—what Chisholm thought was the way many, if not most, people of his class thought. In American political terms, Chisholm was a progressive Roosevelt Republican to Shotwell's E. V. Debs. Had Shotwell—the godfather of the International Labor Organization and a Progressive with pronounced political, cultural, and social views, many of which were almost completely antithetical to Chisholm's—decided to suspend his academic career and throw in with Hooper, the view of the world produced by the *Britannica* might have revealed a radically different planet.

But he didn't. So Hooper accepted Shotwell's decision without apparent rancor. In fact, he appointed him joint assistant editor (with Phillips) and paid him the same salary as the editor in chief—about $15,000. And the equanimous Chisholm apparently was happy to have him.

For the most part, Chisholm and his staff ignored the City gossip and the Hooper-Jackson-Northcliffe theatrics and patiently quilted together the thousands and thousands of entries needed to make a giant encyclopedia. By 1908, some of the staff had been working on the Eleventh Edition for five years, perhaps longer, slowly maturing the articles that would eventually find their way into printer's slips. This all took place in an office so filled with cartons, files, scraps of papers, writers and layabouts, books and notes that it hardly seemed suited to the compilation of a difficult, organized work. In fact, Chisholm and his staff had already moved once, in 1904, relocating their entire operation from one corner of Printing House Square to another. The editorial staff now worked on the third floor of the ancient pile.

As the work passed the 20-, 30-, and 40-million-word marks, the paperwork for the tens of thousands of articles grew more and more dense, one layer of notes covering another, many attached to galleys. The earlier drafts and the card notes and correspondence that were attached to each one of them, all keyed to manuscripts of articles in various stages of development, floated about as editors rushed toward the last stage of editorial work: the publication date in 1910 was only eighteen months away. Tracking the changes in a subject in the real world and noting those changes in the entries themselves—to ensure the encyclopedia's timeliness—became an art. Editors working in different rooms carried dossiers for articles back and forth, consulting over long, library-type tables and making sure the pieces meshed sensibly.

As primitive as this system seems to have been, it was a significant improvement over that used in compiling the Ninth Edition, with its serial publication of twenty-four volumes over the period 1875–1888 (the final volume was published in December of 1888; 1889 is the year of publication conventionally given). Revisions in galleys were a nightmare; Adam W. Black once lamented what he called "that bugbear of all publishers and that apparent delight of most authors, the corrections on the proof-sheets. In our case, these corrigenda amounted to what was equivalent to setting up the twenty-four quarto volumes from beginning to end twice over. That," he added, "formed a rather serious charge in the printer's bill."

Chisholm's office resembled Chisholm's life—he surrounded himself with friends and familiar faces, and he was famous as a club man, with daily visits to the Athenæum Club—even though the *Britannica*'s offices leaned more toward the Drones end of things, with Chisholm often found testing a new putter before a small cluster of amused analysts. Despite the need for organization and efficiency, Hogarth, when she was brought over from the book club, found the office was "one of the worst managed I had ever seen. The clerks boiled water all day long and wasted more time than even in Government offices." Few women worked there, other than the indexers, whose work had been largely overlooked in the effort to simply bring in clean copy, but who had been brought under Hogarth's supervision.

The atmosphere seemed to change, however, as one ascended the editorial hierarchy, from the kettle-watching clerks, past the assistants and the advisers gathered round the assistant departmental editors and the departmental editors, and to the circle of top assistant editors—sixty-four editors altogether—clustered at the bottom of an ascending stair guarded by Chisholm's faithful and diligent assistant, Arthur B. Atkins. Here the air grew more rarified and less steamy, and the desks seemed less chaotic, the work more deliberate.

One pacifying feature of the staff was Chisholm's deputy. Although he had been second—both officially and de facto—to Chisholm for years, Walter Alison Phillips became a central figure in the *Britannica*'s fortunes during the crucial two-year period that began in 1908. Not only was the cousin busy with his editorial duties, he also became a kind of intermediary between the editors and Hooper, with whom he struck a close, if unlikely, friendship—perhaps based on their coincidental connections with the Rocky Mountain West. He had a history with the region and knew it quite well.

His older brother, Lawrence, had lived in Denver at the same time Hooper did, although we don't know of a meeting. He was one of a trio of adventurous Phillips brothers who had left Britain for the American West on a lark in the 1870s, ostensibly as investors in a cattle ranch, but ending up as ranchers and saloonkeepers—one of the brothers, Arthur, fell into the part ownership of a bar and general store at the highest point on the Union Pacific's line. Lawrence had been called to the bar in England before leaving, and returned to practicing law when the cattle business lost its charm for him. Alison, the youngest brother, had stayed in England. For the Eleventh Edition, he wrote several major articles and many minor ones.

In addition to Alison Phillips, Chisholm also had the help of Shotwell—at least in the initial stages—and as an assistant, another ex-colonial, William Edward Garrett Fisher, a frequent contributor to the *Fortnightly Review* and, later, to the *Daily Mail.* His popular book on the Boers had just been published to general approval, not least because of its patriotic sentiment. When Fisher remarked that the Transvaal Railway was crippled by massive "jobbery and bribery," he was sued by the proprietors in London for libel. He took on his own case, told the court that the plaintiffs, the Netherlands Railway Co., were "alien enemies," produced a letter from the railway's manager boasting of the aid the railway had given the Boers, and walked out of court victorious and, for a week or two anyway, quite the hero. In his pieces for the *Fortnightly* and the *Mail,* he had carved out a niche for himself as a chronicler of curiosities; articles, like his "Art of Flying" in the *Fortnightly* ("the announcement of the sad death of Mr. Percy S. Pilcher, from an accident to his artificial wings on the 20th of September, was probably the first intimation that people at large had of his experiments," he wrote in 1899), and his essay on the municipal woes of Glasgow had attracted attention. On the staff, he was often given the offbeat and unusual topics. Others, like Mitchell, who had experience with the work or those who had a history with Chisholm at *The St. James's Gazette*—such as Sala—or who were seen by Chisholm and the others as good editors and administrators were brought in to create a staff of experienced editorial managers who could work congenially under pressure with a very large number of contributors, subeditors, and editorial advisers. "He really did gather round him a galaxy of talent rarely, if ever, equaled amongst the contributors to any other publication," recalled Hogarth.

Chisholm ultimately was able to claim a total of 1,507 contributors, including, as a *Britannica* prospectus put it, "the whole world of scholarship and expert knowledge," including 704 scholars from 146 colleges and universities in 21 countries (and not counting 54 university chancellors and presidents); 168 fellows of the Royal Society; 57 fellows of the British Academy; 47 senior staff members of the British Museum; 238 scholars representing various national libraries, observatories, laboratories, and "learned societies" around the world; 4 Russians; 2 Japanese. Of these, as noted, 35 were women.

A staff in New York, under the supervision of Franklin Hooper and the American historian Charles Crawford Whinery, coordinated the work of the 214 North Americans, including contributors Wright (Carroll, American labor issues) and Wrong (George, Canadian history). In speeches to American audiences, Chisholm made certain to remember "my friend Professor Shotwell of Columbia," and he gave Whinery's work, and that of the North American contributors generally, a great deal of praise, perhaps for the benefit of potential buyers in the U.S. Once, at a banquet at the Plaza where Whinery was in attendance, Chisholm included him in the opening toast, saying, "I cannot pay too high a tribute to the loyalty and efficiency with which Mr. Whinery, in charge of my American office, has carried out this work, in the course of which he has also kept a vigilant eye on the articles for which the London staff were responsible, in order that any work done on those subjects by American writers might not be overlooked." Whinery, in addition to his own entries on La Salle and Lincoln, often sent Chisholm comments on proof sheets suggesting adds and edits and what Chisholm described as "original mind-stuff" that took American research and readers into account, suggestions Chisholm said he was "delighted" to accept.

Administratively, areas of interest were divided among a large number of young university graduates. Each of them was responsible for a list of topics and managed the assignments approved by Chisholm or one of the top editors. Chisholm or one of his deputies directed the copy flow and reviewed articles as they came in to be certain there were no missing elements or parts of an article that were duplicated by another editorial assistant's contributor. Once the articles were approved, they were returned to the editor responsible, who then had to monitor events surrounding his topics to be sure that none of them fell out of date between the time they were accepted and the date of publication—a period that could be as long as seven years. The editorial budget was huge, more than £250,000—all of which came from Hooper and, at least initially, Jackson.

Chisholm rarely scolded or chastised; it didn't seem necessary, something perhaps easier to see at the time than now. Other than Hooper's occasional tantrums, there are few accounts of feuds or bickering or factional infighting in the office, and even the out-of-office advisers and such were for the most part content to do as they were asked. Actually, the only suggestion of infighting is the complete absence of Franklin Hooper's name on much of anything written or spoken at dinners and banquets by Chisholm. Similarly, Franklin Hooper had little to say on the record about Chisholm. But there's also no evidence of a quarrel. For the most part, even difficult situations seem to have passed smoothly. In 1905, when Chisholm had to write to James Alexander Manson, who had been a subeditor of the Tenth Edition, to tell the expert on bowling that "after several years of pleasant association," he would "not be able to retain [Manson's] services on the staff of the E.B.," Manson went without complaint.

A few flare-ups did occur—the quashed "revolt" (on which, see below), for example, or the time Harriet Hennessey, an Irishwoman who had not only "wit and blarney" but also a sharp tongue and a Belgian medical degree, and who was normally a great favorite of Chisholm's, went in to Chisholm to discuss adding new developments in pain management during childbirth to Sir Alexander Russell Simpson's article on obstetrics. On her way back down the steps, she was heard to shout over her shoulder at Chisholm, "Well, at any rate we might have something newer than what Adam did for Eve when he was left alone with her in the Garden of Eden!" Men such as Shotwell, who might have fomented discontent as a simple exercise of workplace politics, opted instead to support Chisholm's effort because they understood and approved of the plan, the man, and his position.

Chisholm was indisputably a British Conservative, but he was also a Victorian skeptic. "He was so strong a politician and so convinced a Tariff Reformer and Constitutionalist that Protection and Die-Hardism had a way of creeping in and upsetting the balance," said Hogarth. "'Chamberlain and I,' he would begin—the irreverent declared that it sometimes became 'I and Chamberlain'—and go off on a dissertation which was really a political speech. When the Parliament Act and the creation of peers were burning questions, we, Liberals on the staff, rejoiced that *Parliament* and *Peerage* were already stereotyped and past any possibility of change. 'Don't you flatter yourselves,' retorted our Tory colleague T. K. Ingram [sic], 'he'll get his own back on *Veto*.'"

CHAPTER 15

THE SINGLE ORGANISM

To fashion the "single organism" that was to be the Eleventh Edition of the *Encyclopædia Britannica*, Chisholm worked to a plan that built on both the Ninth and, especially, the Tenth Editions.

The Ninth Edition was, in a way, most useful as the kind of encyclopedia Chisholm wanted to avoid. Long, disconnected, but very authoritative articles unrelated to anything else in the book—Chisholm called them "a collection of detached monographs of the highest authority and value"—was not the idea, and Chisholm went to great lengths to explain that the Eleventh Edition "is much more than a revision—is, indeed, a new edifice as compared with the structure of the Ninth Edition."

The problem with the Ninth, he wrote in an editorial introduction to the Eleventh, was not caused by editorial incompetence, but by the "system of publication"—the appearance of volumes one at a time. This, he said, meant that the Ninth Edition could "have no proper unity of conception of uniformity of treatment. It cannot be planned from the beginning so as to present at its completion a satisfactory synoptic view of any department of knowledge. The historical record is restricted by the accident of the dates at which the separate volumes are published." This, he said, created a situation in which "the facts included in one volume may contradict those in another." Instead, despite Chisholm's assertions to the contrary, the Tenth Edition in many ways was a prototype for many of the processes, people, and conventions used in the Eleventh. The nine supplemental volumes that, with the Ninth, constituted the Tenth Edition had been published one after the other, but over the course of only nine months, nothing like the sixteen years it had taken to issue the Ninth from the first volume to the last. Nevertheless, Chisholm explained that in his mind, the Eleventh was the "lineal descendant" of the Ninth, "for the name of the Tenth was used only to indicate the incorporation of supplementary volumes which left the main fabric untouched."

He was also sensitive to the recycling of older pieces, from one edition to the next. While admitting that "due acknowledgement must be given to those who kept the sacred fire burning in earlier days," there was a limit to the heat of venerability: Chisholm warned against the model, used in the previous editions, in which "the reverence due to deceased authority was perhaps carried to extreme lengths," citing the Eighth Edition's recycling of Sir Walter Scott's article on "Drama," which had appeared in the Fourth, Fifth, and Sixth Editions unaltered, as his entry in the Seventh admitted.

No doubt marketing concerns were at work, for after the advertising blitz used for both the Ninth and the Tenth, it was important to diminish the value of the older sets and position the Eleventh Edition as a "new edifice." In fact, both the Ninth and the Tenth had substantial impact on the Eleventh, since many entries in the Eleventh were carried over from previous editions. However, the manner in which this was done provides interesting glimpses of Chisholm's careful methods.

One of the most influential articles in the Ninth Edition was the entry on psychology by the Cambridge philosopher-psychologist James Ward. The article positioned Ward far from many of the more controversial theories, including associationism, which the *Britannica* covers in its own confusing and unsigned article only to finally dismiss it. On reading it, William James wrote Ward to say, "I think no competent person will deny that this article, by itself, marks the transition of English psychology from one epoch to another. It will be impossible after it to discuss things from the meagre and superficial standpoint of the classical English school and its critics."

Psychology then was in a transitional period characterized by James as "chaotic fermentation," and Ward's theories fell afoul of those held by Associationists such as E. B. Titchener, an influential British-American (Cornell via Oxford) psychologist who wrote a detailed critique of Ward's Eleventh Edition coverage of psychology for *The American Journal of Psychology*, examining how the original Ninth Edition entry on psychology changed over three editions, through the Eleventh. These notes shed light on how Chisholm shaped older articles to serve in the Eleventh.

Titchener begins by observing that the three articles had been edited with "extreme care; everywhere there is weeding, pruning, dovetailing." The "original" (that is, the Ninth Edition) article was forty-nine pages long. The Tenth reduced this to seventeen pages. But the article in the Eleventh is fifty-eight pages long, and, as Titchener points out, the pages of the Eleventh are larger.

The introductory passages of the three are very similar, "unchanged" in substance, Titchener finds. In section 3, under the heading "General Analysis," he finds that a paragraph on Pragmatism has been deleted. But the following sections, 4 through 8, "practically repeat the ninth edition," Titchener writes. In the ninth section of the entry, "the fine-print discussions of the subjectivity of sensations, of the connection between subjective attention and objective intensity, and of the non-presentability of feeling and attention are . . . omitted." The subentry on the "Subconscious" has been entirely rewritten for the Eleventh and the graduated type size shows that the topic was increased from brevier to long primer. (Alexander Bain, John Stuart Mill's early collaborator and the founder of the journal *Mind*, wanted it raised to pica, to demonstrate its significance.) The subentry devoted to "Sensation, Movement and the External World" derived its title and much of the text from the Tenth Edition. "Sensation" itself is from the Ninth. Most of the remaining subentries survive from the Ninth Edition, although Titchener (who has his own entry) notes that the subentry for "Belief" has been given its own heading and "raised to the dignity of long primer." New material is provided for the subentry on "Presentation of Self, Self-Consciousness and Conduct" while the final subentry on "Freedom" is new to the Eleventh. The subentry on "Relation of Body and Mind" is lifted from the Tenth, as is the appendix, section 48, on "Comparative Psychology." A list of "Authorities" at the end is revised from earlier editions.

Categorization of the entries in the Ninth Edition was made problematic by their structure; as Chisholm noted, "[T]he Ninth Edition was wanting in precisely that character of interdependence in all its parts." And trying to fix that, he added, was impossible without starting over. He gave the Tenth a more conventional structure: the entire work (the Ninth plus the supplemental volumes) was arranged into nineteen straightforward categories, each the bailiwick of an editorial department overseen by category editors who appointed contributors to their sections, with a tier of associate editors and subeditors supporting them:

Law and Government	Art
Military Affairs	Zoology
Medical Science	Naval Affairs
Theology	Biography
Mining	Literature
Botany	Economics
Geography and Statistics	Railways
Astronomy	Music
Mathematics	Games and Sports
Electricity	

For the Eleventh Edition, Chisholm added six principal categories. Where the Tenth used a categorization that avoided over-conceptualization, the new categories were broader and much more conceptual, allowing for flexibility and a framework that reflected the somewhat aspirational galaxy of articles in the Eleventh.

Gone, for example, were "Mining" and "Railways" and "Electricity." Instead, Chisholm folded the former into a category called "Structure of the Earth," which included articles on volcanoes and earthquakes, and the latter two into the broadened "Engineering" category, which contained many of the cutting-edge areas of technological progress, including tunnels, canals, bridges, balloons, flying machines, steam, water power, building, and locomotion, as well as electricity.

Also added to the Eleventh's universe was a category that would have made no sense at all to many readers of the Ninth: "Welfare of the Individual and Social Betterment"—492 articles on subjects such as "Life of the Community and State," legislation, trade and commerce, and finance and history. Also new in the Eleventh: the category "Education," with 172 articles on educational theories, the histories of universities, and entries on specific academies and schools, and an important new category, "The Science of Mankind"—458 sometimes controversial articles reflecting Darwinian revisions of ideas surrounding "the development of the human race and of civilization; races and antiquity of early man," along with entries on mythology and folklore. A major article on "Relics of Early Man" was moved to the category embracing "Art, Monuments and Implements of Antiquity."

Also new: "History of Thought," comprising 643 entries covering some of the hot-button issues of the day in philosophy and ethics, and, reflecting the shapeshifting of spirituality that began in the nineteenth century—and Chisholm's own respectfully curious but skeptical views—a rather lengthy, detailed entry on a topic that captivated many Edwardians, including even Lord Rayleigh: spiritualism. The entry is by the feminist founder of Newnham College, Eleanor Mildred Sidgwick, and includes information on things such as "psychical knockings" and "psychical photography" and connects readers with related entries on conjuring, automatism, divination, crystal gazing, hypnotism, apparitions, hallucinations, and hauntings.

Instead of the "Medical Science" category, the Eleventh takes a more pragmatic view in a category called "Cause, Treatment and Prevention of Disease." It consists of 644 articles, including practical entries on physiology, hygiene, anatomy, surgery, pharmacology, vivisection, and public health.

"Theology" is replaced by a more sociological-anthropological view of comparative religion, with 3,049 articles on primitive, ancient, and non-Christian religions. Topics relating to Christianity (including history, doctrines, and sects) are covered, along with history and criticism of the Bible, the Koran, and other sacred literature. But the Eleventh Edition is not intended to be a tool for Anglican proselytism, and the kinds of controversies that beset the editors of the Ninth do not apply to the Eleventh—which is not to say that Catholic and Protestant leaders were unconcerned with the Eleventh's coverage. Chisholm tried to be fair, but, as we shall see, he did not successfully avoid the displeasure of some religious critics.

In the end, of the 40,000 articles, only 1,674 were left without a category.

Alexander Coleman and Charles Simmons, modern journalists, break down the statistical distribution of entries in the Eleventh Edition this way: geography (29 percent), pure and applied sciences (17 percent), history (17 percent), literature (11 percent), fine arts (9 percent), social sciences (7 percent), and, at the bottom of the list, psychology (1.7 percent) and philosophy (.8 percent), although this kind of enumeration can be misleading. Lewis Campbell's article on Plato alone is sixteen pages long.

The entire project was intended, Chisholm later wrote, to fashion a kind of unified narrative out of many different voices. Compilation of the Eleventh, he wrote, "could proceed in all its parts *pari passu*, the various articles being kept open for revision or rewriting, so as to represent the collective knowledge and the contemporary standpoint of the date which the whole was issued." This was at the center of Chisholm's vision and a reflection of Hooper's all-at-once publishing plan for the encyclopedia. It's not surprising that those he entrusted to help him realize his goal were those he knew well. Journalist-scholars, including Ronald McNeill and Frank Cana and other names familiar to those who had been at Limmer's for Chisholm's big dinner in 1899, moved from slot to slot, doing whatever was asked of them. While others had more fixed roles—scholarly specialist-advisers, such as G. Herbert Fowler, the prominent oceanographer, were easily out of their depth in an area not their own—for the most part, the staff above the adviser level were loyal generalists. Phillips, for example, not only surveyed most entries but, because of his standing as an important younger historian, also took a special interest in the 6,292 historical and political articles in the Eleventh.

Partly, this was a convenient matter of interest. But it also served Chisholm's vision of a sense of woven information in which the warp of his indirect, delegated editorial navigation might be sufficient to prevent unpredictable or eccentric conclusions. For example, Dr. Peter Chalmers Mitchell, secretary of the Zoological Society of London, and Dr. A. B. Rendle, the keeper of the department of botany at the British Museum, were asked not only to contribute articles but also to supervise the creation of others in order to give unity to the whole of the 1,886 entries on subjects botanical and zoological. Chisholm had an instinct for miscellany; he knew that to create a reference work that encompassed all things known meant that the work's editorial cartography had to include all those landmarks, events, personalities, and objects that people would expect to find in an encyclopedia, along with a good dose of things a reader would have never thought of but would be glad (and amused) to find. (See, for example, "Loincloth," vol. 7, p. 226.) Thus Chisholm's article list seems to have been intended to do the wise thing, editorially: meet all reasonable expectations, then exceed them in carefully considered but novel and interesting ways. The editorial staff was enlisted in mapping "the whole field of human knowledge," of course. Chisholm claimed in his introduction that they started "afresh"—although common sense and Hogarth's later admission suggests that the staff started with the 600,000-entry index to the Ninth, at least—"under the advice of specialist departmental advisers, who, in providing for the occupation of the different areas, cooperated with a central editorial staff, comprising many members, each of whom was responsible to the Editor-in-Chief for a particular section of the work."

Most of the latest advances found a place on the list, so of course the sciences were exceptionally well represented in Chisholm's compilation; the volumes feature many, many charts, diagrams, and graphs that add a graphical richness to portions of the text dealing with technical and scientific material. The nineteenth century had been shaped by scientific discovery and the rise of scientism as a form of secular belief—as a transcendent view of existence. The Eleventh would serve as a book of the acts of the scientists of the age.

There are 11,341 entries on geography and cartography in the Eleventh, most of them compiled under the nominal supervision of the geographer Henry Newton Dickson. The world was quickly shedding the mystery of places unknown—the Nile, sourced; the Pole, reached; Livingstone, found a lifetime ago, now as dead as his presumptuous "rescuer," Stanley. The Eleventh was catching up with the world: naturally, it was a kind of top-level gazetteer, examining the trade, customs, religions, arts, crafts, and sciences of the nations of the world, the principal provinces and states, the cities and towns, the rivers, lagoons, and islands of a planet finally and fully charted, known and shown on beautiful maps painstakingly created by the German cartographical firm of Justus Perthes and by Emery Walker, William Morris's mentor. In the selection of entries and on the maps—bound not in a separate volume, as before, but as part of the appropriate articles—the Eleventh Edition was edited the way small-town newspapers are edited: not just the grand cities of the world, but every small hamlet gets its name in the *Britannica*. Mankato, Minnesota, and Superior, Wisconsin, get full-blown articles, but even Mankato, Kansas, and Superior, Nebraska, are in the index and on the beautiful maps, their little dots no doubt making easier the job of the encyclopedia's salesmen working in the hinterlands. (To make room for the dots of the Anglosphere, towns and villages of an equal size in France, China, and elsewhere distant from marketing considerations are generally omitted.) In the great compendium of all known knowledge, the things a reader cares about, the things a reader hopes to find—one's home, school, church, town—all of these details seem to say that though the cosmos is a huge accumulation of data, you, dear reader, are *here*.

Some senior editors, like Edmond Gosse, by now librarian to the House of Lords, took single-handed charge of their own vast empires—the Eleventh contains more than 4,100 entries on literature and writers. Not a few of the contributors were already Victorian cultural celebrities: J. B. Bury, Charles Eliot, Jesse Weston, Frederick Jackson Turner, Algernon Charles Swinburne, Cardinal Gibbons, James Murray, John Muir, Peter Kropotkin, T. H. Huxley, Arthur Symonds, William Michael Rossetti, and Alice Meynell. Moberly Bell, a frequent office visitor, contributed his entry on Nubar Pasha. The machinery of the editing process was harnessed to the clerks and assistants. The *Britannica*'s young and mostly anonymous Edwardian editors were working with the most eminent Victorians—sometimes in revising their work from previous editions. Most of the entries appealed to the hopeful, utilitarian values of the time; there is no "Hate" in the Eleventh, and very little "Love"—and most of that confined to sensible contexts (Christian, Buddhist, Cartesian, Platonic, etc.).

The compass was always Chisholm's; there was never any confusion about who was guiding and shaping the Eleventh Edition of the *Britannica*. At both Printing House Square and High Holborn, his perch was up a flight from the others, where he sat "thinking with his pen," as Hogarth put it—that is, when he wasn't gadding about the office or off at his club or out on the links. He was physically imposing, confident, very happy in his work and at home and even happier in the company he had assembled, his laugh often heard above the others, his discussions animated with an enthusiasm amplified by a taste for amateur dramatics. Nearby was his gatekeeper and private secretary, Arthur B. Atkins, who, Chisholm later wrote, dealt "with all the problems of editorial control." Editors went up with dossiers, notes, and insightful questions, and came down with the clear instructions they felt they needed. Chisholm directly supervised all of the instructions given to contributors assigned major articles, and there are thousands of these.

Shorter pieces he assigned to the editorial staff, thus ensuring that the bulk of the articles were in on time and required little fitting. He guided many of these as well; he had an impressive talent for seeing what a reader would want to know about a given topic, a nearly infallible ability for knowing how to apportion article length according to subject, and an instinctive sense of how to structure the articles themselves.

In the Eleventh Edition, this was a very complicated issue. Each entry of any length was presented in a way that makes the hierarchy of information obvious. Most entries begin in pica, equivalent to 12-point type, but as additional information is insinuated into an entry, the font size drops first to long prime (also called "long primer"), which is 10-point type. The small print comes at the bottom of longer entries in brevier, or 8-point type. The relegation of some subentries to long prime or brevier could be a matter of controversy and argument.

All of this, Hogarth later recalled, was present in the detailed outlines he gave to contributors of important or complex articles. He often used advice given him by the staff's specialists, but regardless of subject matter, the outlines became a sort of conceptual editorial template that he applied to every topic touched by the encyclopedia, including those about which he knew little. Hogarth once noted that the outlines of articles given to contributors by Chisholm might make a better encyclopedia than the one they were all working to produce.

That's not likely, given the Eleventh's "systematic survey of all departments of knowledge," as she described it in her index volume. Chisholm's gift was an editor's skill–knowing what we don't know, and knowing who might. Who else could explain the jeejeebhoy but Sir Mancherjee Merwanjee Bhownaggree, a Parsee and the former Conservative MP for Bethnal Green? Who could trace the outline of "Dust" but John Aitken, the scientific expert on airborne particles, fog, and clouds. And who but Lawrence Chubb, the green-spaces pioneer, could draw a ring around "Smoke"? The subject of children's games was put in the hands of Lady Gomme, who had devoted her life to playground folklore, and the entire English language itself was handed over to Sir James Augustus Henry Murray–James Murray, the man making the dictionary that Oxford would publish the same year the Eleventh appeared. Sidney Low may have been given the celebrated Randolph Churchill but Flora Shaw, Lady Lugard, was given the entire British empire.

Between all these conventional entries were the things-one-never-thinks-of that give any broad reference work its flavor and tone. Sandwiched between the anodyne entry for "Abortion" and Stanley Arthur Cook's elegant and engaging article on Abraham is "Abracadabra," complete in a paragraph that includes not only its Gnostic origins and its pejorative use "by the early opponents of the evolution theory . . . to a conception or hypothesis which purports to be a simple solution of apparently insoluble phenomena," but also the instructions on how to fabricate a Gnostic amulet two different ways. "Adultery" lacks excitement and is a disappointment, but it backs into Haxton's characteristically animated article on "Advertisement," largely reprised from the Tenth Edition. Although an effort was made to avoid text too sere for reading, the Eleventh doesn't exactly brim with epigrammatic style; for a book with so many words, very few find their way into *Bartlett's*. Very few are even contractions. But some articles are more eccentric than others, and among the most peculiar is Haxton's, of course, which stands out as an example of effervescent, pedagogical harassment not far removed in style from the ads used to sell the encyclopedia itself.

Admittedly, Haxtonian prose is an acquired taste, but clearly Chisholm had acquired it, since Haxton's article stretches over five pages of the first volume. (One staff editor, Cecil Weatherly—a barrister and classics scholar, and, later, the editor of *Webster's Handy Modern Dictionary* [1916]—was detailed to add verifiable legal data about the Advertisements Regulation Act and such.) The idiosyncrasies of personal style aren't obviously suppressed in the Eleventh; indeed, the voice of individual writers seems to be preserved, where such a thing can be preserved; many experts the staff selected to write about a topic they know well were not particularly colorful writers, even if they are lucid and authoritative, as, for example, Edward Venables, whose exhaustive study of abbeys is a brilliant monograph of surpassing insight.

But many others convey the lightness of journalism, particularly when the subject was a living person. Biographical entries had been devoted only to the dead in previous editions. The Eleventh was crowded with the living. This practice was the cause of some protests among the older contributors. But it also, of course, emphasized the journalistic tone of things and made the Eleventh "new" in the manner of a yearbook or almanac. The writers for these entries were often surprising choices, assigned articles in the time-honored way of journalists: knowing somebody who knows somebody.

Mrs. Alec Tweedie, for example, the author of brisk and popular travel books (*A Girl's Ride in Iceland, A Winter Jaunt to Norway, Through Finland in Carts*, etc.), who had been one of the women contributors Hogarth had praised at that Savoy dinner, had been selected not because of her famous arctic exploits, or because of any scholarly insights, but because, having befriended the young wife of Mexican president Porfirio Díaz, she had inveigled her way into the Díazes' sunny presidential garden and spent many days there learning what she was convinced was true about Mexico's long-ruling dictator.

She produced two books, *Mexico as I Saw It* and *Porfirio Diaz, Seven Times President of Mexico*, both chatty and sunny as a Mexican patio. Since Díaz had taken power in Mexico just after the first volume of the last major edition of the *Britannica* began appearing in

1875, the need for an entry in the new edition was apparent. Under previous editors, the assignment would have gone to a specialist, to ensure quality—and even then, only if Díaz cooperated by dying first—but the Eleventh Edition was intended for high quality and mass consumption, not for a small market of scholars, so the assignment went to her. After all, she'd met the man. She recalled her pleasant chats and wrote up a brief hagiography, which Chisholm ran. Making entries for living persons was seen as not only vulgar, but risky. Sure enough, six months after her entry appeared, Díaz was in Paris and on the run, accused of fraud and worse.

Few entries were negative; most were at least vaguely uplifting or, at worst, cautionary; the unsigned article on "Adolescence," for example, ends like this:

> The adolescent is prone to special weaknesses and moral perversions. The emotions are extremely unstable, and any stress put on them may lead to undesirable results. Warm climates, tight-fitting clothes, corsets, rich foods, soft mattresses, or indulgences of any kind, and also mental over-stimulation, are especially to be guarded against. The day should be filled with interests of an objective—in contradistinction to subjective—kind, and the child should retire to bed at night healthily fatigued in mind and body. Let there be confidence between mother and daughter, father and son, and, as the years bring the bodily changes, those in whom the children trust can choose the fitting moments for explaining their meaning and effect, and warning against abuses of the natural functions.

Sometimes, the entries are contentious in the way only a certain type of academic can be, as in J. Vernon Bartlet's survey of the Acts of the Apostles: "[T]he Tübingen school did its chief work in putting the needful question, not in returning the correct answer. Their answer could not be correct because . . . their premises were incorrect," says an entry that can not be satisfactory without a full knowledge of the Tübingen school and the claims of Ferdinand Christian von Baur, not a very encouraging prerequisite to use. But for the most part, balance was sought, especially if there was a risk of overpraising those who had already been overpraised. For example, Chisholm, on Lord Acton: "Lord Acton has left too little completed original work to rank among the great historians; his very learning seems to have stood in his way; he knew too much and his literary conscience was too acute for him to write easily, and his copiousness of information overloads his literary style. But he was one of the most deeply learned men of his time, and he will certainly be remembered for his influence on others."

Some entries give delight in their quiet understatement ("There is some reason to believe that excessive absinth-drinking leads to effects which are specifically worse than those associated with overindulgence in other forms of alcohol"—a straight line if ever there was one); others, such as those on Abyssinia and Afghanistan, astound in the complexity of detail and bibliographical references presented—certainly far more than a curious student would expect to find (and perhaps more than is needed) in a general reference work.

Thus, in fewer than 250 pages of the first 976-page volume (which ends with a note on the cannibalistic Androphagi), a reader passes by "Accents" and "Accessories" (both before and after the fact, but neither fashionable); scolds against collectors of natural specimens (in "Acclimatization"); the two dozen charts in Walter Hibbert's "Accumulator" article; a handful of Ozymandiases (the Achaemenes, the Amir of Mascara, Agesilaus); Reverend Thomas Cheyne's remarkable essay on the "strange narrative" of what he calls the Adam myth—the lonely man, the snake, and that woman; and some health advice to live by ("In the close proximity of the fight, where time, assistants, pure water, towels, lotions and other necessaries for carrying out a thoroughly antiseptic operation cannot be forthcoming, gunshot wounds of the abdomen had best not be interfered with"). The amount of information is almost maddening. And this is before a browser even gets to "Boiling to Death" and the other forty thousand useful entries from the letter A to the Zyul-chu River in Tibet, with the maxima and minima of the entire earth in between.

Chisholm apparently welcomed political dissenters to his staff, but he did nothing to hide his own opinions. He passionately disapproved of both Gladstone and Asquith. In common with many Conservatives of the time, he liked to think of himself instead as an unsentimental "progressive"; he wrote poetry dedicated to Canon Barnett, and appreciated the vibrant political and social life of America, often irritating his compatriots by choosing Americans as traveling companions and staff members over Britons. "In America he could salute the New Age," said Hogarth. "In his own country he was afraid of it." Nonetheless, he considered himself an enlightened man on the important issues of the day, and he had no interest in playing the role of ideologue. "He was," wrote Hogarth, "a strange mixture of wide information, combined with an unsophisticated attitude towards many of the problems of modern social life. The lawyer in him disliked irregularities; the historian respected tradition."

Not surprisingly, then, the Eleventh Edition is often marked by an allowance for the potentially incendiary perspective of contributors whose political and social views were often already much better known than Chisholm's. Adelaide Anderson, an activist for women and for workers, writing on labor legislation, for example, produced a very well-tempered but predictable survey of global working-class difficulties. James Bonar's entry on "Socialism," however, must have raised a few Conservative eyebrows. Bonar was prescient on "the coming socialism," and seemed to approve of it, but thought it most likely to manifest as a local matter—an odd view from one of the era's better-known economists. At the same time, entries on "Women" and "Negroes" seem silly and ambiguous, in the case of the former, and simply stupid, in the case of the latter.

Chisholm's strategy mirrored Hooper's. It was predicated on executing Hooper's plan built around an overarching strategy making the Eleventh as up-to-date as possible by publishing the entire set all at once. Despite Jackson's complaints, publishing the encyclopedia serially would have been disastrous to this plan.

For Chisholm, Hooper's goal imposed unique editorial considerations of the production of the encyclopedia. Often articles were not closed until the printer's galley was approved and sent back to Edinburgh, where an army of typesetters was employed. Entries could be updated up to the very last moment before the proofs went into stereotype.

The lessons of the Ninth Edition were given careful consideration. A few veterans of the earlier work were still around.

Most of the fifteen hundred or so expert contributors submitted their entries and were thanked; the process ran smoothly and efficiently, despite the office confusion. However, when the complexity of a topic or the prolixity of a contributor ambushed a subject, the editors took extraordinary, if sometimes futile, steps to correct the problem and get the contributor to help make the article readable by someone who might be expected to buy an encyclopedia like the *Britannica*. Often, Chisholm himself would redirect a lost contributor. He would gather a small group of his editors around a topic, or retire to his desk and work out a detailed plan for a revision and send it off to a contributor in need of guidance. "In those long letters," Hogarth later said, "which he wrote all in his own hand and had duplicated in smudgy copying-books—his office methods were prehistoric and the despair of New York when he and I were over there—with the curious upward slope of the shortening lines, diminishing almost to vanishing point as he got to the bottom of his page, he would build up the framework of an article, forming the words with his lips as he wrote, so that we marvelled why he couldn't dictate them, but he always said he couldn't and never would try. He had his prejudices and he had his weaknesses; but on the whole he had a fine sense of proportion."

Often, his "prejudices" manifested themselves as a loyalty to writers or the ideas that had informed his tastes. Meredith was one of these writers, but in that case, Chisholm was part of a large pack of admirers. He wasn't afraid to go it alone, however. In 1893, when Francis Thompson made his first appearance in print, Chisholm, then an assistant editor at *The St. James's Gazette*, was among the first—if not the first—major critic to praise Thompson's work, even going so far as to seek an autographed copy of "Daisy"—although with careful attention to propriety: "When from . . . Mr. Hugh Chisholm . . . the writer of an appreciative notice in that paper, came a request, reinforcing his printed admiration, for an autograph copy of the 'Daisy', the compliment was made through a third person, and such personalities as his review contained were not based on an acquaintance of the poet." Seventeen years later, he stood by his initial judgment in the article he wrote himself on Thompson for the Eleventh: "Among his work there is a certain amount which can justly be called eccentric or unusual, especially in his usage of poetically compounded neologisms; but nothing can be purer or more simply beautiful than 'Daisy,' nothing more intimate and reverent than his poems about children, or more magnificent than 'The Hound of Heaven.' For glory of inspiration and natural magnificence of utterance he is unique among the poets of his time."

The job required enormous amounts of concentration, of course, but there were only temporary calms in the encyclopedia's offices. Sometimes Chisholm would work himself into a kind of Haxtonian frenzy, then collapse in a chair in Hogarth's office, or pace the floor, talking to himself until he made sense. Hogarth:

> He seemed to need little help and little suggestion; but sometimes he would use me as a listener, to help himself to "clear his mind," as he used to say, by talking a subject out. One could sometimes get in a suggestion then, if one were careful not to break the thread of his argument. To bring him up with a shock did him real injury, physical as well as intellectual, for his brain was a very delicately adjusted mechanism. Those talks showed me another side of him, rather an appealing side. When things went seriously wrong he was like a child put out and needed soothing like a child. He would come in and say, "I don't know what's the matter with me. My brain won't function. I can't get the hang of this," and sit talking until he was cheered up, and then go off work for the rest of that day, taking refuge in the Athenæum. The office staff grumbled sometimes at his short working hours; but on his good days he could make ample amends. No one could turn out a larger quantity of strong, good work in an amazingly short time than he could when he was in the vein.

Chisholm was liked and admired by his staff—not surprising, since he had known many of them from his *St. James's* days: "He came very near being the ideal editor of an encyclopaedia, who should, I take it, be a man of the world as well as a scholar, possessed of the widest knowledge but no pedant," Hogarth said.

> His mind should be evenly balanced, but his imagination must spring ahead of it. He should be able to weigh in the

balance all new subjects, to decide which are mere fads and fashions of the moment and which belong to the future. He must be capable of realising what posterity will want, for he has to anticipate its judgements. Of course he ought to have no prejudices, but we are all human. And he should be able to withstand the verbose and conceited contributor. But it is difficult to keep an expert, or an enthusiast, within his appointed limits, though a due sense of proportion and firmness in maintaining it is the whole duty of an editor.

Keeping the fifteen hundred experts within "appointed limits" required a lot of hand-holding, and in this, not just the *Britannica*'s sixty-four editors but all able-bodied staffers were drafted. Croxton, for example, once found himself being sent to see Sir George Greenhill, one of the world's leading authorities on hydrostatics, dynamics, and ballistics. It was the "Ballistics" entry that was causing consternation. Croxton, whose passion was musical theater and whose previous place of employment had been *The Tatler*—"where flippancy was the keynote"—found himself instantly in deep water.

Sir George was in his quaint chambers in Staple Inn. A question arose about the diagrams illustrating interior ballistics. Pointing to one of the figures, he said, quoting from his article, "On the assumption of uniform pressure up the bore, practically realizable in a Zalinski pneumatic dynamite gun, the pressure curve would be the straight line HK of fig. 3, parallel to AM; the energy-curve AQE would be another straight line through A; the velocity curve AvV of which the ordinate v is as the square root of the energy, would be a parabola; and, the acceleration of the shot being constant, the time-curve AtT will also be a similar parabola." "Quite," I said with reeling brain. And so the conversation went on, until I left Sir George's presence in an almost comatose condition.

As the compilation progressed it became obvious that the entries were running long; the contributors often had much more to say than Chisholm may have wished, and the rapid growth of technologies in the last decade of the previous century and the first decade of the

The Newest Encyclopaedia—A Great Project

The Eleventh Edition of "The Encyclopaedia paedia Britannica"

All who have had the good
fortune to handle and to
consider the new edition of The
Encyclopædia Britannica, which is
published under the auspices of the
Cambridge University Press, can
come to but one decision. Here,
in face of a vast mass of material,
all of it written by the great
specialists in every branch of lite-
rature, of science, and of art, there can be no room for
any verdict other than one of entire approval and indeed
of enthusiastic congratulation. The eleventh edition of
The Encyclopædia Britannica will prove an

fact that the British Empire has
more Mahomedan subjects than
any other country) come from the
United States, being the work of
Professor D. B. MacDonald of
Hartford, and the chapter on The
History of Ancient China is the
work of Professor Hirth of Columbia University.

The Brains of the Whole World
Clearly the editor has tried to get the best men without regard to their nationality. In Physics the book
owes much to Lord Rayleigh, who is Chancellor of the
University of Cambridge, the sponsors of

A Man Easily Can Carry It

Arthur Croxton holding the entire India-paper edition of the Eleventh Edition.

new one—everything from radio signals to X rays to bicycle designers were flying through thin air by 1910—made it hard to plot the volume lengths with precision, and the encyclopedia began adding more and more pages until a whole new volume was necessary—alarming not just Chisholm but also Hooper, who was having bookcases built that were designed to accommodate a set with twenty-eight volumes, not twenty-nine. A quick adjustment was made; a finished standard set would need ten feet of shelving. A much lighter, more compact version would be printed on "Bible," or India, paper.

Keeping some sort of limitations in place was obviously important in terms of production and cost, but it also had an impact on how Chisholm saw the encyclopedia's organization—"planned on uniform lines as a single organism." Chisholm understood the unique anatomy of that organism, so he understood that it was important to keep the project under control; oversized entries or entries that were too technical or too narrow could make the encyclopedia into a different kind of animal. He felt that the vision of the "single organism"—as opposed to, say, a colony of specialized, unrelated organisms—was the only way to avoid the problems that had been inherent with the Ninth Edition. As respected as the Ninth had been for its authoritativeness, he thought it had been created under an "impossible system" that "lacked interdependence," in which no synoptic view could be maintained, no comprehensive plan executed, and only partly because of the long fourteen-year gap between A and Z. The problem wasn't just that the Ninth was out of date, since, as he wrote, in its day the "demand of a modern public for 'up-to-dateness' had not come into existence." It was that it was "a detached collection of monographs," and while those may have been of "the highest authority and value . . . owing to its system of publication, its arrangement was not encyclopædic, and that in preparing an edition which for the first time had the advantage of being systematic in the distribution of its material, there was no way of adapting to its needs what had been written originally on a faulty principle."

This process was a manifestation of Chisholm's faith in "science" as a guiding principle. As Chisholm wrote in the editorial introduction,

> While every individual article in an encyclopædia which aims at authoritative exposition must be informed by the spirit of history, it is no less essential that the spirit of science should move over the construction of the work as a whole. Whatever may be the deficiencies of its execution, the Eleventh Edition has at any rate this advantage to those who use it that the method of simultaneous preparation, already referred to, has enabled every subject to be treated systematically. Not only in the case of "science" itself, but in history, law, or any other kind of knowledge, its contributors were all assisting to carry out a preconcerted scheme each aware of the relation of his or her contribution to others in the same field; and the inter dependence of the related parts must be remembered by any reader who desires to do justice to the treatment of any large subject. Cross-references and other indications in the text are guides to the system employed, which are supplemented in greater detail by the elaborate Index. But the scientific spirit not only affects the scheme of construction as a whole: it has modified the individual treatment. Attention may perhaps be drawn to two particular points in this connexion,—the increased employment of the comparative method, and the attempt to treat opinion and controversy objectively, without partisanship or sectarianism.

Chisholm also felt very strongly that every article should be the beginning of a line of inquiry, not an end in itself. An Eleventh Edition entry should invite the reader to look for more related information, to not feel any question was fully answered until all the references had been followed from one subject to another to another, tracing a path through millions and millions of words. In other words, the authority and credibility of the thing could be seen in its beautifully written entries, but its utility rested on Chisholm's plan, on its cross-references, and especially on the index. The success of the former two qualities can be debated, but the value of the index is obvious and indisputable. In a work so dense and overfilled, without the index the books were more a browser's indulgence than a serious reference work.

Yet the work had languished; the indexers had not been able to keep up, and the publication target was in danger of being lost. Finally, when Hogarth came over from the Times Book Club, which was being reduced to an unexceptional level by Kennedy Jones and Northcliffe's other assistants, she was asked to reorganize the indexers and bring that end of things as current as possible. The index would contain hundreds of thousands of entries; keeping track of it was an enormous job, aside from Chisholm's role perhaps the most daunting task in the entire operation. Hogarth received an unexpected gift from Shotwell, who provided a key innovation that had a very significant impact on how both the index and the entries themselves could be managed together. She fearlessly set about doing the work that had to be done quickly and accurately. It was her first foray into indexing, an exotic art even now. "There is far harder work to be done and more brain needed in indexing than anyone knows who hasn't tried it," she explained later in a memoir.

> Of course I was not, technically speaking, an indexer, and there are technicalities to be learned; but indexing is in the main a matter of imagination, carefulness and common-sense. "To do this work well," as a clever woman on my later staff said to me, "what matters is to have lived." And some of the indexers seemed never to have lived outside offices. . . .
>
> I have said that indexing needs imagination; it also needs

alertness. Many an error we detected and ran to earth, even in the work of the most learned contributors, and, thanks to our system of working on typescript or rough unpaged proof, could get corrected with little trouble or expense. Of course we could only point the errors out, we might not make even the slightest alteration without reference to authority. Solemnity and reverence for scholarship had their uses. In New York, where reverence seemed conspicuous by its absence, the staff working with me on the Twelfth Edition index positively terrified me with their emendations. "I thought it couldn't be that," they would say, even in a subject of which they were completely ignorant, "so I changed it." And to such purpose did they sometimes "change it" that a learned Protestant divine of distinctly Orange sympathies appeared disguised as "the first Roman Catholic ever to be knighted"! His biographer had written "priest," alluding to the infrequent bestowal of knighthood upon a clerk in Holy Orders. But to the proofreader "priest" seemed wrong, and he elected to emend it.

Oddly, none of the indexers of the Ninth Edition were brought on board. The chief indexer of the Ninth, William Cairns, had been hired by A & C Black to pull together the list of Ninth Edition entries. It took him fourteen years, sitting in his little study, reading every word of the fifteen volumes. But he died in 1896, and the others, including George M'Arthur, a chess-playing clergyman, Newnham's Emily Stevenson, and the literary J. T. Bealby, were gone or elsewhere engaged by the time Hogarth began her work.

The women Hogarth supervised were often astonished at what they found in the manuscripts of some of the celebrated experts. Over time, Hogarth observed a growing conceit among the indexers who grew contemptuous of the editorial staff and their far-flung experts. It wasn't until the index cards were examined that the editors evened the contest.

Some very queer results came to light. Slight references to important subjects would be indexed and the main treatment left out, because perhaps the word—Citizenship, Representation, Idealism, or whatever it might be—had not there been used. Superficiality of that sort is a besetting sin in indexers. Looking out for the name, they entirely miss the matter. Again and again we would pull up: "Where is the reference out of the article So-and-so?" someone would ask who really knew the subject, "the main treatment is there," and the reference would have to be hunted up and inserted.

The work sometimes required novel approaches, not all of which produced a predictable result. "I confess," Hogarth later wrote,

> it did give us a shock when *Agapemonites* turned up at the top of the list, headed *Free Churches*. Yet how else could they have been put anywhere else? You couldn't assign them to establishments!... I remember [sixteenth-century prophetess] "Mother Shipton" being tossed backwards and forwards. *Comparative Religion* wouldn't have her, neither would *Folk-lore*. She must either drop out [of the index's alphabetical topic list] or be relegated to the ignominy of *Miscellaneous*. But as that section would have looked like a confession of impotence, we decided to forget her, as well as the marvelous calculating boy [perhaps Jedediah Buxton, a famous 18th century "mental calculator" from Derbyshire], whom our mathematical expert refused to admit amongst mathematicians.

In her accounts, her amusement with Chisholm, her persistent and affectionate deflating of him, her bantering accounts of his peccadilloes, and her use of the transparency that comes with long friendship to prevent even the slightest hint of hagiography all seem to be intentional displays of both familiarity and affection. Who knows how she saw herself in relation to Chisholm that day long ago at Corpus—she records very clear recollections of her first meeting with both Chisholm and W. L. Courtney, her Oxford tutor who was sixteen years her senior, but who greeted her for the first time with a fistful of forget-me-nots purchased "from a woman with a baby, who looked even more tired than I am." Courtney would go on to edit *The Fortnightly Review* and eventually marry Janet Hogarth—but at this stage in their lives, he was merely a favorite tutor, while she had clearly become the big sister Chisholm may not have known he needed. She enjoyed sending him up, as when she reported that he "prided himself on taking an enlightened view of women's capacity." Right, said Hogarth. "If he really made no difference between capacity, wherever you found it, irrespective of sex, you did it without being self-conscious about it." That rather describes Hooper's methods, in fact, and the way he dealt with Hogarth. But it doesn't describe Chisholm's.

> Hugh Chisholm was keen on employing women and theoretically believed in their equality, but he was amusingly frightened of them. Never of me, I think, but then he had known me first when we were both undergraduates at Oxford. The idea, however, of a fuss or an upset amongst the women on his staff filled him with terror. As I have already said, I was brought in to try to straighten out an unsatisfactory state of affairs in the Index department. This provoked at any rate one resignation and a general revolt on the part of the indexers, who appealed to the Editor. Stiffened by "H. E." in the background but in decided trepidation, the Editor upheld me in the measures I was taking. The indexers said they should resign. I did what I always do in an office crisis—I went out to lunch and stopped out for some hours. I even bettered this procedure by going away for the week-end; but, before going, I said to a senior member of the Index staff that, though I should regret parting with them all and hoped that they would not regard themselves as compelled by loyalty to the one who had gone to go with her, I should expect to be told their decision on Monday morning.

The image of Chisholm quailing in his upstairs redoubt while Hogarth sallies forth to lunch may not be entirely fair, but it's probably pretty accurate. By the end of the weekend, Chisholm was more calm. "On Monday," wrote Hogarth, "no one resigned, and the Editor's spirits rose rapidly."

So, the work progressed—almost miraculously. Chisholm may

have been far too loyal to his old *St. James's* cronies—Hogarth records the collective eye rolling at some of their tolerated inadequacies— and everyone was mystified by his penchant for dealing with a set- back by simply disappearing into the dark recesses of the Athenæum Club for an entire day. Everyone at the *Britannica*—with the apparent exception of Chisholm—was aware of the ticking clock. Meanwhile, Hogarth worked without a break from 9:30 a.m. to 8 p.m. daily.

It was a mad place, with men and women doing important work under a murderous deadline in an unusual atmosphere colored by personalities and shaped by dark vicissitudes far from their control, as events would instantly reveal. While Hooper was fighting his battles to make publication possible, Chisholm and his staff were building the *Britannica* right through the summer of 1910, when all the galleys and all the note cards and 44 million words would need to leave the hands of the editors at last.

CHAPTER 16

WAR AND PEACE

Horace Hooper was not a difficult man to read; his motives were always quite clear. He had "the faith and pertinacity of an idealist," according to Chisholm. It was Hooper's idealism that made him what he was, and what had gotten him into his latest predicament. By 1909, he was fifty, and more than thirty years of his life had been spent selling books with apparent sincerity, because he believed good books would help people—and because for thirty years he had found that there was a great deal of profit in doing good.

But Chisholm had also called him "a great business man." Whether or not he was was a matter for dispute, and, ultimately, even a matter for the courts.

What began in late 1907 and early 1908 as a series of petty squabbles and legal skirmishes over inattention (Jackson's) and recklessness (Hooper's) had become by the end of that year a bitterly personal feud. When the two had first started in business in London, Britain was their new world. They had bought country estates and set themselves up as gents; they liked their corner of London society—writers, editors, newspaper types, publishers—and they seemed to enjoy their somewhat marginal place in it. Both men came to be very well known about town, Hooper especially. As Kennedy Jones demonstrated, Hooper was such a familiar face in certain social settings that he could be located by simply going to where he customarily ate his lunch, when he wasn't at High Holborn. Neither seemed to see himself as a would-be Briton; both spent extended periods in America, and neither saw the adventure with the *Britannica* and *The Times* as more than it was.

They had started working together as brothers, and now they were fighting as only brothers can fight. Jackson had endured one too many Hooper blow-ups; he had none of Hooper's idealism; he thought the Eleventh was a mammoth waste of time and a huge risk of money; he thought the budget made profit impossible; he had his own projects to look after; he wanted out. Hooper, frustrated that Jackson couldn't be converted to his missionary zeal, went from hurt to angry. At one point, Hooper offered to sell his stake, and Jackson accepted—only to find that Hooper's offer had only been a tentative one. At another point, Hooper offered to buy out Jackson, but Jackson refused.

Finally, Hooper had called for a meeting of the directors of the American company on November 24, 1908, to confront Jackson and force the company to take measures to ensure the completion of the encyclopedia. Hooper needed credit, and without the backing of the board, it would be hard to come by.

But Jackson refused to attend and, adding a personal jibe, told Hooper that he was obviously a sick man, because if he weren't sick, he wouldn't be dealing with the encyclopedia in such a financially crazy way. He pointed out that since the board had been packed with friendly directors—namely, Franklin Hooper, Charles Whinery, and a Cleveland man named Harris B. Burrows, who ran one of the largest book-and-office-supply companies in America; he was an old friend of Hooper's and served as vice president of the encyclopedia company—the meeting lacked any validity, so, now following the advice of lawyers, he told Hooper he wouldn't attend.

Nevertheless, Hooper tried to entice Jackson to abide by the original arrangement, explaining that no matter their differences, good sense required at least being able to work together toward a mutual goal. "To bring out the new book," Hooper wrote, "it seems very plain that some financing would be necessary to bring us to this point. Even when it comes to buying paper, ads, etc., we need at least 200,000 pounds more. . . . The whole question as to whether or not we should liquidate and close up the business entirely or rather we should raise the money and complete the new book is something so very important that I have as yet been unable to understand your refusal to seriously consider the question."

On November 24, Hooper convened his meeting, and the board duly removed Jackson from any position of responsibility, leaving him a token place on the board. Hooper was given full management responsibility and carte blanche to borrow as much money as he needed to complete the compilation and production of the Eleventh Edition.

Jackson didn't blink. Instead, anxious to avoid legal complications, he started a midwinter round of transatlantic tag and sailed for Britain. Hooper followed, preceded by a volley of letters, warning that the company would be forced "to go ahead without further consultation with you" but determined to deal with Jackson face-to-face.

Jackson waited in London until Hooper's ship from America was nearly there, then quickly returned to the U.S. Of course, Hooper was furious. When another of Hooper's angry letters finally caught up with him, Jackson replied, with injured petulance, "Do you soberly and seriously think that your conduct is fair, even if you believe you are within your legal rights? Do you not realize in your own heart you are merely betraying the confidence I have rested in you and showing yourself to be unworthy of the confidence I have rested in you . . . ? No wonder that consistently in speech and letter you protest your honesty of purpose? Do you not protest a bit too much?" Then he added the rhetorical flourish that has invariably failed to move generations of coldhearted antagonists: he was speaking sternly, he said, "to stimulate your conscience, to arouse your sense of shame or honor . . . to contrast before your own eyes your honest self with your recent conduct. Why not," he demanded, "be honest with yourself and with me and have done with this petty chicanery?" Jackson clung to the claim that any meeting forcing him to surrender power in what he claimed was a partnership would have no standing. He claimed that his partnership agreement with Hooper had been violated. The conflict was now as much a personal dispute as a legal one.

So Hooper's response was to escalate the conflict: What partnership? What agreement? The two men, he argued, had operated on a handshake, setting up back-of-the-envelope, cash-in-a-cigar-box businesses that were never formulated as partnerships—even including Hooper & Jackson Ltd. and the Encyclopædia Britannica Company.

They had done this solely to stay a step or two ahead of tax collectors on both sides of the Atlantic, paying themselves by writing checks when they wished. As a legal tangle, this one had enormous potential for trouble—no doubt why Jackson did what he did and called in the lawyers. Hooper was represented in Chicago by Jacob Newman, and in New York by a team headed by Henry Taft, the brother of the president, and including former New Jersey attorney general Robert McCarter, along with a trio of well-known New York attorneys—Edward S. Leidmann, Henry Wollman, and Francis S. McGrath. He was not going to go for a settlement. To Jackson's threats, he replied, "I shall be only too pleased to have you test the matter of partnership in Court."

On May 27, 1909, Jackson finally sued Hooper in a New Jersey court in a last-ditch effort to take control of the encyclopedia project.

The trial that started that day in New Jersey continued through a series of courts for years—until well after the Eleventh Edition was finally published, in fact. But it was that first month of late-spring skirmishing that inflicted the greatest punishment on Hooper. In his filing, Jackson not only outlined his complaint against Hooper's usurpation of power in a company he maintained was an equal partnership, he also disclosed the manner in which the two of them had operated with casual disregard for tax laws, and, worst of all, he revealed much about the way they had helped Lord Northcliffe seize control of *The Times*.

On June 15, Hooper filed his own detailed affidavit, claiming that there had never been a partnership—only a company. "The only sign on the door of the London office is 'Hooper and Jackson, Ltd.' The only sign on the door of the New York office is 'The Encyclopedia Britannica Company.' Neither the name of Jackson nor myself nor our names together, except with the word 'Limited,' have ever appeared on any door." Rashly, Hooper followed Jackson's lead in claiming influence in the acquisition of *The Times* by Northcliffe and describing the way in which it had been done.

Coming so soon after the debacle in Darling's courtroom, it was exactly the kind of story the press loved, for it validated the narrative constructed around the Americans—that they were vulgar, superficial, tax-dodging, manipulative, combative, and unseemly. For weeks, newspapers in the U.S. and Britain were filled with news of the war between the "encyclopedia men." Details were poured into news columns; in Britain, where lawsuits often had an air of scandal associated with them, news of Hooper and Jackson's involvement with *The Times* was the fuel for gossip up and down Fleet Street. That Northcliffe should have had to rely on subterfuge, stage names, and other masquerades engineered by Americans gave great delight to his many adversaries—and especially to his nemesis Cyril Arthur Pearson, whom he had publicly mortified. *The Times* had always been all about sober propriety, but as the lawsuit documents made clear, the man furthest from propriety was *The Times*'s new proprietor himself.

Northcliffe's reaction was as swift as it was predictable. On June 17, 1909, Hooper received a brief, impersonal note from Moberly Bell saying that Northcliffe had instructed him to cancel the 1903 contract to publish the Eleventh under *The Times*'s name and sponsorship. Hooper had three months to find a way to publish the encyclopedia or close up shop in Printing House Square.

A month or so later, Judge James E. Howell in New Jersey issued an injunction against Hooper, calling the two men "joint adventurers" and ridiculing their improvisational way of doing business. He promised a final ruling soon. Hooper appealed, but he didn't wait. He filed in Britain, telling a Chancery court in London he should be given control of the encyclopedia business, and revealing the perilous state of the enterprise. In New Jersey, the appeals court, in reviewing the *Britannica*'s affairs, reported that "from 1902 to 1908 the business in which the companies were engaged, including the publication of the Encyclopaedia Brittannica [sic], extended all over the civilized world and ran up into millions, the accounts receivable alone . . . amounting to over $ 2,000,000." The pair were each paying themselves $5,000 per month out of the company till. According to Kogan, in the previous six years, Hooper had spent $698,618 on salaries and contributors' fees, leaving him a mere $44,000 cash balance. The *Britannica* had income of $3,000 to $4,000 each month. The editorial staff had been cut to thirty-five—a bare minimum—even as the final crush of deadlines approached. The original budget had been $750,000, but now, Hooper admitted, he needed another $700,000 to get to the end—assuming he could find a publishing partner to replace *The Times*.

So in September 1909, Hooper sent word to Edinburgh to stop

production work, including typesetting. Since late in the spring of 1908, an army of women who had battled their way into the trade had been working on the *Britannica*, where, as one of them coolly pointed out, "You learnt a lot." Now what they were learning was that they were all out of work.

Finally, he sent instructions to Chisholm to give all but the senior editorial staff thirty days' notice and to pack up the office to remove it all to High Holborn. The blizzard of paper settled slowly in drifts around Phillips, Garrett Fisher, and Hogarth as Chisholm perfected his putt. The great *Encyclopædia Britannica* ground to a halt. Hooper was broke, and in a matter of weeks the *Britannica* itself would be without even an office.

The war between Jackson and Hooper became the most pressing matter in the life of those directly associated with the *Britannica*, but it was also the most distant, the most removed from the control of any of them. At one point, a misunderstanding caused Jackson to think he had finally defeated Hooper when he received and accepted an offer to sell, only to find later that the offer had contingencies undisclosed by Jackson's attorney, Sherrerd DePue. No money was ever exchanged; no shares were transferred. Nevertheless, it gave Jackson an opportunity to walk into the New York offices and tell a confused Whinery that his orders from now on would come from Walter Montgomery Jackson, and not Horace Everett Hooper. He even fired off instructions to a bemused Chisholm. Hooper quickly reorganized his company once again, this time adding Garrett Fisher to the board. But they all knew they were out of money and quickly running out of time.

Hooper, by the time the Appeals Court heard his case in November 1909, must have felt exhausted. It had only been thirteen years since he arrived in London with a big idea and no way to make it happen except to talk about it. But eventually, he had talked to the right person at the right time, and it all seemed to come out right, for a while.

But in 1896, Hooper had been an unknown. Moberly Bell couldn't even remember his name after meeting him. Now, nearly a decade into the new century, being unknown in Britain would have carried a distinct advantage, since everyone in publishing knew all about Horace Everett "Hell Every Hour" Hooper. Wasn't he the American who had tricked thousands of unsuspecting Britons into buying an out-of-date encyclopedia by defacing *The Times*'s very serious sheets with half pages of vulgar advertisements and full pages of absurd ramblings? Wasn't he the man who styled himself after Teddy Roosevelt and went about London barking orders in his rat-a-tat twang? He had threatened Englishmen and Englishwomen with his hectoring and dire warnings. "Only one more day!" indeed. They knew Horace Hooper, all right. He was the chap behind the direct marketing campaigns that drove men from Land's End to John o' Groats to curse him from their bathtubs. He had duped innocent British men and women to participate in foolish "contests." He had sent *The Times* into battle with Britain's great and august publishers and had nearly seized control of the nation's Leading Journal. He had corrupted *The Times*'s manager and involved its owner in ridiculous lawsuits. In fact, he was practically a criminal, wasn't he, libeling poor John Murray that way. And now he needed a friend? Not bloody likely.

But to others, Hooper had been exactly what Britain's book business had needed. A little retail innovation, including competition, discount pricing, direct selling, and premium merchandising—none of these had hurt literature, and publishers wise enough to adapt succeeded. Most of all, readers profited: more books were being read by more people. Some 450 years after Gutenberg, the idea of mass marketing—as opposed to simply mass producing—literature and information had finally arrived.

Even with little to keep them engaged, Chisholm and the others kept in close contact with Hooper as he crossed to New York and back with increasing frequency. Alison Phillips, especially, worked closely with Hooper, testing new ideas and sending praise for the work that had been done and especially for the spirit in which Hooper had done it. Hooper rose to Phillips's encouragement.

> I cannot express to you my feelings on reading your letter. For the last four or five years it has been my one great ambition to bring out the 11th edition of the *Britannica*, and make it, from an editorial and scholarly point of view, the greatest book that has ever been published. It is needless for me to add that I

wanted to make money, and more, that I expected to do so; but if it had been for money alone, I would have made that book very different from what it has been made. We could easily have produced a book at half the cost by doing hack work and taking a large share of it from the 10th edition; but I felt I should like to know that I had been instrumental in producing a better book, and in better form, than any other man. This may seem to you like vanity, but it was really a desire to do something that might leave the world a little bit better for my so doing.

The goodness of the book I don't think I deserve great credit for. The conception of the idea was mine, but the carrying out has been due to Chisholm, yourself, and your editorial force, and I don't mind telling you that I really believe it is too great to be crushed by any such methods or suits as Mr. Jackson has started so far, and I still hope that the book comes out, if not under my management, at least under somebody's who is competent and get a good sale of the book. You may rest assured that it took me a long time to make up my mind to give notice to men who had worked so faithfully on the staff down there.

Hooper was also engaged in working out a strategy to do what he had done so successfully before: leverage one major "brand" against another. But now, thanks to Northcliffe's anger, his focus shifted from Britain's greatest newspaper to its greatest universities: Oxford and Cambridge.

In many ways, the alignment of the *Britannica* with a major British university was far more intuitive than the relationship with *The Times* had been. Had Hooper begun there, our story would be far simpler.

With Cambridge and Oxford, the credibility of the institutions overshadowed the *Britannica*'s scholarly pretenses, no matter how justified, with the books that issued from their university presses. A relationship with either would give Hooper a better story to tell and much more to sell. The question was which one of the presses of the great universities most needed the *Britannica*.

Publishing was entering its fourth decade of unprecedented growth in 1910. It seemed that no matter how many books were published, there were buyers waiting for them. It was not only cheap fiction that people were reading, either. In a nation of new readers, all books were new, so classics that might normally have been associated with an academic publisher were flooding the market in cheap editions designed for railway passengers and workingmen and -women. In 1896, George Newnes had launched his "Penny Library of Famous Books." The successful sales of great works in less-than-lasting form encouraged other publishers to enter the market, and by 1900 British publishers were issuing the classics in as many as eighty different "classics" series. J. M. Dent's "Everyman's Library," motivated by a sincere and very widespread belief that good books would create a just nation, was founded in 1906 to publish the 1,000 greatest books of all time, and Dent had 152 of them in print by the end of the first year. Sets of classics had long been a staple of subscription bookmen on the other side of the Atlantic; Charles William Eliot's "five-foot shelf" of Harvard Classics, published by P. F. Collier, made its appearance in 1909. The design and production of these sets of books was intended to inspire reverence, and in this it was occasionally more successful than the content.

George Newnes

Cambridge, bound tightly to the wishes of the professors who formed its University Press Syndicate—the so-called "Syndics"—had retired from this competition into its own academic list.

However, at Oxford a new spirit was governing the place. The press still saw itself as the epitome of academic publishing; its fifteen-member delegacy was a typically cliquish group of scholastics, governed, theoretically, by a secretary. That position was a ditch into which many had fallen.

But during the last twenty years of the nineteenth century, things had changed. A troika of highly entrepreneurial men—including the secretary, Charles Canaan; his young assistant, Humphrey Milford; and Henry Frowde, a man who had joined the press in 1874 from a publishing background and who had no previous Oxford connection—had secured the ability to meet the demands of the growing market by giving the delegates at Oxford the academic turf and leaving the real word of books and readers to Oxford's London office. There, Frowde, who was named publisher, quickly expanded operations, his prestige augmented, in 1881, by his remarkable management of the publication of the eagerly awaited Revised New Testament. Unlikely as it must seem to modern readers, that massive, Harry Potter–sized event saw 1 million copies sold in one day. Under Frowde, the Oxford list grew rapidly as he broadened the market for its books. In 1896, Oxford opened a New York office and had charged into the American market.

Henry Frowde

To respond to the classics mania, Frowde picked up a "World's Classics" series from a bankrupt publisher, printed sets on India paper, and sold them with a bookcase. Compared to Dent's list—or even that of Newnes—it was extremely eccentric, obviously shaped by the peculiar literary preoccupations of the press's bosses. As Oxford University Press chronicler Peter Sutcliffe rightly notes, "Jane Porter's *The Scottish Chiefs* and John Galt's *The Entail, or The Lairds of Grippy* could scarcely be accounted for without a knowledge of Charles Canaan's private reading habits, and Milford's taste for adventure stories can alone explain the inclusion of Mayne Reid's *The Rifle Rangers* and *The Scalp Hunters*." Whatever; the fact is that by 1907, 2 million copies of World's Classics titles had been sold. Frowde became so competitive that he would have books set in type as the expiration of their copyright (in those days, a mere forty-two years) approached, and then wait, watching the hour hand and practically drumming his fingers on the press, until the legally permissible moment arrived.

He seemed like a likely partner for a man such as Hooper. Besides, the *Britannica*'s Oxford contingent, led by Chisholm and Phillips, had already made it clear that they thought the first choice should be their university. It was true that between the two universities, Oxford had a slightly richer patina than Cambridge, especially for Americans, and Phillips, two years older than Chisholm, was not only a well-established scholar in his own right, he also had Merton's flag to hold and was a senior scholar at St. John's as well. *Britannica*'s editorial team enjoyed an insider status at Oxford that none of them had at Cambridge. So, armed with notes and an offer, Phillips and Hooper went up to Oxford, took a room down one of the labyrinthine hallways at the old Mitre, and the next day walked past the Ashmolean, under the imposing Walton Street arch below the press's understated brass letters, and into a door to meet with Canaan.

Maybe they should have started with the enterprising Frowde in London, since, despite the long association he had with Oxford, Phillips knew how difficult his mission was. In theory, the press should welcome an arrangement such as the one Hooper and Phillips offered them, but at Oxford, large-scale reference works were measured against the great dictionary that had been under way there since James Murray, the eccentric president of the Philological Society, brought the project to Oxford in 1879. By 1910, the dictionary that was supposed to have taken ten years to complete was running far behind schedule and was frighteningly over budget. Beyond that, the quick succession of monarchs following Victoria's death caused the university—along with Cambridge, one of the two "privileged" presses given permission to print the established church's prayer books and Bibles—to become bogged down in the revision and production of required replacement texts. The idea of adopting another multivol-

James Murray

ume work without giving the university an ability to control the outcome may not have been a welcome idea.

And then there was the embarrassing lawsuit. But far more problematic was the matter of Hooper, Sickert, and Haxton's approach to advertising. What had made *The Times* solvent would never do, and Haxton's prose seemed incapable of being tranquilized to the level of Oxford sobriety. Nevertheless, the meeting was held and the press was offered a 10 percent royalty. At first, a glimmer of hope: Hooper was asked to wait before offering the encyclopedia elsewhere. But in the end, Oxford passed.

According to one account, Hooper told Phillips he was sure Canaan was suspicious of his motives. "They think I was trying to bribe them. I offered them too much." And he had a point: a massive reference work sure to attract reasonable sales at no financial risk at all to Oxford? It may have seemed too good to be true, especially coming from somebody associated with book wars and the like. "You go to Cambridge now," he told Phillips, "and offer them just half."

Although a century older than Oxford's, Cambridge's university press fit a lower profile. Oxford had its trio of managers pushing for greater revenues from a broader list; Cambridge had only its Syndics; unlike Oxford's fairly broad publishing remit, Cambridge often seemed most invested in publishing academic books they scarcely hoped would find a wider readership; too wide, in fact, might be despised. Still, the press had entered the new century full of hope. In 1891, for the first time, a secretary to the Syndics had been named and given encouragement to negotiate new projects with authors. The post had been taken by Richard T. Wright, a fellow of Christ's College, and he had immediately cast about for a big project that he hoped would succeed financially while meeting the scholastic requirements of the Syndics.

Among Wright's most ambitious projects was one of his own invention: *The Cambridge Modern History*, the university's great gesture of faith in Lord Acton, had been launched just after the turn of the century, but sales were less than hoped, so in 1907 the Syndics approved an ambitious marketing program created by Wright but perhaps influenced by Haxton and Hooper's controversial campaign for the *Britannica*'s Tenth: impressive prospectuses, installment plans, early-ordering discounts. And a bookcase! It was Cambridge's first broadly commercial effort, and while it increased sales and introduced the press to an international community of readers, it hadn't come close to providing Wright with what he felt the press needed if it were going to avoid being eclipsed completely by its great rival.

Hooper and Phillips would have known all of this, of course, since the Cambridge effort to market their *History*s so clearly paralleled their own on the behalf of the Tenth Edition. And they both would have been well aware of Cambridge's association with the Ninth. After all, its most famous editor, William Robertson Smith, had been a Cambridge professor and a Syndic. As Professor John Sutherland Black had told Darwin, Smith, and the others gathered at Christ's College, Cambridge, to celebrate the Ninth Edition, "The *Encyclopædia Britannica* lies under the very immediate, special, and personal obligations to the Fellows of this College. The past Fellows have contributed many valuable articles, and, of the present Society, fully one-half have contributed articles with which honoured names are associated in their several subjects." Things in this respect were not different for the Eleventh Edition, as the Syndics knew.

But the Syndics would have known of Hooper, too. All of the impediments to an agreement he had brought with him to Oxford—the lawsuit, the hyper-marketing, the book war fiasco—also followed along to Cambridge. Indeed, in 1907, Wright and the Syndics had mimicked some of them in launching the *Modern History*. So when, on March 11, 1910–a mere two weeks after winning his New Jersey appeal–the Syndics finally were given Hooper's proposal to publish the *Britannica*, they at least knew the main objections the university community might have to any partnership, and they had experience of the kind of advertising and marketing effort required to sell the set.

As difficult as it was to accept that a man such as Hooper could ever possibly be in partnership with a press as serious as Cambridge's, what the American brought was impossible to ignore. The *Britannica*, the English-speaking world's most famous work of reference, would be published by Cambridge at no cost to the university, all at once all over the world, and with a 5 percent royalty–for doing little more than stamping the covers and title pages with the name and seal of the university.

Wright understood Hooper's vision even more readily than Moberly Bell had. He pressed hard on the Syndics for a whole-hearted embrace not just of the Eleventh but also of the *Britannica* as an ongoing Cambridge enterprise. "In my opinion," he told the professors, "quite apart from the pecuniary gain it would be greatly to the advantage of the University that it should be connected with the publication of this great book, especially if, as might be possible, the connection were made a permanent one and extend to future editions."

There was nothing the Syndics could do but look into the details. A committee was formed, and a three-man delegation dutifully made its way to 152 High Holborn to look at some of the work Chisholm had produced.

The head of the committee was Montague Rhodes James, a forty-eight-year-old medievalist and the provost of King's College, who knew more about ghost stories than any man in England. Although a serious scholar and a dedicated bibliophile, M. R. James was already well known as a writer of supernatural tales intended to be read aloud at night in firelit rooms. As a student, James had been a social chap. In 1889, he had been a charter member of the "TAF"–the Twice a Fortnight Club, an eating and drinking club at King's College domi-

M. R. James

nated by Leslie Stephen's family circle. J. K. "Jem" Stephen, a manic-depressive poet and parodist, was a guiding spirit; E. F. Benson, Walter Crum, Gerald Duckworth, and Walter Headlam were among the other members, of the last two, the first a predator of Virginia Stephen and the second a suitor. Over time, James had become a fixture at Cambridge, widely respected for his academic work and, by the time he was provost of King's and an influential Syndic, a commanding figure. James also apparently fostered a kind of intimidating presence. When, for example, editors and typesetters couldn't read what he had written about the "Christian Renaissance" for the *Modern History*, they paid extra charges rather than simply asking him what the indecipherable marks on the paper meant.

Like Wright, James hit it off with Hooper immediately. The committee spent three days with Chisholm and Phillips looking at edited entries and reviewing the impressive list of contributors. In the wake of a decision by a New Jersey appeals court to set aside Jackson's injunction against Hooper, giving him control of the company and the freedom to move forward, the *Britannica*'s editorial offices, with all their files, tags, notes, and other ephemera, had completed the move to High Holborn. Just enough money was trickling back into the editorial machinery to enable a return to smooth running.

One day, surprisingly, it also brought Jackson back into the High Holborn office, claiming he was done causing legal problems. Hooper calmly looked up at him and said, "Take your place over there and sit down and attend to business." Jackson stiffly took a chair behind a desk, but after an awkward silence he told Hooper he wouldn't be subordinate to those he considered beneath him—especially men such as Harris Burrows and Garrett Fisher.

Hooper flashed. "There is no desire on anybody's part to give you orders. I don't care to give you orders. Why work your imagination as to whether there are orders or not orders to be given to you? Go attend to business." Jackson stood and left, later telling one of Hooper's attorneys, Jacob Newman, that he'd soon be back in court, and he was.

But not in time to stop progress on publication of the Eleventh Edition. At Cambridge, the Syndic committee suggested raising the royalty to 6s. per set sold from 4s. and sent to Wright their recommendation for approval. Wright must have felt he'd face an argument from some of the other Syndics, since he delayed convening a meeting to approve the agreement until midsummer 1910 to allow James and the others to continue to examine entries supplied to them by Chisholm. Besides, at both Oxford and Cambridge, administrators such as Wright had learned long before that summer provided unusual opportunities for progress, since almost nothing could disturb the estival plans of entitled dons; Benjamin Jowett, for example, had taken advantage of the phenomenon of academic warm-weather hibernation to push through the approval of Philip Lyttelton Gell as secretary of the Delegacy of Oxford University Press in 1884, albeit to disastrous results.

So Wright waited until July 8, 1910, to schedule a meeting to approve Hooper's offer. To preempt what would likely be the Syndics' biggest objection, an amendment was added stipulating that all advertising had to be approved by Cambridge. A few weeks later, on July 31, the contract was signed. According to its terms, Hooper had eight weeks to produce the entire work for approval in anticipation of a publishing date of December 1. The immediate effect of this was to open the large and necessary lines of credit that had been previously choked by the lawsuit and the ending of the agreement with *The Times.*

So Hooper had a new home for his encyclopedia and enough money to finish the work, and Cambridge University Press had a new reference series to publish, one that would couple the name of the ancient, elite university with the democratizing goals of Hooper's *Britannica*. It was not going to be a placid marriage.

CHAPTER 17

THE DREADNAUGHT LAUNCH

The news of the agreement between the *Britannica* and Cambridge University Press traveled slowly. From Britain, where the focus in publishing circles often was more on Hooper than on the books he published, the editor and critic James Milne, a popular *New York Times Saturday Book Review* columnist, gave readers early if incorrect news: "Some particulars reach me of the new edition of the 'Encyclopædia Britannica' which the 'Times' newspaper is to pubish [sic] this Winter"—along with the news from Oxford that the *OED* would also be making a winter 1910 appearance.

A few days after this report appeared, the university issued a statement about agreement, and offered an explanation of its motives, other than money. "It is only through the medium of the printing press that the modern university can establish and maintain relations with the whole English-speaking world. The present time seems appropriate for an effort toward thus signally extending the intellectual and educational influence of the University of Cambridge." The university had examined and approved the "solid and scholarly foundations" of the new edition.

The first response to word from London's book crowd that Hooper and Cambridge had come to an agreement on the encyclopedia was surprisingly optimistic. Writing in *The New York Times Saturday Book Review* under a headline reading "The Taking Over of the 'Encyclopædia Britannica' by the Cambridge University Press," Milne—at the time the literary editor of the *Daily Chronicle*, the founder of *Book Monthly*, and a popular *New York Times Saturday Book Review* columnist—reflected the London view:

The other week I was able to say something in advance about the coming new edition of the "Encyclopædia Brit," as that great work is always called in catalogues. Somewhat earlier I had occasion to say a word about the history of the Cambridge University Press. Now the "Encyclopædia Brit" and the Cambridge University Press come together in the news, given forth as I write, that the latter has taken over the control and copyright of the former. In other words, the new issue of the "Encyclopædia Britannica," although it has been prepared under the auspices of *The Times* newspaper, is to be published by the University of Cambridge. One wonders whether the London *Times* or Cambridge University is most to be congratulated on this arrangement—one because an encyclopaedia is not naturally part and parcel of the activities of a newspaper, the other because it is the natural work of a great and learned institution.

Milne praised the *Britannica*'s staff ("The editor in chief has been Mr. Hugh Chisholm, whose name stands well alike in English scholarship and in the higher ranks of journalism"), gave voice to what most assumed to be the case with respect to the *Britannica*'s new publisher ("it is now hoped that the work has found a permanent abiding place at Cambridge"), and promised "a Dreadnaught launch in literature, for never before has such a large reference work been prepared as a complete thing and so published."

The trigger had been pulled. Thousands of copies of a "book" of 44 million words began to roll off the presses in Britain and the U.S. The Cambridge University Press had been swamped by the demands made in the production of the *Modern History*, so production of the *Britannica* was farmed out to printers all over Great Britain—at least five in all. In the U.S., R. R. Donnelley and Sons had been given the contract to do the work after being persuaded by Hooper, who had their representative met at the docks by a royal railway carriage chartered for the trip to London.

Only a month passed between the Cambridge announcement and the celebrations of it. The "Dreadnaught launch" of the Eleventh Edition began with another series of dinners in London and

"The only book, except the Bible, which has followed the Anglo-Saxon around the world."

New York given by Chisholm. The first of these, held on October 21 at Claridge's, was a highly elevated sort of affair, with tables packed full of literary celebrities, political figures and academics from Cambridge, and the usual tableful of journalists. Hooper had planned every detail, including the music, and the leather-covered menu—matching the Eleventh's binding. Even the boxes holding cigars were made to look like volumes of the Eleventh. While the other dinners were held specifically to thank the contributors, this one was to thank Cambridge for giving the *Britannica* the university's blessing. But so energetic had the *Britannica*'s editors been, it was impossible to convene a large gathering of scholars without also finding plenty

The invitation to celebrate the Eleventh Edition

of contributors in the net. Certainly that was true of the man at the center of the event, Lord Rayleigh, Cambridge's chancellor.

And some of those present had not only been contributors to the Eleventh, they had also been at that dinner at Limmer's for Chisholm only twelve years earlier—Frank Cana and Sidney Low, among others. Characters from the recent past of the *Britannica* were there: Adam Black, Moberly Bell, Godfrey Walter, Donald Mackenzie Wallace, George Earle Buckle. R. T. Wright, secretary of Cambridge University Press, was seated at a table surrounded with Phillips, Garrett Fisher, and Franklin Hooper on one side, and J. A. Spender, Duckworth, and Heinemann on the other. Other Syndics, including James, their chairman, were scattered here and there. Gosse was sitting in the distance with Ronald McNeill and T. A. Ingram. The *OED*'s James Murray was seated next to the etymologist Walter William Skeat. Sprinkled liberally throughout the room were the Cambridge academics, listed by the title of their university office—the Quick Professor, the Plumian Professor, the Knightsbridge Professor, the Slade Professor, the Public Orator! The Disney Professor was present, as was Reverend Principal Skinner. The Esquire Bedells were there, presumably there to look after the chancellor, and so were the masters of the various colleges. The heads of the British Museum, the British Academy, and the Royal Society were all there—only fitting, since all three institutions had provided hundreds of contributors to the Eleventh.

Lord Rayleigh sat in the middle of the High Table, sandwiched between Whitelaw Reid, the American ambassador, and the venerable John Morley, *The Fortnightly Review*'s editor emeritus, recently ennobled and named chancellor of Manchester University. Nearby was S. H. Butcher, only weeks from death, who gave a spirited and witty toast in his capacity as president of the British Academy and MP for Cambridge Univer-

John William Strutt Rayleigh

sity, reciting from what must have sounded like a point provided by Hooper or Chisholm: "Now for the first time the book, though of immense variety, is itself a unit. Hitherto you have had curious inconsistencies and discordant articles introduced in different volumes. Sometimes it has happened formerly that the same man writing under the letter A, afterwards under the letter M, and still more under the letter Z, each time contradicts what he said before. . . . The old kind of Encyclopaedia that I mentioned might be described in a single line: 'Monstrum horrendum informe, ingens, cui lumen ademptum.' [Laughter and cheers.]"

When his turn came, Rayleigh was too clever to "enter into the credits of the New Edition"—even though he'd written the article on argon for the Tenth, and articles on light and optics for the Ninth, as well as the entry for "Sky," all of which also appeared in the Eleventh. Instead, he explained who really bought books like the *Britannica* by linking it to its previous, celebrated editor. "I knew the former editor, the vivacious and almost omniscient Robertson Smith. It comes back to me that in reply to a question of mine he told me that the circulation of the *Encyclopædia Britannica* was largely in the Western States of America, where it was the custom for the head of the family to read it out after dinner. I confess the idea of certain articles relating to the Wave Theory, Optics, and so on—pernicious nonsense, as we have heard—being read out in family circles on the prairie, rather tickled me," even if it didn't exactly brighten Adam Black's evening.

The London dinners continued one after the other, many at the Savoy, and, in New York, at the Plaza. In early January, Chisholm and Alison Phillips crossed from England to host a dinner for the American contributors and other notables—including Alexander Graham Bell, House Speaker Joseph Cannon, Admiral Dewey, Cardinal Gibbons, Oliver Wendell Holmes, Charles Evans Hughes, Henry Cabot Lodge, J. Pierpont Morgan, Elihu Root, Woodrow Wilson, and the presidents of Yale and Harvard—at the Plaza on January 21, 1911. Chisholm delivered what had, since he first delivered it at Claridge's, become his set speech:

> An encyclopaedia, of necessity, is, in a way, a cooperative work, but the mere collecting of the contributions of a number of distinguished authors does not make a work really cooperative, and what we have done in this particular edition is to make it co-operative by the use of the instrument which has existed in my editorial staff. That is really the distinguishing feature of this new edition. Robertson Smith pointed out, in the preface to the index volume of the Ninth Edition, that the use of authors' initials at the end of the articles was not designed to lighten the responsibility of the editors. 'No editor can possess the knowledge which would enable him to control the work of his contributors in all the subjects treated of in the *Encyclopædia Britannica*, but no effort has been spared on the part of the editorial staff to secure the accuracy or efficiency of every contribution.' That statement of Robertson Smith's I regarded, when I took up this work, as representing the tradition of the *Encyclopædia Britannica* . . . but I made up my mind that I had at any rate got to have a command of all the knowledge that would enable me to control them. It is perfectly certain I could not have it myself, so I had to get round me . . . enough men of different capacities, selected for that purpose because of their different knowledges, to enable me to pull all the strings under proper advice and to have control over every

single article that appeared in the book. That was the only way of making that book uniform and a single book, edited from first to last in exactly the same spirit and exactly on the same lines. That is at any rate what we attempted to do.

And he concluded always with praise for his new publisher, Cambridge: "I believe that Cambridge, by selling the book and disseminating through all its educational channels the contents of the book, will really be doing a great work in advancing popular culture and in carrying out the mission which is confided to our great universities."

Advertisements began appearing almost simultaneously with the Cambridge announcement in late summer. Alison Phillips was detailed with holding Hooper and Sickert in check to avoid inviting the wrath of the Syndics. But it was impossible to contain Hooper sufficiently to give reassurance to those at Cambridge who were certain that the marketing of the *Britannica* would besmirch the name of the university. He needed to advertise in order to recoup his investment, and Cambridge University was perhaps not the best institution to determine how popular works of reference should be sold. The ads soon began featuring Haxton's familiar don't-wait, ticking clock augmented by Sickert's flamboyant and hyperbolic description of the feat of publishing the newest *Britannica* (fifteen hundred miles of thread! ten tons of glue! etc.). And for America, where much larger sales could be anticipated, Hooper had in mind an ad plan designed by Haxton that would cost $1 million. Worried about Hooper's marketing techniques, the university began imposing restrictions it didn't even observe for its own books, and at one December 1910 meeting the worried Syndics devoted time to describing how the *Britannica* could articulate its relationship with Cambridge as the copyright holder.

They would perhaps have been mollified if they had known how little Haxton was able to contribute to the campaign. Although Hooper still counted on Haxton to help him, the adman's visits to London were now only occasional. "[A] breakdown in health had removed him from the regular staff," Hogarth later recalled. Sometimes it was difficult for her and the others to watch. Once, for example, when Hogarth proposed a particularly complex solution to an indexing problem at one lunch meeting with Haxton and Hooper, Haxton said, "Miss Hogarth, you are wanting to qualify for where I have been—a s-s-s-sanatorium."

As the sales effort drove toward the first shipment of volumes in late December, Cambridge began finding itself in the unfamiliar role of defending its role in publishing the encyclopedia, with Hooper's familiar nemesis, the Booksellers' Association, leading the charge in the pages of the *Publishers' Circular*. Their complaints: the 7.5 percent royalty offered booksellers for forwarding orders was "miserable," and the money being spent on *Britannica*s would mean less money being spent buying the books of British authors. As the criticisms mounted, the pages of the *Circular* grew increasingly shrill. They didn't like the *Britannica*'s offer to buyers of the Tenth to give them a £5 discount, but most of all they didn't like Hooper and felt Cambridge should be chastened for yielding to "this latest effort of heaven-born American-cum-British genius." In response, the press canceled its advertising schedule with the *Circular*. But once the first volumes began shipping, the press, worried about losing the goodwill of booksellers in supporting their other titles, turned on a new strategy of distancing itself from Hooper and reminding publishers of Cambridge's support during the book war.

All the animosity that could be generated by a Hooper-Haxton-Sickert marketing effort came to bear on the *Britannica*. The words of Hugh Chisholm, spoken only weeks earlier at Claridge's, suddenly seemed wildly optimistic. "I do not think," he had said, "there is anything in this new edition, with all its modern handling of serious subjects, which can reasonably be a cause of offense."

CHAPTER 18

OFFENSES

The first reviews of *Britannica*'s Eleventh Edition were overwhelmingly positive; *The Athenæum*, perhaps the most influential of review periodicals, in evaluating the encyclopedia's coverage of classical literature, said, "[W]e can heartily congratulate the editors on their excellent performance. . . . If we were to begin to enumerate things well done, the task would be endless." Virtually every important review on both sides of the Atlantic carried approving notices.

But if Chisholm thought he'd avoided giving offense, he was quickly corrected. The Eleventh Edition gave plenty of offense.

And it continues to do so in ways that didn't generate widespread outrage one hundred years ago. Scattered through the volumes are commonplace views of the time, now refined by events and consensus wisdom into hot outrages. The entries "Negro" and "Ku Klux Klan" are especially repellent to a modern mind. Disentangling those offensive views from the more comprehensive opinions and "discoveries" that in turn informed them may be asking for the impossible.

The entry by Thomas Athol Joyce, the British Museum's chief ethnographer, on "Negro" ethnography is the obvious example here. Because of its notoriety, it may be one of the Eleventh's best-known articles. It's an entry that has given offense since the day it first saw ink, and its offensiveness continues to grow with every passing year. There is no reasonable modern explanation for Joyce's views.

But how can we understand that a man such as Joyce could maintain that blacks were "mentally inferior" to whites? Even if they were measured "by tests taken directly from the environment of the white man, as for instance in tests in mental arithmetic." Joyce asserted that "skill in reckoning is necessary to the white race . . . but it is not necessary to the Negro." While Joyce noted that blacks outperformed whites in "acuteness of vision, hearing, sense of direction and topography," he said they also have hair resembling wool and carry a "characteristic odour"; and, at puberty, "sexual matters take the first place in the Negro's life and thoughts."

Whence such views? And how could they have ever appeared in print in a serious publication? A more reasoned, intelligent, and useful statistical review adjoined Joyce's. Written by Walter Francis Willcox, the former director of the U.S. Census and Cornell's great statistician, it directed readers to works by Booker T. Washington and W. E. B. Du Bois. Willcox's entries continued to appear in the Twelfth and Thirteenth Editions, and he must have been disappointed to have been tandomed with (and often blamed for) Joyce's views.

The explanation may seem impossible today, but perhaps Joyce didn't realize his views were unorthodox; at the time, and under the sway of Darwin, maybe they weren't. Apparently, neither Joyce nor Chisholm had stated any objection to the "Negro" entry in the Ninth, written by a contributor named Filippo Manetta, a man perhaps unqualified to write the entry but with views that were unexceptional then (but would today rightly be considered blatantly racist).

At the time—and certainly not intended to excuse Chisholm's editorial insensitivity—natural selection and its various consequent "sciences" (including eugenics, especially) were reflections of evolutionary assumptions that were deeply held by the intellectual class and its higher journalists. There was no indication of public disapproval when the *Britannica,* with Athol Joyce's entry, appeared (which is not to say that disapproval did not exist), because Joyce reflected what those familiar with contemporary ethnography considered to be scientifically correct. Those beliefs were also deeply racist and in turn gave sanction and impetus to racist impulses that extend to the present day.

Darwin's views, and not just the racist ones, were welcomed by many thoughtful Victorians, including religious leaders. Charles Kingsley, who was a prominent clergyman (he was the queen's chaplain from 1859 until 1875), writer (*The Water Babies*), lecturer in

Thomas Athol Joyce

modern history at Cambridge, and generally understood to be an open-minded and thoughtful chap, enjoyed a lively correspondence with Darwin, privately ridiculing the anti-evolutionary posture of old-school theological literalists, such as the bishop of Oxford. When the bishop dismissed natural selection at a hunting party to which Kingsley had also been invited, Kingsley defended Darwin—then hurriedly wrote to tell the great scientist what he had done, and to extend the conversation to the topic of race. Kingsley said that on the idea of an "intermediate" species between man and the apes, there was no need for evidence. "To me, it seems strange that we are to deny that any Creatures intermediate between man & the ape ever existed, while our forefathers of every race, assure us that they did—As for having no historic evidence of them—How can you have historic evidence in pre-historic times? Our race was strong enough to kill them out while it was yet savage—We are not niggers, who can coexist till the 19th century with gorillas a few miles off."

Darwin agreed, repeating—and not for the first time—his horror at the thought that he might have some kinship with the "naked painted, shivering hideous" natives of Tierra del Fuego he had seen during his famous voyage. The idea of it was "more revolting than my present belief that an incomparably more remote ancestor was a hairy beast." Added Darwin, "It is very true what you say about the higher races of men, when high enough, replacing & clearing off the lower races. In 500 years how the Anglo-Saxon race will have spread & exterminated whole nations; & in consequence how much the Human race, viewed as a unit, will have risen in rank." This is of a piece with other comments by Darwin that must have reflected a contemporary view of a racial superiority that would lead, Darwin promised, to "the less intellectual races being exterminated." Joyce's racism, as seen in his entry, was a reflection of the racism not just of the time but also of his professional class, and the scientifically anointed process of "selection" that made seeing other races as inferior a necessary part of being a modern man, educated in the sciences and subscribing to the dominant scientific theory.

The *Britannica*'s mostly British staff could certainly be accused of indifference and worse. Janet Hogarth provides some clue to the general level of racial consciousness on the staff when she tells what she thinks is an amusing story from her indexing career: "I shall never forget ... when a card came to light inscribed: 'Christianity, unsuited to negroes.'"

But "Christianity, unsuited to negroes" *is* one of Joyce's findings, and thus it is Chisholm, who believed equally in the claims of science and in social justice, if only in service to British and American English-speaking men and women, who ultimately must be held to account for the entry, which obviously did not go onto the page unexamined. Maybe Joyce's warning that "it's not fair to judge of [a black person's] mental capacity by tests taken directly from the environment of the white man" was enough to mollify Chisholm and the other editors. But it's hard to imagine the effect on a young black reader in 1911 encountering this line in the local library: "[T]he Negro would appear to stand on a lower evolutionary plane than the white man, and to be more closely related to the highest anthropoids. ... Mentally the Negro is inferior to the white." This, from the world's most celebrated ethnographer in the pages of the world's most eminent encyclopedia. Common sense might have prevented the *Britannica* from falling into the apparent absurdities of some of these widespread interpretations of Darwin's theories, at least as they pertain to race, and contributing to the century's dismal record of racial equality by enshrining it as a scientific assumption. The Eleventh Edition was also unkind to Native Americans, Southeast Asians, the Chinese, Afghans, Arabs, and Caribbean people. The biases must have been considered so commonplace that they were invisible, especially to men and women of the educated classes.

In fact, the Darwinian hypotheses about races also frame the general dismissal by the "higher journalists" of the day of religion's claims. There is something familiar in the contemporary descriptions of the ludicrousness of the religious beliefs of "lower orders" of men and women, especially blacks.

Perhaps that's the nature of social progress. Chisholm, no doubt like Joyce, would have not wished to be seen as the backward thug who today would normally be associated with such views.

Assumptions, of course, are often unconscious. Chisholm's were shaped by a belief in rationality and modernism as defined by contemporary Darwinian logic. The belief was more dangerous because, as Hooper and Chisholm both assumed, surely, every creature living in the first decade of the twentieth century should aspire to the state of the educated, civilized Englishman. Chisholm's assumptions were harmonious with Joyce's remarks, themselves examples of a racism based not on hatred or fear so much as on a faith in the science of the day. It's unsurprising, if also deeply unfortunate, that this racism should also permeate the Eleventh Edition of the *Encyclopædia Britannica*.

Other entries attracted criticism from offended historians. While some may have had an axe or two to grind, they also had valuable points to raise about the *Britannica*'s editorial process. *The American Historical Review*, for example, had never had many kind words for Walter Alison Phillips. Even his most widely admired book, *European History, 1815–1899*, had been dismissed by the *AHR*, whose reviewer, Charles M. Andrews, complained, "[A]lthough Mr. Phillips has made an important addition to the small stock of good books on the nineteenth century he has not furnished the history that many expected him to write. The field is still open to anyone who desires to produce a good text-book covering the period since 1815." (As it happens, Phillips's book filled that very function for a half century.)

The *AHR* did applaud the Eleventh's generous coverage of arts and letters, and praised Shotwell's "History" entry for its "learning and eloquence." But mostly the reviewer, George Lincoln Burr, yearned for the Ninth Edition and its unedited versions of Mark Pattison's "Erasmus" instead of the new crop of younger historians working under Chisholm. And that was the problem: "Neither Mr. Chisholm nor Mr. Phillips was known to the world of readers

George Lincoln Burr

by work in any period save the most modern; their colleagues were scarcely known at all." Burr lamented the large number of unsigned articles and the use of "the most accessible sources." He continued:

> The most daring of the staff is indisputably Mr. Phillips. With a temerity almost appalling he ranges over the whole field of European history, political, social, ecclesiastical, now astonishing us by the keenness of his fresh research, now perpetuating some venerable error. Whether such work be keen or careless is, however, little to the point: the grievance is that it lacks authority. This too—this reliance on editorial energy instead of on ripe special learning—may, alas, be counted an "Americanizing": for certainly nothing has so cheapened the scholarship of our American encyclopaedias. But it is an Americanizing few Americans will welcome.

For the future there is one great reassurance. Now and henceforward the *Britannica* is under the care of the University of Cambridge. That transfer came too late to be of serious moment to the eleventh edition; but it may well mean everything to those that follow. May it hasten the day when it shall be the editor's function to select its authors and aid them, but not do their work.

Burr's criticism of the *Britannica*'s "scarcely known" writers— including those the *AHR* had previously reviewed—seems ill-informed, however, and his appeal for authority seems misplaced coming from a man who was self-taught in history beyond his undergraduate degree. However, his targeting of the minor articles does address a possible weakness in Chisholm's strategy. The "unsigned article" debate was still current in periodical publishing until 1974, after all.

Psychologists were offended. Like Burr, E. B. Titchener, reviewing the *Britannica* for *The American Journal of Psychology*, complained more about what the Eleventh had omitted than what it said. The *Britannica*'s entry for the Ninth, Tenth, and Eleventh Editions had been written by the same contributor—Professor James Ward. Titchener complained, reasonably, that perhaps someone more current might have done better work, since, as he explained, "the intervening years" since the Tenth Edition in 1902 "were notable in the history of psychology." Freud and Jung had both been published by the time of the Eleventh, and, Titchener wrote,

[T]hey were years of rapid horizontal expansion, during which laboratories were equipped, journals were founded, and comparative psychology and mental pathology made unwonted progress. It may well be the case that psychology outgrew its strength, that a "thorough scrutiny of methods" is needed before the new results "can be safely or systematically incorporated into the science": at any rate there is good material mixed with the bad, sound with the flimsy: and the superficial extension of psychology, the widespread adoption of the psychological attitude, is itself a sociological phenomenon of the first importance.

None of this, Titchener said, was evident in the Eleventh.

> Professor Ward is . . . less interested in these things than in
> the "signs of life" shown by the "old" psychology. He had
> himself discussed, in the *Naturalism and Agnosticism* of 1899,
> the great questions of the perception of an external world and
> of the relation of the body and mind. He had also published
> in 1893-4 two articles on *Assimilation and Association*, in which
> Höffding's "quality of familiarity" and "tied ideas" were turned
> to account for a genetic study of ideation. James' apologetic
> paper on the "Physical Basis of Emotion" came out in 1894;
> von Ehrenfel's *Gestaltqualitäten* appeared as "forms of combi-
> nation" in Stout's *Analytic Psychology* (1896). It is still the "old"
> psychology, then, that the supplementary article expounds
> and advances; the sections on the Experimental Investiga-
> tion of Memory and on Comparative Psychology are as nearly
> perfunctory as the writer's critical acumen and philosophical
> conscience will allow. And so we are not surprised—though
> many of us, no doubt, have been disappointed—to find that
> the revised article of 1911 is, in all essentials, simply a skillful
> blend of the articles of 1886 and 1902.

Titchener also found that the editor had failed to deliver on a
widely heralded innovation—the arrangement of entries on a "dictionary plan" as opposed to a "treatise plan." In this, Titchener said,
the *Britannica* failed to deliver what the editor had promised.

Hogarth's testimony in the two memoirs she wrote touching on
the *Britannica* provide insights that go beyond the mechanics of the
encyclopedia's editorial processes. She brought with her an impressive educational background, a valuable work experience, a long history of friendship with Chisholm and many of the others, and also
something else unique to the top editors' table: a woman's perspective. To what extent this was appreciated at the time may not be clear,
but it certainly is interesting now.

The paralytic political polarization with which most Americans
are now familiar is something Edwardians would have recognized
too. The transition from Victorian paradigms of stability, tradition,
sobriety, patriarchy, and public morality to a period of unsettled

debate leading up to the outbreak of war in 1914 may have eased some of the social stratification of an earlier time, but it also divided Britons into new strata in which party affiliation was often inconsequential, and in which social class, if not entirely incidental, was certainly not a determining factor.

The leadership of the women's suffrage movement, for example—as with its iteration six decades later—may have been dominated by educated middle- and upper-middle-class women, such as those at the *Britannica*'s dinner for the women contributors, but thousands of regular members were factory workers and others, with especially strong representation from the north. Their strategies varied. Some were Pankhurst "suffragettes," members of the Women's Social and Political Union, which favored overt social action, disruptions, property destruction, and even physical violence. Others, such as those in the National Union of Women's Suffrage Societies, were "constitutional suffragists" who attempted to unify the movement behind less confrontational methods, often arguing their cause in print or using what Hogarth described as "Parliamentary tactics," which, she thought, had virtue: "There was nothing undignified in these repeated petitions, and processions, and Bills, and ministerial pledges"—even if the latter were, "apparently, made to be broken."

In 1909, a quarter-million Britons signed a petition against parliamentary suffrage; the next year, seventy thousand more joined them. Hogarth was one of these, and so were several other women contributors to the *Britannica*. When Mary Ward created the Anti-Suffrage Society, Hogarth had been among the founders. One of her anxieties at that December 1910 dinner was that her most public reputation was associated with the anti-suffrage campaign, an issue that had the nation in turmoil. By 1910, most women could vote in county and borough elections, but not for members of Parliament. As the pressure for change increased, the divisions between those who opposed the vote and those who favored it deepened.

Hogarth and others were appalled by what they feared were the rude excesses of the suffrage movement. Hogarth's appeals in the press and elsewhere had been directed mostly against militant suffragettes, those who claimed the right to use violence in their campaign, but also against suffragists generally, since she saw their tactics as a threat to the progress already made by women such as her. Her language was often blunt, easy to misunderstand but not easily forgotten, and her apparent vehemence diverged from her fiancé's views (W. L. Courtney was a supporter of the feminist cause) and from Chisholm's as well. In 1895, Chisholm was arguing (anonymously, it must be said) in *The Fortnightly Review* for Oxford and Cambridge to drop their absurd refusal to grant women graduates the degrees they had earned. Two months earlier, and in the same journal, Hogarth was attacking "*fin-de-siècle* authoresses" such as Victoria Cross (Annie Sophie Cory)–whose "Theodora: A Fragment" had just appeared in *The Yellow Book*–as "literary degenerates" for promoting the "delirious fancies of the victims of sex mania." In the *Fortnightly*, she wrote,

> If the century as a whole has progressed by leaps and bounds, women have advanced at an almost immeasurable speed. Small wonder, therefore, that their self-control has not kept pace with the demands upon their nervous energy. When half-education has given way to a completer training, and when the independent woman attains the years which bring the philosophic mind, perhaps she may discover new objects upon which to expend her emotions.

Although contemporary perceptions suggested that many, if not most, women were on the anti-suffrage side, Hogarth's opinion was not a view warmly welcomed by most of those with whom she associated, especially in connection with her duties at the *Britannica*. After all, it was Hogarth who called women entering the workforce the "Monstrous Regiment of Women" (paraphrasing John Knox) and wondered in another *Fortnightly Review* article what to do with this "innumerable host, blindly bent on forcing its way into the professions"–especially journalism, where Hogarth felt they could find only disappointment, yet a direction popular women's magazines had urged them to go. If women must work, she wrote, the state should help them find work as schoolteachers and in other positions likely to avoid costing men jobs. She was very well connected, and her essays, letters, and articles were widely discussed and quite influential. Barely a fortnight before the dinner for the women contributors, the struggle for women's suffrage for the first time had turned violent in a "Black Friday" demonstration intended to force action on a bill that would have given the parliamentary vote to women of property. It was one of many such skirmishes; from a publicity point of view—women in the news!—it was very helpful to the *Britannica*'s proprietor, but the whole thing was often perhaps more than a little intimidating to Janet Hogarth.

Hooper had always known it was important to the *Britannica* that it be associated with the suffragists' cause. Like the women contributors at Hogarth's dinner, those invited represented an interesting and quite progressive slice of British life—a cluster of high-table celebrity suffragists and their supporters, gathered, whether they knew it or not, less for self-congratulation and more for marketing an encyclopedia intended for middle-class homes where the tools for learning were often selected by aspiring women. They were the sociopolitical set, growing in influence and dedicated to working on behalf of women's autonomy and self-definition. Henry James had called them "New Women," and their endorsement of the *Britannica* (and their identification with it) was critical.

A brief vignette from that December 1910 dinner may be useful in illustrating Hooper's ambition in uniting the *Britannica* with those at the forefront of social change. The head table that night stretched nearly the length of the hall. In the center sat the editor, Hugh Chisholm, affable, tall, and athletic looking, despite the chainless pince-nez. He was buttressed on one side by Lady Strachey, mother of Lytton (and many other Stracheys) and a leader of the Mud March of '07. On Chisholm's other side was Millicent Garrett Fawcett, one of the formidable Garrett sisters (her sister, Elizabeth Garrett Anderson, was one of those first-to women of the time—first female doctor, first female mayor, first female medical school dean, etc.)—and the well-known cofounder of Newnham College, Cambridge, a women-only institution that produced many suffrage leaders, including her.

Higher education for women—neither Oxford nor Cambridge awarded degrees to women at the time—was a common topic, so arranged in the front of the room was the mistress of Girton, E. E. Constance Jones, and the slightly scandalous Margaret "Meta" Tuke, the pioneering woman scholar who was a familiar traveler on Newnham's famous corridor. All around were other suffragists, educationalists, and anti-vivisectionists, not all of them *Britannica* contributors (in fact, most of them were not). Emily Davies and Sophie Bryant, both quite well known for their feminist commitments, were there– although neither had written for the *Britannica*. Charlotte Despard, a member of the Women's Social and Political Union, and the only bona fide "deeds not words" Pankhurst-style suffragette present, was prominent at the head table. Alice Bruce, the shy co-principal of Somerville College, one of Oxford's first women-only colleges, was in the back of the room, as were May Morris, Mrs. Alec Tweedie, and a number of other well-known women.

And the anti-suffrage cohort, though small, was represented as well. In addition to Hogarth, there was also Mrs. Humphry Ward, Matthew Arnold's niece, at the time the most popular woman writer in England and perhaps the world, a passionate campaigner for the education of poor women and children, a cofounder of the Women's National Anti-Suffrage League, and a strong advocate of women's involvement in local elections (though not in the parliamentary vote). Mary Ward had contributed the article on the writer John Lyly to the *Britannica*, but it was the editor of the *Britannica* who had contributed the article on Mary Ward, observing in his entry that her then controversial but now nearly forgotten novel *Robert Elsmere* had become "the talk of the civilized world."

Mrs. Humphry Ward, "the most popular woman writer in England and perhaps the world"

Like Gertrude Bell, Flora Shaw, and many others, the suffrage movement– and especially its militant wing–had long been a threatening embarrassment to many in Hogarth's circle. "Many of us," she wrote, "feared that Pankhurst militancy was going to wreck most of what professional women had won."

There were sometimes deep divisions between these groups of women. Take, for example, the stories on a single newspaper page—page 10 of *The Times* for October 9, 1909—involving both militant suffragettes and anti-suffrage types (suffragists were little in the news that day, apparently). The events reported took place just two days before the anniversary of the founding in 1903 of the WSPU. That day, it was reported, the Liberal prime minister, Herbert Asquith, a determined foe of the vote for women, was traveling south through the country surrounded by Scotland Yard detectives, and announcing his refusal to meet with the suffragette agitators—which may be why he was under wraps as plain "Mr. Evans." David Lloyd George, the chancellor, was also given to traveling incognito, and for the same suffragette-dodging reasons. Tempers were high. Scotland Yard was investigating a report that two suffragettes were plotting to assassinate the prime minister. Only a month before, jailers had begun force-feeding women imprisoned for criminal vandalism and other crimes; the forcing of tubes and all that was abhorrent to many. Meanwhile, at the Bow Street police court, fiery Emmeline Pankhurst was being fined £100 for "obstructing the police in the vicinity of the House of Commons," thus setting up an appeal before the High Court to test whether or not the prime minister could be petitioned by causing an obstruction. At a WSPU meeting in Newcastle-on-Tyne, Emmeline's daughter, Christabel, was shouted down by "a body of college students" who stood in the rear whistling, singing, and playing various musical instruments, probably badly. While Christabel Pankhurst was gleefully pointing out to the reporters that the leaders of the government were "enemies of liberty" who "must go about protected . . . until women get the vote," four other suffragettes were being arrested for throwing rocks through the windows of the Newcastle Liberal Club.

At the bottom of the page, there was a letter to the editor from Janet Hogarth:

Sir,—The letters which have appeared in your columns during the last few days encourage me to ask a question which

Emmeline Pankhurst is taken into custody in May 1914.

has recently been much in the minds of many moderate and thoughtful people. Is there no way out? Must this most harmful agitation continue? Can we not at least call a truce to what threatens to become civil war amongst women?

It is agreed on all sides that a general election lies in the near future. Only the fanatical few suppose that that election will turn upon any issue except the financial policy of this country and the constitutional position of the House of Lords. The enfranchisement of women has not the ghost of a chance of being made a test question. On the other hand, the next six months will give women important opportunities for strengthening their influence on local government, if they do not throw away the bone whilst grasping at the shadow.

Would it be quite impossible to agree to differ upon the question of obtaining the Parliamentary franchise, which is after all a question of the future, and to concentrate our united efforts upon securing adequate representation upon the borough councils in November and the County Council in March? Our suffragist friends can hardly object to this additional chance of demonstrating their fitness for performing civic duties; many anti-suffragists will welcome the opportunity of taking their proper share in useful social work. Mrs. Steel in your columns to-day laments "the absolute lack of any real employment for unmarried middle-class women." But the deficiency is in the workers, not the work. From all sides we hear a lack of women candidates; the harvest is plentiful enough, it is the labourers that are few. And with all this work waiting to be done, need we waste our time and our nerves and our energy in obstructing the work of Government and calling each other names? Who knows? Perhaps if we all set to work to cultivate our own garden, that great field of educational and social work lately opened to us by our admission to local administration, we should wake up some day to find that the field had enlarged its borders, or else that our energies were best directed to intensive, instead of extensive, cultivation.

The Eleventh Edition was a small garden indeed. To the extent that their social and political views were known, they mostly reflected Chisholm's own somewhat aloof views, and those reflected a kind of enlightened version of the prevailing views on what at the time was called the "Woman Question," which, for men, reduced to a question about the noise outside. Moberly Bell, in discussing a suggestion for a "Woman's Supplement," said he failed "to recognize the [difference between the] reading requirements of an intelligent woman and an intelligent man: What are the subjects that appeal exclusively to women, and cannot come in the columns of *The Times*? I know of none but women's dress. I can see no more reason why intelligent people should be divided according to sex than according to their height or the colour of their hair."

Chisholm was similarly convinced that his view on the Woman Question was intelligent and sufficiently up-to-date. Like many men of his time and ours, he seemed to view the Woman Question in a literal way, as if there were a Woman Answer, and the more promptly and efficiently that Answer was provided, the less ado there'd be. This, of course, drove Hogarth mad.

Chisholm may have possessed the raw materials for intellectuality, but by temperament he was a journalist; to him all ideas had the potential to become an issue. "He was always," wrote Hogarth, "a little inclined to generalise from a single instance and to start off like a crusader, to champion some quite well-established cause as though, having just discovered its justice himself, he must at once convert the world to his opinion."

For instance, he had very strong views on one of the more obvious inequities of the time: the failure of universities to treat men and women equally. Until the middle of the nineteenth century, the idea of giving women an education equal to that given men was almost unthinkable. Aside from a few female visionaries, nobody even raised the issue much until after the education reform acts of the latter part of that century. The College for Women (later Girton College, Cambridge) in Hertfordshire had been established in 1869, but the first university degrees weren't awarded until 1878 by the University of London. Oxford and Cambridge were among the last to adjust to the rising educational levels of women; Cambridge didn't deal equally with men and women until after the Second World War.

In 1895, Chisholm adopted the issue after watching his sister, Grace, treated unfairly by both Oxford and Cambridge. In an article for *The Fortnightly Review*, Chisholm wrote anonymously about her remarkable achievement in 1892 as an undergraduate at Girton, sitting the first part of her tripos and finishing with a first—then signing up to take the Final Honour School of Mathematics exam at Oxford. She passed that exam with a first, as well, giving her a double-first from Britain's two greatest universities in the space of two weeks' time. But that success would not give her a university degree from either. So she learned another language and went to another country and went to yet another university that also denied women degrees— Göttingen, the Prussian university under the direction of the Kaiser. The university abandoned tradition and awarded her a doctorate *multa cum laude*, its first given to a woman.

Grace Chisholm Young, Chisholm's brilliant sister, "a young
English lady, who could not get a degree at Oxford or Cambridge"

Chisholm was outraged. He wrote:

If young ladies may drive alone in hansom cabs, go without
chaperons to dances, ride bicycles in knickerbockers, have
latchkeys, and play cricket, or even football, there can be
nothing very alarming in their using their brains to such effect
that they pass the most difficult examinations, and come out
above their male competitors. . . .

[B]ut neither this nor that will probably have been of so much positive effect in determining the degree question in England, as the fact that a young English lady, who could not get a degree at Oxford or Cambridge, has just been allowed the full reward of her abilities at one of the Prussian universities— Göttingen. If the typical country of reactionary ideas about women and their place in life—if Germany, with its hausfrau ideal and its Emperor William, allows such an innovation, why is it, people may ask that . . . an Oxford first-class woman could not receive the same honour in her own country? If it was only prejudice that stood in the way, it must be time to drop prejudice. . . .

If properly qualified English women need University degrees, they will have them. In point of fact, they can get them practically everywhere but at Oxford, Cambridge, and Dublin; and the refusal there is unjust, unpatriotic, financially foolish, and educationally mischievous. Common sense must at length prevail.

Hogarth claimed that she found Chisholm's eloquent rant an "amusing instance" of his chauvinistic naïveté—especially when his *Fortnightly* piece ended with a reassurance that "even when Oxford and Cambridge fall into line with the other Universities, there will still be a large majority of the nicest and most highly cultivated women, just as we see them now, who will never have had the least inclination to pass an examination or take a degree." (However, Hogarth herself had begun to equivocate a mere eight years later, when she wrote the chapter on "Education and Professions: The Higher Education of Women" in the first volume of *The Woman's Encyclopedia*.)

And even before his degree campaign in the *Fortnightly*, Chisholm had risen to champion the distribution of George Moore's *Esther Waters*, allying himself not only with Conan Doyle but also with Sarah Grand, the pioneer of the New Woman movement in literature, against W. H. Smith's refusal to offer the book to readers based on the disapproving view of William Faux, an influential Smith's manager. The scuffle had dominated the book pages of *The Morning Chronicle* in the spring of 1894.

Commercial discrimination against literature friendly to feminist views and the refusal of the great universities to award degrees to deserving women were marrow issues of principle that he could grasp easily. The issue of women-in-general was a little more daunting. As Hogarth later wrote,

> Being much pressed by overmatter, and having already exceeded his prescribed limits by as much as a whole volume, [Chisholm] was anxious not to give more space than need be to any article under W. So I vividly remember a winter afternoon, when he called me "into counsel," as he called it, in the editorial sanctum, which, being interpreted, meant that, whilst I sat meekly by the fire, he walked up and down, expounding to me that the then position of women as an integral part of the human race made it unnecessary to write about them as though they were a race apart! I cordially but respectfully agreed, and we decided that only a few columns, chronicling the suffrage movement and certain educational advances need be inserted in Vol. XXVIII.

And what a strange article it is. While many of the major articles in the Eleventh Edition were unsigned, "Women" bore an author's initial–"X"–but, of course, the index of contributors offers no key, although it was written under very close scrutiny by Chisholm and perhaps even by Hogarth. Modern feminists find the "Women" article ambivalent, to say the least, and criticize it for its "evasiveness about the suffrage issue." It's true that the article doesn't pronounce a finding on the issue of the parliamentary vote. Chisholm may have thought that covering that debate was the work of the newspapers. But its sentiments aren't very well hidden, either. The very first paragraph suggests a credible polemic, and indicates pretty clearly the mind of encyclopedia.

> WOMEN. The very word "woman" (O. Eng. *wifmann*), etymologically meaning a wife (or the wife division of the human race, the female of the species *Homo*), sums up the long history of dependence and subordination, from which the women of to-day have only gradually emancipated them-

selves in such parts of the world as come under "Western civilization." Though married life and its duties necessarily form a predominant element in the woman's sphere, they are not necessarily the whole of it; and the "woman's movement" is essentially a struggle for the recognition of equality of opportunity with men, and for equal right irrespective of sex, even if special relations and conditions are willingly incurred under the form of partnership involved in marriage. The difficulties of obtaining this recognition are obviously due to historical causes combined with the habits and customs which history has produced.

There are many ways to begin an encyclopedia article about the sex of half the human race, but launching it from a consideration of emancipation certainly suggests a point of view. Hogarth, writing about this entry much later, laughs at Chisholm's careful editing, saying, "By 1910 he has got a little farther in his progress towards feminism," and it's very true that the *Britannica* wasn't exactly in the forefront of what, at the time, was radical social change, but that might not have been its job. Besides, it was a good measure better than Smellie's article under "Woman" in the first edition, which read, "The female of Man. See *Homo*."

And, in fact, Chisholm was almost certainly more sympathetic to the women's suffrage movement of the time than was Hogarth. After all, she, along with Gertrude Bell, Mary Ward, and a few others, were founding members of the Anti-Suffrage Society, which had early success, despite the fact that, as Hogarth later remarked,

Gertrude Bell

"It was our fate, as Antis, to attract all the ultra-feminine and the ladylike incompetents." Of all of them, only Gertrude Bell, Hogarth said, could deliver a decent speech. In a signed article in the 1913 *Britannica Year-book*, edited by Chisholm, she was more explicitly anti-suffragette–if not also anti-suffrage–blaming the parliamentary failure of suffrage acts and the final withdrawal of the Franchise Bill in February 1913 on a long series of violent episodes, including theater fires, bombings, assaults on the prime minister and other MPs, and especially the four days of vandalism that began March 1, 1912, in which "a number of women, armed with hammers, went out and broke the plate glass windows of the principal London shops," and blaming the violence on the leniency of officials who failed to inflict the punishments meted out. She contrasted this with the progress made by the mostly peaceful suffrage movement in California and elsewhere.

Three decades later, she finally had caught up with some of Chisholm's more pragmatic views–not to mention her husband's more progressive politics.

> We were on the wrong track, I think now; we had put our money on the wrong horse. But we had no desire to stop the women's movement. We merely wanted to regulate its pace and to prevent a noisy minority from bringing us all into discredit. From the first, though I have seen the contrary stated in semi-official publications, Mrs. Humphry Ward and her followers advocated an extension of women's work and powers in local government, and the opening to them on equal terms of professional opportunities. Probably we should have done better to turn ourselves into a right wing of the constitutional suffragists. Perhaps even we should have smiled on the suffragettes. After all, "Qui veut la fin"–when you want a thing very much, it does not always answer to be too squeamish about methods.

The New York Times was surprisingly hostile to the new edition. A confusing review by the folklorist Joseph Jacobs in the paper's February 19, 1911, book section sketched the history of the *Britannica* through the Ninth Edition. "Ten years after the completion of the ninth edition," Jacobs wrote, "*The Times* newspaper of London induced thereto by two ingenious American gentlemen, conceived the idea of selling a reprint of the edition at a reduced price to its readers and others, and succeeded beyond all expectation, incidentally involving itself in a quarrel with the whole publishing world of England. . . . Encouraged by its first success, it planned and carried out a supplement in nine volumes [the Tenth] . . . containing a new alphabet of articles intended . . . to last for 'the present generation.'" He praised a great deal of the new material in the Eleventh—especially the geography articles that caused Jacobs to call the Eleventh a "glorified gazetteer." That came as no surprise to Jacobs, who credited Chisholm's "excellent text-book on Commercial Geography" for the strength of the coverage. If the Tenth was supposed to be an encyclopedia for "the present generation," Jacobs felt the Eleventh had helped make that true by including far too much of the older editions:

> I have made a few necessarily rough calculations, which appeared to show that the tenth, or supplementary, edition rewrote about a quarter of the ninth and added about the same amount in new topics; thus a mere re-arrangement in one alphabet of the ninth and tenth editions would have made the present edition differ essentially from the ninth in close on half of its articles. . . . [I]t is probably that two-thirds of the topics of the eleventh edition differ entirely from the ninth, while most of the remainder has been brought up to date, especially with the bibliographies. The amount of change from the tenth edition is more difficult to estimate but, even with the new geographical, biographical, military and dictionary articles, there is probably not more than a fifth of the contents that is absolutely new.

Chisholm, who was in New Orleans to promote the Eleventh when Jacobs's review appeared, protested:

> While I naturally appreciate the compliments paid to me, as editor, by Dr. Joseph Jacobs in his able review of the first four-

teen volumes of the new editions of the *Encyclopædia Britannica*, which was printed in *The Times* of last Sunday (Feb. 19), I must ask you to allow me to correct one misapprehension into which he has fallen. My namesake, Dr. George Chisholm, the geographer, and myself are two totally distinct persons. I am not the author of his excellent text-book on Commercial Geography, and Dr. Jacobs has attributed the strength of the geographical side of the new edition to a wrong cause. His praise for the geographical articles is none the less welcome, and, I believe, deserved; but, if they are as good as he says, it is not because the editor-in-chief was himself a specialist in geography, but because, in the organization of the editorial staff, I from the first provided for a geographical department, ably manned within, and in touch with a number of expert geographers without. It has been my own duty to direct the work in all departments, with the assistance of others who has special knowledge in each, and I imagine that it was only in this way that the attempt could be made, as to the success of which the critics and the public must judge, to preserve that uniformity, unity and organic character in the construction of the whole work, which in my editorial introduction I have ventured to claim for the Eleventh Edition.

Catholics and Protestants were each offended by the *Britannica* for being too charitable and biased on both sides. For Protestants, the "errors" of the Ninth Edition had not been sufficiently expunged and there were too many articles covering Catholic topics. For Catholics, the articles covering Catholic topics—and Christianity in general—were not adequately embracing of certain dogmatic views. *The New York Times* carried a one-sided report typical of many:

CATHOLICS ATTACK NEW ENCYCLOPEDIA

ELEVENTH EDITION OF THE *BRITANNICA* IS CALLED "UNSCHOLARLY, SECTARIAN AND OFFENSIVE."

MANY PASSAGES CITED

The New York Times's story, which was carried without comment from anyone associated with the *Britannica*, was one of several that reported the anger at the *Britannica*'s coverage. The National Federation, a Catholic organization, had formed "a special committee of prominent priests and laymen who made a compilation of some of the alleged prejudiced passages offensive to Catholics." The committee, reported the newspaper, had passed a furious resolution:

> Whereas, The treatment of religious subjects in the eleventh edition of the *Encyclopædia Britannica*, particularly in matters in which the Catholic Church is concerned, is unscholarly, sectarian, and offensive.
>
> Be it Resolved, That we protest against this manifestation of prejudice in a work which bids for public patronage as a scholarly, impartial, and urbane publication.

The committee had a long list of complaints. They didn't like the entries on "Religion, Inspiration, Revelation, Liturgy, Mass, Theology, Marriage and Divorce, Absolution, Asceticism, Casuistry, Celibacy, Excommunication, Holy Water, Relics, Images, the Virgin Mary, or even the Catholic Church."

In addition, the report declared, "[o]f the 40,000,000 [sic] words in over 4,000,000 lines of the twenty-eight volumes, the Vulgate has enough to fill only five and one-half lines and God only twenty-six!"

Competent Catholics were not permitted, according to the report, to read or suggest revision of the numerous articles in which Catholics are specially interested. "Of the 1,500 contributors to the new *Britannica*, about fifteen are really Catholic, only ten of whom are recognized authorities in religious subjects."

The report concluded, "The entire encyclopedia is a sad manifestation of anti-Catholic animus, and must henceforth, for Catholics and all fair-minded Protestants, be considered as a storehouse of traditions, errors, prejudices born of a spirit of religious animosity and rancor long since happily repudiated by well-bred people."

Chisholm again responded, this time somewhat impatiently. "As I am at present advised," Chisholm told *The Times* in a letter, "these critics approached the subject in a spirit which makes a fair controversy impossible." He was not, he insisted, interested in any religious polemic at all; if anything, the Eleventh Edition was rational-Anglican and therefore incapable of accommodating religious mysteries of any kind, including the Catholic variety. "Everybody knows that the *Encyclopædia Britannica* is not itself a Catholic work, England is not a Roman Catholic country, and Catholics, whether in America or elsewhere, cannot reasonably suppose that they will find their point of view dominating the theological article of such a work. What are errors to them happen to be very often conclusions of standard theological and historical criticism as understood in the wider sphere outside that of dogmatic Roman Catholicism."

Finally, there was one other important group of people offended by the *Britannica*—and it was the group that ultimately had the most impact on the *Britannica*'s future: Cambridge academics.

R. T. Wright and M. R. James's summertime agreement had always been vulnerable to criticism. The faculty at Cambridge saw their positions as something a little loftier than they were; after all, most Cambridge profs, like most academics in most places, drew their salaries, taught a few courses, retired, and were promptly forgotten.

But while they lived and breathed, their insistence on importance and the power that entailed was their most cherished prerogative, and for the scholars associated with the university's press, attaching the name of the University of Cambridge to something so marinated in commerce as Hooper's *Encyclopædia Britannica* was an unforgivable act. They felt somehow soiled by the association.

For a year, Wright and James had been fearless champions of the *Britannica*. Wright and Chisholm had toured India together to plump for sales there, and James had put his name to a sales pamphlet that defended—indeed, celebrated—the intellectual quality of the encyclopedia. Other booklets and pamphlets were produced to feature the encyclopedia's most famous contributors, their portraits lined up row upon row, from statesmen to sportsmen, like a scrapbook of tobacco-card heroes. A prospectus bound in boards displayed the *Britannica*'s features, including an insert of pages printed on Bible paper, and individual brochures were produced to explain the various bindings available. There was, admittedly, an emphasis on affordability and on the necessity of being better informed than the neighbors, but the selling points were all about quality. The Cambridge imprimatur was not wasted by Hooper.

In fact, the Cambridge association was offensive to more than just the prickly academics at Cambridge. It also offended Oxford graduates who were nervous about giving Cambridge the keys to the *Britannica*, no matter how much Cambridge didn't want them. A correspondent, identified only as "Y.Z." and soon to be disappointed, wrote in 1910 to *The New Age*, a socialist periodical, and spoke no doubt for other concerned, if not offended, Oxford types:

> The precise reasons which have led to the remarkably abrupt change in the ownership of the copyright of the Eleventh Edition of the "Encyclopædia Britannica" at the eleventh hour of its preparation are by no means clear, and have given rise to much speculation on the part of outsiders and the reading public generally. It was *a* matter for congratulation however to all who appreciated the excellent manner in which the Supplement of the Ninth Edition was brought out, to find that the editorship remained in the hands of Mr. Hugh Chisholm, who by the way, is an Oxford man, as a wholesome antidote to the predominant influence of Cambridge. There are of course many and serious objections to a single university possessing the monopoly in such a publication.
>
> Cambridge fads, which are innumerable, will no doubt prevail, as in so many publications of the "University Press." If the Roman Curia succeeds in purchasing the twelfth edition it would be going one better. So we would advise those with a mission and enough money to keep their eyes open. Mrs. Eddy may be a good bidder and win the thirteenth. To be logical, indeed, we see no reason why there should not be such trusts for propaganda in all schools of thought, if only to prove their absurdity. It seems a pity that the "Encyclopædia Britannica" should be dominated by any particular schools of thought.
>
> Mr. Chisholm will, we trust, see that it is free from this objection this time. But the complaint has been urged before now that there is an ill-bred tendency on the part of Cam-

bridge professors to push their own "policy" or views against all others. In this respect indeed German scholarship is vastly superior to that of the Cambridge schools at the present day. There is a scrupulous and chivalrous feeling of fair play towards others which is singularly lacking in such writings as, for instance, those of Sir J. J. Thomson on electricity.

Your esteemed contemporary the "Outlook," from which you differ widely in politics, has in its issue of February 5th, 1910 (and the "Electrician" many times), directed attention to this fact, and something should be done to elevate the tone of English morals in science; if nothing else. Mr. Chisholm will no doubt see that the "Encyclopædia Britannica" is free from blemishes in this respect. For science is not religion, nor Cambridge an Insurance Company for professors' "policies."

But a lot had happened in that year, and for the sidelined academics at Cambridge, as for the nervous managers of the Oxford University Press, too much of it had taken place in the muddy marketplace. Advertising was the culprit, of course. Yet it was advertising that had made the whole enterprise successful, and while the university wished to restrain Hooper, Haxton, and Sickert from the excesses of competitions and the like, the university's press understandably was interested in encouraging people to buy the books.

The sales effort had been steady and sustained in the United Kingdom, where virtually every English-speaking newspaper of size in Britain and the English-speaking world received promotional messages from the *Britannica*. In six months, from the official (but generally ignored) publication date of November 1, 1910, through May of the following year, Hooper bought as much as $800,000 worth of advertising and promotion. The campaign brought back the familiar charges of American vulgarity in selling things, although in the U.S. the campaign was much less restrained. There wasn't much Cambridge could do about the way Hooper sold books to his fellow Americans, after all.

Early in the spring of 1911, a date was set—May 31—at which time it would be decided how many sets to produce. Those who signed up before that date were assured a *Britannica*. Their less enlightened friends and neighbors would have to wait. The hurry-last-day theme set by Haxton a decade earlier was trotted out again, to spectacular effect. On May 31, when the newspaper ads screamed "last day," Hooper made sure it was a day to remember.

> That was a stirring day on West 32nd Street. Messenger boys filed into the Builders' Exchange Building in a stream. The bags of the letter carriers grew more plethoric with each delivery. The order clerks in the *Britannica* offices on the tenth floor forgot their lunch in their vain endeavors to keep the stacks of letters and telegrams from toppling. Oliver McKee, the English sales manager in charge, came near to uttering an exclamation, so nearly did he come to losing his reserve, as his excited assistant reported the doings. One of the final orders was from a corporation head who asked for fourteen sets, one for his yacht, one for his home, and the rest for his executives.

Even if that unnamed executive was Hooper (and there's no evidence it was), by the time the sun rose on June 1, thirty-two thousand sets of the *Britannica* had been sold in a variety of bindings and papers. Hooper had spent $75,000 on ads during the month of May alone, and it had been money well spent.

Hooper's spectacular success was seen with horror in Cambridge. A year after the publication of the *Britannica*, new Syndics were to be appointed by the university senate. Those whose hands had been dirtied by the *Britannica* affair were the victims of a witch hunt mounted by Archdeacon William Cunningham, a fellow of Trinity, a sometime lecturer in history, and the author of several CUP titles. After reviewing the prospectus for the *Britannica*, in which the relationship with Cambridge was explained, he had but one persistent question: "When did the Syndics of the Press begin to be responsible for this important and long-continued editorial supervision?" Answers given by James and others didn't satisfy him, because that wasn't the kind of satisfaction he wanted.

Finally, on December 1, 1911, just before the naming of new Syndics, a letter from Cunningham and six other disapproving colleagues made its way to the letters page of *The Times:*

With reference to the appointment of members of the Senate to serve on Syndicates of Cambridge University, the following protest has been issued:–

THE SYNDICS OF THE PRESS
AND THE "ENCYCLOPÆDIA BRITANNICA"

The appointment of members of the Senate to serve on the different Syndicates will in the usual course be made at the Congregation on Thursday, December 7. We fear that the reappointment of any one who has shared the responsibility of the Syndicate in undertaking the publication of the "Encyclopædia Britannica" might be regarded as the formal acceptance by the Senate of a policy which we believe is very generally condemned by members of the University, and against which we wish to protest. No information has been given as to the rights which the University has acquired and the obligation which the University has incurred, but the publication of this work, although it has been undertaken by the Syndics on their own authority, has not been treated as a transaction in the ordinary course of their business. It has been represented as the direct act of the University in its corporate capacity; statements have been put forward that the University has undertaken the publication as part of a definite educational policy and the prefatory note prefixed to the first volume and dated from Cambridge suggests to anyone who is not acquainted with the facts that the University is responsible for the preparation and publication of the work. We believe that the reputation of the University has been injured by the representations which have been made; that this reputation has suffered, and is suffering, by the methods taken to advertise the work; and on these grounds we enter our protest.

Any member of the Senate who wishes to join in this protest is requested to send his name to Archdeacon Cunningham, Trinity, or L. Whibley, Pembroke, not later than Monday, December 4.

Then, only a few days later, they declared a "victory."

Our protest has already served its purpose; it has made clear to the public that the responsibility for the publication and advertisement of the "Encyclopædia Britannica" rests with the Syndics, and not with the University; it has prevented the possibility of any misinterpretation of the Senate's attitude, which would have been natural, if the re-appointment of any Syndic had been proposed and tacitly accepted.

The sound and fury ebbed with the year. The *Britannica*'s end-papers may have borne the seals of all the Cambridge colleges, and the spine and cover of each volume may have displayed the seal of the university and the words "Cambridge University Press," but thanks to the protesting archdeacon, nobody would get the wrong idea about Cambridge's involvement.

Chisholm had understood the potential threat that could come from irate academics and had been very careful in addressing the university's role in his prefatory note:

The present publication of the new *Encyclopædia Britannica* by the University of Cambridge is a natural step in the evolution of the university as an educational institution and a home of research. The medieval University of Cambridge began its educational labours as an institution intended almost exclusively for the instruction of the clergy, to whose needs its system of studies was necessarily in a large measure accommodated. The Revival of Learning, the Renaissance and the Reformation widened its sphere of intellectual work and its interests, as well as its actual curriculum. The 19th century saw the complete abolition of the various tests which formerly shut the gates of the English universities against a large part of the people. The early establishment in Cambridge of special colleges for women was also a sign of expanding activities. About the same time the University Extension movement, first advocated at Cambridge in 1871 on the ground that the ancient universities were not mere clusters of private establishments but national institutions, led to a wider conception of the possibilities of utilizing the intellectual resources of the universities for the general diffusion of knowledge and culture; and the system of Local Examinations brought the university into close contact with secondary education throughout the country. But the public to which the University of Cambridge thus appealed, though wider than that of the college lecture-rooms, was still necessarily limited. Practically it is only through the medium of the University Press that Cambridge can enter into and maintain direct relations with the whole of the English-speaking world. The present time seems appropriate for an effort towards thus signally extending the intellectual and educational influence of the university.

To this end, the University of Cambridge has undertaken the publication of the *Encyclopædia Britannica*, and now issues the Eleventh Edition of that work. These twenty-eight volumes and index aim at achieving the high ambition of bringing all extant knowledge within the reach of every class of readers. . . . This Eleventh Edition of the *Encyclopædia Britannica* is now, therefore, offered to the public by the University of Cambridge in the hope and belief that it will be found to be a trustworthy guide to sound learning, and an instrument of culture of world-wide influence.

It was a silly incident, but for Hooper the immediate protest by Cunningham and the others yielded to the inescapable fact that the university's most famous professors were among the *Britannica*'s celebrated contributors.

But just as there had been no future for the *Britannica* at Printing House Square two years earlier, now there was no future at Cambridge. Hooper's ambitious, forward-looking proposals for an extensive home study course that he believed would carry Cambridge and the *Britannica* into the parlors of the civilized world were casually dismissed, and other ideas intended to harness the *Britannica*'s marketing muscle to Cambridge's authority—as he had done before with *The Times*—were easily turned away. Cambridge did not care to be a global university. He was restrained again and again by the new secretary, A. R. Waller, who had replaced Wright in 1912. The smallest hint of marketing vulgarity was suddenly offensive. At one point, Cambridge even forbade him to use lantern slides in sales presentations for the encyclopedia: too colorful.

Chisholm was given what Janet Hogarth later described as a "provisional but quite definite" offer of the editorship of *The Times* by Lord Northcliffe in 1912. He accepted, and agreed to take up the post as soon as he returned from a promotional tour of the U.S., a promise made to Hooper. Hogarth enjoyed the premature announcement of the job, which Chisholm discussed with many of the audiences he met there.

> So definite was the prospect that he had thought himself justified in confiding it to the best of his university staff and expressing a hope of being able to find them future posts.
>
> We who were left behind, still struggling with the printing and proof-reading of the Index Volume, used to lighten our evening labours by getting someone to read aloud to us the flaming accounts which our American press-cutting agents sent us of his triumphal progress through the West. As he got nearer the Pacific the tides of enthusiasm seemed to rise higher and to carry the editor with them, for on one occasion he went so far as to tell his audience that he hoped to be in a position to exercise an influence upon international politics and would see to it that British-American friendship should be strengthened and deepened. "Good old chief," interjected an irreverent member of the staff. "Another glass of champagne and he'd have promised them a sympathetic Ambassador!"

But when Chisholm returned, he discovered that Northcliffe had reneged. The editorship of *The Times* was given by Northcliffe instead to Geoffrey Dawson, who went on to promote Hitler and appeasement and Chamberlain's Munich compromise, and then to Wickham Steed, who used *The Times* to promote the "Protocols of the Learned Elders of Zion." In the years preceding the Second World War, not a word was published concerning anti-Semitism in Nazi Germany.

Chisholm didn't sever ties with the *Britannica* completely. In 1913, as war loomed, Chisholm and Courtney produced *The Britannica Year-book*—called "Wisdom Without Waiting" by the parodists at *Punch*. It was to be the first of the encyclopedia's annual updates, covering events from 1910 to the end of 1912. But no new project immediately appeared, so in 1912 Chisholm accepted a seat on the board of *The Times* and a key position on the staff as city editor, where he skirmished with those eager to protect their investments and fearful of war with Germany.

It's impossible to know what kind of editor of *The Times* Chisholm would have made—neither the editorship of *The St. James's Gazette* nor the *Britannica* is usefully analogous. His own very successful stint as city editor during the First World War—mindful of *The Times*'s influence and assiduous in repelling threats against it, is probably a better indicator—as in the Rothschild case, when Nathan, the famous and influential banker, anxious about his European portfolio and the effects of war on the European economy, summoned Chisholm and abruptly demanded that *The Times* reflect a more pacifistic, pro-German policy. Chisholm returned to Printing House Square, dutifully presented Baron Rothschild's demands—and insisted they be ignored, and they were.

But he saw the *Year-book* through production in 1912 and even went to New York to read proofs. The book had heavy coverage of American and British geography, politics, and finance, and a pronounced modernist tone in which science was featured and the recent history of all things was described invariably as "progress"—until, in 1914, all progress came to a halt.

At some point, Chisholm had set down his premonitions about a world still undocumented by his *Britannica*:

> I dream that I am in a peasant's hut in some obscure corner of Russia. The room is large and low, with three windows, white-washed walls, and very little furniture. In front of the house stretches a broad plain which loses itself in the far distance, over which hangs like a roof a mountainous, gray sky.
>
> I am not alone: There are about ten men in the room, very simple, plainly-dressed people: They move silently, as it were gliding to and fro, avoiding each other, but continually casting anxious glances at one another.
>
> None of them know how they came there or what sort of people the other are. Anxiety and depression are to be read on every face: They all step in turn to the windows, and look as if expecting something.

Now they turn again and wander restlessly up and down. A little boy, who is among them, moans from time to time in a thin, monotonous voice: "Papa, I'm afraid!" This whimpering fairly makes me sick. I too am beginning to be afraid,—but of what? I do not know: I merely feel [that] some terrible misfortune is approaching. The little boy goes on whimpering. Oh! If we could only get away from here! How close it is, how sultry, how oppressive . . . But escape is impossible. The sky is like a pall, there is not the slightest breeze, the air seems dead.

Suddenly the boy calls from the window with a terrified voice: "Look, look! The earth has fallen away."

What! Fallen away? . . . It is a fact: There had been a plain in front of the house: Now it stands on the summit of an enormous mountain! The horizon has fallen down, sunk away: And close to the house yawns a steep, black, gaping abyss!

We all press round the window . . . Our hearts stand still with fear. "Look there!—There," whispers my neighbor. Now over the whole, wide, boundless waste, suddenly something begins to move, as if little round hills were rising and falling. We scream!—We all thought at once. It will engulf us. But how can that be? How can it rise in its might to the height of this lofty summit? Meanwhile it rises ever higher and higher. Now there are not merely little hills visible here and there in the distance . . . A single, mighty, monstrous wave sweeps across the whole circle of the horizon. It is flying towards us! Like an icy whirlwind, it approaches, circling like a dark abyss of Hell. Everything about begins to tremble: And there, in that hurrying chaos, a thousand-voiced brazen clangor crashes and thunders and roars.

Ah! What howling—groaning! It is the Earth, moaning with terror.

Its end has come! Universal destruction! The little boy goes on whimpering . . . I turn to cling to my companions: But suddenly we are all overwhelmed, buried, drowned, swept away by that pitch-black icy monstrous wave.

Darkness—eternal darkness!

Almost breathless, I awake.

The war changed everything, as wars do. Certainly little in Hooper's world was left intact. Sales of the *Britannica* steeply declined even as a "Handy edition" was introduced in 1915 in the U.S.—smaller, cheaper, same contents. Hogarth set aside her children's encyclopedia. Sickert was sent back out to the colonies. Haxton was sent to South America to sell *Britannica*s—partially, no doubt, out of spite at Jackson, who was selling his own version in Buenos Aires and elsewhere. Haxton did not succeed, although it must be noted that Jackson had the distinct advantage of publishing an encyclopedia in Spanish—unlike Hooper's.

Immediately after the war, Hooper and Chisholm met on the pavement in front of New York's Lotos Club, where Chisholm was a member. The *Times* archive has a copy of the telegram Chisholm sent the next day resigning from his post and from his seat on *The Times*'s board. On it, a flurry of handwritten notes. "What does this mean?" reads one. In 1922, the Twelfth Edition—a three-volume "war edition"—appeared, again edited by Chisholm, with Hogarth's snappy assistance.

The two men should have had another decade or two to pursue their dreams of a British-American Anglosphere the size of the earth. But Hooper gave up Pendell Court and settled for Cheverells, a swank, 113-acre estate in Bedford Hills, where his wife, Harriet Meeker, had successfully launched a local career as an interior decorator and consulting architect. Hooper died—a bad heart—in 1922, just before the new volumes of the Twelfth Edition were published, and a year before his partner-nemesis, Jackson. Chisholm eulogized Hooper in print as a great publisher, and so did others, of course. John St. Loe Strachey, then editor of *The Spectator*, ran an anonymous obituary, possibly by Walter Alison Phillips, that surveyed Hooper's rapid rise in London, ending with this:

> It is the opinion of many that Mr. Hooper's success lay in his boldness and "dash" as an advertiser and a salesman, but the truth lies more in his immutable faith in the intelligent ambition for education of the great mass of the people. Many well-known professional educators have done less for the enlightenment of the world, and he leaves behind him a finer

monument than many of us could wish for in the work to which he devoted his life.

To this, Strachey added this note:

It is a great pleasure to us to publish this just and reticent appreciation of Mr. Hooper's work. We are especially glad to see his zeal for education emphasized, for that was the central aspiration of his mind. He was a warm, unswerving and true friend of this country—or, as we should prefer to put it, he recognized the paramount unity of the English-speaking race.

Then, two years later, Chisholm died, too—according to family stories, the victim of a botched appendectomy—after lingering for a couple of days in a nursing facility. *The Times* commemorated him with a curt and lifeless obituary. His body was taken by the London Necropolis & National Mausoleum Company railway out to Brockwood in the company of his wife and his three sons.

Sickert and Haxton died at about the same time, the latter, an inmate at St. Johnland, then a home for the poor in Kings Park, New York, the former at age fifty in Madrid, where he was visiting with his wife, Elizabeth Kennedy, a singer he married in 1908. The reaction of Haxton's son (and any other survivors) isn't known, but Oswald's sudden death stunned Sickert's family and his many friends. He had been away after yet another very long journey in support of the *Britannica* and was preparing to finally return to England.

Janet Hogarth Courtney outlived them all by more than thirty years, writing clever, amusing, and witty memoirs about journalists, writers, editors, feminists, and freethinking positivists. And she never could quite leave behind the *Britannica*. She and Beatrix Chisholm remained friendly and, as "Aunt Janet," she knew the children well. In a letter to Chisholm's widow, she wrote, "I would love to come to lunch one day and to tell you a tale of an abortive attempt some of us made years ago to re-capture and rescue the E.B. from permanent Americanisations which will amuse you." Her accounts are the principal source of what is known about the personalities behind Hooper's great project.

Hooper's dreams died before he did, as often happens, and he knew it along with his sentimental affection for a set of British values that, if they ever existed, certainly had vanished in the war. The ownership of the *Encyclopædia Britannica* passed from Cambridge University Press, happy to be rid of it, to Sears, Roebuck, who, ironically, marketed it with considerably less panache than Haxton and Sickert had provided on behalf of *The Times* or even Cambridge. It was as if exhaustion, caused by the energy necessary to generate plausible hyperbole in a market turned deeply sour and pessimistic, had set in for good. J. Louis Garvin edited the *Britannica* next, with Franklin Hooper, as always, on duty in New York. But in 1940, Hooper, who enjoyed demonstrating his reckless skills as a pedestrian on the streets of New York, was struck by a truck on a quiet country lane and he died, too.

CHAPTER 19

POSTSCRIPT

The *Britannica*'s Eleventh Edition is the last great English-language encyclopedia. As a general reference work, it's unrivaled, as unique now as when it was published.

Readers realized instantly that despite the recycling of entries from earlier *Britannica* editions, the Eleventh was unlike any of those—especially, the Ninth, in which some entries massaged eloquence out of science while many others spun lead from art. That edition's collection of scholarly essays was linked only by stitches, boards, and binding tape. The price and the sheer heaviness of the material and the writing—not to mention the object itself—combined to limit its usefulness and only made a ready market for all those snappy, abridged, "Americanized" editions. As mentioned above, entire books were repurposed from overlong entries in the Ninth, so unrelated were the articles to each other.

And the Eleventh Edition certainly wasn't like the relatively light and apparently random compendium of information found in *Chambers' Cyclopædia*, the first of these general works. Chambers seemed to contain everything, yet nothing it contained seemed to matter. Yet Denis Diderot's famous *Encyclopédie* had started with Chambers as its model; Diderot simply made more of it, adding more and more entries until its size suggested ostensible utility.

When Chisholm began his work, it had been 160 years since Diderot published his massive aggregation of articles by accomplished men with specialized interests. The *Encyclopédie* had never been a useful model for English encyclopedias—although in one important respect it was more "modern": it contained nearly twice as many entries, at only half the length of the Eleventh. Moreover, it was a collection with an obvious political mission, thus authoritative the way the Catholic catechism was authoritative. As the Eleventh said in its entry on the French work, Diderot "sought . . . to guide opinion." The Eleventh can't be said to have intentionally provoked dispute. Chisholm seemed genuinely surprised at the criticisms leveled at the work. He meant no offense even while giving so much to so many.

Diderot hoped his work would change how people thought. But Diderot was a revolutionary and a philosopher. Chisholm was a journalist. His work was intended to reflect what was known. He didn't need to create a way to "guide opinion," and besides, he knew revolution wasn't necessary. By 1910, the Goddess of Reason had already triumphed and the Church was in intellectual disarray. Chisholm's intention seems to have been what he said it was in his editorial introduction to the Eleventh: to create a secular Beatrice—"a trustworthy guide to sound learning, and an instrument of culture of world-wide influence."

On the face of it, creating a "trustworthy guide" is a fairly friendly ambition for a reference work. No wonder the Eleventh's companionship still elicits a kind of affected, clubby comfort, like a pipe next to the fire or a massive pile of highly detailed chintz; those with a taste for the wry can easily read it as an experimental fiction about a place that nearly existed, once. The Eleventh has a personality that can't be easily overlooked: it's plausible, reasonable, unruffled, often reserved, completely authoritative. It makes no apologies for its point of view; indeed, it doesn't seem to realize it even has one. To Chisholm and his editors, it was just the facts, laid out in a helpful and logical fashion. Chisholm had shown the readers of the *Britannica* what they had hoped was their world, and a great measure of the Eleventh's success was due to its ability to so solidly build on that set of shared assumptions.

Looking at it now, we can't say exactly how the Eleventh's world is different from ours, other than the props and sets. Maybe it isn't different after all; fundamentally, not much has changed. As noted, most of the familiar things with which we are now surrounded also existed in some form in 1910—airplanes, cars, communists, telephones, rockets, microscopes, recorded music, psychologists. A clever reader of the Eleventh could follow the simple rill that from that reservoir also produced television and satellites and polio vaccines. The twentieth century seems like a century of radical innovation, but it can also be seen as a century of logical extrapolation, the Rome to the long nineteenth-century's Greece, an era in which engineers spoke the language of visionaries. And it was English.

What better time to be a Briton or an American? From Harvard to Cambridge to Stanford to Yale to Oxford, the planet was trussed in the expertise of imperial achievement and Yankee energy. Nothing threatened the muscular dominance of the English language or of the educated class who had provided the bricks for the magnificent creation Hooper and Chisholm had made from nothing more than an idea or two. Yes, there were very few Americans, and even fewer women, involved in the great project, but no matter, for those who wrote for the *Britannica* spoke for all of humankind.

Had it misspoken? Well, in those offending articles, certainly. But those errors are visible mostly in hindsight. Otherwise, its failings were in what had been left unsaid or in what it said at insufficient length. And beyond the quibbles of a few reviewers, most readers found few errors of any kind. Instead, they found that life was so mysterious that only experts could explain it all, and Chisholm gave them that explanation in a systematic, clear, and final statement of what was correct and what was incorrect, what was true and what was not true—which is, of course, very close to a moral claim of being able to decide what's right and what's wrong. A hopeful, educated man or woman of 1910 could open a volume of the *Britannica* and see that all the people and places were accounted for, and all the bits and pieces, buildings, monuments, and ditches of the entire planet were measured in length or weight or height and put in their proper place. The known world was alive with details and minutiae, down to the first primordial globule. It's still a wonderful place to visit on a lazy afternoon.

Try it. Sets of the Eleventh are still ubiquitous, online and off-. For a modern reader, the book's utter lack of anarchy encourages ironic comparisons of the entries in its columns. "Steam Engines" seems to deserve its several pages. But next door, the many thousands of words by Carl Pulfrich on the stereopticon, that antique-shop-and-parlor staple? This most rational of all publishing enterprises is a bad influence on a sober reader; it's difficult to pick up a volume and pass from one entry to another without being ambushed by imagination. The Argentinian fantasist Jorge Luis Borges finds unseemly gaps in future editions compared to the Eleventh; his discussion of the entry on John Wilkins and his "analytical language" contains his well-known list of animal types ("Those that tremble as if they were mad," "those that at a distance resemble flies") taken from an invented Chinese encyclopedia, the *Celestial Emporium of Benevolent Knowledge*. Is the *Wunderkammer* of the Eleventh any less fanciful? Characters carefully documented and emerging larger than life are on nearly every page (see, for instance, John Gully, who beat up a giant and fathered twenty-four), alongside exciting descriptions of plants and flowers best read aloud in unctuous, twee tones ("The filaments elongate rapidly at flowering-time, and the lightly versatile anthers empty an abundance of finely granular pollen through a longitudinal slit"—and this is happening in your front yard in front of the children *right now*). Colorful genealogies ("Sir Harbottle's eldest daughter, Mary, married Sir Capel Luckyn, Bart") and found poems are everywhere—and, when not found, mined; in 1957, Richmond Lattimore distilled the entry on "Hara-kiri" to what he called a sonnet, but really the poetry remained on the *Britannica*'s page.

Borges has a point; maybe on some level, all encyclopedias are artifice and invention, a way of slicing and dicing that which ought not be minced. They are certainly invented in the mind of the reader who takes in the wide horizon of a thousand entries and makes a landscape that fits the known facts; and really, they are invented in their very construction, like elaborate, richly sourced folktales, the story of the world and all creation, what we know so far, literally catalogs of received wisdom. As Janet Hogarth Courtney pointed out, the manner of the Eleventh's compilation—taking a previous collection of all-that-is-known and improving and expanding it—was not unusual. "Of course every encyclopædia cribs from its predecessors as much as it dares, keeping one eye on the laws of copyright," she wrote. "But it is *de rigueur* to pretend that it starts with a blank page." This pretense, she wrote, "is maintained even by the staff.

To assume airs of omniscience whilst really ransacking the reference books of the habitable world, running your facts to earth in *Brockhaus* or *Meyer*, *La Grande Encyclopédie* or *Larousse*, whilst pretending to recover them from the recesses of your own richly stored mind, is a pose which naturally deceives no one inside the office, not even yourself. But there is something in the atmosphere of encyclopædias, in their *aura*, so to speak, which does tend to self-conceit, and it needs a perpetual play of humour to preserve a sense of proportion." This extends even to those who write about encyclopedias and who can then claim to have been "over" or "through" the whole thing, but who, when questioned, have to run and look it up *again*—of course.

Fortunately for the Eleventh Edition's staff, many dozens of encyclopedias had been published by the time Chisholm started his work. In a way, that contributed to the sense that the Eleventh was like nothing before, because the world wasn't like what it was before. The Eleventh was an anticipated thing; as noted, it could hardly be otherwise after the promotion of the Tenth. Readers could be forgiven for assuming the Eleventh Edition would be a kind of ultimate encyclopedia: the expectations of readers were that as each year, month, day passed, knowledge also grew apace, and therefore so would encyclopedias.

But they didn't. After the Eleventh came a series of encyclopedias containing as many—or even more—articles. But in each case the entries grew shorter, less certain, much less authoritative, until we come to today. From the Twelfth Edition onward, it's possible to trace a degradation of sustained thought. Shorter and shorter, more and more simple, that's the way of publishers of encyclopedias (and books and magazines and discs and websites and podcasts and tweets). As newspaper pages shrink in size, so, apparently, do the ideas they contain. That kind of regression can only be expected in a world where authority is up for grabs, the thing separating right from left, Republican from Democrat, scientist from clergy, green from not-so-green. Great institutions cling to their claims of authority— their "brands"—for dear life, for without them, they would vanish into a sea of discount nonentities. The *Britannica* still uses experts for this reason, but "authority" is always highly qualified, now that one person's expert is another's propagandist.

Hans Koning wrote that for him—and his argument is so compelling that it might work for many of us—the Eleventh is the "last" *Britannica*: "One rang in the age of reason," he said, "the other rang it out." Subsequent *Britannicas*—with their Micro- and Macropedias—were not encyclopedias "in the precise sense that the word had been used between 1751 and 1910. A circle of all human knowledge with a single center or point of view was no longer possible. . . . Only one concept of the world—the teleological—was the true one. Thus, the cross-referencing of facts and theories, which is of the essence for an encyclopedia, came naturally; its writers shared a common rationality, and even a common idea of human destiny. The world [of the Eleventh] was a rational and ultimately a harmonious place."

The ability of Chisholm to seize the *Britannica*'s moment in history in an orderly, systematic, and all-encompassing way was an astonishing feat, but no less astonishing, at least to the Eleventh's readers, was the time itself. For them, for more than a century—one could argue, since the days of the plague—civilization's trajectory had been rising with momentary dips caused mostly by those French with their revolutions and emperors, and occasionally by the more belligerent followers of what the Eleventh called the "Mahommedan Religion."

To most of those living and working in the English-speaking world—and definitely for readers of the *Britannica*—the outlook was for continued rosiness. United by culture and language—with a quarter of the world's surface occupied by the empire, and with the United States holding sway over North and South America—the ongoing story of civilization had been reduced to working out some of the technical problems associated with quotidian existence—how to make trains run faster, telescopes see farther, limbs heal quicker. Social issues were trifles in the world of the *Britannica*; religion was a respectable, if irrelevant, concern of the editors, and the humanities were documented to give the proper mix of erudition and pleasure. The main thing was *progress*.

In the Eleventh, optimism was the logical conclusion to every line of inquiry, and proof of progress was everywhere you looked, on nearly every page. In his editorial introduction, Chisholm used the word so often, it took on a nearly percussive effect. The Eleventh explained everything that was explainable, just as the ads had promised. We knew whence we came and we knew how we'd arrived at the dawn broken by the *Britannica*'s bright appearance, shining the light of absolute certainty everywhere. It was all there. You could look it up. Being able to do so provided readers a great deal of comfort and reassurance.

It also provided a way of seeing contemporary intellectual life. While some older contributors to the Ninth Edition declined to write for the Eleventh because of Chisholm's decision to include entries on those still living, in the Eleventh Edition all things and most people are connected if not in fact, then in understanding. Biographies of modern politicians are not presented in a way that differs from those of ancient kings or warriors or philosophers; they are often very highly detailed with personal information—we find that the peculiar social theorizer Jonas Hanway, for example, was the first Londoner to carry an umbrella and was passionately opposed to tea drinking and *tipping*, of all things, and that Lady Hamilton's husband, Sir William, may have missed his wife's well-publicized dalliance with Nelson because the old gent was completely senile. (As a rule, browsers note, the best moments of a life in the Eleventh come at the end, in a by-the-way last few sentences, where there seems always to be a place for eccentricities when they are germane, or even nearly so.) Of course, some entries cover the lives of contributors to the Eleventh. This is especially affecting when we see how narrowly they beat their deadlines—for example, the article on that scholar of Arabic, Michael Jan de Goeje, whose life, we realize, concluded just as his work was going to press, his editor still sighing with sorrow and relief.

In some cases, characterizations that seem delicate for the time even veer toward awkward gossip. Chisholm, for example, who wrote the article on Oscar Wilde, found that the revelations that came out during his libel case against the Marquess of Queensberry were "fatal" ones. Even after nearly a decade, he wrote, "It is still impossible to take a purely objective view of Oscar Wilde's work. The Old Bailey revelations removed all doubt as to the essential unhealthiness of his personal influence; but his literary genius was none the less remarkable, and his plays were perhaps the most original contribution to English dramatic writing during the period." And while most biographies detoured gingerly around controversial themes, as did Chisholm's of Wilde, some waxed on the very qualities that might make some of the *Britannica*'s more prim readers blush, however mildly. John Burroughs, the great naturalist and essayist, on Walt Whitman, for example, was emphatic and straightforward: "His *Leaves* radiates democracy as no other modern literary work does, and brings the reader into intimate and enlarged relations with fundamental human qualities—with sex, manly love, charity, faith, self-esteem, candor, purity of body, sanity of mind. He was democratic because he was not in any way separated nor detached from the common people by his quality, his culture, or his aspirations. He was bone of their bone and flesh of their flesh."

But this was an uncharacteristic tone. The Eleventh has almost nothing in it that might excite, no entry on "manly love" or even on sex; and readers are provided excitement only after it's been draped in euphemism. There is, however, a very long, very dry article on prostitution.

But in terms of mechanics, technology, tools, tubes and beakers, artillery and all things military, iron and railways—the Eleventh Edition has it covered, completely. Koning pointed out that by his count the number of words devoted to hydraulics and hydromechanics alone exceeded 110,000, or more than three-quarters the length of the book you're reading now. The Eleventh may carry the pretensions of the high Victorian classicism that informed its editor, but it's indisputably a work of his Edwardian exuberance and optimism. The entire world waited only to be mapped, examined, improved, and explained. For Chisholm, Hooper, and all the others who wrote, edited, compiled, published, and purchased the Eleventh, it was a 44-million-word preamble to a whole new century.

And what a century! The twentieth century must have seemed as unlimited to Britons and Americans as it did to Janet Hogarth and the female contributors. Optimism had always been a Victorian trait, but only for the middle class. For the first time ever, optimism seemed at least understandable, even among the poor. Civilization, as they knew it, seemed to be working itself out, and where it didn't work, it could be fixed with a little charity, some glue, and a bit of jolly inventiveness. The Victorians saw the world as a massive *project*, one still in the process of being shaped, but which seemed to show great promise. And as Victorian anxiety began turning into Edwardian certainties, as the empire outlived its empress yet nevertheless grew stronger, the project of civilization took on an elegance that was hard to ignore.

It was the nineteenth, not the twentieth, century that had given the public square to science and banned the rest; an educated elite—men such as Chisholm—was pitted against the rest of the world, all black, yellow, brown, non-U, non-important, irrational. Many Edwardians would certainly be alarmed at some of the consequences of the way political theorists have interpreted one form or another of "rationalism" to produce the "scientific" policies of Germany, Russia, and China during the 1900s. But the genial acceptance of a secularized way of understanding humankind's place in the world would be quite familiar to every educated Edwardian. So would our public intellectuals and pundits, the perhaps not always worthy inheritors of the "higher journalism" mantle. The views and movements that seem modern now were also modern a century ago. Only the stereopticon view of our own recent history draws an incompatible distinction between then and now. Even unproductive rhetoric is similar: disputes marked by furious exchanges—such as that between Herbert Spencer and Frederic Harrison, both on approximately the same side in the nineteenth century's culture wars—contributed little to the lasting memory of either man, for there is none, although both at the time were as celebrated as any modern pundit. What those polemics brought wasn't the enlightenment of a well-formed argument. It was polarization and the death of good faith as an operating principle in public debate.

The Eleventh Edition freezes these discussions, while opening the doors on new ones. For those who see the Eleventh as a snapshot of a golden age before the Fall have misread the encyclopedia, just as Chisholm mistook the significance of his own vocabulary of enlightenment. The belief in the unquestioned benefits of Progress embraced by Chisholm and all his colleagues and friends, editors and contributors, not to mention readers, may have been misleading, since the nineteenth century progressed to the twentieth—and the twentieth has been the most homicidal and barbaric century of them all.

One measure of that barbarism is that there's no authoritative, credible place to examine the facts as a means to finding truth. The three new volumes of the Twelfth–focusing, at Hooper's insistence, on the war–marked a retreat from the earlier editions. Optimism in the aftermath of war seemed ludicrous. Hooper, his commercial instincts excited, was clear in his expectations and expressed them in a note to Hogarth, sent in June 1920: "These volumes ought to be made up so that the history of the War dominates the whole book. . . . [W]e cannot get the military side or the historical side too well done. . . . Literature, for instance, is one of the subjects that can be passed over with great ease and not do much harm, and it is quite within a possibility that this is true of art."

Hooper's dream was long dead. Nevertheless, in 1920, Hogarth was summoned to High Holborn again, this time as deputy editor to assist Chisholm and a staff of four others in creating the three-volume Twelfth Edition. "The 'E.B.' offices were left desolate. We dug out the old reference books from under a pile of dusty papers," she wrote. "It was incredibly difficult to pick up the threads, to dis-inter from dust-heaps the records of 1911. As far as we could, we did it and started afresh, with something of the same spirit but little of the old gaiety. We were all much older, by far more than the ten years' interval. Behind us stood the War." In 1922, writing his editorial introduction to the three volumes that with Eleventh constituted the Twelfth Edition, Chisholm observed that creating a whole new encyclopedia the size and scope of the Eleventh after the First World War was an impossibility: "Neither the minds nor the wills that are required for such an undertaking are any longer obtainable in any corresponding degree, nor probably can they be again for years to come." What Chisholm called "war-weariness" had made it impossible to carry on as before. He was quite right, of course.

In 1831, John Stuart Mill observed, "The first of the leading pecu-liarities of the present age is, that it is an age of transition. Mankind have outgrown old institutions and old doctrines, and have not yet acquired new ones." Mill was describing a linear notion of historical development that had begun with the Enlightenment and led, after many, many iterations, first to the articulation of what some scholars called an "ideology of transition." Indeed, Victorians, whose sensibilities are so well represented in the Eleventh, were consumed with the idea that their age was an age of anxious transition—not, as one would assume, from an age of Napoleonic warfare, but from a foggy *medieval* past. Thackeray is the one who pointed out that he was from an age of horses and coaches and was surprised to find himself living in an age of steam locomotives.

Finally, in the decades ending the nineteenth century and the first decade of the twentieth, the ideology of transition gave way to what perhaps we can call an "ideology of Progress"—a belief as global (and as rigidly enforced) as Catholic dogmatic theology was six hundred years ago, an ideology that made something by definition dynamic into a paradoxically static sensibility: transition *is* Progress and Progress is the destination. What does it matter where it leads? The Eleventh was a long list of things that are secular, rational, scientific, measurable, and therefore modern; but it's impossible to use the Eleventh to chart the progress of love or the slow defeat of hatred.

But for those who have wandered into its many volumes, only to emerge a day later, blinking, the Eleventh shines, still. It's a fount of nostalgia for eggheads, the definitive survey of a middle earth of Edwardian tranquility, filled with magic squares and "Invincible" engines and the serious, well-dressed Swedes of the Philanthropic Exegetic Society. Meanwhile, only four editions later, the *Britannica* is stuck forever in a state of constant revision, competing unsuccessfully against Wikipedia, the very antithesis of the Eleventh (on which, ironically, it is built), but perfect for our own transitional, consensus-driven period, in which, according to the Department of Education, the vast majority of U.S. public schools are failing in their mission just as miserably as their British counterparts are failing in theirs. Mostly, we call this "Progress."

Even the most visionary of Edwardians would never have ventured to guess that a deeply held belief in the ideology of Progress would lead eventually to the first twenty-four hours of the Battle of the Somme, let alone to all of this.

Acknowledgments

The author wishes to thank nearly as many people who helped with the creation of this text as helped Chisholm build his own book—about fifteen hundred souls. Since that's not possible, let me run the risk of missing the many generous and helping hands who helped lift this book, none of whom have any responsibility for the errors.

I am grateful to my family most of all—my wife, April, and my three clever daughters, Hattie, Maggie, and Anna—for their patient reading and rereading of endless pages.

I received early encouragement for this project from Professor Anthony Grafton at Princeton, from Professor Alan Macfarlane at Cambridge, and from Professor Anthony O'Hear at the Royal Institute of Philosophy. Once the work was under way, librarians and researchers came to the rescue. For an author working far from English-language research libraries, this was an unusual project to undertake, and the research work was fairly intense, so I owe many thanks to many people, including Karen Kriberney in Portland, Julie Anne Lambert at Oxford's Bodleian Library, and Austin Ashley, who helped me find material in Cambridge. My friends Georg Kajanus and Barbie Wilde helped find material in *The Times*'s archive, with the essential assistance of Nick Mays and Eamon Dyas, while Christine Hultgreen and Tony Hutchinson provided great logistical (read food and shelter) help. Anne Chisholm relayed a few messages to her family members, opening some very helpful doors. Andrea Schwartz at the Harvey A. Andruss Library of the Bloomsburg University of Pennsylvania, in Bloomsburg, uncovered a very hard-to-find item for me. Friends, including Harry Stein, Jennifer Metcalf, Priscilla Turner, and Jenny Tripp provided very valuable help in managing such a long manuscript. I also wish to thank Rachel Youdelman, who sought in vain for a photo of Haxton; Marilyn Beyer, who kindly provided a photo of Alison Phillips, and Don Montague, who provided additional family background; the Resource Sharing Department of the University of Kansas, who unearthed material relating to Henry Williams Chisholm; Mr. Maarten Witkam, of Leiden, Netherlands; and David Rumsey, of Cartography Associates. I received invaluable collegial support from Mr. Ferdi McDermott and the teaching fellows at Chavagnes International College and the Chavagnes Studium. I owe thanks to the late Herman Kogan, whose book *The Great EB* provided a kind of compass for me. This work occupied me for many years, and so I hope those I have forgotten at this very moment will forgive me.

Finally, Victoria Wilson, my editor at Knopf, helped shape and guide this project; without her faith and patience, this book would not exist.

The Pirate Publishers: The "Reprint Hyaenas"

Alvin Johnson's *New Universal* wasn't the *Britannica*'s only competitor. The end of the nineteenth century was a kind of golden age of self-improvement of all kinds, in the U.S. as in Britain, and erudition was just another form of fitness for the growing middle class. Appleton's *New American Cyclopedia*, edited by Charles Anderson Dana and George Ripley—two influential journalists who worked together on Horace Greeley's *New York Tribune*—was first published between 1857 and 1863. Reissued between 1873 and 1876 as *The American Cyclopædia* in "16 large volumes, each containing 750 two-column pages" for $3.50 a volume (with an 1878 "General and Analytical Index" sold separately), Appleton celebrated the set's American provenance and tried to capitalize on the *Britannica*'s pervasive British condescension toward most things American. It armed its salesmen with pamphlets called "The Encyclopedia Britannica: Is It Adapted for American Circulation?" and announced its native virtues proudly in its advertising, while condemning the *Britannica*'s "godlessness."

An anti-*Britannica* campaign was supported by more serious critics of the Ninth Edition, as well. "Even when American subjects find a place in the *Encyclopædia Britannica* under their proper titles," complained Oliver Wendell Holmes in a May 1878 issue of *The Washington Evening Post*, "the treatment in nine times out of ten is so defective, so incomplete, and often so erroneous, as to become ludicrous, affording a sense of amusement rather than of instruction."

The American publishers of the authorized *Britannica* shot back from on high, calling the Appleton encyclopedia "unsafe" for reference purposes. Appleton won the prize for most sets sold—estimates run as high as 3 million volumes. But ironically, the competition solidified the *Britannica*'s reputation as the definitive encyclopedia. No one was measuring the success of their encyclopedia by how well it compared to *Johnson's New Universal Cyclopædia*, for example.

However, the strongest competition to Scribner's and Little, Brown's *Britannica* didn't come from the likes of Johnson. It came from those "pirate" publishers whose outlaw sets of the *Britannica* outsold the authorized volumes by as much as ten to one. Ethically minded Americans found this disregard for the property of others appalling. The American Copyright Committee sometimes organized a little outrage in New York City, and occasionally brought embarrassment to trade publishers who attempted to do meekly what the pirates did so well.

Disapproval had almost no effect. People bought books much as they accepted ideas, and the merchandising and retail elements were very far in the background. Books of all kinds and from all nations thus filled the shelves of American shopkeepers and the suitcases of the traveling men. The various editions of the *Britannica* were often the biggest prize, and had been since Thomas Dobson's pirated version of the Third Edition was first published in 1789. Dobson was a Scottish immigrant with Scottish sensitivity toward British attitudes. His eighteen-volume edition disposed of the word "Britannica"—and the dedication to the king—and instead featured entries rewritten to eliminate bias (or, some might say, to substitute his own) and hundreds of altered illustrations. The Dobson edition, which was owned by George Washington, Thomas Jefferson, Benjamin Franklin, Alexander Hamilton, and fifteen hundred other Americans, was followed over the years by other pirated versions of subsequent *Britannica* editions, usually sold at a much cheaper price than either the originals or the authorized American editions.

All intervening editions had sold well in America, but the first volumes of the Ninth began appearing as an obsession for self-improvement was spreading quickly in America, putting the set in more demand than any of the previous editions. Already praised widely for scholarship and carrying an aura of intellectual brilliance, the first pirated Ninth was published by James M. Stoddart in Philadelphia; the volumes appeared nearly simultaneously with those in Britain. Where previous pirates had to wait for new plates to be made, inviting a delay that authorized publishers used to their advantage, Stoddart bought plates from a printer's assistant who stole the things and spirited them off to Stoddart as soon as they came off the presses of one of Black's printers, Neill & Co., in Edinburgh. The scoundrel was arrested and locked up for twenty days.

Black's and Scribner's Sons wanted to stop the proliferation of unauthorized editions before it got out of control, so, in 1879, they sued Stoddart—and lost. The judge, Arthur Butler, declared that the law allowing the publication of a work in America that was protected by copyright in Britain might be morally suspect, nonetheless "it is supposed to have an influence upon the advance of learning and intelligence." That, Butler said, explained why "the public policy of this country . . . is in favor of such republication."

The decision had a predictable effect: during the 1880s, as new volumes continued to appear in Edinburgh, the economy boomed and the number of pirate publishers in America grew, and by the time the last volume of the Ninth Edition was published, several hundred thousand sets had been ordered from unauthorized publishers. The versions each differed, some a little, some a lot—often by eliminating material, but sometimes by having new material edited and incorporated into the set, thus providing publishers and salesmen with a "unique" encyclopedia. By 1890, customers could order a set of pirated *Britannica*s from Funk & Wagnalls for $40, while Wanamaker's sold their pirated version for $2 less. But Isaac Funk was a severe Prohibitionist and public moralizer, while John Wanamaker was a prominent business leader, and, at the time, postmaster general, and the press wasted no time shaming them. The *New York Post* blasted "the mania for robbing the Messers Black," while *The New York Times* called it "The Black Robbery," causing both Funk & Wagnalls and Wanamaker's some embarrassment. But meanwhile, Little, Brown's official version was selling for $225—about the list price charged for a set in London—so even the passage of the International Copyright Act in 1891 did little to slow the number of variations of the *Britannica* published in America.

Among the most enterprising of these highly entrepreneurial publishers—"reprint hyaenas," in the words of a Scribner's representative in Chicago—was an Irish-Canadian man from Toronto named Alexander Belford. Like Hooper (and, interestingly, many other pirate publishers), Belford was a man of limited education but extraordinary energy, whose cheap reprint company, run in partnership with his two brothers in Toronto, then in Chicago, was as shady as it was profitable.

Belford was the scourge of British and American trade publishing in those days, reviled as an ignorant thief, stupidly stealing the work and ideas of his betters—until, that is, he married Helen, the daughter of Andrew McNally, a partner in the famous map-making company, and a man at the pinnacle of local social success. Belford instantly became immensely wise, and as his pockets deepened, his wisdom increased, until he, too, reached a perch near the top of Chicago society, where others sought his company and counsel.

But even then, he was a particular nemesis of Clemens, who unsuccessfully fought the Belford brothers in court over the release in Canada of a cheap edition of *Tom Sawyer* in late July 1876. Clemens had published the book in Britain on June 9, 1876, in an attempt to gain the protection of an imperial copyright. But by doing so, he unwittingly supplied the Belfords, then still in Toronto, with a product irresistibly popular to book buyers. While Clemens's publisher delayed publication of the book, Belford flooded the American market with the Canadian version.

"Belford Bros., Canadian thieves, are flooding America with a cheap pirated edition of *Tom Sawyer*," Clemens wrote angrily to a business associate. "I have just telegraphed Chatto to assign Canadian copyright to me, but I suppose it is too late to do any good. We cannot issue for 6 weeks yet, & by that time Belford will have sold 100,000 over the frontier & killed my book dead. This piracy will cost me $10,000, & I will spend as much more to choke off those pirates, if the thing can be done."

But it couldn't. Clemens was furious, and his only weapon was a sharpened lampoon, so he created a character called Jack Belford, "the black-souled pirate himself," in his play *Cap'n Simon Wheeler, the Amateur Detective*. It wasn't $10,000 of pleasure, perhaps, but it was a laugh.

The business arrangements of these bookmen were as erratic as their literary tastes. Alexander Belford, for example, was often in partnership with another school dropout (also of Irish stock, also Canadian) named James "Uncle Jim" Clarke, a man described by a good friend as a "violent Irishman," with a large, sad face, a thick shock of hair, and a drooping mustache that made an accidental smile invisible. Together, Belford, Clarke & Co. came to dominate bookselling and distributing not only in Chicago, but throughout the West. In 1890, they had a very successful outing with an unofficial version of the Ninth Edition of the *Britannica*, called *The Americanized Encyclopædia Britannica Revised and Amended*. Belford and Clarke revised and amended fourteen volumes out of the set, printed Christopher Marlowe's epigram, "Infinite riches in a little room," at the top of the pages, and claimed that it contained "all that is important to know, in a nutshell—compact, reliable and intelligible." (And a couple of years later, the pair reissued it as *The Home Encyclopedia*, calling it a "magnificent monument of Genius.")

Belford was impulsive and energetic, prone to occasional detours to experiment with corporate grandeur. In December 1892, for example, Belford and three other reprint publishers announced the formation of the Werner Company. *The New York Times* reported on page 1 that it would be "the largest complete printing and publishing company in the world." During its brief, incandescent moment, perhaps it actually was.

Clarke, however, was more methodical than most pirate publishers, carefully considering his various options and always looking out for new talent, new partners, and new books. Operating from the Belford-Clarke offices in the Adams Building at Wabash and Congress Streets in Chicago, Clarke published Dickens and Thackeray, among many others, while, in partnership with Belford, he ran the book departments in many downtown stores. These were self-contained, autonomous operations. Retailers who balked at the arrangement soon found that Belford, Clarke & Co. had installed complete book departments in nearby haberdashers or other shops, where underpriced titles lured consumers away. Soon, cities and towns across the country had Clarke's (or Belford, Clarke) bookstalls in most large stores, while small shops were opened on the fly for a limited time and used to dispose of overstocked books—a retail technique Belford called "hippodroming."

The Text of Henry R. Haxton's First *Times* Advertisement for the Ninth Edition, March 23, 1898

[in small type, occupying all of page 15]

The Times

OFFERS THE

"ENCYCLOPÆDIA BRITANNICA"

(NINTH EDITION. THE COMPLETE 25 VOLS.)

FOR A PRELIMINARY PAYMENT OF

ONE GUINEA,

AND 13 MONTHLY PAYMENTS OF ONE GUINEA EACH

AFTER THE SET IS DELIVERED

THE 1898 IMPRESSION IS NOW ON THE PRESSES AND WILL SOON BE IN THE BINDER'S HANDS. THE SPECIAL PRICE IS OFFERED ONLY TO SUBSCRIBERS WHOSE NAMES ARE ENROLLED BEFORE THE DATE OF PUBLICATION. PROVISION HAS BEEN MADE FOR NO MORE THAN THE EXPECTED NUMBER OF PROMPT APPLICATIONS.

THE TIMES, enlarging the policy adopted in issuing *The Times Atlas*, is enabled to offer its readers the opportunity of acquiring a most important work of reference at a peculiarly advantageous price. The new offer is the result of an arrangement made with the well-known publishing house of A. and C. Black, and concerns their library of universal knowledge, the "Encyclopædia Britannica." This great national work, first published in 1771, has been revised and enlarged from time to time, and the sale of the existing edition—the ninth—has been so large that fresh printings have been continually required. The sale of the work has, however, been in great measure confined to libraries and clubs, and to such private persons as could, without inconvenience, purchase a costly book. The publishers' catalogue price was £37, and the greater number of copies sold have been supplied by booksellers who gave no very material discount to their customers. THE TIMES is now, however, by the terms of its contract with the publishers, in a position to accept advance subscriptions for the 1898 impression of the "Encyclopædia Britannica" (9th edition) at prices, and upon conditions, which will place a number of early copies within the reach of a larger public.

The "Encyclopædia Britannica," is already known to every one, but it is of interest, in connexion with the present remarkable offer, to note the proportions of its component parts. It consists of twenty-four massive volumes of about 850 pages each, and a twenty-fifth volume containing an elaborate index to the whole. In addition to the 30,000,000 words which fill its 22,000 pages of letter-press, it contains 338 full-page plates and 671 maps and plans. There are over 9,000 other illustrations. Over 1,100 writers contributed to the work, and a sum of more than £60,000 was paid for the manuscript alone. Its exquisite printing, and the care with which it is bound, combine with the editorial outlay to make it the most costly work ever offered to the public.

THE "ENCYCLOPÆDIA BRITANNICA" embraces all branches of human knowledge, and was written by specialists of the highest distinction. Not only men of learning: scholars, divines, masters of science and philosophy; but also men of action: statesmen, soldiers and sailors, financiers, jurists and surgeons, artists and engineers, manufacturers, sportsmen and travellers have contributed to the pages of the "Encyclopædia Britannica."

To the casual inquirer it presents all the advantages which a library of a thousand chosen volumes yields to the trained scholar who is thoroughly acquainted with each of the thousand. It may indeed be said to be the essence of all books, ancient and modern, prepared for convenient use. The contents of the twenty-four massive volumes are placed in alphabetical order, and a copious index, occupying the twenty-fifth volume, facilitates cross reference. In the desire to secure convenient disposition of the contents, the quality of interest has not, however, been sacrificed.

THE "ENCYCLOPÆDIA BRITANNICA" is not a mere aid to

memory, to be hastily consulted in moments of emergency; it is not only the greatest of works of reference, but it is

A LIBRARY IN ITSELF, a collection of admirable treatises upon all conceivable subjects. Even the most recondite branches of learning are treated without a trace of pedantry. The volumes are

EMINENTLY READABLE.

The great *litterateurs* of our day wrote for it, and every one of them was proud to do his best in such goodly company. The "Britannica" appeals to men—and women—who have already enjoyed the fullest opportunities of education, who desire to refresh and clarify impressions already received.

THE LITERARY QUALITY

of the Encyclopædia gives it rank among our classics. The wide knowledge and keen sense of fitness that guided the Editors to their happy choice of specialists may be illustrated by the mention of one exquisite combination. Swinburne, on Keats, writes not only with the authority of scholarship, but with the even more distinctive authority of a peculiar sympathy in a common craft. Some, indeed, among contemporary writers may be said to have done their most faultless work in the pages of the "Britannica." Canon Farrar's article on the earthly life of Our Saviour is not more than twenty thousand words in length, but its concision brings out to their best advantage the remarkable qualities that made the "Life of Christ" so deservedly esteemed. It is the outcome of a full mastery tuned up to tense expression. Turning to the article on Béranger, a delicate elaboration of phrase betrays the touch of Robert Louis Stevenson. When Cable writes on New Orleans, the reader need not be surprised to find in the article passages which have been quoted a hundred times. For no writer, not even Dickens, seems so sensitive to impressions of place as the author of "Dr. Sevier" and "Old Creole Days." New Orleans is not only Mr. Cable's home; it is, as it were, his art. Andrew Lang, again, takes the key which his admirers most appreciate when he writes upon Mythology. No subject, unless it be ghosts (and Mr. Lang brings them before us under the heading "Apparitions"), lies closer to Mr. Lang's heart than folk-lore. With his lasting interest in myths and their origin, and his wide knowledge he ranges from Greece to Polynesia, he puts before his readers a complete review of the comparative mythologies of civilized and savage peoples, and his critical faculty enables him to present and discuss with great effectiveness the systems of Prof. Max-Müller and Mr. Herbert Spencer.

EVERY contributor to the "Encyclopædia Britannica" is a master of his subject, and a master, too, of that method of treatment which best fits his subject. For even the least picturesque of sciences have a technique of style. The late Professor [Arthur] Cayley said that the value of a treatise on pure mathematics depended rather upon the order of its statement than upon its predications; and his article on Functions shows that even the most abstruse discussions may display a beauty of construction that brings their complicated formulae into distinct relation to literary style.

THE HISTORY OF THE "BRITANNICA"

is closely connected with the history of the intellectual and material progress during the past century. Its successive imprints bear these dates:—1771 (first edition), 1776, 1784 (second edition), 1787, 1797 (third edition), 1801, 1810 (fourth edition), 1817 (fifth edition), 1823 (sixth edition), 1827, 1842 (seventh edition), 1853, 1861 (eighth edition), 1875, 1889, 1894, 1896 (ninth edition).

Through all these changes the "Encyclopædia Britannica" has occupied a position of peculiar authority. German and French works of general reference are, in their respective countries, the subject of constant discussion and controversy, but the impartiality and sincerity, the scholarship and precision of the "Britannica" are unquestioned. The whole body of human knowledge has changed since the first edition of the "Britannica" appeared in 1771, and the enlargements and revision of the work have kept pace with the march of learning. But the fine sense of responsibility which animated "A Society of Gentlemen" (as the quaint old title-page describes the first editors) has proved a lasting tradition. No contributor has ever been asked to write upon a subject which he has not made especially his own, and no personal or corporate bias has ever been suffered to interfere with the broad honesty of the work.

The success which attended the efforts of the various editors has received generous recognition from the most intelligent and critical classes. To professional men the work is almost as necessary as the text books of their respective callings, and it is certainly not too much to say that no one book has contributed so much to the cause of informal education in this country as has the "Britannica." In America, where the slipshod condition of the law of copyright permitted the sale of pirated, mutilated, and cheaply-printed counterfeits of the work, more than four hundred thousand sets have been sold within the past twenty years, and reprehensible as is the condition of public sentiment which permits such an iniquity, the proverbial intelligence of all classes in the United States is in great measure due to the eagerness with which they have seized the opportunity of supplementing hasty and careless schooling by the study of the great British classic. There, as in Germany, every one reads and thinks; and the knowledge of foreign countries and foreign markets, the eager ambition and the versatile ingenuity which are shown by the Americans may in some measure be ascribed to the widespread use of the "Britannica."

The "Britannica" is essentially the production of men who wrote out of the fulness of knowledge. The wonderful story of the 19th Century is told by the men who made its greatness; the history of modern progress in the arts, sciences, and industries has the glow that only a soldier can give to the tale of a campaign; for the men who fought against ignorance, and brought enlightenment to their generation, themselves tell how the light was spread.

When the first edition of the "Encyclopædia Britannica" was completed, a hundred and twenty-seven years ago, THE TIMES was not yet in existence. It cost more to travel from Plymouth to Inverness than it costs to-day to travel from Plymouth to Hong-kong. Every signboard was a picture, for not one man in a score could read, popular government was a farce, labour was servitude, slavery existed under the British flag, candles were luxuries, gaslight unknown, the steam-engine and the electric telegraph not yet introduced, barracks and prisons were pesthouses, medicine and surgery were little better than guesswork, bull-baiting and bear-fighting were regarded as manly British sports. To whatever aspects of life attention is directed the material and intellectual condition of the English people was, in 1771, so far below our present standards of comfort and efficiency that a truthful picture of the life of that period seems almost incredible. Superstition and prejudice governed the lives of rich and poor alike; a sort of Chinese respect for the customs and traditions of the past made all attempts at progress appear revolutionary. Cotton and woollen goods were still woven by hand; iron was hammered and not rolled; the alternation of crops was unknown—the farmer grew corn, year after year, until the land was exhausted, and then left it foul with weeds for years. Bone and guano fertilizers had not been introduced, the draining and reclamation of low-lying land was regarded as a visionary project. Yet the farmer and manufacturer of that day bear the scrutiny of modern criticism better than the classes who were supposed to be vastly their superiors. The professional classes were stubbornly opposed to progress of any sort, and corruption was not uncommon among both the legislative and judicial authorities.

At the end of the last century a sudden and irresistible sense of impatience seems to have been born in the nation, and at the cost of strenuous and continued effort all the conditions of life were changed for the better. It is not too much to say that the English are to-day, of all the people of the earth, the best governed and the most law-abiding, the most comfortable and the soundest of body and mind—in all respects, the happiest. There is yet much to be done, and we are doing it, but, as we look back at the dirt and darkness of the past, we may well feel that we have put our house in order, and that it is time to look about us and see what our neighbours are doing. They, too, have been changing their conditions of life. Some of them burned down the old houses and built anew, with more haste than wisdom; some of them seized the houses that others had built; while others were hewing down forests and finding room to build. But, on the whole, none of them has made better men than we have made of this period of unrest. If, at first glance, there is any cause for dissatisfaction, any one respect in which comparison fails to satisfy our national pride, it is in connexion with our informal education. Our schools are good, and their doors are open to every one; our Universities send out, year after year, young men of the highest culture and the soundest sense of right and wrong. But in no class is it so general a practice as it should be to follow and supplement the routinary education of our earlier years by thoughtful reading. We all read the newspapers, if nothing else, and our Press, for trustworthiness, clearness, fairness, fearlessness, and absolute honesty of purpose, compares favourably with that of any other country. It supplies, to even a most hasty reader, a fund of general information which is not to be despised. It is, however, the function of the newspaper to tell the news of the day rather than to recapitulate. An intelligent comprehension of current events requires a certain familiarity with historical, political, geographical, and scientific facts. If in the hurry of life a man has neglected to acquire these facts, or suffered them to escape his memory, he is constantly meeting, in the column of his newspaper, allusions which mean nothing to him. The reports, for instance, of military activity on the northern frontier of India are bewildering to a reader who does not understand the remarkable conditions, both natural and political, which make the sterile and silent Himalaya so fertile a source of clamour. The situation in China at the present moment affords another example. Since the first Europeans visited China, in 1260, the struggle to break down Chinese exclusiveness has been always increasing. But even the events of forty and fifty years ago, important as they were to British commerce, are little known to the average newspaper reader. We cannot carry all knowledge in our heads, anymore than a carpenter can carry all his tools in his apron, but we can know where to find what we want in the tool chest. The reader who, when he is at a loss to understand what he reads, dismisses the subject with a vague sense of confusion, is doing himself harm. The habit of resolving doubts, of turning to books for information, is the note of all progress. It is a good habit that grows as fast as any bad habit. The only encouragement it needs is that the information should be found when it is sought.

It is not, however, as a mere training of the mind that this sort of secondary education is of importance. The development of new markets for British manufactures, the perfecting of British industries, is a matter of vital importance to every class. Every little bye-election, every opportunity for the assertion of public opinion, every utterance that goes to the making of public opinion, every individual determination of a vexed question is of moment. No man has a right to enjoy the protection and peace which is assured to him by the Government unless he is doing his best to promote good government, and no man can intelligently pass an opinion upon the questions of the day unless he keeps his mind fresh and active by frequent reference to the best accounts of what has already been done at home and abroad. It is impossible to evade the responsibilities of self government. Every man influences the men about him. The casual opinion which he expresses, in conversation with a friend, is, in its degree, an exercise of power. To speak without knowledge on such an occasion is a breach of confidence. When it is possible for a man to have a proper library of reference in his house, it is his duty to have it. It is not enough that one should have, at a club or a library, occasional access to the pages of the "Britannica," it should be always at hand, a silent invitation to thought and study.

TO-DAY THE TIMES will Open the Subscription List for ITS DISTRIBUTION of the

ENCYCLOPÆDIA BRITANNICA (Ninth Edition) at an UN-PRECEDENTED PRICE and for

SMALL MONTHLY PAYMENTS.

FOURTEEN GUINEAS in FOURTEEN PAYMENTS of ONE GUINEA EACH. ONLY ONE GUINEA in CASH is to be paid by the subscriber UNTIL AFTER THE COMPLETE SET HAS BEEN DELIVERED.

THE TWENTY-FIVE SPLENDID VOLUMES, complete and unabridged, published by Messrs. A. and C. Black. The same size, the same contents, the same coloured plates, steel plates and wood-cuts, the same high quality of paper, printing, and binding as in the sets sold at the higher prices.

THE PRICE at which THE TIMES offers the "ENCYCLOPÆ-DIA BRITANNICA" is LOWER THAN the LOWEST WHOLE-SALE PRICE at which the work has ever been sold. The publishers' catalogue price for purchasers at retail was £37.

THE TIMES has obtained the exclusive privilege of distributing the 1898 impression of the "ENCYCLOPÆDIA BRITAN-NICA," now on the Presses, at this special price, to those who enrol their names before the date of publication. The printing is rapidly proceeding, and the volumes will soon be in the binders' hands. Applications will be consecutively numbered, and the sets will be delivered in rotation. The first subscriber will receive the first set, and so on until the offer is withdrawn. THE TIMES reserves the right (which will be exercised only in the case of unforeseen circum-

---

[COUPON]

The Times
Reprint of the
"ENCYCLOPÆDIA BRITANNICA."

To Mr. George Edward Wright, *"The Times,"* Printing House Square, London, E.C.

Herewith remittance for One Guinea. Kindly reserve for me one set of the "Encyclopædia Britannica" (Ninth Edition) bound in (a), for which I agree to make to you or to any one you may appoint further payments amounting to (b) _____ Guineas, at the rate of One Guinea per month, the first of the payments to be made against delivery, as below agreed, of the twenty-five volumes of the "Encyclopædia Britannica," and the remaining payments on the corresponding day of each succeeding month until complete. Until such payments are complete, I engage that the volumes, not being my property, shall not be disposed of by sale or otherwise.

I further agree that, if, owing to unforeseen circumstances of which you shall be the judge, the volumes cannot be delivered at the date mentioned, the return of the deposit of One Guinea to me shall cancel this agreement.

I further request that the "Encyclopædia Britannica," be delivered to

NAME. . . . .

ADDRESS . . . .

. . . .

If without the London postal district add name of London station, shipping office, or forwarding agent here . . . .

SIGNATURE . . . .

ADDRESS . . . .

. . . .

(a) Insert here "cloth," "half morocco," or "full morocco."
(b) Insert here "thirteen" if cloth binding is chosen,
                "seventeen" if half morocco binding is chosen
                "twenty-four" if full morocco binding is chosen.

stances) to cancel any order on returning the preliminary payment of one guinea. THE TIMES does not guarantee that all orders will be filled, but provision is made for the expected quotum of PROMPT APPLICATIONS.

HALF MOROCCO and FULL MOROCCO BINDINGS may be had for a few more monthly payments.

A SUCCESSFUL MERCHANT'S
APPRECIATION OF
THE "ENCYCLOPÆDIA BRITANNICA"

In addressing a meeting of his constituents in North Derbyshire, the late Sir William Jackson referred to his early struggles, and said the reading of the "Encyclopædia Britannica" had formed his character as it then existed. In his master's office, he said, there was a copy of the "Encyclopædia Britannica," which he studied night and day, storing his mind with knowledge of every sort. He always attributed his success in life to the fact of having studied the "Encyclopædia Britannica." During the last forty-eight years, he had been in the four quarters of the globe; and there was scarcely a port to which a ship could go that he had not had commercial relations with. He first began with the West Coast of Africa, and his ships were found from Sierra Leone to the Cape of Good Hope trading with the natives. Where did he get his knowledge regarding the tribes? From the "Encyclopædia Britannica." As the divine reads the Bible to enable him to preach, so did he (Sir William) read the "Encyclopædia Britannica" to obtain knowledge of the world. Wherever he had transactions—whether it was with the Indies or the Cape of Good Hope, with Hottentots, Boers, Dutchmen, Englishmen, Mussulmans, or Hindus—he found in the "Encyclopædia Britannica" the information he required regarding the manners and customs of the people. He traded as far as California, buying raw hides, and carrying salt from the Cape de Verd Islands to pay for them, before an ounce of gold was found there. He had also whalers in the north, and he had always looked at the "Encyclopædia Britannica" to get the information he desired. When a mere lad he had made up his mind to get on in the world, and it was the education derived from the "Encyclopædia Britannica" which moulded his character and qualified him in after life to achieve both wealth and position.

DISTINGUISHED CONTRIBUTERS.

Among the eleven hundred writers whose articles appear in the ninth edition of the "Encyclopædia Britannica" are these representative men of our time:

Rt. Hon. James Bryce	Rt. Hon. Prof. Max Muller	Dean Farrar
Lord Kelvin	Lord Rayleigh	Lord Grimthorpe
Alg. Chas. Swinburne	Sir W. Crookes	Principal Tullock
Alex. Bain	Rt. Hon. John Morley	Prof. Skeat
Bishop Of London	Mrs. Humphry Ward	Prof. Ray Lankester
"Cavendish"	Sir Arch. Geikie	Sir Fredk. Pollock
Sir Robert Ball	Sir George Reid	Lord Houghton
Elie Reclus	Sir Richd. Temple	Sidney Colvin
Sir Walter Besant	Sir Norman Lockyer	Prof. Saintsbury
Dean Bradley	Sir R. Strachey	Prof. Sully
Prof. Jerb	Sir W. W. Hunter	Edmund Gosse
Andrew Lang	Prof. Sidgwick	Rt. Hon. Leon'd Courtney
Sir Rutherford Alcock	W. E. Henley	Edmund Warre
Prof. Caird	W. M. Rossetti	Sir Fredk. Abel
Mrs. M. G. Fawcett	Prof. Dewar	Gen. Maurich
Austin Dobson	Rev. H. R. Haweis	Grant Allen
Canon Rawlinson	Geo. W. Carle	St. George Mivart
Prof. Huxley	Matthew Arnold	Robt. Louis Stevenson
W. M. Morris	John Addington Symonds	Prof. Romanes

To select, in this fashion, the names of but one contributor out of every score who collaborated upon the "Encyclopædia Britannica" is not an altogether satisfactory process.

In reading over these names one is at any rate impressed by the fact that contributors to the "Encyclopædia Britannica" are not merely specialists with great information, but original thinkers. They are the men who have themselves influenced our thoughts and beliefs, have directed, even created, contemporary taste and learning. The "Britannica," in fact, was made by the men who have made our time. Its pages, therefore, bear the priceless impress of individuality of living, authoritative personality. And of the great variety in these characteristic currents of thought, the scanty enumeration of contributors will afford some notion. Each one of the eleven hundred authors was invited to write for the "Britannica" because he possessed special knowledge which did not lie within the competence of any among his colleagues. Such dissimilarity among the writers is an essential merit in a work of general reference, and there arises an almost grotesque incongruity when an attempt is made to think of such divergent capacities in the block. One common quality, however, binds the name just cited. The Encyclopædia gave no hospitality to the sort of "harmless drudges" who used to compile works of reference when the world was younger. Nor is the "Britannica," indeed, in any sense a compilation. The names given here were selected because they are at the moment very much before the public. They bring home to the reader's mind the vivid and immediate interest of the work. To the student of any special art or science, other names in the full roster might appeal with greater force, but to every general reader this list of acknowledged celebrities will convey some sense of the distinction which characterizes the contents of the volumes.

PRESS AND OTHER OPINIONS

"The 'Encyclopædia Britannica' is the one work to which every inquirer first addresses himself, with the certainty of finding firm ground beneath his feet."–The Times.

"The most extensive collection of accurate knowledge that has been brought together since the revolution produced by the consistent application of the historical method to all branches of thought."–The Athenaeum.

"To own a set of the 'Encyclopædia Britannica' is to acknowledge one's self as recognising the best there is in literature."–Gladstone.

"A work of national importance."–Birmingham Post.

"Men of science, theologians, philosophers, Oriental scholars, geographers, artists, those engaged in practical pursuits, all alike will turn to these pages for the last word that has been said on their own special subject by the highest authorities. Even statesmen will not disdain to look for the most recent information concerning the countries and the peoples with which they have to deal. To some readers the biographies, to others the historical sketches, will prove the most interesting. Despite the oft-quoted paradox of Charles Lamb about 'books that are no books,' we undertake to affirm that any person who takes pleasure in reading would be well provided with literature if shut up for several days and nights in company with a single volume. . . . Our own feeling at the present moment is as if we had been guests at some great feast of wit and learning, where the very excellence and variety of the entertainment had blunted the normal faculty of appreciation."–The Pall Mall Gazette.

"Un monument littéraire auquel l'Europe savant tout entière a collaboré."–Le Figaro.

"A critique which should do justice to this stupendous and admirable publication would in itself occupy the whole space at our command. Wherever we have opened these volumes, we have been instructed and delighted by the concise, yet exhaustive, manner in which each of its vast range of subjects is handled."–The Westminster Review.

"It has been said that a man shut up in a prison or on a desert island, and allowed one printed volume to while away his weary hours of loneliness, would do most wisely in choosing for that purpose a volume of a good Cyclopaedia. As to this we can speak all the more freely, because, having taken up the new edition of the 'Encyclopædia Britannica' with the intention of reviewing certain articles contained, we suddenly discovered, after the lapse of an hour or so, that the time which should have been devoted to reading and noting these articles had been consumed in a desultory reading of articles on all kinds of other subjects. We found ourselves acquiring a store of knowledge about Clocks, Coleoptera, and Cookery; we dipped into Confucius, and revived our memories of the once fashionable Croquet; and we paid flying visits to Dahomey and Damascus."–The Saturday Review.

"Professor Baynes has taken the only safe method of securing articles that shall embody the fullest and highest and most accurate knowledge, viz., by obtaining the services of those who have proved themselves to be at the summit in their particular departments. To the present and to the future generations, therefore, this Ninth Edition of the 'Encyclopædia Britannica' must be regarded as indicating the highest tide-mark of the science, literature, and art of the time."–Nature.

"This great Encyclopædia in some sense registers both the past and present achievements of human knowledge in a most interesting and trustworthy manner. The Editors do not require their contributors to simply inform the readers concerning the lore of bygone times, but to keep them well and truly informed about the work, the thoughts, and the facts of the present day."–The Christian World.

The Rev. Charles Spurgeon said in recommending the "Britannica":–"If all other books were destroyed, the Bible alone excepted, the world would have lost but little of its information."

"The Contributors are widely scattered not only over the British Isles, but also over the world. It draws its supplies from the four quarters of the globe."–The Scotsman.

"Many will be glad to know where they can conveniently find a good exhibition of even the most advanced views which they know to be current in the world, but which are not to be met with in the 'Speaker's Commentary,' even in Smith's 'Dictionary of the Bible,' and for them the 'Encyclopædia Britannica' will be very serviceable. Nothing, indeed, can be more useful, either to the student, or to the busy man of the world, or to the professor of a limited library, than to have upon the shelf a book which may be trusted to present in a compendious form a clear statement of all that is at present known or thought on any subject by those who have made that subject their special study."–The Guardian.

"The education received at school or college is but a beginning and is valuable inasmuch as it trains the mind and habituates it to continuous application and study."–Smiles

---

PRICES FOR THE 25 VOLS.
CLOTH BINDING, with Gilt Tops...............£14
Or 14 guineas in Monthly Payments.

PUBLISHERS' CATALOGUE–PRICE £37.
HALF MOROCCO (which we recommend)...............£18
Or 18 guineas in Monthly Payments.

PUBLSHERS' CATALOGUE–PRICE £45.
FULL MOROCCO, Full Gilt Edges, a sumptuous binding
for special purposes...............£25
Or 25 guineas in Monthly Payments.

"The [Tenth Edition of the] *Encyclopædia Britannica*: A Retrospect," by Hugh Chisholm, *The Times*, December 18, 1903

We hear occasionally nowadays some rather glib and contemptuous talk about the ubiquity and excess of advertisement. It is only human nature to be ungrateful for an expedient which has really increased our opportunities and our comforts enormously, but which to the unconsidering mind becomes, in some of its forms and as a thing by itself, a pestering nuisance. No product of the human hand or mind can obtain a market outside the very narrowest sphere without advertisement of some sort, and the sort of advertisement depends upon the stage of social organization reached by the community concerned. For the diffusion of information of all kinds, no engine of modern civilization can compare with the great daily newspaper, and it was not long before its columns were found to be a better medium even than the booksellers' counters for attracting purchasers. Nobody, so far as I know, has ever thought it strange to see publishers' advertisements in the newspapers, though it is still very commonly forgotten how much better a newspaper the reader gets for his money by reason of the advertising revenue which the proprietor obtains from this and other sources. At all events, it would not have needed the exceptional imaginative faculty of such a writer as Mr. H. G. Wells (whose *Anticipations* contains some curious prophecies as to the future evolution of newspapers) to lead to the reflection that the indirect connexion of the newspaper with the publishing business could hardly stop at this point. The newspaper having been proved to be the best medium for obtaining purchasers for books, it was inevitable that sooner or later a proprietor would ask himself why he should not be the owner of the book which he was offering for sale; and, in England, any one who reasoned this out would have naturally expected *The Times* to start the new experiment. As a matter of fact, it was in the United States that it was first tried, which only shows that our American cousins think a little faster than we do and are less restrained by the fetters of tradition; but, before the proprietors of *The Times* obtained their interest in the "Encyclopædia Britannica," they had already taken several steps toward enlarging their sphere of operations beyond the production of the daily newspaper which by common consent was the greatest in the world. . . .

Among publishing experts generally, the proposal of *The Times* to sell on these terms so ambitious and cumbrous a book as the "Encyclopædia Britannica" was regarded at first as doomed to failure. They thought that the field was exhausted, and, so far as the instalment plan was concerned, they said, quite candidly, that the probable number of defaults and withdrawals would be fatal. But the reception given by the public to the offer made by *The Times* upset all calculations. The merits of the book itself, the additional prestige it acquired from its new backing, the effect of the publicity now for the first time given it by constant and elaborate advertising, and lastly—but not the least important point—the honesty and educability of the book-buying public had all been under-estimated. While fewer than 10,000 sets had been sold in the previous 23 years, *The Times* disposed of about that number more in the course of four months. After August 6, 1898, the price was slightly raised, and more than 30,000 had been sold when a further large sale was effected by an arrangement with the *Daily Mail* which enabled people of smaller incomes to purchase at the same prices, but with smaller instalments.

The special features of this "record" in publishing—as it then was— were the introduction of the instalment system and the employment of large advertisements. As regards the latter, some reflections may be permitted. They had two different objects, both essential to the success of the enterprise. In the first place, it was necessary to describe the nature of the contents of the work and to interest a widespread public in it. Ordinary publishers' advertisements previously had been composed merely of announcements of the title of a book, with perhaps a quotation from a review, and only a small space had been occupied by each. *The Times* began by devoting a whole page, undivided by columns, to a detailed account of the scope of the

"Encyclopædia," which itself was interesting to readers; and the subsequent advertisements, in its own columns and outside, were on a similar scale. Nor was the attempt to bring home the character of the book confined to newspaper advertisements. An elaborate pamphlet, with abundant extracts from its pages, was widely circulated, while innumerable explanatory letters were sent at intervals to any persons who might be expected to become subscribers. It is always possible to make fun of people who appear to have only one idea, and the devices adopted for interesting the public in the "Encyclopædia Britannica"—novel, varied, and picturesque as they were—have been the subject of some clever skits and a good deal of satirical parody. Nobody minds this poking of fun so long as it is not malicious. But while anybody with a sense of humour can appreciate the comical side of a persistent and vigorous attempt to rouse preoccupied or negligent humanity to a sense of its own interests, by bombarding the portals of the mind from every conceivable vantage-ground, this, after all, is the essence of clever advertising, and in the long run its only proper test is its success, provided always that the thing advertised really is what it is claimed to be.

The second object which *The Times* had in view was to explain the new system of payment. It is curious how slow the public are to understand a novelty like this, but experience shows that they require to be instructed over and over again before they can appreciate the simplest change from time-honoured methods. It might have seemed a fairly easy thing to grasp, that subscribers might either pay the whole price at once, or might divide it over monthly instalments; but, though the convenience of this system has since been recognized, and it has been very widely imitated, it required at the outset repeated explanations in the advertisement columns before intending purchasers could be satisfied in what way to comply with the directions. Thus it happened that in starting the sale of the reprint of the Ninth Edition, a substantial part of the need for extensive advertising arose from the necessity of overcoming the inertia of the public and accustoming them to the instalment system of payments, which provides an easy method for people of moderate incomes, and especially those whose salaries are paid monthly, to become the owners of costly works otherwise beyond their means.

In selling the Ninth Edition, *The Times* also made it better adapted for household use by supplying a revolving bookcase to hold the 25 volumes, and subsequently another to hold the 35 volumes of the Tenth Edition. How popular this feature has been may be judged from the fact that, while only 200 were at first offered, 33,200 have been sold. . . .

The final stage of the enterprise of *The Times* came, therefore, when it offered the Tenth Edition temporarily on the instalment plan, and at a cheap rate, with a view to supplying a yet further section of the public. After the large sale of the Ninth Edition and supplement separately, it might have been supposed that the number of people who could afford to have the work in their own houses could no longer be a large one; but again the results have upset all such calculations. By means of the extensive advertising employed, a very large new public has been discovered. It is, no doubt, easy for fastidious people to carp at the amount of "booming" which has been resorted to. Conservative Englishmen, who, having bought the "Encyclopædia Britannica" themselves, or being amply provided with extensive libraries, get tired of seeing its merits thrust before them in large type every morning at breakfast in their newspapers, are apt to forget that their copy of the paper cannot be printed specially for them, and that there are plenty of people who, strange to say, are still making up their minds whether to buy or not. It is, of course, possible that the modern extension of advertising—which is itself to some extent due to what *The Times* has done with the "Britannica"—may defeat its own object by paralysing the ordinary man's power of attention. But only those who are engaged in the business can tell whether they have exhausted the possibilities of reaching enough new clients to make their expenditure profitable. I heard only the other day of a member of the present Cabinet who professed not to have noticed *The Times* offer of the "Encyclopædia Britannica"; and this would seem to indicate that the advertising department had still—in spite of all its efforts—fallen short of its object.

The actual results prove that, while the efforts made to stimulate the public into equipping themselves with the "Encyclopædia Britannica" have been unexampled, the response has been also on an unprecedented scale in the history of publishing. In the course of the 300 weeks during which the sale has lasted more than 1,500,000 volumes weighing more than 5,500 tons have been sold and will have been delivered on an average of more than 5,500 a week during the whole period of 5¾ years. The largest sales on any one day exceeded £30,000, and in any one week £100,000. The largest despatch on one day was 503 sets weighing over 60 tons. The packing cases used for despatching sets could, if arranged in a solid block form an edifice as big as St. Paul's Cathedral and the Houses of Parliament combined. The P.O. has been kept very busy, and while it has benefited by nearly £60,000 spent in stamps, it has been the medium of bringing in over 1,200,000 cheques and postal orders. The transmission of so large a number might have been expected to be accompanied by occasional losses in the post, but these have been trifling—only 52 in all. From time to time there have been great difficulties in getting binders to bind the sets fast enough to meet the demand, and also in obtaining leather for the full morocco three quarter levant and half morocco bindings. Suffice it to say that altogether over 500,000 goats have been requisitioned, while the amount paid by binders for gold leaf alone for the lettering and edges has been more than £50,000. Over 200,000 people have written to *The Times* to enquire about the book. There have been altogether 2,153 who have for one reason or another made default in their instalment, and 158 sets of the work have somehow got into the category of "lost, stolen or strayed." The staff employed in the department has varied from 100 to 475 persons. I am enabled to give some idea of the amount of advertising done by means of the following figures. One whole page advertisement in *The Times* is ascertained to have been the means of attracting buyers to the amount of £8,000, for the orders were received on forms cut from the pages. The cost of all the circulars sent to individuals was £90,000, and as regards to newspaper advertising, which cost altogether £203,000, the total space occupied has been the equivalent of 5,160 columns of the daily papers and 3,400 pages of weekly papers and magazines. In *The Times* itself, during the 5¾ years, a space of 890 columns was devoted to advertising the "Encyclopædia," an amount which spread over the whole period is equivalent to less than half a column a day.

 The Times has then made a gigantic commercial success out of a situation which the publishing world regarded at the outset as offering no reasonable expectation of profit. It is amply entitled to the reward of its enterprise. Without its dauntless faith in the prosecution of a good object the venture must have failed. Countless letters received in connection with the recent competition—an ingenious device for stimulating among the new possessors of the "E.B." an intelligent and systematic habit of using it—have proved how widely the advantage of possessing the work is recognised. It is easy enough for the cynic to sit in the seat of the scornful and to disparage the educational influence that may be exercised by the introduction of the "E.B." into so many house-holds. But those who consider seriously the importance of a more earnest adoption throughout the nation of the means for a sound education will not despise this contribution towards the acceptance of a higher intellectual standard. In these days of frivolous, inaccurate and slipshod journalism it is a contribution worthy of the traditions of *The Times*. Nor can the work done by *The Times* in that respect end with their service to contemporary culture. In its production of the New Volumes the continuously progressive ideals of the earlier publishers of the "Britannica"—regarded as a classical British embodiment of scholarship and science—have been kept steadily in view in a manner that must operate advantageously upon any future edition of the work, and by deliberately including among the editors and contributors the ablest specialists of the United States it has given practical recognition of the community of intellectual interests between this country and America and has thus made the Tenth Edition representative of the best thought of the whole English-speaking world.

Haxton on Advertising

Haxton's article on "advertising" as it appears in the *Eleventh Edition:*

Before discussing in detail the methods of advertising in periodical publications it may be well to complete, for the use of the general reader, a brief survey of the whole subject by examining the two other classes of advertisement. The most enthusiastic partisan of advertising will admit that posters and similar devices are very generally regarded by the public as sources of annoyance. A bold headline or a conspicuous illustration in a newspaper advertisement may for a moment force itself upon the reader's attention. In the French, and in some English newspapers, where an advertisement is often given the form of an item of news, the reader is distressed by the constant fear of being hoodwinked. He begins to read an account of a street accident, and finds at the end of the paragraph a puff of a panacea for bruises. The best English and American journals have refused to lend themselves to this sort of trickery, and in not one of the best journals printed in the English language will there be found an advertisement which is not so plainly differentiated from news matter that the reader may avoid it if he sees fit to do so. On the whole, then, newspaper advertisements ask, but do not compel attention. The whole theory of poster advertising is, on the other hand, one of tyranny. The advertiser who pays for space upon a hoarding or wall, although he may encourage a form of art, deliberately violates the wayfarer's mind. A trade-mark or a catch-word presents itself when eye and thought are occupied with other subjects. Those who object to this class of advertisement assert, with some show of reason, that an advertisement has no more right to assault the eye in this fashion than to storm the ear by an inordinate din; and a man who came up behind another man in the street, placed his mouth close to the other's ear, and bawled a recommendation of some brand of soap or tobacco, would be regarded as an intolerable disturber of public peace and comfort. Yet if the owner of a house sees fit to paint advertisements upon his walls, his exercise of the jealously guarded rights of private property may not lightly be disturbed. For the most part, both law and public opinion content themselves with restraining the worst excesses of the advertiser, leaving many sensitive persons to suffer. . . .

The preparation of advertisements for the periodical press has within the last twenty years or so become so important a task that a great number of writers and artists—many of the latter possessing considerable abilities—gain a periodical livelihood from this pursuit. The ingenuity displayed in modern newspaper advertising is unquestionably due to American initiative. The English newspaper advertisement of twenty years ago consisted for the most part of the mere reiteration of a name. An advertiser who took a column's space supplied enough matter to fill an inch, and ingenuously repeated his statement throughout the column. Such departures from this childlike method as were made were for the most part eccentric to the point of incoherence. It may, however, be said in defence of English advertisers; that newspaper publishers for a long time sternly discountenanced any attempt to render advertisements attractive. So long as an advertiser was rigidly confined to the ordinary single-column measure, and so long as he was forbidden to use anything but the smallest sort of type, there was very little opportunity for him to attract the reader's attention. The newspaper publisher must always remember that the public buy a newspaper for the sake of the news, not for the sake of the advertisements, and that if the advertisements are relegated to a position and a scope, in respect of display, so inferior that they may be overlooked, the advertiser cannot afford to bear his share of the cost of publication. Of late *The Times*, followed by almost all newspapers in the United Kingdom, has given the advertiser as great a degree of liberty as he really needs, and many experienced advertisers in America incline to the belief that the larger licence accorded to American advertisers defeats its own ends. The truth would seem to be that the advertiser will always demand, and may fairly expect, the right to make his space as fantastic in appearance as that allotted to the editor. When some American editors see fit to print a headline in letters as large as a man's hand, and to begin half-a-dozen different articles on the first page of a newspaper, continuing one on page 2, another on page 4, and another on page 6, to the bewilderment of the reader, it can hardly be expected that the American advertiser should submit to any very strict code of decorum. The subject of the relation between a newspaper proprietor and his advertisers cannot be dismissed without reference to the notable independence of advertisers' influence, which English and American newspaper proprietors authorize their editors to display. Whenever an insurance company or a bank goes wrong, the cry is raised that all the editors in Christendom had known for years that the directors were imbeciles and rogues, but had conspired to keep mute for the sake of an occasional advertisement. When the British public persisted, not long ago, in paying premium prices for the shares of over-capitalized companies, the crash had no sooner come than the newspapers were accused of having puffed promotions for the sake of the money received for publishing prospectuses. As a matter of fact, in the case of the best dailies in England and America, the editor does not stand at all in awe of the advertiser, and time after time the Money Article has ruthlessly attacked a promotion of which the prospectus appeared in the very same issue. It is indeed to the interest of the advertiser, as well as to the interest of the reader, that this independence should be preserved, for the worth of any journal as an advertising medium depends upon its possessing a bona fide circulation among persons who believe it to be a serious and honestly conducted newspaper.

E. B. Titchener's Content Analysis

E. B. Titchener's detailed critique of the Britannica's *coverage of psychology is a useful look at the way in which major articles evolved over time. James Ward, the contributor selected by Hugh Chisholm, wrote three articles on psychology in a row in the Ninth, Tenth (called "the supplementary" by Titchener), and Eleventh Editions. In the excerpt below, Titchener shows how they changed, edition to edition.*

The supplementary article occupies 17 pages; the original article required 49. The article of 1911 occupies 58 of the slightly larger pages of the new *Britannica.*

The Introduction (§ 1. The Science of "Mind"; § 2. Standpoint of Psychology) is substantially the same as the article of 1886. Here, as throughout,—the statement may be made once for all,—the author has revised with extreme care; everywhere there is weeding, pruning, dovetailing; but the substance of the two preliminary sections is unchanged. Under *General Analysis* we have first, in § 3. the discussion of Experience from the tenth edition: the paragraph on Pragmatism is omitted. Sections 4–8 then practically repeat the ninth edition; the fine-print discussions of the subjectivity of sensations, of the connection between subjective attention and objective intensity, and of the non-presentability of feeling and attention are, however, omitted. A new § 9 is devoted to *Attention.* The *Theory of Presentations* opens (§§ 10–12) with the familiar treatment of the Psychological Individual, the Presentation Continuum, and Retentiveness; an interpolated § 13 gives a brief note on Assimilation; and the discussion of Relativity follows (§ 14), thus changing places with that of Subconsciousness. Professor Ward has entirely rewritten this latter section, § 15, and has raised it–if not, as Bain counselled, from brevier to pica, at least–from brevier to long primer: the core of doctrine remains unchanged. Section 16, *Sensation, Movement and the External World*, owes its change of title, its introduction, and its conclusion, to the tenth edition; the treatment of the characteristics of sensation is expanded from the ninth. *Perception* (§§ 17–20) and *Imagination or Ideation* (§§ 21, 22) stand with a few omissions–compensated, as most of the omissions of the article are, by later additions–as they stood before. A new § 23, on the *Genesis and Development of Ideation*, comes in from the tenth edition. Sections 24, 25, *Mental Association and the Memory-Continuum*, and §§ 26–29, *Reminiscence and Expectation: Temporal Perception*, repeat the ninth edition; a critical note is added on the relation of successive to simultaneous association, and on the notions of "form" and "law" of association. Then comes the excursus (from the tenth edition) on *Experimental Investigations Concerning Memory and Association*. The sections on *Feeling* (§§ 31–33) are as they were. *Emotion and Emotional Expression*, from the tenth edition, follows as § 34; *Emotional and Conative Action*, § 35, stands unaltered. The treatment of *Intellection* and *Categories* is extended by the introduction of § 39, *Objects of Higher Order: Their Analysis and Genesis*, from the tenth edition; otherwise there is practically no change in §§ 36–42. *Belief* is then given a separate heading, and raised to the dignity of long primer. The subject-matter of *Presentation of Self, Self-Consciousness and Conduct* (§§ 44–46) has been newly articulated, and the concluding note on Freedom has been rewritten. Section 47, *Relation of Body and Mind*, comes from the tenth edition, as does also the appendix, § 48, on *Comparative Psychology*. A revised list of *Authorities* brings the article to an end.

Hugh Chisholm's Response to Joseph Jacobs's Unfavorable Review in *The New York Times*

While I naturally appreciate the compliments paid to me, as editor, by Dr. Joseph Jacobs in his able review of the first fourteen volumes of the new editions of the *Encyclopædia Britannica*, which was printed in *The Times* of last Sunday (Feb. 19), I must ask you to allow me to correct one misapprehension into which he has fallen. My namesake, Dr. George Chisholm, the geographer, and myself are two totally distinct persons. I am not the author of his excellent text-book on Commercial Geography, and Dr. Jacobs has attributed the strength of the geographical side of the new edition to a wrong cause. His praise for the geographical articles is none the less welcome, and, I believe, deserved; but, if they are as good as he says, it is not because the editor-in-chief was himself a specialist in geography, but because, in the organization of the editorial staff, I from the first provided for a geographical department, ably manned within, and in touch with a number of expert geographers without. It has been my own duty to direct the work in all departments, with the assistance of others who has special knowledge in each, and I imagine that it was only in this way that the attempt could be made, as to the success of which the critics and the public must judge, to preserve that uniformity, unity and organic character in the construction of the whole work, which in my editorial introduction I have ventured to claim for the Eleventh Edition.

It would be perhaps ungracious of me to criticise some of the less favorable comparisons which Dr. Jacobs draws between the new edition and the Tenth, which, being composed of supplementary volumes (of which I was the acting editor) added to those of the

Ninth, was in its nature a stopgap, pending a complete new edition, and could not be made satisfactory even by means of the index. It was obviously impossible for Dr. Jacobs, after a few hours' use, as he himself points out, to make more than a very cursory examination of a number of volumes containing about twenty-four millions of words. But when he estimates that not more than one-fifth of the contents, as compared with the Tenth Edition, is absolutely new, his arithmetic is certainly faulty. My own opinion is that not more than one-fifth has appeared before, if as much. It is difficult sometimes to compute arithmetically the amount of change involved when revision is made of an earlier article, but Dr. Jacobs himself mentions as repeated from the previous edition articles which in fact have gone through considerable revision for the new one. A very careful count, from the same point of view of comparison, was made for me in our London office as regards a single volume, taken haphazard from those of the new edition, and it was found that only sixteen per cent. represented matter which had appeared in the Tenth. . . .

I should not have been surprised if any one confusing the Eleventh Edition with the Tenth were to express surprise at the large amount of apparently valuable matter which had not been repeated; but, in the circumstances, it does seem strange that even a cursory examination should suggest the opposite. When I began, nearly eight years ago, to consider the planning of the Eleventh Edition, I expected to be able to use again a considerable proportion of what had appeared in the Tenth Edition, but experience proved this to be impracticable in a work which was to represent contemporary scholarship and opinion.

It has been my duty at various times to become acquainted with the structure of all the preceding editions, and I know it to be a fact that no previous edition has been so original in its matter, as compared with its predecessor, as that which I have had the honor of directing to its conclusion. I feel, therefore, in justice to the large number of contributors whose work is involved—and of whom Dr. Jacobs himself is one—that I must ask you to let me correct the somewhat hasty impression which he has obtained in this respect.

Hugh Chisholm's Eulogy of Horace Everett Hooper

From the Saturday Review *(UK) 8 July 1922, pp. 56–7*

A GREAT PUBLISHER

By Hugh Chisholm

(The sudden death on June 13th, in New York, of Mr. H. E. Hooper, the proprietor and publisher of the "Encyclopædia Britannica," has removed a remarkable personality, whose association with the "Times" during 1898–1908 made something like an epic in the history of English Publishing.)

Horace Everett Hooper was born at Worcester, Mass., U.S.A., on December 8, 1859. By parentage he was of English descent on both sides, his father's family having settled in New England about 1650, while his mother was a descendent of John Leverett, governor of Massachusetts in 1672–1679, son of Sir John Leverett of Boston, Lincolnshire. Having been educated in the public schools of Worcester, Mass., and Washington, D.C. (to which city the Hooper family moved in 1873), he started in business in early life, at Denver, Col., and subsequently had a varied experience of bookselling and advertising in New York and elsewhere. In 1893, in Chicago, he took part in organizing the Western Book and Stationery Company, which operated in several of the larger Western American cities. In 1895, he formed a company in New York for popularizing the sale of the "Century Dictionary," and the success of this enterprise led to its extension into wider fields. In 1897, with Mr. Walter Jackson as his partner, Mr. Hooper came to London, and arranged with Messrs. A and C Black, the owners and publishers of the "Encyclopædia Britannica," for the issue of a reprint of the 9th Edition of that work, which had been brought out, in 25 volumes, between 1875 and 1889; and shortly afterwards, he purchased the copyright. He made an arrangement with the *Times* by which the latter undertook to publish the reprint, at about half the price at which the 9th Edition had been sold, and to promote its sale in all English-speaking countries. The result of Mr. Hooper's introduction of what were then in England novel methods of American book-advertising, together with the provision of facilities for payment by monthly instalments (on what came to be known as "The *Times* System"), was that the sale of the "Encyclopædia Britannica" was widely extended and popularized. During the next few years over 70,000 sets of the reprint were sold, whereas up to 1898 only about 10,000 sets of the 9th Edition had been sold by Messrs. Black in Great Britain. In continuance of this arrangement with Messrs. Hooper and Jackson for the publication of the "Encyclopædia Britannica," the *Times*, in 1899, took in hand the preparation of a Supplement in ten New Volumes, completed in 1902, bringing the volumes of the 9th Edition up to date and forming with them the 10th Edition, of which a further 30,000 sets were sold.

A yet larger enterprise was then entered upon. The editorial staff which had been engaged at Printing House Square for making the New Volumes of the 10th Edition was in 1903 considerably enlarged, and an elaborate organization was created for the preparation of an entirely new edition, to be published after an interval of eight years. Up to 1908, when the work on the new 11th Edition "Encyclopædia Britannica" was already far advanced, its headquarters remained at the *Times* office. Meanwhile the relations between Mr. Hooper and the management of the *Times* had become continuously closer. In association with Mr. Moberly Bell he took an active part in its business affairs, and it was on his initiative, and under his direction, that the *Times* Book Club was started. In 1905 the "Historians' History of the World," the production of which, in 25 volumes, had been promoted by Mr. Hooper, was published and sold by the *Times*. In 1908, however, about a year after Mr. Hooper's partnership with Mr. Jackson in their own business had been dissolved and he had acquired its entire control the connection between him and the *Times* was brought to an end, on its chief proprietorship passing into the hands of Lord Northcliffe. The headquarters of the "Encyclopædia Britannica," together with the whole of the editorial staff, were consequently transferred to the offices of the Encyclopædia Britannica Company, at 125 High Holborn. There the editorial work of the 11th Edition was carried to completion, and in 1911 was published, in 29 volumes, by the Cambridge University Press under a similar arrangement with the Syndics of the Cambridge Press to that previously made with the *Times*. Mr. Hooper, as president both of the Encyclopædia Britannica Company in England, and also the corresponding company in the United States, had charge of its sales throughout the world; and by the end of 1921, though during the war the sale was necessarily interrupted except in the United States so long as that country remained neutral, it had amounted to about 225,000 sets, either in the original large volumes known as the "Cambridge issue" or in the small-sized "Handy Volumes," which were brought out in the United States in 1916. Finally, the preparation of a Supplement in three New Volumes (30, 31 and 32), conceived so as to convert the 11th into a 12th Edition by adding the history of the World War and accounts of all other important later developments during the decade, was initiated by Mr. Hooper in 1920. These New Volumes were completed last March and are now in course of delivery to purchasers.

Mr. Hooper's success in the particular field of publishing and bookselling to which he specially devoted himself was, no doubt, largely dependent on his genius for advertising and his powers of salesmanship. The organization which he gathered round him for this purpose in London from 1897 onwards, as well as in New York, was highly skilled and highly paid, and it was engaged from time to time in the interests of large undertakings other than his own. It would probably be admitted that no man in the advertising business had done more in his time to revolutionize the art of publicity in this country but it was the faith and pertinacity of an idealist that made Mr. Hooper a great businessman, and it was this element in his character that will always be associated with his memory in the minds of those who knew him most intimately. When in 1900 I was originally invited by Mr. Arthur Walter and Mr. Moberly Bell, on behalf of the *Times*, to take the place of Sir Donald Mackenzie Wallace in directing its production of the New Volumes of the 10th

Edition of the "Encyclopædia Britannica," which were completed in 1902, I was not aware that Messrs. Hooper and Jackson had anything to do with that undertaking, nor was it for some little while that I became personally acquainted with either of them. It was only in 1903, when I was entrusted with the preparation of the new 11th Edition, that I came into direct relations with Mr. Hooper, and up to 1908 this was still as representing the *Times* in this connection. But during those years, and later, I came to regard him with ever increasing respect, affection and confidence. As editor of the 10th, 11th and 12th Editions of the "Encyclopædia Britannica," I could not have had a more loyal, a more generous or a more helpful employer as its proprietor. His acquisition of the copyright in that work, with its long-established tradition of scholarly accuracy and authority, and his devotion to the object of bringing it up to date in later editions, were founded on his belief that the introduction of this "library of knowledge" into the home of the public at large, with its progressive accretion of authoritative information on every sort of subject, was the best way of democratizing the means of self-education, and that, the more persons he could bring to buy it and habitually consult its pages, the more advanced would be the general standard of intelligence and culture. While leaving the editorial responsibility to my unfettered control, he threw all his remarkable energy and inventiveness into the details of the printing, manufacture and sale, and into the elaboration of his "campaigns" of publicity, sparing no pain and no money in the pursuit of the ideal he had set before himself.

It was an essential part of this ideal that the educational influence of the "Encyclopædia Britannica"—as a standard British work, English-edited, but representing the disinterested critical co-operation of selected expert authorities from every quarter, American and international—should be a potent instrument for bringing all the English-speaking peoples on a common footing of mutual understanding. For many years he had made his home in England, and it was his passionate ambition to forward Anglo-American solidarity in every possible direction. He was twice married, and is survived by a widow and by sons by both marriages. His eldest son by his second marriage went into the British Army as a private at the age of 18 during the war.

Notes

PROLOGUE

xi A century later: Robert Collison, *Encyclopedias: Their History Through-out the Ages* (Kingston-upon-Thames: Hafner Publishing Co., 1966).

xv "attains the dignity": Cited in an advertisement in *The Times*, February 2, 1911, p. 4, for the Eleventh Edition.

xvi "making the work": "Editorial Introduction," *Encyclopædia Britannica*, 11th ed., vol. 1.

xvi Chisholm introduced the: For a very useful account of the women contributors, see Professor Gillian Thomas's *A Position to Command Respect: Women and the Eleventh Britannica* (Metuchen and London: Scarecrow Press, 1992). There have been several efforts to give a brief history of the eleventh edition. Herman Kogan's *The Great EB: The Story of the Encyclopædia Britannica* (Chicago: University of Chicago Press, 1958) is the one best known, but its vague (or nonexistent) attributions and inaccuracies are problems for readers. But Professor Thomas's pocket history in *A Position to Command Respect* is excellent and recommended.

xvii "To keep the": Mrs. Alec Tweedie, *Thirteen Years of a Busy Woman's Life* (London: John Lane, 1912), p. 296.

xvii "one of the": And certainly more auspicious than the banquet for the Ninth Edition, where the leading contributors, "a distinguished company of literary and scientific men," supped while one remarked that "the voices of the ladies" invited to a reception following dinner could be heard through the door to an adjoining room. From the booklet *Celebration Banquet*, Encyclopædia Britannica, *Ninth Edition, Cambridge, 11th December 1888*, p. 24. The speaker was the historian John Sutherland Black, whose biography of W. Robertson Smith, the editor of the Ninth Edition, would appear in 1912.

CHAPTER 1. PLYMOUTH 1896

4 Even in the: Mark Rinella and Whitney Walton, "Planned Serendipity: American Travelers and the Transatlantic Voyage in the Nineteenth and Twentieth Centuries," *Journal of Social History* 38, no. 2 (winter 2004): 365–83.

6 Hooper had established: From the Eleventh Edition, on "Bookselling":

> Coming between the publisher and the retail bookseller is the important distributing agency of the wholesale bookseller. It is to him that the retailer looks for his miscellaneous supplies, as it is simply impossible for him to stock one-half of the books published. In Paternoster Row, London, which has for over a hundred years been the centre of this industry, may be seen the collectors from the shops of the retail booksellers, busily engaged in obtaining the books ordered by the book-buying public. It is also through these agencies that the country bookseller obtains his miscellaneous supplies. At the leading house in this department of bookselling almost any book can be found, or information obtained concerning it. At one of these establishments over 1,000,000 books are constantly kept in stock. It is here that the publisher calls first on showing or "subscribing" a new book, a critical process, for by the number thus subscribed the fate of a book is sometimes determined.

6 Hooper's starting inventory: As the Eleventh Edition, again in the article on "Bookselling," points out, America's rising rate of literacy was closely tied to intellectual property theft: "[W]ith the spread of newspapers and education there also arose a demand for books, and publishers set to work to secure the advantages offered by the wide field of English literature, the whole of which they had the liberty of reaping free of all cost beyond that of production. The works of Scott, Byron, Moore, Southey, Wordsworth, and indeed of every author of note, were reprinted without the smallest payment to author or proprietor. Half the names of the authors in the so called 'American' catalogue of books printed between 1820 and 1852 are British. By this means the works of the best authors were brought to the doors of all classes in the cheapest variety of forms."

8 For agents representing: Sacvan Bercovitch and Cyrus R. K. Patell, *The Cambridge History of American Literature* (New York: Cambridge University Press, 1994), p. 44.

8 Other Twain prospectus: A small portfolio of these has been assembled by Stephen Railton for "Mark Twain in His Times," Electronic Text Center, University of Virginia.

11 Robert Collison traces: Robert Collison, *Encyclopedias: Their History Throughout the Ages* (Kingston-upon-Thames: Hafner Publishing Co., 1966), p. 22.

12 in 1859: Malcolm Woodfield, "Reviewing After 1860: R. H. Hutton and the 'Spectator,'" *Yearbook of English Studies* 16 (1986): 74–91. By 1922, the number of periodicals in the UK had ballooned to more than *fifty thousand*; David Finkelstein, *Victorian Studies* 52, no. 3 (2010).

12 and biblical scholar: As so described in the Eleventh Edition, which concludes its entry on Robertson with this sentence: "The sweetness and purity of his nature combined with his brilliant conversational powers to render him the most delightful of friends and companions." Herman Kogan, *The Great EB: The Story of the Encyclopædia Britannica* (Chicago: University of Chicago Press, 1958), discusses Robertson's role in detail on pp. 52–69.

14 From the first: J. D. Newth, *Adam & Charles Black 1807–1957: Some Chapters in the History of a Publishing House* (London: Adam & Charles Black, 1957). Johnson, one of a breed of Yankee entrepreneurial encyclopedia publishers, felt he understood the American character better than English academics did, so he blanketed newspapers with ads touting his own encyclopedia, while damning the *Britannica* for, among other things, its size and scope ("An Expensive, Cumbersome, and Almost Useless Work for Practical People . . .") and especially for its skepticism of biblical literalism in entries such as T. H. Huxley's on "Evolution": "If evolution is true, the Bible is false. The Bible is true, and evolution is a malicious diabolic lie!" (pp. 42–43). The straw man in Johnson's argument was to hang on for more than a century, suffering repeated blows from both sides in this odd, nearly senseless dispute. See appendix A for more on the unofficial *Britannica* publishers.

15 "The barn itself": *Rocky Mountain News*, May 9, 1890, p. 5.

15 a major Chicago: Kogan, *The Great EB*, p. 71.

17 The huge World's: "Chicago," Encyclopædia Britannica Online, accessed January 12, 2008, http://britannica.com.

17 One such journalist: To account for Haxton's presence, some reason-

able speculation: Hearst had paid \$7,500 for the confession of H. H. Holmes, one of America's most prolific serial killers, sometime toward the end of 1894. Holmes's infamous "Castle," where many of his murders were committed, was in the Englewood district of Chicago, and Hearst carried a stream of reports from the city. Haxton was one of Hearst's favorites.

CHAPTER 2. THE ADMAN

20 "never could": Elizabeth Robins and Joseph Pennell, *The Life of James McNeill Whistler* (Philadelphia: Lippincott, 1911), p. 284. "Fancy Jim" appears here and on an inscription page of a copy of *The Gentle Art of Making Enemies* (1890) published in a limited edition by Brentano's in Paris given by Whistler to Haxton over Whistler's famous "butterfly" signature. Many thanks to Phil Bishop, of Mosher Books, who once owned the copy and provided me with useful scans.

20 In early 1894: Henry Haxton, *Hippolyte and Golden-Beak: Two Stories* (New York: Harper Bros., 1894). "The author, though he writes from the wilds of Wisconsin [a hoax, as indicated by Haxton's place-name, "Lake Tired-Canoe"], appears to be an Englishman. Both stories are well told, and provided with startling denouements." *Dial*, August 16, 1895, p. 95. Haxton curried Whistler's favor, for Whistler knew everyone. For example, Mary, the older sister of Janet Hogarth, whom we just met delivering her speech, was a Whistler friend. So were many other painters and writers who struck up relationships with each other independent of Whistler's direct involvement. Judging from the inscription in a copy of his book in my own collection, Haxton was at least acquainted with Xavier Martinez, a young California tonalist who was studying in Paris at the time. Everybody, it seems, knew Whistler.

20 "Mr. Bassett is": Times change; *New York Times*, March 3, 1895, p. 27. The book has been serialized online by *The Fortnightly Review*, http://fortnightlyreview.co.uk.

23 "the boat davits": *San Francisco Sunday Examiner*, April 2, 1888.

23 Death-in-the-bay exposés: And not just in San Francisco. As a twenty-year-old cook on the clipper ship *Loch Awe* docked in Lyttelton, New Zealand, Haxton had gone to retrieve the ship's steward from a bar at 8:30 the evening of August 29, 1880. There was a splash. The next day, Haxton reported the steward missing, but his hat found, and police discovered his body floating in the water about four yards from the

gangway. An inquest ruled "found drowned" and suggest putting nets under gangways to keep stumbling sailors out of the sea. *Star*, September 4, 1880, p. 3, http://paperspast.natlib.govt.nz/.

23 When they found: *San Francisco Examiner*, January 4, 1890. An independent source is Emily Dow Partridge Young, whose diary covers her visit to San Francisco at the time. It may be found online at http://partridge.parkinsonfamily.org.

23 The *Examiner*'s coverage: *Life*, August 25, 1961, p. 76.

24 the schooner Stevenson: Henry Meade Bland, *Stevenson's California* (San Jose: Pacific Short Story Club, 1924), p. 34. Dates from Edinburgh Napier University's RLS website, http://robert-louis-stevenson.org.

24 "Mr. Stevenson has": June 24, 1888. The article, "A Man of Letters," is a long and rambling one, filled with impassioned speeches on history, anthropology, George Meredith, writing technique, and even word choice ("My special distaste is the use of any foreign word") attributed to Stevenson, interrupted by Haxton's sycophantic asides ("All this, it should be remembered, is a sick man's talk—a man bedridden, half the time, in pain always. If only men in health all thought as robustly!"). It's obvious that the twenty-eight-year-old Haxton was awestruck by the fragile thirty-eight-year-old Stevenson. Haxton's "word of prose"—he rarely used a single word when a thousand would do—already had the sideshow tone and dense texture that shocked readers of *The Times* would later find familiar: "Mr. Stevenson's words have been noted with almost literal accuracy—and one cannot but be impressed by the similarity of his talk to his work. The quaint terms of phrasing, the happy extraction of fresh metal from a word which other men would think had been tortured out of everything but the useless quartz, are not, plainly enough, the result of study—they are flashes of spontaneous ignition, appearing in the quiet evening of desultory chat as often as in the set show of a book. . . . [W]ork must be easy to a man who ordered his dinner or muttered in his sleep in epigrams." The piece has now been published in *The Fortnightly Review*'s series online, http://fortnightlyreview.co.uk.

24 He had met: Emily Wortis Leider, *California's Daughter: Gertrude Atherton and Her Times* (Stanford: Stanford University Press, 1991), p. 116.

24 after Jackson's death: Kate Phillips, *Helen Hunt Jackson: A Literary Life* (Berkeley: University of California Press, 2003), p. 273.

26 leaving his rooms: San Francisco City Directory, May 1890.

27 And when news: Thomas had toured Australia, where she described

herself to a reporter from the *South Australian Advertiser* as "a common-place every-day sort of leading lady" [24 November 1886, p. 8], and New Zealand and, after her eventful visit to San Francisco, returned to England and the London stage, where she appeared fairly frequently in supporting roles into the 1920s. She was also active in the suffrage movement, and played the unnamed "working woman" in the Royal Court Theatre's 1907 production of Elizabeth Robins's *Votes for Women*—according to *The Guardian* (March 19, 2003) the first suffragette play. The performance was noted by critics ("just the rasping Cockney tones, the termagant attitude, that are required," said *The Illustrated London News*); in fact, her forte was stealing entire plays as a secondary character. Her daughter (born in 1879, and not fathered by Haxton, apparently), Elie Malyon, had a long and interesting career as a character actress. However, Haxton apparently did have a daughter, May, born in 1885. She appears on several passenger lists traveling with her father and in a *Brooklyn Eagle* story from 1909 announcing the comings and goings of the summer season.

27 "'What has become'": Answering this question exactly is work for another day, but a curious example of Haxton's domestic confusion may be found in a notice in the New York *Evening Telegram*, dated July 7, 1889, concerning the formation of something called the "Mariposa Musical Society." Its members were "California people who reside in this city, and who are musically inclined." Among its number was Michael Banner, a famous young violin virtuoso; Edgar Kelly, a popular songwriter; and "Mrs. H. R. Haxton, elocutionist." And Agnes did try, at least for a time, to hold on to her San Francisco connection. *The San Francisco Blue Book* for 1890 lists her as "Mrs. H. R. Haxton (nee Agnes Thomas)" among the members of "The California Colony in New York." She lived in the large building at 42 West 35th Street. Whether the two divorced before Haxton married Sara Thibault is not known. The Mariposa Musical Society announced that it would perform a concert at the Chickering that fall.

27 "[R]umor says he": *San Francisco Call*, April 26, 1891, p. 12.

27 But eventually: By 1901, Sallie and the child were boarders in the home of a railway worker named Arthur Pepper in St. John's Wood, near Finchley Road. On one of her trips to the U.S. Sallie told immigration authorities she was "coming home to the U.S.A," but the next year she was back in England again, and this time for good. She was still in the gossip columns as late as 1905 when the *Oakland Tribune*

(March 11, p. 22) remembered her as "one of the beauties of the Southern Set." But her friends began to fall out of touch, and, without money, she tried to sue Haxton (along with the Hooper & Jackson company) in 1908. When she died alone, in 1923, the *San Francisco Chronicle* (September 17) misspelled her last name twice in her brief obituary.

28 following the map: Janet E. (Hogarth) Courtney, *Recollected in Tranquillity* (London: Heinemann, 1926), p. 210. Given their hurry to reach London, this seems to be a bit of embroidery. Trains met arriving ships, and the ride to London took only hours.

CHAPTER 3. PRINTING HOUSE SQUARE

30 "The London *Times*": *The Times* was less kind to Lincoln. The paper's description of the address the president gave at Gettysburg: "The ceremony was rendered ludicrous by some of the sallies of the poor President. . . . Anything more dull and commonplace it would not be easy to imagine." Quoted by Daniel Finkelstein, *The Times*, June 2, 2008.

33 Unfortunately: F. Harcourt Kitchin, *Moberly Bell and His Times: An Unofficial Narrative* (London: Philip Allen & Co., 1925), pp. 198ff.

34 *The Times*'s printer's: S. V. Makower, *Some Notes Upon the History of "The Times," 1785–1904* (1904), p. 13.

34 The Walter family: Bowman, p. 304, among many other sources. Stanley Morison et al., *The History of "The Times" 1884–1912: The Twentieth Century Test* (London: The Times, 1947) also provides great detail.

35 In 1885: Morison et al., *History of* The Times, p. 115.

36 more than £200,000: At least £12 million in 2009, but probably much more. A note about the tricky business of historical conversions: £1 in 1890 was worth about £60 ($100 or so) in 2009, according to the helpful calculator available online at Britain's National Archives website, http://nationalarchives.gov.uk/currency/results.asp. However, using the GDP deflator at http://measuringworth.com yields a modern (2007) value of just over £100. The same source shows that a dollar in 1890 was worth $22.46 in 2007, roughly the same as the 5:1 ($:£) exchange rate used in 1890.

36 Although Walter took: Morison et al., *History of "The Times,"* pp. 45ff. Pigott's name also appears as "Piggott."

38 "a man of": E. H. C. Moberly Bell, *The Life and Letters of C. F. Moberly Bell* (London: Richards Press, 1927), p. 18.

38 "Let's go and": Ibid., p. 22.

CHAPTER 4. THE CAIRO CORRESPONDENT

42 By August: See Michael Christopher Low, "Empire and the Hajj: Pilgrims, Plagues, and Pan-Islam Under British Surveillance, 1865–1908," *International Journal of Middle East Studies* 40, no. 2 (May 2008): 290a. See also *Reports of the Medical Officer of the Privy Council and Local Government Board, Issues 5–8* (1875); J. N. Hays, *Epidemics and Pandemics: Their Impacts on Human History* (Santa Barbara, CA: ABC-CLIO, 2005), pp. 267–79.

42 "So you've come": E. H. C. Moberly Bell, *The Life and Letters of C. F. Moberly Bell* (London: Richards Press, 1927), p. 25.

45 "Thus between the": Ibid., p. 26.

47 When Mowbray Morris: Arthur Irwin Dasent, *John Thadeus Delane, Editor of "The Times"–His Life and Correspondence*, vol. 2 (London: John Murray, 2008), p. 292. I contrive a probable truth here. I find no document showing that the two met, but it seems highly unlikely they would not have. Morris's condition was grave when he came to Egypt, and it's not probable that the paper's most familiar person there would have been kept away. Morris died the next year, replaced as manager by John Cameron Macdonald. A very shy man, Morris had been born in Jamaica in 1816, he had worked at *The Times* as manager for more than twenty years, and his roots ran deep into Printing House Square, but other than a simple death notice his passing went unremarked; his paper published no obituary for him. He was a brother-in-law of John Delane, one of *The Times*'s most famous editors. Indeed, Delane was editor at the time of Morris's death. Morris's son, who shared his father's given name, was a drama critic and editor (of *Macmillan's Magazine*, among others), but he was best known in London for his unpaid debts. The discovery of this vice by his father while in Egypt is said to have hastened the old man's demise.

CHAPTER 5. THE ASSISTANT MANAGER

50 a job as: Sample question: "How is it that the firing of heavy artillery causes rain to fall in the neighbourhood?" Sidney Dark, *The Life of Sir Arthur Pearson, BT., G.B.E.* (London: Hodder and Stoughton, 1925), p. 35.

52 He was also: In Egypt, however, he was much more comfortable playing the newspaper publisher. He tried for years to get *The Levant Herald* to publish a Cairo edition. When that failed, he formed a small

company and published *The Egyptian Gazette*. It was not a failure, but it didn't produce enough income to feed his ambitions, either.

52 "have been born": E. H. C. Moberly Bell, *The Life and Letters of C. F. Moberly Bell* (London: Richards Press, 1927), p. 141.

53 "We are little": Ibid., p. 133.

54 when advertisers would: A few years later, Alfred Harmsworth described the price of such arrogance: "An advertising agent once told me that his father, many years ago, had been insulted by the Advertisement Manager of *The Times*. That insult cost the paper £120,000." Bowman, p. 323.

54 In 1852: Sir Edward Cook, *Delane of "The Times"* (London: Constable & Co., 1916), p. 2.

54 Meanwhile: Stanley Morison et al., *The History of "The Times" 1884–1912: The Twentieth Century Test* (London: The Times, 1947); Bowman, p. 304.

56 As the votes: Bell, *The Life and Letters of C. F. Moberly Bell*, p. 188.

57 1897: This date may be very esoterically controversial, so often has it been reported as 1898, first by Herman Kogan (*The Great EB: The Story of the Encyclopædia Britannica* [Chicago: University of Chicago Press, 1958], pp. 81ff), apparently. But the note to Arthur Walter in Moberly Bell's own hand retailing a *second* meeting with Hooper and Clarke is unmistakably dated "26/2/97" and it mentions a meeting with the pair "last Tuesday," thus setting this first meeting on the 23rd. It would seem that 1897 would make more sense than 1898 in any case, since the first advertisement for *The Times Edition of the Encyclopædia Britannica* is dated March 23, 1898. It's unlikely that Hooper and Clarke could have had the fulfillment mechanism in place, and only barely likely that Haxton could have written his thousands of words of advertising copy, so quickly—Kogan claims that it all came together in a week. (Sadly, Kogan's papers, said by his son to have been deposited with the book and manuscript in Chicago's Newberry library, have disappeared.) Clarke was also occupied with his *Britannica–New York Times* scheme of 1897. Morison et al.'s *History of "The Times"* (p. 442) gives the date of the meeting as 1897, but almost immediately follows with 1898 as the date when Hooper and Jackson made their proposal. That may be true for Hooper and Jackson, but the agreement accompanying the 1897 note is identical with the arrangement discussed by Hooper and Clarke (interestingly, after their first meeting, Moberly Bell remembered Clarke, but not Hooper—only a "second person") as it obtained

in 1898. The note from Bell to Arthur Walter is in the *Times* archives, London.

58 It was a: *Andrees Handatlas.*

58 Bell offered it: *The Times,* April 8, 1895, p. 12. For the information on the German edition, I am indebted to Mr. Maarten Witkam of Amsterdam.

59 When Hooper and: The Savoy: Kogan, *The Great EB,* pp. 81ff. Most recapitulations of this come from Kogan, and he didn't make his sources known. He has only Hooper and Haxton in London and Edinburgh at the time, and, as noted above, Kogan also has the meeting with Moberly Bell at *The Times* taking place in 1898, with prefatory discussions with Clarke and Hooper taking place during that year, when it was, in fact, a year earlier, just after Hooper and Haxton's meeting with the printer in Edinburgh, according to the memo in the *Times* archives. Clarke was also frequently in London on business.

60 Haxton and Hooper: That this meeting took place, there is little doubt. But alas, there's no documentation of it, either, so we can't say if Clarke was present too. Dr. Iain G. Brown, principal curator, Manuscripts Division, at the National Library of Scotland, told me, "No record of the meeting with the U.S. publishers had been preserved [in the R & R Clark Collection]. At least it is not obvious where such a record might be: that is the more accurate thing to say."

60 Clark had been: Kogan, *The Great EB,* p. 76. Kogan's source is unknown.

61 Black snatched the: J. D. Newth, *Adam & Charles Black 1807–1957: Some Chapters in the History of a Publishing House* (London: Adam & Charles Black, 1957), p. 7, says £6,150, but the company history transposes the 5 and the 1. See http://acblack.com.

61 The first volume: *Edinburgh Literary Journal,* January 30, 1830, p. 8.

61 Others wrote exhaustively: Kogan, *The Great EB,* pp. 31–39.

63 In 1891: His obituary appeared in *The Athenæum,* June 4, 1898, pp. 724–25.

63 How Hooper and: The agreement apparently didn't preclude the right to manufacture and sell sets not printed in Edinburgh.

64 It was growing: It appears that Werner had two versions of the *Britannica* to offer that year. In addition to *The New American Supplement to the Latest Edition of the Encyclopædia Britannica,* about which more below, they also published *The Americanized Encyclopædia Britannica, Latest Edition,* in twelve volumes, in 1897. The "latest edition" was, of

course, an edited and greatly distilled version of the Ninth–the edition with the Marlowe epigram atop each page–as opposed to the supplement, which added five volumes to an Americanized Ninth.

CHAPTER 6. THE AMERICAN SCHEME

65 "found out things": J. D. Newth, *Adam & Charles Black 1807–1957: Some Chapters in the History of a Publishing House* (London: Adam & Charles Black, 1957), p. 66.

65 a guinea: A guinea is 21 shillings–£1 1s.–and equal to about £63 ($120) in 2008. In 2008 equivalencies, the previous list price of the *Britannica* had been £2,220, or about $4,200. The *Times* edition would sell for less than half that–just over £900 ($1,700), if purchased on time. If a customer paid cash, and many did, the price was £860 ($1,600).

66 "The proposal is": Newth, *Adam & Charles Black*, p. 67.

66 "Before we publish": Ibid.

67 Dawson: Geoffrey Dawson, at the time the Johannesburg correspondent for *The Times*. He was promoted to editor in 1912 and served until 1914, then again from 1923 to 1941. His presence at the meeting is unexplained, although Moberly Bell habitually worked with his door open and rarely discouraged staff visits.

67 C Moberly Bell: February 26, 1897, *Times* archives, *Encyclopædia Britannica* box and folders, *News International,* London.

68 "Arthur Fraser Walter": Ibid.

69 "to restrain the": *New York Times*, April 16, 1893, p. 4.

69 "In view of": *New York Times*, April 24, 1893, p. 3.

69 "The St. Paul": *New York Times*, June 18, 1890, p. 4.

71 "After some years": Day Otis Kellogg, DD, "Publisher's Preface," *New American Supplement to the Latest Edition of the Encyclopædia Britannica: A Standard Work of Reference in Art, Literature, Science, History, Geography, Commerce, Biography, Discovery and Invention,* 5 vols. Werner Company, 1897).

72 John Sherman: Camp also covered the same topic for the *Britannica*'s Tenth and Eleventh Editions.

73 in a lavish: April 29, 1897, p. 4.

73 The review was: The importance of the contributors may be measured thusly: few of them were used as contributors to the Tenth or the Eleventh Editions. Instead, many of them appeared as entries themselves. The notion of a *Britannica* contributor writing an encyclopedia entry on a person who contributed to a rival encyclopedia is interesting,

but of course official status doesn't necessarily confer useful editorial expertise. One more thing *The New York Times* noted in that April 29, 1897, review: there were events described in the encyclopedia that had occurred as recently as the previous February.

75 Hoboken: *New York Times*, May 24, 1897, p. 4. The name at that address is apparently fictitious, if census records are correct.

75 "You can get": *New York Times*, May 1, 1897, p. BR8.

76 On March 23: The full text of the remarkable ad can be found in the appendix of this book.

76 Readers were by: *The Times*, December 25, 1896, p. 11.

76 And so on: Ibid.

76 "It is a": *The Times*, April 8, 1895, p. 12.

77 Haxton filled the: The complete text appears in an appendix to this book.

77 "society of gentlemen": In reality, a printer, an engraver, and a writer named Smellie. See above for that whole story.

80 discussed in universities: See chapter 9.

80 More than once: Herman Kogan, *The Great EB: The Story of the Encyclopædia Britannica* (Chicago: University of Chicago Press, 1958), pp. 99–100.

81 But the very: In fact, a newspaper story at the time reported the theft of a set of *Britannicas*. Street value? Five pounds.

82 "As stated in": Ibid.

83 Just two sentences: quoted in Kogan, *The Great EB*, p. 88.

83 nearly half what: Ibid., pp. 83–84.

83 "We have let": E. H. C. Moberly Bell, *The Life and Letters of C. F. Moberly Bell* (London: Richards Press, 1927), p. 244.

83 Nonetheless: Kogan, *The Great EB*, p. 88.

84 "Dear Mr Haxton": Bell to Haxton, January 30, 1899, *Times* archives.

85 In 1900: Stanley Morison et al., *The History of "The Times" 1884–1912: The Twentieth Century Test* (London: The Times, 1947), p. 446.

CHAPTER 7. TEN

86 The pairing of: Much of this description of the Hooper-Jackson arrangement appears in Herman Kogan (*The Great EB: The Story of the Encyclopædia Britannica* [Chicago: University of Chicago Press, 1958]), who was often unclear about how he matched certain of his statements with his sources. In this case, it seems likely that Kogan's principal source may have been Margaret Schneider, one of Jackson's former

employees. *Publishers Weekly* also contained information on this, but the accounts frequently conflicted.

86 There was also Jackson's: *Publishers Weekly*, July–December 1894, p. 971.

87 These carried the: *Publishers Weekly*, March 31, 1923, pp. 1079–81.

87 being careful always: This was done not by changing the cash price but by extending the payment plan so smaller payments were made over a longer time, the better to accommodate the more modest budgets of *Mail* readers.

89 Their companies were: Kogan, *The Great EB*, p. 105, and *New York Times*, May 29, 1909, p. 1. The Cox family details come from Henry Miller Cox, George William Cocks, and John Cox, *The Cox Family in America* (New York: Privately published, 1912), pp. 229–30. Passenger lists are found in most genealogy resources.

93 "his knowledge": *The Times*, January 11, 1919. This quote is from Wallace's obituary, in which *The Times* describes him as a "savant" three times in the space of several hundred words.

94 "dealing with recent": *New York Times Saturday Review of Books and Art*, April 26, 1902, p. BR1.

101 "Well": Quoted by John Steele Gordon in "Mephistopheles of Wall Street," *American Heritage Magazine* 4, no. 8 (December 1989). Hadley also is usually cited as the man who, on passing the entrance to New Haven's Grove Street Cemetery and reading there the inscription "The Dead Shall Be Raised" is supposed to have said, "They certainly will be if Yale University wants this land." Credit is also made on behalf of most Yale presidents, however.

101 "undaunted by his": "Encyclopædia," Encyclopædia Britannica Online, 2009, http://britannica.com.

CHAPTER 8. A DINNER FOR MR. CHISHOLM

104 Unlike the Savoy: The stable boys may have had the better lodging. According to R. H. Gronow, Limmer's "was the most dirty hotel in London; but in the gloomy, comfortless coffee-room might be seen many members of the rich squirearchy, who visited London during the sporting season. This hotel was frequently so crowded that a bed could not be obtained for any amount of money; but you could always get a very good plain English dinner, an excellent bottle of port, and some famous gin-punch."

And that was in 1814. Rees Howell Gronow, *Reminiscences of Captain Gronow: Being Anecdotes of the Camp, the Court and the Clubs, at the Close of the Last War with France* (London: Smith, Elder & Co., 1862); this book has been reprinted many times since. This passage appears in the Kessinger reprint of 2004 on p. 38.

There are many true tales set in Limmer's, and I won't retail all of them—just a few. Once, for example, in 1833, George Payne, a wealthy sportsman and inveterate gambler, sat up all night playing cards with one of Britain's richest aristocrats, Albert Denison, Lord Londesborough, until his lordship was some £30,000 lighter—at which time Londesborough "proceeded to the adjoining temple of Hymen at St. George's, Hanover Square, to be married to his first wife." John Seaverns, *Sporting Anecdotes* (London: Hamilton Adams & Co., 1889). The first wife, Henrietta Weld-Forester, more than made up for the gambling losses: she was among the richest heiresses in England.

Even the barmen at Limmer's were the stuff of legend. An example from Lord William Lennox's wonderful *Tracy Hamilton, or the Adventures of a Westminster Boy* (London: William Shoberl, 1851): "No sooner had we drawn up at this far-famed hotel of olden times, the record of which would furnish many an interesting anecdote of life, ay, even of death—than I was most warmly welcomed by that celebrated character, Mr. Collin, immortalized in song by a genuine descendant, in birth, wit, and talent of that brilliant genius—[Charles] Sheridan.

"The couplet runs as follows:—

> *My name is John Collin, head waiter at Limmer's,*
> *At the corner of Conduit Street, Hanover Square;*
> *My chief occupation is filling up brimmers,*
> *To solace young gentlemen laden with care.*

Bartender lore says that at some point, John Collin became Tom Collins, and his celebrated concoction, the gin punch mentioned by Captain Gronow above, lives on in memory, if not always clearly.

In 1876, the place was rebuilt and thoroughly sanitized and came into use as a favorite venue for dinners such as Chisholm's, as well as for regular meetings of exclusive clubs such as the Sette of Odd Volumes—forty men (and a few women) who would meet regularly for supper, during which time one of the "odd volumes" would present a paper on some obscure topic, then pass around the document bound beautifully as a small book. (The Sette's 214th meeting had been scheduled for Limmer's a couple of weeks before Chisholm's dinner, but was postponed until January 1900.) By the 1890s, the place was so hygienic that in 1893 the Society of Laryngology, Otology, and Rhinology of Paris held their annual dinner there. Still, Limmer's legend was built on many little milliner's girls and not so much on ENT men or Odd Volumes. As late as 1896, writers such as Sir Arthur Conan Doyle, who captured Limmer's seedy importance to the sporting crowd in *Rodney Stone*, were still trading on Limmer's edgy charm, as were Chisholm's hosts.

104 "many a little": Real name: Charles Molloy Westmacott. Bernard Blackmantle, *The English Spy: An Original Work Characteristic, Satirical, and Humorous, Comprising Scenes and Sketches in Every Rank of Society, Being Portraits Drawn from the Life*, illustrations by Robert Cruikshank (London: Sherwood, Jones, and Co., 1825), vol. 1, p. 170.

106 Virginia Stephen: In "A Sketch of the Past," one of the five brief memoirs in Woolf's *Moments of Being*.

106 In all: Philip Waller's *Writers, Readers & Reputations* (New York: Oxford University Press, 2006), pp. 85ff, offers a succinct appraisal.

108 as he later: Theodore Andrea Cook, *The Sunlit Hours* (London: Nisbet & Co., 1925), pp. 192–200.

108 His grandfather: H. W. Chisholm, "Recollections of an Octogenarian Civil Servant," *Temple Bar* 91 (January–April 1891), pp. 33–34. This rambling, four-part memoir includes microscopic details concerning paperwork and individuals, including his great-aunt, a London policeman, an Italian on a train, and a swindling hotelier in Switzerland—but not the names of his children or his wife.

109 In 1790: Grenville succeeded his cousin, William Pitt the Younger, as prime minister in 1806. Grenville's "Ministry of All the Talents"—a unity government formed in wartime and lasting just over a year—succeeded in ending the British slave trade but failed to find a way to make peace with France or do much else. Grenville's government finally collapsed over the issue of Catholic emancipation, a persistent political problem, especially at the beginning of the nineteenth century.

109 Chisholm: H. C. Williams, p. 37, and additional information contained in notes written by Laurence Chisholm Young before he died, aged ninety-five, on Christmas Eve in 2000. Laurence, a great-grandson of Henry and the son of Hugh Chisholm's sister, taught in Cape Town and at the University of Wisconsin. He was one in a line of brilliant Chisholm-Young mathematicians that extends to this very day. His

daughter, Professor Sylvia Wiegand, is a well-known mathematician at the University of Nebraska and is actively involved in encouraging women to enter her field. Laurence's notes are hosted online by the School of Mathematics and Statistics at the University of St. Andrews, http://turnbull.mcs.st-and.ac.uk/history/.

110 A year later: Janet E. (Hogarth) Courtney, *An Oxford Portrait Gallery* (London: Chapman & Hall, 1931), p. 108. Helen Chisholm died in 1909.

110 "As for little": HWC to AC, November 21, 1866. The correspondence cited in this chapter is in the possession of the Chisholm family.

111 He was sent: Parliament was not convinced by Chisholm, however. "It is to be regretted that this country takes no part in this new scientific institution," he wrote. H. W. Chisholm, *On the Science of Weighing and Measuring and Standards of Measure and Weight* (London: Macmillan and Co., 1877), p. 129.

112 "Recollections of an": Serialized in *Temple Bar* (January–April 1891).

115 as Rudyard Kipling: *The St. James's Gazette* published Kipling's first story to appear in England, according to Low's account. Major Desmond Chapman-Huston, *The Lost Historian: A Memoir of Sir Sidney Low* (London: John Murray, 1936).

117 It was an: Ibid., pp. 94–97. Several months later, a public dinner, very much like Chisholm's, with many of the same guests (and perhaps even in the same place), was given for Low, and since Chisholm was asked to give one of the toasts, the friendship between the two men must have survived this episode.

117 the word more: "The publicist proper is he who delivers his views on public affairs in the Press; but the excellence of his articles may nevertheless be consistent with the journal being a disastrous failure," Chisholm explained later in his entry on "Newspapers" in the *Britannica*.

118 At one point: G. R. Searle, *A New England?: Peace and War 1886–1918* (New York: Oxford University Press, 2005), p. 194. Searle, citing others, aptly calls Toynbee Hall "a kind of finishing school for the next generation of social 'experts,' civil servants, politicians, and academics" and settlements like it "manor for new urban squirearchy."

119 "another man Spender": HC to EC, October 1889. This is someone Chisholm would later come to know better as J. A. Spender, the Liberal writer, who sat on Gosse's left at Chisholm's dinner; he's the uncle of Stephen Spender, the late poet. Smith went on to become a Labour

activist and "social investigator." Andrew Saint calls him a "proto-Fabian," in *Politics and the People of London: The London County Council, 1889–1965* (London: Continuum International Publishing Group, 1989), p. 72.

119 "We were accompanied": HC to EC, October 1889.

119 "I began to": Ibid.

119 "Yesterday evening was": HC to Helen Chisholm, undated.

120 "Indeed I am": HC to EC, undated.

122 a champion of: M. J. Kelly, *The Fenian Ideal and Irish Nationalism, 1882–1916* (Boydell & Brewer Ltd., 2006), p. 79.

122 For each of: In the possession of his grandson, Hugh R. Chisholm. For many years, he managed to combine his interest in esoteric spiritualism and performance in interesting ways. In 1904, for example, he appeared at the spring recital for the Sesame Club, a forward-looking group advocating education and rich in political progressives and theosophists. With the composer looking on, he performed Sir Arthur Somervell's "Maud," a thirteen-part song cycle based on the Tennyson poem.

CHAPTER 9. THE SUPPLEMENTAL VOLUMES

125 "Come see me": MB to HC, February 27 and March 9, 1900. Both letters are in the *Times* archives.

126 "Messrs. Hooper and": F. Harcourt Kitchin, *Moberly Bell and His Times: An Unofficial Narrative* (London: Philip Allan & Co., 1925), pp. 124ff.

127 "good company and": E. H. C. Moberly Bell, *The Life and Letters of C. F. Moberly Bell* (London: Richards Press, 1927), p. 248.

128 "My machine has": Hooper to Bell, undated 1901, *Times* archives.

128 "He liked to": Kitchin, *Moberly Bell and His Times*, p. 21.

128 "He was": Ibid., pp. 130–32. This Stracheyesque little libel—written after Moberly Bell, Hooper, and Chisholm had all departed—stuck. Hooper is described as a "ranker" and worse fairly often in subsequent accounts, often with the comment attributed to Moberly Bell, who, of course, never said it, nor thought it. Kitchin's account has a great deal of useful detail, but his intense dislike of "American" innovations, and, in the case of the *Britannica*, of the innovator himself, is palpable. What Kitchin didn't mention—but Janet Hogarth, who knew him well, did—was that "years afterward, this man [Kitchin], who had given all the help he could to Hooper's opponents at a time of stress, fell deservedly upon evil days and applied to 'H.E.' for help." Janet E.

(Hogarth) Courtney, *Recollected in Tranquillity* (London: Heinemann, 1926), pp. 206–07. Neither she nor Hooper, and certainly not Kitchin, say whether it was given.

130 "There are special": *The Times*, December 18, 1903. The article is "The 'Encyclopædia Britannica.' A Retrospective." The fairly exhaustive account of Chisholm's work on the Tenth Edition will be found there; it is the source for many of his comments on the topic of the supplemental volumes.

130 Many of the: Herman Kogan, *The Great EB: The Story of the Encyclopædia Britannica* (Chicago: University of Chicago Press, 1958), p. 90.

133 "Moberly Bell": Kitchin, *Moberly Bell and His Times*, p. 124.

134 In early 1902: Kogan, *The Great EB*, p. 96.

134 "[T]he whole work": *The Times*, December 18, 1903, p. 7.

135 "I have a": Bell to Haxton, January 3, 1903, *Times* archives.

136 "bade in English": "Encyclopædia Britannica Dinner," promotional booklet, 1902 (?).

CHAPTER 10. HALF A MILLION GOATS

142 He was contestant: *The Times*, December 1, 1903, p. 8.

143 "The strongest inducement": *The Times*, April 1, 1903, p. 13.

143 "It is useless": *The Times*, April 2, 1903, p. 4.

144 "*WARNING:* ATTEMPTED FRAUD": *The Times*, April 30, 1903, p. 4.

145 "A mass of": *The Times*, April 27, 1903, p. 4.

146 "Your advt on": Moberly Bell to Haxton, July 13, 1903, *Times* archives.

146 "on that day": Moberly Bell to Haxton, July 14, 1903 [misdated as June], *Times* archives.

148 "When in 1888": *The Times*, October 8, 1903, p. 12.

148 "Our last bit": December 8, 1903, from Deborah Alcock to Susan Kift, cited in Elisabeth Boyd Bayley, *The Spanish Brothers (Deborah Alcock): Her Life and Works* (London: Marshall Brothers, 1914), e-text available at http://telusplanet.net.

149 Not only did: Leslie Ashe and Arthur Carson Roberts, *The Times Competition. The Answers of the First Prize-Winner. The Questions. Answers of the Second Prize-Winner. Notes* (1904).

149 "already familiar to": Noted in Stefan Collini, *Absent Minds: Intellectuals in Britain* (Oxford: Oxford University Press), p. 27.

149 "the column of": Herman Kogan, *The Great EB: The Story of the Encyclopædia Britannica* (Chicago: University of Chicago Press, 1958), p. 101.

The dating error is Kogan's; Boulanger's missed chance had come a decade earlier.

150 "object [of the": Thomas Russell, *Commercial Advertising: Six Lectures at the London School of Economics and Political Science* (New York and London: G. P. Putnam's Sons, 1920), p. 223.

150 "Well do I": Max Pemberton, *Lord Northcliff: A Memoir* (London: Hodder & Stoughton, 1922), p. 131.

152 "the most entirely": Denys Sutton, ed., *Letters of Roger Fry*, vol. 2 (London: Chatto & Windus, 1972), pp. 546–67.

152 "a clique of": Carl Spadoni, "The Curious Case of *The Cambridge Observer*," *Russell* 2, no. 1 (1982), http:// digitalcommons.mcmaster.ca /russelljournal/vol2/iss1/12.

152 published by Fisher: Published by Unwin in the "Pseudonym Library" series and dedicated to Edward Marsh. A year earlier, Sickert and some Cambridge friends, including S. V. Makower, collaborated on another "Pseudonym" title, *The Passing of a Mood*, dedicated to Elizabeth Robins.

152 which apparently was: Haxton's book received a few, mostly favorable, reviews, but he did very little, other than write a dedication containing a personal and idiosyncratic reference ("Fancy Jim"), which would cause anyone to attribute the book to him. Oswald's *Helen* is a slight and delicate work—much like Oswald himself—in which two characters, an ambitious writer and a freshly liberated woman, are revealed in elaborate detail. It is to novels what buckwheat porridge is to breakfasts. Plot: boy meets girl, they meet, marry, nearly divorce, but don't. The manuscript was shown by Oswald to those he thought might help improve it, including, even, Frank Harris. Marsh (pp. 52–53), who gave the book an edit before publication, recalled in 1939, "[Oswald] wrote with infinite pains and utter integrity a novel . . . but nobody read it. Such fire as he had was banked under his 'artistic conscience'; he kept his tone so perfectly that nothing stood out; he was so careful not to say too much that he seemed to be saying nothing at all."

152 After one such: Arthur Waley, *Nō Plays of Japan* (London: Allen & Unwin, 1921), pp. 306–16.

153 "Books!": Kogan, *The Great EB*, p. 106, among many other places. The story is a favorite.

153 "It was one": Swanwick, p. 352.

153 "With a voice": Arthur Croxton, *Crowded Nights—and Days* (London: Sampson Low, 1931), pp. 139–40.

154 "Flight was useless": F. Harcourt Kitchin, *Moberly Bell and His Times: An Unofficial Narrative* (London: Philip Allen & Co, 1925), p. 135.

154 "You have made": Kogan, *The Great EB*, p. 100.

154 "Perhaps nothing has": W. L. Alden, "Mr. Alden's Views," *New York Times*, May 2, 1903, p. BR12.

155 the pair had: See *War of the Wenuses*, by Graves and Lucas, 1898, the story of an invasion of earth by the inhabitants of "the pale pink planet Wenus," all of whom are "astral women, with eyes that are to the eyes of English women as diamonds are to boot-buttons, astral women, with hearts vast and warm and sympathetic . . . regarding Butterick's with envy, Peter Robinson's with jealousy, and Whiteley's with insatiable yearning, and slowly and surely maturing their plans for a grand inter-stellar campaign."

155 *Wisdom While You*: There couldn't have been many hard feelings, since Lucas wrote the *Britannica*'s entries on Jane Austen and Charles Lamb. See also Philip Waller's *Writers, Readers & Reputations* (New York: Oxford University Press, 2006), p. 69. The pair collaborated on many parodies—notably *Signs of the Times, or the Hustlers' Almanac for 1907*.

157 It exceeded in: Ibid.

158 Their work filled: *New York Times*, April 26, 1902, p. BR1.

CHAPTER 11. ANGLOSPHERE

159 "all the": "Hugh Chisholm Here," *New York Times*, December 16, 1902, p. 2. The article doesn't mention it, but he would have been traveling with his family.

161 "it is the": Hugh Chisholm, "Anglo-American Relations Vis-à-vis the Other Great Powers," an address given before the Victorian Club at Boston, January 20, 1903 (Boston: Victorian Club, 1903), pp. 11–12.

162 but one estimate: Herman Kogan, *The Great EB: The Story of the Encyclopædia Britannica* (Chicago: University of Chicago Press, 1958), p. 108.

163 *Lay of the Bell*: Translated by A. G. Foster-Barham, a friend of Phillips's, and published in 1896 by Unwin.

163 "Now we can": Kogan, *The Great EB*, p. 110.

164 "Your letter of": Hooper to Bell, January 19, 1903, *Times* archives. Eccentricities in the original. There's a curious postscript scrawled on this note: "Feel greatly relieved that you cannot cut yourself when shaving any more." Perhaps he was referring to Moberly Bell's adoption of King Gillette's safety razor, first made widely available in 1902. (Or maybe Bell was growing a beard.)

167 They all offered: Both letters appeared in the *New York Times*, June 17, 1909, p. 4.

168 "I return you": FCMB to HRH, April 21, 1904, *Times* archives.

168 "I find that": FCMB to HRH, April 27, 1904, *Times* archives.

170 "In an advertisement": *The Times*, June 23, 1904.

172 "It led to": *The Times*, September 9, 1904, p. 9.

173 "Dear Mr. Bell": Hooper to Moberly Bell, November 4, 1904, *Times* archives. There's another postscript scrawled at the bottom of the last page of this letter: "Your note of today just received. If I can help you any in regard to these letters, of course I will come and talk with you. Shall I keep the 750 letters that you have sent up, here?"

176 "Haxton": F. Harcourt Kitchin, *Moberly Bell and His Times: An Unofficial Narrative* (London: Philip Allen & Co, 1925), pp. 166–69.

177 "I don't think": Hooper to Moberly Bell, July 3, 1905, *Times* archives.

178 "For all his": Kogan, *The Great EB*, p. 114.

178 "The revenue for": Stanley Morison et al., *The History of "The Times" 1884–1912: The Twentieth Century Test* (London: The Times, 1947), p. 447.

CHAPTER 12. PLAN B: THE BOOK WAR

185 "The scheme": E. H. C. Moberly Bell, *The Life and Letters of C. F. Moberly Bell* (London: Richards Press, 1927), pp. 251–52.

186 "[Subscribers] will have": *The Times*, September 9, 1905, p. 9. Although clearly a promotion, the story was listed as a "special article"–"The Times and Its Readers"–along with "The Land of the Anatolian Railway–IV" and "Grouse Driving: A Retrospect."

187 "I got your": *New York Times*, June 17, 1909.

190 "I have taken": Bell, *The Life and Letters of C. F. Moberly Bell*, pp. 253–54.

191 "Messrs Hooper and": "The Times Book Club TTBC History," handwritten manuscript by Ethel Jeanes, *Times* archives.

191 "save 12s. and": *Times Literary Supplement*, October 6, 1905, p. 323.

192 "[t]hat of the": Bell, *The Life and Letters of C. F. Moberly Bell*, p. 262.

193 "a set of": Janet E. (Hogarth) Courtney, *Recollected in Tranquillity* (London: Heinemann, 1926), p. 167.

193 "Hooper saw the": Ibid., p. 204. Hogarth devoted two full pages of her memoir to a catalog of examples of Hooper's generosity and competence. Sick maids were tended at his expense; he gave extraordinary attention to the families of his employees; he managed by encouragement rather than by intimidation; etc.

194 "the club-room and": Ibid., p. 206.

194 Hogarth quickly set: Ibid., pp. 176–77, 180.

195 "It is the": *The Times*, May 1, 1906, p. 15.

196 "mob in Oxford": Courtney, *Recollected in Tranquillity*, p. 172.

196 "select books for": Ibid.

197 "As this was": Sir Frederick Macmillan, *"The Net Book Agreement 1899" and "The Book War 1906–1908," Two Chapters in the History of the Book Trade, Including a Narrative of the Dispute between The Times Book Club and The Publishers' Association by Edward Bell, M.A., President of the Association 1906–1908* (Glasgow: Robert Maclehose & Co., Ltd., University Press, 1924), pp. 40–41. Like Kitchin's book, this little volume has permanently tarnished both Moberly Bell's and Hooper's reputations. When the British Library published a book in 2010 called *Book Makers: British Publishing in the Twentieth Century*, the author, Iain Stevenson, citing Macmillan's booklet, described Moberly Bell as a "swivel-eye obsessive" and Hooper as "a crook." A recapitulation of this affair will be found in *Publishers Association 1896–1946* with an epilogue by Reginald J. Kingsford (Cambridge, 1970).

198 "You do not": Bell, *The Life and Letters of C. F. Moberly Bell*, p. 267.

199 "whether they begin": *The History of the Book War: Fair Book Prices Versus Publishers' Trust Prices* (London: The Times, 1907), pp. 46–47.

199 "Nothing would give": *The Times*, May 6, 1908, p. 17.

200 A sympathetic member: The first of these appeared on December 3, 1906.

CHAPTER 13. CHAOS

202 They were certain: Except where noted, the sources for much of the data in this chapter are from chapters 14, 16, 17, and 18 in Stanley Morison et al., *The History of "The Times" 1884–1912: The Twentieth Century Test* (London: The Times, 1947), and from associated appendices, and from Herman Kogan, *The Great EB: The Story of the Encyclopædia Britannica* (Chicago: University of Chicago Press, 1958), pp. 127–43.

203 Walter had ignored: E. H. C. Moberly Bell, *The Life and Letters of C. F. Moberly Bell* (London: Richards Press, 1927), pp. 274–75.

207 "If Mr. Walter": At the time, Northcliffe was willing to pay as much as £1 million for the paper, so it's doubtful that Hooper could have outspent him in the event Walter had decided to sell. Besides, at least in 1900, that wasn't part of Northcliffe's plan. Northcliffe to R. D. Bluemenfeld, R.D.B.'s diary, London, 1930, p. 95, cited in Morison et al., *The History of "The Times,"* vol. 3, p. 439.

207 "found a great": Janet E. (Hogarth) Courtney, *Recollected in Tranquillity* (London: Heinemann, 1926), pp. 219–20.

214 After a day: Max Pemberton, *Lord Northcliffe: A Memoir* (London: Hodder & Stoughton, 1922), p. 134.

215 "Mr. Pearson": *New York Times*, January 7, 1908, p. 1. That sentence, like several others, also appeared in Northcliffe's *Daily Mail* on the same date, suggesting a complicity in orchestrating so much of this publicity.

218 "That," his daughter: Bell, *The Life and Letters of C. F. Moberly Bell*, p. 286.

218 "I want you": Ibid., p. 288.

227 "Mr. Darling": *New York Times*, October 28, 1897, p. 7.

227 "[A] worse piece": *New York Times*, October 31, 1897, p. 1.

227 a comment: These examples were compiled by Malcolm Weatherup on March 31, 2008, for the *Townsville Bulletin*; see http://townsville bulletin.com.au.

228 "It might only": *The Times*, May 6, 1908, p. 17.

228 "That might increase": *The Times*, May 8, 1908, p. 8.

229 "I do not": Ibid.

229 "What was said": Ibid.

229 "With his few": Courtney, *Recollected in Tranquillity*, p. 207.

230 "I am against": Kogan, *The Great EB*, p. 140.

230 "Mr. Murray is": *The Times*, May 8, 1908, p. 8.

231 " 'Mr. Bates' ": Actually, Alfred Butes.

231 "neither Mr. Moberly": Sir Frederick Macmillan, *"The Net Book Agreement 1899" and "The Book War 1906–1908," Two Chapters in the History of the Book Trade, Including a Narrative of the Dispute between The Times Book Club and The Publishers' Association by Edward Bell, M.A., President of the Association 1906–1908* (Glasgow: Robert Maclehose & Co., Ltd., University Press, 1924), pp. 67–75. The Publishers Association by then must have been used to meeting behind Bell and Hooper's backs. Within days of announcing his intention to buy *The Times*, and without notifying Hooper or anyone at either *The Times* or the book club, Northcliffe had convened a meeting of publishers, including Macmillan, with the aim of ending the book war immediately. "They are quite willing to come to an arrangement," he reported back to a surprised Walter, "and I do not think there is likely to be any difficulty in settling matters. Their principal feeling is one of bitter personal enmity against Hooper and Moberly Bell, whom they consider have treated them both unfairly and insultingly."

231 "had gone looking": *The Times*, May 9, 1906.

232 "Think of Kennedy": Courtney, *Recollected in Tranquillity*, p. 211.

CHAPTER 14. HIGH HOLBORN

233 He had virtually: It was published by his Grolier, Inc., as *The Book of Knowledge: The Children's Encyclopedia* and was one of the most successful subscription publication ventures in history. George H. Doran, *Chronicles of Barabbas: 1884–1934* (New York: Harcourt, Brace and Company, 1935), pp. 102–03, and *Publishers Weekly*, March 31, 1923, pp. 1079–81, Jackson obituary.

234 "junior *Britannica*": Hogarth wrote about the work, which occupied her in 1914 and 1915, after the war had started: "It was to be made up of shortened, brighter versions of the 'E.B.' articles, with lots of pictures in it of Oswald Sickert's selection. I was doing the Bible articles, and through those blazing August weeks sat in the window of a quiet Surrey cottage looking down from a height over waving cornfields, still writing peacefully of *Ehud, Eli, Ephesians, Esther, Eve*. It was an unspeakable help to me in keeping my own mental balance; but what could be the use of it when Namur had fallen, Liège was sacked, and the flower of the British Army was falling back from the Mons?" Courtney, *Recollected in Tranquillity* (London: Heinemann, 1926), p. 243.

234 "I have had": Herman Kogan, *The Great EB: The Story of the Encyclopædia Britannica* (Chicago: University of Chicago Press, 1958), p. 146.

235 "making a fool": Courtney, *Recollected in Tranquillity*, pp. 208–11.

235 "his nimble brain": Ibid., p. 213.

236 "There never was": Ibid., p. 224.

236 "Where would you": Ibid., p. 213.

237 "Until one became": Arthur Croxton, *Crowded Nights–and Days* (London: Sampson Low, 1931), p. 143.

237 Hooper instantly produced: Courtney, *Recollected in Tranquillity*, p. 214n. Kogan (*The Great EB*) for some reason reports this differently, saying it was for £60, although his account is clearly borrowed from Hogarth. Mitchell was a lecturer in Classics at the University of London; he assigned the archaeological portion of the Sicily article to Thomas Ashford, the director of the British School of Archaeology at Rome. The entry for Corsica was far less substantial and is unsigned.

237 "I have had": James T. Shotwell, *The Autobiography of James T. Shotwell* (New York: Bobbs-Merrill, 1961), p. 61. Shotwell was co–assistant editor at the beginning stages of the compilation, working in London.

After his return to New York, he worked with Charles Whinery in the New York office and contributed more than 250 articles, including the major article on "History," to the Eleventh.

238 "A British editor": Courtney, *Recollected in Tranquillity*, p. 230.

238 Certainly: A British editor was seen as a necessary ornament for some time. The Thirteenth (1926) and Fourteenth (1929) Editions of the *Britannica* were both edited by J. L. Garvin, who had been given his start by Hogarth's husband, W. L. Courtney, at *The Fortnightly Review*, and who had risen to prominence as a newspaper editor, including a successful run at *The Observer*. His politics and worldview were quite consistent with Chisholm's. Franklin Hooper coedited the Fourteenth Edition with Garvin and became editor in chief in 1932. By then, Sears, Roebuck had owned the *Britannica* for more than ten years.

239 In fact: Shotwell, *The Autobiography of James T. Shotwell*, p. 61.

240 "that bugbear of": *Celebration Banquet* (booklet), Encyclopædia Britannica, *Ninth Edition, Cambridge, 11th December 1888*, p. 23.

240 "one of the": Courtney, *Recollected in Tranquillity*, p. 212.

241 and as an: He is described in various places as both an American and a Cape Town journalist. He may have been both, of course.

241 "Art of Flying": *Fortnightly Review*, November 1899. The article is now available online at http://fortnightlyreview.co.uk.

242 a *Britannica* prospectus: L126pp, published in 1911.

242 A staff in: The Honorable Carroll Davidson Wright and Professor George McKinnon Wrong.

242 at a banquet: January 21, 1911.

243 "delighted" to accept: "Remarks Before the Dinner to the American and Canadian Contributors," January 21, 1911, at the Plaza, New York City.

243 more than £250,000: A current dollar equivalent is hard to estimate, but a little under $30 million would be a conservative figure; it is likely much higher.

243 "after several years": HC to Manson, undated, author's collection.

244 "Well, at any": Courtney, *Recollected in Tranquillity*, p. 227.

244 "'Don't you flatter'": Ibid. The riposting editor was Thomas Allan Ingram, MA, LLD (Trinity College Dublin).

CHAPTER 15. THE SINGLE ORGANISM

245 "have no proper": Hugh Chisholm, "Editorial Introduction," *Encyclopædia Britannica*, 11th ed., vol. I., p. xii.

246 confusing and unsigned: "Association of Ideas," *Encyclopædia Britannica*, 9th ed., vol. 2, p. 730.

246 "I think no": Ralph Barton Perry, *The Thought and Character of William James*, vol. 2 (1936), p. 59.

246 as "chaotic fermentation": Ibid., p. 53.

247 A list of: E. B. Titchener, "The Psychology of the New 'Britannica,'" *The American Journal of Psychology*, vol. 23, January 1, 1912, pp. 37–58. Titchener's very detailed review (see Appendix E in this volume) ends with this jibe aimed toward Chisholm: "My general impression, after this survey, is that the new *Britannica* does not reproduce the psychological atmosphere of its day and generation. . . . We still find 'inconcinnities,' not only of secondary articles with main article, but of two adjacent columns of the same article; and we find men signing articles and writing books some years after the recorded date of their deaths. Despite the halo of authority, and despite the scrutiny of the staff, I do not hesitate to say that the great bulk of the secondary articles in general psychology—articles of the type of Affection, Apperception, Cognition, Intellect—are not adapted to the requirements of the intelligent reader; and that many of them might as well have been left out."

250 Alexander Coleman and: Alexander Coleman and Charles Simmons, eds., *All There Is to Know: Readings from the Illustrious Eleventh Edition of the Encyclopædia Britannica* (New York: Simon & Schuster, 1994), p. 32.

253 "with all the": Chisholm, "Editorial Introduction," p. xiii.

254 "systematic survey of": *Encyclopædia Britannica*, 11th ed., vol. 29, p. 879.

254 But some articles: An excerpt from Haxton's article appears as an appendix to this book.

256 Sure enough: Everybody knew Mrs. Alec. Mr. Alec, an insurance man, had died in 1896 after eleven years of marriage, leaving Ethel with two sons and, so she claimed, no money. She managed, through vivaciousness and tireless authorship, to live a very comfortable slightly upper-middle-class life and remain in society. She painted, she volunteered, she cultivated a very wide circle of influential friends; she wrote about anything and everything, travel, fiction, newspaper fodder, biography, memoir—she even wrote a book that plunged her deeply into the debate over British and Danish methods of butter production. Her books were described as "light," "pleasant," "sprightly," "chatty," and "long" in *The Westminster Gazette*, *Punch*, *The Times*, and other national papers. *The Saturday Review* described her as "[a] monument of discursive energy." She knew "everything and everybody," said *The Pall Mall Gazette*, and they were only talking about Finland. Her dinner parties

were not, perhaps, legendary, but they were very frequent. She made all her guests sign her tablecloths, and she followed their pencil strokes with embroidery thread and a keen sense of entrepreneurialism. Eventually, she wrote about those tablecloths; the list of names dropped is a late Victorian A-minus list. And "Mrs. Alec," as she was known her entire life, was a passionate supporter of women's rights.

257 And this is: For an entertaining collection of articles from the Eleventh Edition, see Coleman and Simmons, *All There Is to Know.*

258 "He was": Janet E. (Hogarth) Courtney, *An Oxford Portrait Gallery* (London: Chapman & Hall, 1931), pp. 156–57.

258 Bonar was prescient: "The hungry generations have trodden the working man down too much to make him instantly or even speedily fit to do the work of government himself," Bonar wrote. "He is of like passions with ourselves. He will be perfectly qualified in process of time to share in such responsible work. But at present he needs training."

259 "In those long": Courtney, *An Oxford Portrait Gallery*, p. 226.

259 Meredith was one: It was rare to read criticism of Meredith in the literary papers of the day. Sidney Low was not willing to let the common view of Meredith's work go unchallenged. Edmund Gosse, an early friend of Meredith's, and normally a reliable supporter, had finally had enough of Meredith's opiate prose. In the *Gazette* in November 1895, he wrote,

> There is an unfailing law in literature which determines that if a writer of strong individuality has indulged a mannerism in early life, that wilful peculiarity of style shall grow upon him and shall render his latest productions a vexation to his critics. Mr George Meredith is a novelist to whom in no small degree has been given the quality of genius. But when he was young he was not content to shine: he desired to dazzle also, and he soon adopted the deplorable habit of saying nothing simply or easily, but always in the oddest language possible, with the maximum of effort. When he was at the height of his power the images which flooded his mind were so brilliant, the flow of them so copious, that he constantly overruled this tendency and wrote—never, it is true, simply—yet often vehemently and nobly. But with the increasing and inevitable languor of years his imagination has grown less active, and he has allowed it—without conscious affectation, we are sure—to take refuge beneath the increasing extravagance of his artificial dic-

tion. We hardly know how to say it without seeming to pay less than respect to a very distinguished and original writer, but it must be said—the Alexandrian extravagance of Mr Meredith's style has now reached such a pitch that it is difficult to enjoy and sometimes impossible to understand what he writes. In the *Amazing Marriage* we seem to be listening without a break to a rhapsody of Sir Piercie Shafton's.

259 "When from": Everard Meynell, *The Life of Francis Thompson* (London: Burns & Oates, 1913), p. 140.

260 "He seemed to": Courtney, *An Oxford Portrait Gallery*, p. 228.

260 "His mind should": Ibid.

261 "Sir George was": Arthur Croxton, *Crowded Nights–and Days* (London: Sampson Low, 1931), p. 146. Kogan (*The Great EB: The Story of the Encyclopædia Britannica* [Chicago: University of Chicago Press, 1958], p. 90) tells a similar story about Franklin Hooper being presented with an entry called "Algebraic Forms." He couldn't understand it at all, so he gave it to one of his assistants, Edward S. Holden, a well-known astronomer, and asked him to read it. Holden gave up on it and sent it to Simon Newcomb, a math professor at Johns Hopkins University. "It's magnificent, although I am not sure it is all clear to me. But it's really magnificent." Hooper killed the entry, saying it was "too magnificent." Gillian Thomas (see below) tells of Chisholm sending a note off to A. J. Hipkins, the author of the "Pianoforte" entry, suggesting he could stop in at Broadwoods, Hipkins's shop, "to talk over the changes" he wanted to suggest. Gillian Thomas, *A Position to Command Respect: Women and the Eleventh Britannica* (Metuchen and London: Scarecrow Press, 1992), p. 1.

262 A much lighter: From the Eleventh's article "Paper," by Garrett Fisher:

In 1841 an Oxford graduate brought home from the Far East a small quantity of extremely thin paper, which was manifestly more opaque and tough, for its weight, than any paper then made in Europe. He presented it to the Oxford University Press, and in 1842 Thomas Combe, printer to the University, used it for 24 copies of the smallest Bible then in existence—Diamond 24mo. These books were scarcely a third of the usual thickness, and were regarded with great interest; one was presented to Queen Victoria, and the rest to other persons. Combe tried in vain to trace the source of this paper. In 1874 a copy of this

Bible fell into the bands of Henry Frowde, and experiments were instituted at the Oxford University paper-mills at Wolvercote with the object of producing similar paper. On the 24th of August 1875 an impression of the Bible, similar in all respects to that of 1842, was placed on sale by the Oxford University Press. The feat of compression was regarded as astounding, the demand was enormous, and in a very short time 250,000 copies of this "Oxford India paper Bible" had been sold. . . . Its strength was as remarkable as its lightness; volumes of 1500 pages were suspended for several months by a single leaf, as thin as tissue, and when they were examined at the close of the exhibition, it was found that the leaf had not started, the paper had not stretched, and the volume closed as well as ever. The paper, when subjected to severe rubbing, instead of breaking into holes like ordinary printing paper, assumed a texture resembling chamois leather, and a strip 3 in. wide was found able to support a weight of 28 lb without yielding. The success of the Oxford India paper led to similar experiments by other manufacturers, and there were in 1910 nine mills (two each in England, Germany and Italy, one each in France, Holland and Belgium) in which India paper was being produced.

According to the dramatic scene described by Kogan in *The Great EB* (p. 145), Phillips proposed what Kogan called a "precedent setting" solution to fitting the encyclopedia into the bookcase: printing the set on India, or "Bible," paper. Kogan reported that this suggestion was made by Phillips over lunch with Hooper at the Café Royal. Hooper, he wrote, was at first dismissive. "But after a few minutes, Hooper interrupted Phillips, crying, 'Yes, by God! It can be done!'" As indeed it already had been done many times before. Oxford's "World's Classics" series, for example, had always been published in an India-paper edition. The so-called "Bible paper" stock was all the rage. It had already been made famous by Colonel Keith Young, who described it as the medium ("the secret of its manufacture is said to be known to only three living persons") on which was written the smuggled Cossid letter written during the Indian Mutiny in 1857. (See appendix I in Henry Wylie Norman and Mrs. Keith Young, eds., *Delhi–1857: The Siege, Assault, and Capture as Given in the Diary and Correspondence of the Late Colonel Keith Young, C.B., Judge-Advocate General, Bengal* [London: W. & R. Chambers]). In the *Britannica* itself, Garrett Fisher certainly praised the stuff lavishly, as cited above.The bookcases were not an issue at all. It's highly unlikely that Hooper wouldn't have considered such a useful text stock for a book whose chief drawback, after price, was size and weight. Each standard volume is bound in full Morocco leather, weighs eight pounds, four ounces, and is three inches thick. Each volume of the India-paper edition is one inch thick, bound in supple, flexible leather, and weighs two pounds, fourteen ounces. Besides, it wouldn't have solved the problem of those bookcases; using India paper would have made matters worse. The India-paper volumes are about an inch thick, while the regular volumes are three times that; reducing the seven feet of the Eleventh to less than three would have required a completely different case–which was, in the end, what was made for the India-paper editions, sales of which would far outstrip the regular-paper editions. One case, with a slanted shelf and a flat reading table above, was called a "Chippendale" model; another was tall and thin, with a vertical stack of slips for each volume; the standard case was a two-shelf version about sixteen inches wide, on legs. There was also a "traveling" set that fit all twenty-nine volumes neatly in a long "Vuitton" case–an elongated paperboard box decorated in the Vuitton pattern of quatrefoils, flowers, and "LV" logos.

India paper was a huge selling point. A promotional piece showed the remarkable qualities of the paper. In a series of photographs, an India-paper page of the *Britannica* was folded into a long, thin strip and tied in knots, then passed through a "lady's ring," crumpled into a tight little ball, smoothed out a bit, and then, finally, pressed with a hot iron, which returned "the page back absolutely to its original state." The India-paper editions were popular because they would lie flat; ink appeared crisper and richer on their bright pages, and each volume was covered in supple, black sheepskin. The regular edition weighed 250 pounds or so; the India-paper edition about 65. Hooper persuaded Arthur Croxton to be photographed for publicity holding an entire India-paper set in his arms. The photo made him a bit famous, he reported.

262 "planned on uniform": Hugh Chisholm, "Editorial Introduction," *Encyclopædia Britannica*, 11th ed.

263 "a detached collection": Ibid., p. xii.

263 "While every individual": Ibid.

264 hundreds of thousands: The index to the Tenth Edition contained 600,000, but it was simpler, without the complexity of the Eleventh's.

264 keeping track of: Just keeping track of the article authors was difficult enough. An overlapping of responsibility had resulted in duplicate sets of initials being used to identify authors of major articles. The problem was fixed in indexing by putting an asterisk next to the set of initials attached to the article that fell first in the volumes. Otherwise Haxton, as HRH* the author of the "Advertisement" article, would have been credited also with writing about ceramics and plates (the field of expertise claimed by Harry Reginald Holland Hall, a second HRH, sans *). Haxton may have broken many plates in many hotels and halls, but it's doubtful he knew what he was breaking.

264 Hogarth received an: James T. Shotwell, *The Autobiography of James T. Shotwell* (New York: Bobbs-Merrill, 1961), p. 62. Shotwell's system was soon adopted by *The Times* itself. Describing it is best left to Hogarth:

> We had a very ingenious system, simplicity itself when you had thought of it, but no one ever did think of it until an American on the "E. B." staff had a bright idea. We had little square blocks made up of slips of lined paper and cards alternating, and with a slip of carbon deftly inserted by a clip between paper and card we could move along rapidly, making every reference entry in duplicate. The paper slips we kept in the actual order in which the references appeared upon the printed page, or even upon the typescript, or MS. for that matter. The cards went into a common stock and were sorted into alphabetical sequence and ranged in order in their cabinets. In this way the "E. B." could be indexed almost as it was written, before it was even set up and long before it was paged. Should an article be subsequently altered, cut, or scrapped, you had only to find its own little bundle of slips, take out any references to what had dropped from the text, and find and remove their corresponding cards from the embryonic index in the cabinets. By various mechanical devices, quite simple and needing only a steady and careful clerk to work them, slips were stamped with a mark for which later the correct page number could be substituted, these numbers being transferred to the edited cards when the index had reached its final stage.

Simplicity itself. It's not clear whether Hogarth knew that Shotwell had been her inventive benefactor, since she didn't name him. He had returned to New York in 1905, but continued to do work for the encyclopedia. His article on "History" is an important statement of his philosophy of history. Hogarth quote is from Janet E. (Hogarth) Courtney, *Recollected in Tranquillity* (London: Heinemann, 1926), pp. 234–35.

264 "Of course I": Ibid., pp. 233–35.

265 "Some very queer": Ibid.

266 "I confess": Ibid., pp. 238–39.

266 "from a woman": Janet E. (Hogarth) Courtney, *The Making of an Editor: W. L. Courtney 1850–1928* (London: Macmillan and Co., 1930), p. 7.

267 "Hugh Chisholm was": Courtney, *Recollected in Tranquillity*, p. 230.

268 Meanwhile, Hogarth worked: Ibid., p. 252.

CHAPTER 16. WAR AND PEACE

270 a Cleveland man: William Ganson Rose, *Cleveland: Making of a City* (Kent, Ohio: Kent State University Press, 1950), p. 394.

270 "To bring out": Herman Kogan, *The Great EB: The Story of the Encyclopædia Britannica* (Chicago: University of Chicago Press, 1958), pp. 148ff. Kogan's detailed account of the legal battle between Jackson and Hooper is the source for the otherwise unattributed letters and comments in this chapter. Other sources, cited, seem to corroborate Kogan.

272 He was not: *New York Times*, June 16, 1909, p. 4.

272 "The trial that started": Court of Errors and Appeals. 76 N.J. Eq. 592 (N.J. 1910). Among the revelations, "From 1902 to 1908 the business in which the companies were engaged, including the publication of the *Encyclopaedia Britannica*, extended all over the civilized world and ran up into millions, the accounts receivable alone, at the time of the filing of the bill, amounting to over $2,000,000."

273 In New Jersey: From Justice James B. Dill's decision, *Jackson v. Hooper,* Court of Errors and Appeals. 76 N.J. Eq. 592 (N.J. 1910). The second set of figures in this paragraph come from Kogan, *The Great EB*, pp. 148–55.

274 Since late in: David M. McKitterick, *A History of Cambridge University Press*, vol. 3 (Cambridge: Cambridge University Press, 2006), p. 188. McKitterick's highly readable account of the *Britannica-CUP* episode is invaluable.

274 "You learnt a": Siân Reynolds, *Britannica's Typesetters: Women Compositors in Edwardian Edinburgh* (Edinburgh: Edinburgh University Press, 1989), p. 100.

275 "I cannot express": Kogan, *The Great EB*, p. 155.

277 J. M. Dent's: Peter Sutcliffe, *The Oxford University Press: An Informal History* (Oxford: Oxford University Press, 1978), pp. 141–44. May I just say, incidentally, that this book is a delight, written with authority and not a little wit. Innocent passersby will see you reading *The Oxford University Press: An Informal History* and laughing out loud and think it's a prank. These books—this one and McKitterick's *History of Cambridge University Press*, cited above—are rewarding for any student of publishing, and both are immensely engaging.

278 on India paper: Frowde capitalized grandly on the popularity of India paper; indeed, it was Frowde who did most to perpetuate the notion that "the secret of its manufacture is said to be known only to three living persons"—Frowde being one who wished he could be all three.

279 Frowde became so: Sutcliffe, *The Oxford University Press*.

279 By 1910: There are several histories of the *OED*. Of the two most recent, Simon Winchester's *The Meaning of Everything: The Story of the Oxford English Dictionary* (Oxford: Oxford University Press, 2003) is a highly entertaining account of Murray's grand project; Lynda Mugglestone's *Lost for Words: The Hidden History of the Oxford English Dictionary* (New Haven: Yale, 2005) lightly augments great Winchester's tale, but is a far heavier academic treatment. Murray's contribution to the Eleventh was, of course, the entry for "English Language." His eldest daughter, Hilda, a formidable scholar in her own right, collaborated with her father in its authorship. Murray was also accorded a biographical entry in the encyclopedia.

280 "You go to": Kogan, *The Great EB*, p. 157.

281 The post had: Michael H. Black, *A Short History of Cambridge University Press* (Cambridge: Cambridge University Press, 2000), p. 36.

281 It was Cambridge's: McKitterick, *History of Cambridge University Press*, vol. 3, p. 159.

281 "The *Encyclopædia Britannica*": *Celebration Banquet* (booklet), Encyclopædia Britannica, *Ninth Edition, Cambridge, 11th December 1888*, p. 25.

281 All of the: McKitterick, *History of Cambridge University Press*, vol. 3, p. 189: "It is inconceivable that some Syndics at least did not remember the fuss over the tenth edition, or that Wright did not know of Hooper's late activities."

282 "In my opinion": Syndicate minutes, March 11, 1910, cited in ibid., p. 190.

283 were among the: Sarah M. Hall, *Before Leonard: The Early Suitors of Virginia Woolf* (London: Peter Owen, 2006), pp. 52–53. The TAF is also in L. P. Wilkinson's *A Century of King's, 1873–1972* (Cambridge: King's College, 1980), p. 32. Jem Stephen died during a manic episode in 1892.

283 When, for example: McKitterick, *History of Cambridge University Press*, p. 158.

284 Jackson stood and: Kogan, *The Great EB*, pp. 159–60. Kogan is the only source for these exchanges, and as noted elsewhere he does not reveal his sources.

284 According to its: McKitterick, *History of Cambridge University Press*, p. 190.

CHAPTER 17. THE DREADNAUGHT LAUNCH

286 "Some particulars reach": James Milne, *New York Times Saturday Book Review*, August 27, 1910, p. BR6. (The column carried a dateline of August 17, but was published on the 27th.)

286 "solid and scholarly": James Milne, *New York Times Saturday Book Review*, September 10, 1910, p. BR6. Milne's chatty, personal letters from London appeared weekly from 1909 until 1911.

287 "The other week": Ibid. Hogarth mentions that the *Britannica* was always called "the EB" in the encyclopedia's offices.

287 Milne praised the: Ibid.

287 Thousands of copies: David M. McKitterick, *A History of Cambridge University Press*, vol. 3 (Cambridge: Cambridge University Press, 2006), pp. 190–91, offers a very good summary of the production details, including information on the machining of plates and the names of the printers.

287 In the U.S.: Herman Kogan, *The Great EB: The Story of the Encyclopædia Britannica* (Chicago: University of Chicago Press, 1958), p. 161.

288 Even the boxes: Ibid.

290 " 'Monstrum horrendum informe' ": Translation of "Monstrum horrendum informe, ingens, cui lumen ademptum": "A huge, hideous, formless monster deprived of vision," from *The Aeneid*, Book III. Gone are the days when Virgil can be counted on to deliver a good laugh.

292 December 1910 meeting: Syndics minutes, December 16, 1910.

293 "Miss Hogarth": King's Point, New York, according to census records. Janet E. (Hogarth) Courtney, *Recollected in Tranquillity* (London: Heinemann, 1926), p. 238.

293 But once the: McKitterick, *A History of Cambridge University Press*, vol. 3, pp. 189–90.

CHAPTER 18. OFFENSES

294 "[W]e can heartily": *The Athenæum*, August 26, 1911, p. 239.

297 "It is very": The letters are collected online at the Darwin Correspondence Project, a joint venture of the American Council of Learned Societies and Cambridge University. The exchange cited is located at the following URLs: Kingsley to Darwin: http://darwinproject.ac.uk /entry-3426; Darwin's reply: http://darwinproject.ac.uk/entry-3439.

297 "the less intellectual": Frederick Burkhardt and Sydney Smith, eds., *The Correspondence of Charles Darwin, 1858–1859* (Cambridge: Cambridge University Press, 1992), p. 345. I am indebted to Professor Anthony O'Hear for this reference, cited in his 2009 essay "Darwinian Tensions," published online at http://fortnightlyreview.co.uk.

298 Common sense might: Indeed, Darwin's racial views, filtered through Joyce, continue to be influential to some. In January 1999, a "historical revisionist" magazine, *The Barnes Review*, published "Is There a Negro Race?" under Joyce's name. The publisher of *The Barnes Review* also publishes books such as *The Auschwitz Myth* and *Anne Frank's Diary a Hoax*. It seems that Joyce followed Darwin straight to well-deserved ignominy.

The Eleventh Edition's "Ku Klux Klan" entry, written by W. L. Fleming, a Louisiana history professor, suffers from the same sort of inept editing. To contemporary readers, whether or not the entry contains any facts would have been secondary to the larger inaccuracies conveyed by absent context.

298 "[A]lthough Mr. Phillips": Charles M. Andrews, *American Historical Review* 7, no. 54 (July 1902): 784–86.

299 "The most daring": George Lincoln Burr, *American Historical Review* 17, no. 1 (October 1911): 103–09.

300 publishing until 1974: When John Gross, then editor of *The Times Literary Supplement*, the last major bastion of unsigned reviews, finally, and famously, banned the practice. "There are many occasions on which a reader is entitled to ask on what authority a judgment or opinion is being advanced," he wrote in the *TLS* on June 7, 1974. "There are even occasions when the whole import of a review depends on knowing the identity of the reviewer."

301 In this: E. B. Titchener, "The Psychology of the New *Britannica*," *American Journal of Psychology* 23 (1912): 37–58.

302 Hogarth was one: A very interesting and useful survey of the *Britannica*'s women contributors can be found in Gillian Thomas, *A Posi-*

tion to Command Respect: Women and the Eleventh Britannica (Metuchen and London: Scarecrow Press, 1992). Dr. Thomas's survey of the Eleventh Edition is brisk and more accurate than Kogan's (*The Great EB: The Story of the Encyclopædia Britannica* [Chicago: University of Chicago Press, 1958]), and augmented by a collection of insightful, well-informed biographical sketches.

303 "If the century": Janet Hogarth, "Literary Degenerates," *Fortnightly Review* (April 1895): 586–92. See also Victoria Cross, *Anna Lombard*, ed. Gail Cunningham (Birmingham: University of Birmingham Press, 2003), p. xi.

303 After all: "New Careers for Women: Journalism," *Ladies' Pictorial* (November 1893): 34, cited in Lorna Shelley, "Female Journalists and Journalism in Fin-de-siècle Magazine Stories," *Nineteenth-Century Gender Studies* 5, no. 2 (summer 2009), accessed October 10, 2011, http://ncgsjournal.com/issue52/shelley.htm.

303 She was very: See "Regiment," *Fortnightly Review* 68 (December 1897): 926–36; "Degenerates," *Fortnightly Review* 57 (April 1895): 586–92; and Robert F. Haggard, *The Persistence of Victorian Liberalism: The Politics of Social Reform in Britain, 1870–1900* (Westport, CT: Greenwood Press, 2001), p. 107.

306 "Sir,–": *The Times*, October 9, 1909, p. 10. An even more militant position was marked by her in a June 1897 *Fortnightly Review* article titled "The Monstrous Regiment of Women" (pp. 926–36): "There are few aspects of the Eternal Feminine more disheartening to contemplate than the alarming increase of that monstrous regiment of women which threatens before long to spread throughout the length and breadth of this city of London." One might, with cause, suggest that this isn't just anti-suffrage, but simply anti-woman, but that would be to ignore the way in which Hogarth reflected not an eccentric view, but that of the majority of Britons, men and women, at the time.

308 "to recognize the": E. H. C. Moberly Bell, *The Life and Letters of C. F. Moberly Bell* (London: Richards Press, 1927), p. 250.

309 "He was always": Janet E. (Hogarth) Courtney, *An Oxford Portrait Gallery* (London: Chapman & Hall, 1931), p. 132.

309 In an article: "An Oxford B.A." [Hugh Chisholm], "University Degrees for Women," *Fortnightly Review* (June 1895): 895–903. Grace had gone to Germany with two American students as part of an experiment, but the lack of respect shown her and another gifted Cambridge woman, Philippa Fawcett, caused a great uproar. It is probably not without

reason that an important meeting of the Oxford Association for the Education of Women was held within a fortnight of the day when Göttingen University made an Englishwoman its first Prussian "Fräulein Doktor."

309 The university abandoned: In Britain, University College London began admitting women to degree courses in 1878.

311 Hogarth claimed that: Courtney, *An Oxford Portrait Gallery*, p. 133. "An Oxford B.A.," "University Degrees for Women."

311 "Education and Professions": *The Women's Encyclopedia* (London: Chapman & Hall, 1903).

311 The scuffle had: Grant Richards, *Author Hunting, by an Old Literary Sportsman: Memories of Years Spent Mainly in Publishing 1897–1925* (New York: H. Hamilton, 1934), p. 54.

312 "Being much pressed": Courtney, *An Oxford Portrait Gallery*, p. 135.

312 While many of: Ironically, "X" is also credited as one of the authors of the article on George Henry Lewes, the founding editor of *The Fortnightly Review*, whose most-remembered contribution to journalism is his insistence on signed articles. There are many anonymous articles in the Eleventh Edition; the identity of "X" is one of the encyclopedia's mysteries. Suspects include Morley, Harrison, Chisholm himself, or possibly James Louis Garvin, one of Northcliffe's best editors, who later edited his own editions (Thirteen—a three-volume supplement to Eleven and Twelve—and the twenty-four-volume Fourteen) of the *Britannica*.

312 Modern feminists find: Thomas, *A Position to Command Respect*, p. 38.

312 "WOMEN": *Encyclopædia Britannica*, 11th ed., vol. 28, p. 782.

313 "By 1910 he": Courtney, *An Oxford Portrait Gallery*, p. 135.

313 "It was our": Janet E. (Hogarth) Courtney, *The Women of My Time* (London: L. Dickson, 1934), p. 174.

314 She contrasted this: "The Woman Suffrage Movement," *The Britannica Year-book* 1913 (London: Encyclopædia Britannica Company, 1913), pp. 87–90.

314 Three decades later: It must have been interesting at breakfast in the Courtney home; in 1913, Chapman & Hall published W. L. Courtney's collection called *The Soul of a Suffragette and Other Stories*. The suffragette in the title piece was a bomb thrower, but with a great big heart.

314 "We were on": "The Woman Suffrage Movement." One wonders how these friendships matured after that set of battles was over. I have an interesting 1920 "association copy" of *Freethinkers*. The volume is

inscribed by Courtney curtly and simply: "To Mrs Humphrey Ward, with gratitude. The author."

315 "I have made": *New York Times*, February 19, 1911, p. BR86.

315 "While I naturally": *New York Times*, March 5, 1911, p. BR128. Professor Jacobs was indeed an important contributor to the Eleventh, authoring "Jew, The Wandering," "Nethinim," "Passover," "Purim," and "Tabernacles, Feast of," according to the index. The full text of Chisholm's interesting response appears in an appendix to this book.

317 "The entire encyclopedia": *New York Times*, September 29, 1911, p. 6.

319 "The precise reasons": *New Age*, October 6, 1910, p. 547.

320 Early in the: David M. McKitterick, *A History of Cambridge University Press*, vol. 3 (Cambridge: Cambridge University Press, 2006), pp. 192–93.

321 "That was a": *Publishers Weekly*, June 24, 1911, cited in ibid.

322 "With reference to": *Times*, December 1, 1911, p. 14.

323 "Our protest has": Ibid., p. 6.

324 forward-looking proposals for: However, they may be examined in the Cambridge University Press archives.

325 "So definite was": Janet E. (Hogarth) Courtney, *An Oxford Portrait Gallery* (London: Chapman & Hall, 1931), pp. 138–39.

326 "I dream that": "The Destruction of the World: A Dream." Undated handwritten ms.

328 113-acre estate: *New York Post*, July 9, 1925, p. 21. For these details, I am indebted to Patrick Baty (http://patrickbaty.co.uk/).

328 "It is the": *The Spectator*, July 21, 1922, p. 13.

329 then a home: Whether Haxton died in poverty isn't known. But in 1911, Hooper engineered a lawsuit against Jackson (as Hooper & Jackson) to give Franklin and Haxton a share of the profits of the Eleventh Edition. The Kings Park records were apparently destroyed in a fire; remaining records are archived, but not available to researchers. Although census records show him in residence after 1920, St. Johnland has no records showing him there at all; it's not known if Haxton's records survived the blaze.

329 He had been: Matthew Sturgis, *Walter Sickert: A Life* (New York: HarperCollins, 2005), p. 541, and Swanwick, p. 352.

329 "I would love": 401. Personal correspondence (undated).

CHAPTER 19. POSTSCRIPT

331 *Chambers' Cyclopædia*: The Schwenck-like subtitle of the *Chambers' Cyclopædia*: "An Universal Dictionary of Arts and Sciences: Contain-

ing the Definitions of the Terms, and Accounts of the Things Signify'd Thereby, in the Several Arts, both Liberal and Mechanical, and the Several Sciences, Human and Divine: the Figures, Kinds, Properties, Productions, Preparations, and Uses, of Things Natural and Artificial; the Rise, Progress, and State of Things Ecclesiastical, Civil, Military, and Commercial: with the Several Systems, Sects, Opinions, etc; among Philosophers, Divines, Mathematicians, Physicians, Antiquaries, Criticks, etc.: The Whole Intended as a Course of Ancient and Modern Learning."

331 Yet Denis Diderot's: The University of Wisconsin has put a digital version of *Chambers' Cyclopædia* online at http://digital.library.wisc.edu/1711.dl/HistSciTech.Cyclopaedia; the Eleventh is online in various "user-edited" formats; the *Encyclopédie* can be found at a magnificent University of Chicago site, http://encyclopedie.uchicago.edu/.

334 his discussion: In "John Wilkins' Analytical Language," nightmare fodder for Janet Hogarth, *Selected Non-Fictions* (New York: Penguin, 2000), p. 231.

334 Richmond Lattimore: Lattimore in *The New Yorker*, January 26, 1957, p. 36.

334 "is maintained even": Janet E. (Hogarth) Courtney, *Recollected in Tranquillity* (London: Heinemann, 1926), pp. 232–33.

336 Hans Koning wrote: In *The New Yorker*, March 2, 1981, pp. 67–83.

338 "His *Leaves* radiates": *Encyclopædia Britannica*, 11th ed., vol. 28, p. 610.

340 "These volumes ought": Courtney, *Recollected in Tranquillity*, p. 221.

340 John Stuart Mill: In "The Spirit of the Age," *Examiner*, January 9–May 29, 1831.

341 "ideology of transition": Mary R. Anderson, "Cultural Dissonance and the Ideology of Transition in Late-Victorian England," *Victorian Periodicals Review* 26, no. 2 (1993).

341 Indeed: Walter E. Houghton, in *The Victorian Frame of Mind* (New Haven: Yale, 1957), discusses this in entertaining detail in his introduction.

APPENDIX A. THE PIRATE PUBLISHERS: THE "REPRINT HYAENAS"

345 Reissued between 1873: Appleton, it should be noted, was one of the few American publishers to routinely pay British writers royalties, even though no copyright statute required them to do so. Sidney Eisen, "Frederic Harrison and Herbert Spencer: Embattled Unbelievers," *Victorian Studies* (September 1968): 49.

345 "The Encyclopedia Britannica": Ibid.

345 while condemning the: J. D. Newth, *Adam & Charles Black 1807–1957: Some Chapters in the History of a Publishing House* (London: Adam & Charles Black, 1957), p. 44.

345 "Even when American": Ibid.

345 The American publishers: Herman Kogan, *The Great EB: The Story of the Encyclopædia Britannica* (Chicago: University of Chicago Press, 1958), p. 67.

346 The Dobson edition: Robert D. Arner, *Dobson's Encyclopædia: The Publisher, Text, and Publication of America's First Britannica, 1789–1803* (Philadelphia: University of Pennsylvania Press, 1991), p. 213.

346 Alexander Hamilton: Richard B. Sher, *The Enlightenment and the Book: Scottish Authors and Their Publishers in Eighteenth-Century Britain, Ireland and America* (Chicago: University of Chicago Press, 2007), p. 559.

347 The scoundrel was: Newth, *Adam & Charles Black*, p. 45.

347 "the public policy": Ibid., pp. 44–45.

347 "The Black Robbery": Ibid., p. 47. A half century later, however, *The New York Times* reflected benignly (and somewhat oxymoronically) on what it called the "ethical piracy" of James Clarke in Clarke's September 6, 1945 (p. 25) obituary—understandable since, as we shall see, *The Times*, after much condemnation of other newspapers, soon jumped on the encyclopedia bandwagon too.

347 But meanwhile: Newth, *Adam & Charles Black*, pp. 48–49. Inexplicably, Newth has the date as 1889.

348 "Belford Bros.": Clemens to Moncure D. Conway, November 2, 1876, Hartford, Conn. (UCCL 01386), University of California, http://mark twainproject.org.

348 Clemens was furious: Barbara Schmidt, "A Closer Look at the Lives of True Williams and Alexander Belford," paper presented at the fourth International Conference on the State of Mark Twain Studies, Elmira, New York, August 18, 2001, http://twainquotes.com/TWW/TWW .html.

349 "violent Irishman": George H. Doran, *Chronicles of Barabbas: 1884–1934* (New York: Harcourt, Brace and Company, 1935), p. 100.

349 And a couple: Kogan, *The Great EB*, p. 69.

349 "the largest complete": *New York Times*, December 12, 1892. The company lasted until 1900, when it was acquired by Arthur J. Saalfield of Akron, Ohio, whose interest was in children's books. Saalfield Publishing continued the Werner imprint for a brief period. Saalfield itself

continued in existence until 1977. Its catalogs, publications, artwork (including a Shirley Temple paper-doll book nearly three feet tall), and other archival material are housed in the Department of Special Collections and Archives of the Kent State University Libraries. Edith Serkownek of Kent State University's Special Collections sent me the following helpful note:

> According to a January 13, 1900, newspaper clipping from the [Akron] *Beacon Journal,* "The trade and subscription department of the Werner company has been transferred to the Saalfield Publishing Company." The article goes on to state that the Werner company was to continue in the business of "book manufacturing, printing and lithography." According to a 1951 KSU Master's thesis, *A History of the Saalfield Publishing Company* by Viola A. Smith, "Business went on very much the same as before except that Mr. Saalfield was now the owner of the book publishing department; the Werner Company confined itself entirely to the printing business." According to another paper (unsigned and untitled) found in the administrative files, A. J. Saalfield originally obtained rights to the Werner Company's fictional titles resulting from the fact that Saalfield had signed as a co-guarantor on a $125,000 note that Paul Werner took out and subsequently did not [repay]. "Arthur didn't have the money, but the court allowed him to use the inventory of Werner's finished books—including [the] Encyclopedia Britannica—as collateral to borrow money to pay the note." [Smith.] In a transcript of a talk given by Henry R. Saalfield to the Friends of the Libraries at KSU on April 13, 1978, Saalfield states, "Grandfather endorsed a huge financial obligation for the Werner Co. which was defaulted so that he had to pay it all off himself. In exchange, he acquired the plates, copyrights and full ownership of the Werner books in the publishing department." Whatever the circumstances, it does appear that the Werner company continued to exist for a time following the founding of the Saalfield Publishing Company.

The debts incurred by Werner must have been due largely to the company's very ambitious efforts to produce an Americanized *Britannica* "Tenth Edition," about which see chapter 8.

349 Clarke: Clarke, for example, collected a bunch of columns written by George Peck for a newspaper and bought the rights for $1,000. Out of the clippings came *Peck's Bad Boy*, a title that sold in the millions. Peck went on to become governor of Wisconsin, while Clarke later "voluntarily paid handsome royalties to the author," reported *The New York Times*, September 6, 1946, p. 6.

349 Operating from the: Schmidt, "A Closer Look at the Lives of True Williams and Alexander Belford."

349 Soon: *Publishers Weekly*, October 20, 1906, pp. 1098–99. The University of Iowa librarian Sidney F. Huttner's "*Lucile* Project" website was helpful in pointing out this source, http://sdrc.lib.uiowa.edu/lucile/index .html.

APPENDIX B. THE TEXT OF HENRY R. HAXTON'S FIRST *TIMES* ADVERTISEMENT FOR THE NINTH EDITION, MARCH 23, 1898

361 "Sir Fredk. Abel": Sir Frederick Abel, a chemist and the co-inventor of cordite, was not, in fact, a listed contributor. He did have a biographical entry under his own name, however.

APPENDIX E. E. B. TITCHENER'S CONTENT ANALYSIS

375 "The supplementary article": *The American Journal of Psychology*, vol. 23, January 1, 1912, pp. 37–58. The full review is available online at https:// archive.org/details/jstor-1413113.

APPENDIX F. HUGH CHISHOLM'S RESPONSE TO JOSEPH JACOBS'S UNFAVORABLE REVIEW IN *THE NEW YORK TIMES*

377 Dr. Jacobs: *The New York Times*, March 5, 1911, p. BR128. The index shows that Professor Jacobs was indeed an important contributor to the Eleventh, authoring "Jew, The Wandering," "Nethinim," "Passover," "Purim," and "Tabernacles, Feast of."

Index

Page numbers in *italics* refer to illustrations.

ILLUSTRATION ACKNOWLEDGMENTS

Every effort has been made to accurately determine the rights status and ownership of the images in this book. They are believed to be in the public domain, with the exceptions listed below:

page 6 *Western Publishing Advertising Card.* From the author's collection.

   7 *Woodbury Mansion.* From The Denver Public Library, Western History Collection. Orin Sealy. X-27124. Used with permission.

  30 *John Walter I.* From *The History of the Times.* Published by The Times, Printing House Square, London. Courtesy of The Times (London).

  31 *John Walter II.* From *The History of the Times.* Published by The Times, Printing House Square, London. Courtesy of The Times (London).

  32 *John Walter III.* From *The History of the Times.* Published by The Times, Printing House Square, London. Courtesy of The Times (London).

  37 *CF Moberly Bell.* From *The History of the Times.* Published by The Times, Printing House Square, London. Courtesy of The Times (London).

  48 *John Cameron Macdonald.* From *The History of the Times.* published by The Times, Printing House Square, London. Courtesy of The Times (London).

  49 *John Delane.* From *The History of the Times.* Published by The Times, Printing House Square, London. Courtesy of The Times (London).

  51 *George Buckle.* From *The History of the Times.* Published by The Times, Printing House Square, London. Courtesy of The Times (London).

58   The Times *Atlas*. From The David Rumsey Map Collection and used with permission.

93   *Donald Mackenzie Wallace*. From *The History of the Times*. Published by The Times, Printing House Square, London. Courtesy of The Times (London).

107   *Limmer's Menu*. From the collection of Rory Chisholm MBE and used with permission.

111   *Grace and Hugh Chisholm 1872*. From the collection of Rory Chisholm MBE and used with permission.

112   *Anna Louisa Bell and Eliza Chisholm 1907*. From the collection of Rory Chisholm MBE and used with permission.

121   *Eliza Beatrix Harrison Chisholm*. From the collection of Rory Chisholm MBE and used with permission.

124   *Hugh Chisholm's three sons: Archie, John, and Hugh*. From the collection of Rory Chisholm MBE and used with permission.

137   From the National Portrait Gallery, London: *Earl of Selborne*. © National Portrait Gallery, London.

162   *Walter Alison Phillips*. From the collection of Marilyn Beyer and used with permission.

183   *The Grand Canal with Santa Maria della Salute, Venice*, by Mary Hogarth. © Leeds Art Museum and Galleries.

210   From the National Portrait Gallery, London: *Lord Northcliffe*. © National Portrait Gallery, London.

219   From the National Portrait Gallery, London: *Kennedy Jones*. © National Portrait Gallery, London.

A NOTE ON THE TYPE

This book was set in Garamond, a typeface originally designed by the famous Parisian type cutter Claude Garamond (1480–1561). This version of Garamond was drawn by Günter Gerhard Lange (1921–2008) and released by the Berthold type foundry in 1972. Lange based his Garamond revival on a combination of models found in specimen sheets from both Paris and Antwerp.

Claude Garamond is one of the most famous type designers in printing history. His distinguished romans and italics first appeared in *Opera Ciceronis* in 1543–1544. While delightfully unconventional in design, the Garamond types are clear and open, yet maintain an elegance and precision of line that mark them as French.

Composed by North Market Street Graphics,
Lancaster, Pennyslvania

Printed and bound by Berryville Graphics,
Berryville, Virginia

Designed by Betty Lew